HUMAN SEXUALITY: CONTEMPORARY PERSPECTIVES

Edited by
Eleanor S. Morrison
and
Vera Borosage

Michigan State University

with the assistance of
Judith A. Arrigo

MAYFIELD PUBLISHING COMPANY

To our students, who are our continuing teachers

Copyright © 1973 by Eleanor S. Morrison and Vera Borosage
First edition 1973

Library of Congress Catalog Card Number 72-97843
International Standard Book Numbers: 0-87484-256-5 (paper)

Manufactured in the United States of America

Mayfield Publishing Company
285 Hamilton Avenue, Palo Alto, California 94301

This book was set in Trade Gothic Light and Times Roman by
Typographic Service Company and was printed and bound by the
George Banta Company. The designer was Nancy Sears; the editors
were Alden C. Paine and Barbara Pronin; production supervisor was
Michelle Hogan. Cover design by Ireta Cooper.

CONTENTS

iii

Part 5   SOME PUBLIC ISSUES

Part 6   SOME PERVASIVE
SEXUAL MISCONCEPTIONS

Contents

PREFACE

The idea for this book arose during the teaching of a course on human sexuality and the family at Michigan State University. Although material on sexuality proliferates, it is difficult to find a range of viewpoints gathered under one cover. We therefore hope that students will find this collection of readings provocative and that teachers will find it a useful means of providing diverse materials in the convenient form of a single book.

Judith Arrigo, while a graduate assistant in the Department of Family and Child Sciences at Michigan State University, doggedly pursued copyright permissions, raised practical questions, represented the student's perspective to the editors, and efficiently executed innumerable details in the preparation of the manuscript. We are particularly grateful to Richard Whalen, Professor of Psychobiology at the University of California, Irvine, for his constructive help and criticism in the planning of the book. Wendy and Stephanie Morrison were of great help in preparing materials for review and publication.

As our dedication suggests, we are especially grateful to students who, in the experimental stages of our course in sexuality, have contributed their perspectives, criticism, and enthusiasm.

INTRODUCTION: A HUMANISTIC APPROACH TO TEACHING HUMAN SEXUALITY

Perhaps no aspect of modern American life is more riddled with contradiction and paradox than human sexuality. "Sexual revolution" notwithstanding, there is still widespread ignorance and misinformation about human sexual functioning and a persisting reticence on the part of parents and teachers about being candid with the young about sex. The intimate and delicate fabric of sexual interaction is often sullied by overemphasis on sexual competence, technique, and achievement on the one hand and by inhibition and fear on the other. Rollo May's characterization of our culture as schizoid with regard to sex is pointedly accurate. Both as individuals and as a culture, including the so-called "youth culture," we appear free and open about sexual matters but are still "hung up" sexually in innumerable ways.

Almost all cultures have regarded sex in a specialized way, as evidenced by its recurrence in symbol, myth, ritual, and mores. And there is sound basis for this tendency. The sexual is distinguished from other physiological functions in its reciprocal and vital aspects. First, sex alone requires another human being for optimal accomplishment; second, sex alone can create new life. Sexuality has communal as well as individual implications and is for that reason a source of continuing concern with regard to protecting human beings, especially young people, from destructive and exploitative modes. It is precisely with regard to "protection" that much of the distortion enters. Restrictive, hypocritical, and repressive laws, codes, and rules enacted by one segment of the population to "protect" another have often resulted in unfair double standards for old and young, white and black, men and women, and sexual encounter has too often been accompanied by shame, guilt, or stealth.

In this book, the term "sexuality" covers much more than the merely biological or reproductive meanings often employed in sex education courses or sex talks between parents and children. Sex is, in fact, only a small part of sexuality. As Thomas Driver has observed, "Sex is what you are born with; sexuality is who you are." Sexuality is, then, an integrated, individualized, unique expression of self. Although I, for example, am a woman, my sexuality, or sexual self-identification, has wide parameters. My sexuality, though based on biological data, is not determined by this alone but also by cultural, psychological and personality factors, and by family experience, all of which produce a certain sexual style. My sexuality, then, is my particular style of femaleness. In personality or sexual interaction, I may be assertive or docile, homosexual or heterosexual, "feminine," "masculine," or "androgynous," according to the traditional definitions of sexual role. I may be a mixture of all of these, depending on circumstances, partner, and my individual values, experiences, and preferences.

The assumption underlying these statements, and the selection of readings in this book as well, is that sexuality involves a great many more factors than genitalia alone. Value identification, decision-making, and reflection on personal experience are all involved in the process of understanding human sexuality. In assembling this anthology, an attempt was made to select materials that not only represent the pluralism of sexual values in contemporary America, but also ones that might catalyze reflection and interaction about sexual life styles.

Beyond the purely physiological aspects of sexuality, there is strong disagreement on many sexual concerns and issues, including homosexuality; pornography; autoeroticism; marital, premarital, and nonmarital contracts; contraception; abortion; women's and men's liberation; sex and racism; and personal/impersonal sexual interaction. Every student approaches the study of human sexuality with personal opinions about all sorts of sexual matters ranging from when to talk with children about sex to the acceptability of oral-genital sex. The intention of this book is to enable students to become more consciously aware of their own and others' value positions and sexual lifestyles.

The challenge is to find ways of teaching and learning at the college and university level that emphasize the human and existential aspects of human sexuality while at the same time providing a solid foundation of research-based information. It is often assumed in the academic world that "objective" information suffices for an understanding of sexuality; but to accept that assumption is only to perpetuate the split between cognitive knowledge and full personal understanding. For the fully human dimensions of human sexuality to be explored, intellectual grasp and immediate personal experience must somehow be integrated.

In our view, learning about human sexuality must include a personal focus —reflecting on, and grappling with, one's own experience, knowledge, convictions, and values—tested against the experiences, attitudes, beliefs, insights, and values of persons from different cultural and family traditions. It is hoped that discussion and interchange will accompany the reading of these selections, many of which are polemical rather than "objective" and were deliberately selected to trigger reaction and interaction.

To learn about human sexuality is to deal not only with information about gonads, orgasm, and coitus but also with a kind of personal knowledge about oneself and one's sexual role. This is not to belittle the crucial importance of accurate cognitive information but only to add to it the existential. Among the significant results of the work done by Masters and Johnson at the Reproductive Biology Research Foundation in Saint Louis has been the discovery of the complex and intriguing ways in which the mind, feelings, and inner perceptions affect the sexual functioning of the body. In both the laboratory research and the clinical therapy program, Masters and Johnson have found that an individual may be sexually dysfunctional, not so much from physiological disorder as from a disorder of attitude and feeling—that is, the sexual apparatus may be perfectly capable of functioning but is nevertheless operationally dysfunctional because of the person's fears or apprehensions about his or her anatomy specifically or of themselves as persons generally.

Students are encouraged to reflect critically upon their feelings and attitudes toward their own sexuality, the sexuality of others, and the cultural setting in which sexual functioning occurs. If some of the articles herein appear too "subjective," too "radical," or too "traditional," our catalytic purpose will have been achieved.

Eleanor S. Morrison

Part 1
DEVELOPMENT AND SEXUALITY

PSYCHOSEXUAL DEVELOPMENT

William Simon and John Gagnon

The continuing controversy concerning whether human sexual development is primarily influenced by "nature" or "nurture" is the main focus of this section. Although the three articles that follow take an essentially cultural ("nurture") rather than biological ("nature") stance, they should not be interpreted as obviating the importance of physiological, genetic, and hormonal factors. The issue will reappear in Part 2, where the argument concerning whether anatomy is destiny, in the Freudian sense, will be examined.

To Simon and Gagnon there is no significant continuity between childhood experiences which appear sexual to adults and genuine adult sexuality; indeed, they regard the idea of sexual development as largely a social invention. In the "nature-nurture" controversy, they argue that "the sexual is precisely that realm where the sociocultural forms most completely dominate biological influences." They deny that sexual behavior is a necessary cover for an intense primordial urge that must constantly be kept in check, taking the position that human sexual behavior is essentially learned behavior— "scripted" is their word.

Some interesting and controversial issues are raised in this article.

1. Despite their penchant for a sociocultural interpretation, they suggest, for instance, that male sexual development proceeds "naturally" from the biological development of genitalia, whereas the female has to *learn* how to be sexual.

2. They doubt that an inherent "natural" chemistry would produce sexual excitement in foreplay without the complex set of symbolic interpretations that individuals have learned to associate with foreplay.

3. They see the courtship and dating period as a time when men and women train one another to be sexual in ways hitherto omitted from their individual training—i.e., the man trains the woman to be genitally sexual, and the woman trains the man to be emotionally and relationally sexual.

Erik Erikson has observed that, prior to Sigmund Freud, "sexologists" tended to believe that sexual capacities appeared suddenly with the onset of adolescence. Sexuality followed those external evidences of physiological change that occurred concurrent with or just after puberty. Psychoanalysis changed all that. In Freud's view, libido—the generation of psychosexual energies—should be viewed as a fundamental element of human experience at least beginning with birth, and possibly before that. Libido, therefore, is essential, a biological constant to be coped with at all levels of individual, social, and cultural development. The truth of this received wisdom, that is, that sexual development is a continuous contest between biological drive and cultural restraint should be seriously questioned. Obviously sexuality has roots in biological processes, but so do many other capacities, including many that involve physical and mental competence and vigor. There is, however, abundant evidence that the final states which these capacities attain escape the rigid impress of biology. This independence of biological constraint is rarely claimed for the area of sexuality, but we would like to argue that the sexual is precisely that realm where the sociocultural forms most completely dominate biological influences.

It is difficult to get data that might shed much light on the earliest aspects of these questions: Adults are hardly equipped with total recall and the preverbal or primitively verbal child does not have ability to report accurately on his own internal state. But it seems obvious—and it is a basic assumption of this paper—that with the beginnings of adolescence many new factors come into play, and to emphasize a straight-line developmental continuity with infant and childhood experiences may be seriously misleading. In particular, it is dangerous to assume that because some childhood behavior appears sexual to adults, it must be sexual. An infant or a child engaged in genital play (even if orgasm is observed) can in no sense be seen as experiencing the complex set of feelings that accompanies adult or even adolescent masturbation.

Therefore, the authors reject the unproven assumption that "powerful" psychosexual drives are fixed biological attributes. More importantly, we reject the even more dubious assumption that sexual capacities or experiences tend to translate immediately into a kind of universal "knowing" or innate wisdom—that sexuality has a magical ability, possessed by no other capacity, that allows biological drives to be expressed directly in psychosocial and social behaviors.

The prevailing image of sexuality—particularly that of the Freudian tradition—is that of an intense, high-pressure drive that forces a person to seek physical sexual gratification, a drive that expresses itself indirectly if it cannot be expressed directly. The available data suggest to us a different picture —one that shows either lower levels of intensity, or, at least, greater variability. We find that there are many social situations or life-roles in which reduced sex activity or even deliberate celibacy is undertaken with little evidence that the libido has shifted in compensation to some other sphere.

A part of the legacy of Freud is that we have all become remarkably adept at discovering "sexual" elements in nonsexual behavior and symbolism. What we suggest instead (following Kenneth Burke's three-decade-old insight) is the reverse—that sexual behavior can often express and serve nonsexual motives.

No Play Without a Script

We see sexual behavior therefore as *scripted* behavior, not the masked expression of a primordial drive. The individual can learn sexual behavior as he or she learns other behavior—through scripts that in this case give the self, other persons, and situations erotic abilities or content. Desire, privacy, opportunity, and propinquity with an attractive member of the opposite sex are not, in themselves, enough; in ordinary circumstances, nothing sexual will occur unless one or both actors organize these elements into an appropriate script. The very concern with foreplay in sex suggests this. From one point of view, foreplay may be defined as merely progressive physical excitement generated by touching naturally erogenous zones. The authors have referred to this conception elsewhere as the "rubbing of two sticks together to make a fire" model. It would seem to be more valuable to see this activity as symbolically invested behavior through which the body is eroticized and through which mute, inarticulate motions and gestures are translated into a sociosexual drama.

A belief in the sociocultural dominance of sexual behavior finds support in cross-cultural research as well as in data restricted to the United States. Psychosexual development is universal—but it takes many forms and tempos. People in different cultures construct their scripts differently; and in our own society, different segments of the population act out different psychosexual dramas—something much less likely to occur if they were all reacting more or less blindly to the same superordinate urge. The most marked differences occur, of course, between male and female patterns of sexual behavior. Obviously, some of this is due to biological differences, including differences in hormonal functions at different ages. But the significance of social scripts

Psychosexual Development

5

predominate; the recent work of Masters and Johnson, for example, clearly points to far greater orgasmic capacities on the part of females than our culture would lead us to suspect. And within each sex—especially among men—different social and economic groups have different patterns.

Let us examine some of these variations, and see if we can decipher the scripts.

Childhood

Whether one agrees with Freud or not, it is obvious that we do not become sexual all at once. There is continuity with the past. Even infant experiences can strongly influence later sexual development.

But continuity is not causality. Childhood experiences (even those that appear sexual) will in all likelihood be influential not because they are intrinsically sexual, but because they can affect a number of developmental trends, *including* the sexual. What situations in infancy—or even early childhood—can be called psychosexual in any sense other than that of creating potentials?

The key term, therefore, must remain potentiation. In infancy, we can locate some of the experiences (or sensations) that will bring about a sense of the body and its capacities for pleasure and discomfort and those that will influence the child's ability to relate to others. It is possible, of course, that through these primitive experiences, ranges are being established—but they are very broad and overlapping. Moreover, if these are profound experiences to the child—and they may well be that—they are not expressions of biological necessity, but of the earliest forms of social learning.

In childhood, after infancy there is what appears to be some real sex play. About half of all adults report that they did engage in some form of sex play as children and the total who actually did may be half again as many. But, however the adult interprets it later, what did it mean to the child at the time? One suspects that, as in much of childhood role-playing, their sense of the adult meanings attributed to the behavior is fragmentary and ill-formed. Many of the adults recall that, at the time, they were concerned with being found out. But here, too, were they concerned because of the real content of sex play, or because of the mystery and the lure of the forbidden that so often enchant the child? The child may be assimilating outside information about sex for which, at the time, he has no real internal correlate or understanding.

A small number of persons do have sociosexual activity during preadolescence—most of it initiated by adults. But for the majority of these, little apparently follows from it. Without appropriate sexual scripts, the experience remains unassimilated—at least in adult terms. For some, it is clear, a severe reaction may follow from falling "victim" to the sexuality of an adult—but, again, does this reaction come from the sexual act itself or from the social response, the strong reactions of others? (There is some evidence that early sexual activity of this sort is associated with deviant adjustments in later life. But this, too, may not be the result of sexual experiences in themselves so much as the consequence of having fallen out of the social main stream and, therefore, of running greater risks of isolation and alienation.)

In short, relatively few become truly active sexually before adolescence. And when they do (for girls more often than boys), it is seldom immediately related to sexual feelings or gratifications but is a use of sex for nonsexual goals and purposes. The "seductive" Lolita is rare but she is significant: she illustrates a more general pattern of psychosexual development—a commitment to the social relationships linked to sex before one can really grasp the social meaning of the physical relationships.

Of great importance are the values (or feelings, or images) that children pick up as being related to sex. Although we talk a lot about sexuality, as though trying to exorcise the demon of shame, learning about sex in our society is in large part learning about guilt; and learning how to manage sexuality commonly involves learning how to manage guilt. An important source of guilt in children comes from the imputation to them by adults of sexual appetites or abilities that they may not have but that they learn, however imperfectly, to pretend they have. The gestural concomitants of sexual modesty are learned early. For instance, when do girls learn to sit or pick up objects with their knees together? When do they learn that the bust must be covered? However, since this behavior is learned unlinked to later adult sexual performances, what children must make of all this is very mysterious.

The learning of sex roles, or sex identities, involves many things that are remote from actual sexual experience, or that become involved with sexuality only after puberty. Masculinity or femininity, their meaning and postures, are rehearsed before adolescence in many nonsexual ways.

A number of scholars have pointed, for instance, to the importance of aggressive, deference, dependency, and dominance behavior in childhood. Jerome Kagan and Howard Moss have found that aggressive behavior in males and dependency in females are relatively stable aspects of development. But what is social role, and what is biology? They found that when aggressive behavior occurred among girls, it tended to appear most often among those from well-educated families that were more tolerant of deviation. Curiously, they also reported that "it was impossible to predict the character of adult sexuality in women from their preadolescent and early adolescent behavior," and that "erotic activity is more anxiety-arousing for females than for males" because "the traditional ego ideal for women dictates inhibition of sexual impulses."

The belief in the importance of early sex-role learning for boys can be viewed in two ways. First, it may directly indicate an early sexual capacity in male children. Or, second, early masculine identification may merely be an appropriate framework within which the sexual impulse (salient with puberty) and the socially available sexual scripts (or accepted patterns of sexual behavior) can most conveniently find expression. Our bias, of course, is toward the second.

But, as Kagan and Moss also noted, the sex role learned by the child does not reliably predict how he will act sexually as an adult. This finding also can be interpreted in the same two alternative ways. Where sexuality is viewed as a biological constant which struggles to express itself, the female sex role learning can be interpreted as the successful repression of sexual impulses. The other interpretation suggests that the difference lies not in learning how to handle a preexistent sexuality but in learning how to *be* sexual. Differences between men and women, therefore, will have consequences both for *what* is done sexually, as well as *when*.

Once again, we prefer the latter interpretation, and some recent work that we have done with lesbians supports it. We observed that many of the major elements of their sex lives—the start of actual genital sexual behavior, the onset and frequency of masturbation, the time of entry in sociosexual patterns, the number of partners, and the reports of feelings of sexual deprivation— were for these homosexual women almost identical with those of ordinary women. Since sexuality would seem to be more important for lesbians—after all, they sacrifice much in order to follow their own sexual pathways—this is surprising. We concluded that the primary factor was something both categories of women share—the sex-role learning that occurs before sexuality itself becomes significant.

Social class also appears significant, more for boys than girls. Sex-role learning may vary by class; lower-class boys are supposed to be more aggressive and put much greater emphasis on early heterosexuality. The middle and upper classes tend to tolerate more deviance from traditional attitudes regarding appropriate male sex-role performances.

Given all these circumstances, it seems rather naive to think of sexuality as a constant pressure, with a peculiar necessity all its own. For us, the

crucial period of childhood has significance not because of sexual occurrences but because of nonsexual developments that will provide the names
and judgments for later encounters with sexuality.

Adolescence

The actual beginnings and endings of adolescence are vague. Generally, the
beginning marks the first time society, as such, acknowledges that the individual has sexual capacity. Training in the postures and rhetoric of the sexual
experience is now accelerated. Most important, the adolescent begins to
regard those about him (particularly his peers, but also adults) as sexual
actors and finds confirmation from others for this view.

For some, as noted, adolescent sexual experience begins before they are
considered adolescents. Kinsey reports that a tenth of his female sample and
a fifth of his male sample had experienced orgasm through masturbation by
age 12. But still, for the vast majority, despite some casual play and exploration that post-Freudians might view as masked sexuality, sexual experience
begins with adolescence. Even those who have had prior experience find that
it acquires new meanings with adolescence. They now relate such meanings
to both larger spheres of social life and greater senses of self. For example,
it is not uncommon during the transition between childhood and adolescence
for boys and, more rarely, girls to report arousal and orgasm while doing
things not manifestly sexual—climbing trees, sliding down bannisters, or
other activities that involve genital contact— without defining them as sexual. Often they do not even take it seriously enough to try to explore or
repeat what was, in all likelihood, a pleasurable experience.

Adolescent sexual development, therefore, really represents the beginning
of adult sexuality. It marks a definite break with what went on before. Not
only will future experiences occur in new and more complex contexts, but
they will be conceived of as explicitly sexual and thereby begin to complicate
social relationships. The need to manage sexuality will rise not only from
physical needs and desires but also from the new implications of personal
relationships. Playing, or associating, with members of the opposite sex now
acquires different meanings.

At adolescence, changes in the developments of boys and girls diverge and
must be considered separately. The one thing both share at this point is a
reinforcement of their new status by a dramatic biological event—for girls,
menstruation, and for the boys, the discovery of the ability to ejaculate. But
here they part. For boys, the beginning of a commitment to sexuality is

*Psychosexual
Development*

primarily genital; within two years of puberty all but a relatively few have had the experience of orgasm, almost universally brought about by masturbation. The corresponding organizing event for girls is not genitally sexual but social: they have arrived at an age where they will learn role performances linked with proximity to marriage. In contrast to boys, only two-thirds of girls will report ever having masturbated (and, characteristically, the frequency is much less). For women, it is not until the late twenties that the incidence of orgasm from any source reaches that of boys at age 16. In fact, significantly, about half of the females who masturbate do so only after having experienced orgasm in some situation involving others. This contrast points to a basic distinction between the developmental processes for males and females: males move from privatized personal sexuality to sociosexuality; females do the reverse and at a later stage in the life cycle.

The Turned-on Boys

We have worked hard to demonstrate the dominance of social, psychological, and cultural influences over the biological: now, dealing with adolescent boys, we must briefly reverse course. There is much evidence that the early male sexual impulses—again, initially through masturbation—are linked to physiological changes, to high hormonal inputs during puberty. This produces an organism that, to put it simply, is more easily turned on. Male adolescents report frequent erections, often without apparent stimulation of any kind. Even so, though there is greater biological sensitization and hence masturbation is more likely, the meaning, organization, and continuance of this activity still tends to be subordinate to social and psychological factors.

Masturbation provokes guilt and anxiety among most adolescent boys. This is not likely to change in spite of more "enlightened" rhetoric and discourse on the subject (generally, we have shifted from stark warnings of mental, moral, and physical damage to vague counsels against nonsocial or "inappropriate" behavior). However, it may be that this very guilt and anxiety gives the sexual experience an intensity of feeling that is often attributed to sex itself.

Such guilt and anxiety do not follow simply from social disapproval. Rather, they seem to come from several sources, including the difficulty the boy has in presenting himself as a sexual being to his immediate family, particularly his parents. Another source is the fantasies or plans associated with masturbation—fantasies about doing sexual "things" to others or having others do sexual "things" to oneself; or having to learn and rehearse available but proscribed sexual scripts or patterns of behavior. And, of course, some guilt and anxiety center around the general disapproval of masturbation. After the early period of adolescence, in fact, most youths will not admit to their peers that they did or do it.

Nevertheless, masturbation is for most adolescent boys the major sexual activity, and they engage in it fairly frequently. It is an extremely positive and gratifying experience to them. Such an introduction to sexuality can lead to a capacity for detached sex activity—activity whose only sustaining motive is sexual. This may be the hallmark of male sexuality in our society.

Of the three sources of guilt and anxiety mentioned, the first—how to manage both sexuality and an attachment to family members—probably cuts across class lines. But the others should show remarkable class differences. The second one, how to manage a fairly **elabo**rate and exotic fantasy life during masturbation, should be confined most typically to the higher classes, who are more experienced and adept at dealing with symbols. (It is possible, in fact, that this behavior, which girls rarely engage in, plays a role in the processes by which middle-class boys catch up with girls in measures of achievement and creativity and, by the end of adolescence, move out in front. However, this is only a hypothesis.)

The ability to fantasize during masturbation implies certain broad consequences. One is a tendency to see large parts of the environment in an erotic light, as well as the ability to respond, sexually and perhaps poetically, to many visual and auditory stimuli. We might also expect both a capacity and need for fairly elaborate forms of sexual activity. Further, since masturbatory fantasies generally deal with relationships and acts leading to coitus, they should also reinforce a developing capacity for heterosociality.

The third source of guilt and anxiety—the alleged "unmanliness" of masturbation—should more directly concern the lower-class male adolescent. ("Manliness" has always been an important value for lower-class males.) In these groups, social life is more often segregated by sex, and there are, generally, fewer rewarding social experiences from other sources. The adolescent therefore moves into heterosexual—if not heterosocial—relationships sooner than his middle-class counterparts. Sexual segregation makes it easier for him than for the middle-class boy to learn that he does not have to love everything he desires and therefore to come more naturally to casual, if not exploitative, relationships. The second condition—fewer social rewards that his fellows would respect—should lead to an exaggerated concern for proving masculinity by direct displays of physical prowess, aggression, and visible sexual success. And these three, of course, may be mutually reinforcing.

In a sense, the lower-class male is the first to reach "sexual maturity" as defined by the Freudians. That is, he is generally the first to become aggressively heterosexual and exclusively genital. This characteristic, in fact, is a distinguishing difference between lower-class males and those above them socially.

But one consequence is that although their sex lives are almost exclusively heterosexual, they remain homosocial. They have intercourse with females, but the standards and the audience they refer to are those of their male fellows. Middle-class boys shift predominantly to coitus at a significantly later time. They, too, need and tend to have homosocial elements in their sexual lives. But their fantasies, their ability to symbolize, and their social training in a world in which distinctions between masculinity and femininity are less sharply drawn, allow them to withdraw more easily from an all-male world. The difference between social classes obviously has important consequences for stable adult relationships.

One thing common in male experience during adolescence is that while it provides much opportunity for sexual commitment in one form or another, there is little training in how to handle emotional relations with girls. The imagery and rhetoric of romantic love is all around us; we are immersed in it. But whereas much is undoubtedly absorbed by the adolescent, he is not likely to tie it closely to his sexuality. In fact, such a connection might be inhibiting, as indicated by the survival of the "bad-girl-who-does" and "good-girl-who-doesn't" distinction. This is important to keep in mind as we turn to the female side of the story.

With the Girls

In contrast to males, female sexual development during adolescence is so similar in all classes that it is easy to suspect that it is solely determined by biology. But, while girls do not have the same level of hormonal sensitization to sexuality at puberty as adolescent boys, there is little evidence of a biological or social inhibitor either. The "equipment" for sexual pleasure is clearly present by puberty but tends not to be used by many females of any class. Masturbation rates are fairly low, and among those who do masturbate fairly infrequent. Arousal from "sexual" materials or situations happens seldom, and exceedingly few girls report feeling sexually deprived during adolescence.

Basically, girls in our society are not encouraged to be sexual—and may be strongly discouraged from being so. Most of us accept the fact that while "bad boy" can mean many things, "bad girl" almost exclusively implies sexual delinquency. It is both difficult and dangerous for an adolescent girl to become too active sexually. As Joseph Rheingold puts it, where men need only fear sexual failure, women must fear both success and failure.

Does this long period of relative sexual inactivity among girls come from repression of an elemental drive or merely from a failure to learn how to be sexual? The answers have important implications for their later sexual development. If it is repression, the path to a fuller sexuality must pass through processes of loss of inhibitions, during which the girl unlearns, in varying degrees, attitudes and values that block the expression of natural internal feelings. It also implies that the quest for ways to express directly sexual behavior and feelings that had been expressed nonsexually is secondary and of considerably less significance.

On the other hand, the "learning" answer suggests that women create or invent a capacity for sexual behavior, learning how and when to be aroused and how and when to respond. This approach implies greater flexibility: unlike the repression view, it makes sexuality both more and less than a basic force that may break loose at any time in strange or costly ways. The learning approach also lessens the power of sexuality altogether; all at once, particular kinds of sex activities need no longer be defined as either "healthy" or "sick." Lastly, subjectively, this approach appeals to the authors because it describes female sexuality in terms that seem less like a mere projection of male sexuality.

If sexual activity by adolescent girls assumes less specific forms than with boys, that does not mean that sexual learning and training do not occur. Curiously, though girls are, as a group, far less active sexually than boys, they receive far more training in self-consciously viewing themselves—and in viewing boys—as desirable mates. This is particularly true in recent years. Females begin early in adolescence to define attractiveness, at least partially, in sexual terms. We suspect that the use of sexual attractiveness for nonsexual purposes that marked our preadolescent "seductress" now begins to characterize many girls. Talcott Parsons' description of how the wife "uses" sex to bind the husband to the family, although harsh, may be quite accurate. More generally, in keeping with the childbearing and child-raising function of women, the development of a sexual role seems to involve a need to include in that role more than pleasure.

To round out the picture of the difference between the sexes, girls appear to be well-trained precisely in that area in which boys are poorly trained— that is, a belief in and a capacity for intense, emotionally-charged relation-

Psychosexual Development

ships and the language of romantic love. When girls during this period describe having been aroused sexually, they more often report it as a response to romantic, rather than erotic, words and actions.

In later adolescence, as dates, parties, and other sociosexual activities increase, boys—committed to sexuality and relatively untrained in the language and actions of romantic love—interact with girls committed to romantic love and relatively untrained in sexuality. Dating and courtship may well be considered processes in which each sex trains the other in what each wants and expects. What data is available suggests that this exchange system does not always work very smoothly. Thus, ironically, it is not uncommon to find that the boy becomes emotionally involved with his partner and therefore lets up on trying to seduce her, at the same time that the girl comes to feel that the boy's affection is genuine and therefore that sexual intimacy is more permissible.

In our recent study of college students, we found that boys typically had intercourse with their first coital partners one to three times, while with girls it was ten or more. Clearly, for the majority of females first intercourse becomes possible only in stable relationships or in those with strong bonds.

"Woman, What Does She Want?"

The male experience does conform to the general Freudian expectation that there is a developmental movement from a predominantly genital sexual commitment to a loving relationship with another person. But this movement is, in effect, reversed for females, with love or affection often a necessary precondition for intercourse. No wonder, therefore, that Freud had great difficulty understanding female sexuality—recall the concluding line in his great essay on women: "Woman, what does she want?" This "error"—the assumption that female sexuality is similar to or a mirror image of that of the male— may come from the fact that so many of those who constructed the theory were men. With Freud, in addition, we must remember the very concept of sexuality essential to most of nineteenth century Europe—it was an elemental beast that had to be curbed.

It has been noted that there are very few class differences in sexuality among females, far fewer than among males. One difference, however, is very relevant to this discussion—the age of first intercourse. This varies inversely with social class—that is, the higher the class, the later the age of first intercourse—a relationship that is also true of first marriage. The correlation between these two ages suggest the necessary social and emotional linkage between courtship and the entrance into sexual activity on the part of women. A second difference, perhaps only indirectly related to social class, has to do with educational achievement: here, a sharp border line seems to separate from all other women those who have or have had graduate or professional work. If sexual success may be measured by the percentage of sex acts that culminate in orgasm, graduate and professional women are the most sexually successful women in the nation.

Why? One possible interpretation derives from the work of Abraham Maslow: Women who get so far in higher education are more likely to be more aggressive, perhaps to have strong needs to dominate; both these characteristics are associated with heightened sexuality. Another, more general interpretation would be that in a society in which girls are expected primarily to become wives and mothers, going on to graduate school represents a kind of deviancy—a failure of, or alienation from, normal female social adjustment. In effect, then, it would be this flawed socialization—not biology—that produced both commitment toward advanced training and toward heightened sexuality.

For both males and females, increasingly greater involvement in the social aspects of sexuality—"socializing" with the opposite sex—may be one factor that marks the end of adolescence. We know little about this transition, especially among noncollege boys and girls; but our present feeling is that sexuality plays an important role in it. First, sociosexuality is important in family formation and also in learning the roles and obligations involved in being an adult. Second, and more fundamental, late adolescence is when a youth is seeking, and experimenting toward finding, his identity—who and what he is and will be; and sociosexual activity is the one aspect of this exploration that we associate particularly with late adolescence.

Young people are particularly vulnerable at this time. This may be partly due to the fact that society has difficulty protecting the adolescent from the consequences of sexual behavior that it pretends he is not engaged in. But, more importantly, it may be because, at all ages, we all have great problems in discussing our sexual feelings and experiences in personal terms. These, in turn, make it extremely difficult to get support from others for an adolescent's experiments toward trying to invent his sexual self. We suspect that success or failure in the discovery or management of sexual identity may have consequences in personal development far beyond merely the sexual sphere— perhaps in confidence and feelings of self-worth, belonging, competence, guilt, force of personality, and so on.

Psychosexual Development

15

Adulthood

In our society, all but a few ultimately marry. Handling sexual commitments inside marriage makes up the larger part of adult experience. Again, we have too little data for firm findings. The data we do have come largely from studies of broken and troubled marriages, and we do not know to what extent sexual problems in such marriages exceed those of intact marriages. It is possible that, because we have assumed that sex is important in most people's lives, we have exaggerated its importance in holding marriages together. Also, it is possible that, once people are married, sexuality declines relatively, becoming less important than other gratifications (such as domesticity or parenthood); or it may be that these other gratifications can minimize the effect of sexual dissatisfaction. Further, it may be possible that individuals learn to get sexual gratification, or an equivalent, from activities that are nonsexual or only partially sexual.

The sexual desires and commitments of males are the main determinants of the rate of sexual activity in our society. Men are most interested in intercourse in the early years of marriage—woman's interest peaks much later; nonetheless, coital rates decline steadily throughout marriage. This decline derives from many things, only one of which is decline in biological capacity. With many men, it is more difficult to relate sexually to a wife who is pregnant or a mother. Lower-class adult men receive less support and plaudits from their male friends for married sexual performance than they did as single adolescents; and we might also add the lower-class disadvantage of less training in the use of auxiliary or symbolic sexually-stimulating materials. For middle-class men, the decline is not as steep, owing perhaps to their greater ability to find stimulation from auxiliary sources, such as literature, movies, music, and romantic or erotic conversation. It should be further noted that for about 30 percent of college-educated men, masturbation continues regularly during marriage, even when the wife is available. An additional (if unknown) proportion do not physically masturbate but derive additional excitement from the fantasies that accompany intercourse.

But even middle-class sexual activity declines more rapidly than bodily changes can account for. Perhaps the ways males learn to be sexual in our society make it very difficult to keep it up at a high level with the same woman for a long time. However, this may not be vital in maintaining the family, or even in the man's personal sense of well-being, because, as previously suggested, sexual dissatisfaction may become less important as other satisfactions increase. Therefore, it need seldom result in crisis.

About half of all married men and a quarter of all married women will have intercourse outside of marriage at one time or another. For women, infidelity seems to have been on the increase since the turn of the century—at the same time that their rates of orgasm have been increasing. It is possible that the very nature of female sexuality is changing. Work being done now may give us new light on this. For men, there are strong social-class differences—the lower class accounts for most extramarital activity, especially during the early years of marriage. We have observed that it is difficult for a lower-class man to acquire the appreciation of his fellows for married intercourse; extramarital sex, of course, is another matter.

In general, we feel that far from sexual needs affecting other adult concerns, the reverse may be true: adult sexual activity may become that aspect of a person's life most often used to act out other needs. There are some data that suggest this. Men who have trouble handling authority relationships at work more often have dreams about homosexuality: some others, under heavy stress on the job, have been shown to have more frequent episodic homosexual experiences. Such phenomena as the rise of sadomasochistic practices and experiments in group sex may also be tied to nonsexual tensions, the use of sex for nonsexual purposes.

It is only fairly recently in the history of man that he has been able to begin to understand that his own time and place do not embody some eternal principle or necessity but are only dots on a continuum. It is difficult for many to believe that man can change, and is changing, in important ways. This conservative view is evident even in contemporary behavioral science; and a conception of man as having relatively constant sexual needs has become part of it. In an ever-changing world, it is perhaps comforting to think that man's sexuality does not change very much and therefore is relatively easily explained. We cannot accept this. Instead, we have attempted to offer a description of sexual development as a variable social invention—an invention that in itself explains little and requires much continuing explanation.

SEXUAL INTIMACY

Desmond Morris

This unique selection, while not "developmental" in the conventional sense (i.e., infancy-childhood-youth-adult progression), traces a twelve-stage sequence in the pattern of human courtship, in which the gradual process of building human love proceeds from attraction through trust to intimacy. While variations are often to be found in this pattern, Morris represents the sequence as virtually universal in pair-formation, and the process of growing intimacy as a uniquely human phenomenon.

The progress from first attraction to final trust is nearly always a long and complex sequence of gradually increasing intimacies, and it is this sequence that we must now examine.

To do so, the simplest method is to take a pair of "typical lovers," as seen in our Western culture, and follow them through the process of pair-formation from first glimpse to ultimate copulation. In doing this we must always remember that there is in reality no such thing as the "typical lover," any more than there is the "average citizen" or "man in the street." But it helps if we start out by trying to imagine one, and then, afterwards, consider the variations.

All animal courtship patterns are organized in a typical sequence, and the course taken by a human love affair is no exception. For convenience we can divide the human sequence up into twelve stages, and see what happens as each threshold is successfully passed. The twelve (obviously over-simplified) stages are these.

1. *Eye to body.* The most common form of social "contact" is to look at people from a distance. In a fraction of a second it is possible to sum up the physical qualities of another adult, labelling them and grading them mentally

in the process. The eyes feed the brain with immediate information concerning the sex, size, shape, age, coloring, status, and mood of the other person. Simultaneously a grading takes place on a scale from extreme attractiveness to extreme repulsiveness. If the signs indicate that the individual in view is an attractive member of the opposite sex, then we are ready to move on to the next phase in the sequence.

2. *Eye to eye.* While we view others, they view us. From time to time this means that our eyes meet, and when this happens the usual reaction is to look away quickly and break the eye "contact." This will not happen, of course, if we have recognized one another as previous acquaintances. In such cases, the moment of recognition leads instantly to mutual greeting signals, such as sudden smiling, raising of the eyebrows, changes in body posture, movements of the arms, and eventually vocalizations. If, on the other hand, we have locked eyes with a stranger, then the rapid looking away is the typical reaction, as if to avoid the temporary invasion of privacy. If one of the two strangers does continue to stare after eye contact has been made, the other may become acutely embarrassed and even angry. If it is possible to move away to avoid the staring eyes, this will soon be done, even though there was no element of aggression in the facial expressions or gestures accompanying the stare. This is because to perform prolonged staring is in itself an act of aggression between unfamiliar adults. The result is that two strangers normally watch one another in turn, rather than simultaneously. If, then, one finds the other attractive, he or she may add a slight smile to the next meeting of glances. If the response is returned, so is the smile, and further, more intimate contact may ensue. If the response is not returned, a blank look in reply to a friendly smile will usually stop any further development.

3. *Voice to voice.* Assuming there is no third party to make introductions, the next stage involves vocal contact between the male and female strangers. Invariably the initial comments will concern trivia. It is rare at this stage to make any direct reference to the true mood of the speakers. This small talk permits the reception of a further set of signals, this time to the ear instead of the eye. Dialect, tone of voice, accent, mode of verbal thinking and use of vocabulary permit a whole new range of units of information to be fed into the brain. Maintaining this communication at the level of irrelevant small talk enables either side to retreat from further involvement, should the new signals prove unattractive despite the promise of the earlier, visual signals.

4. *Hand to hand.* The previous three stages can all occur in seconds, or they may take months, with one potential partner silently admiring the other

from a distance, not daring to make vocal contact. This new stage, the hand to hand, may also take place quickly, in the form of the introduction handshake, or it is likely to be delayed for some considerable time. If the formalized, nonsexual handshake does not come into operation, then the first actual body contact to occur is likely to be disguised as an act of "supporting aid," "body protection" or "directional guidance." This is usually performed by the male towards the female and consists of holding her arm or hand to help her cross a street, or climb over an obstruction. If she is about to walk into an obstacle or danger spot, then the hand of the male can quickly take the opportunity to reach out swiftly and take her arm to alter her course or check her movement. If she slips or trips, a supporting action with the hands may also facilitate the first body contact. Again, the use of acts which are irrelevant to the true mood of the encounter is important. If the body of the girl has been touched by the man in the act of assisting her in some way, either partner can still withdraw from further involvement without loss of face. The girl can thank the man for his help and leave him, without being forced into a position where she has to deliver a direct rebuff. Both parties may be well aware that a behavior sequence is just beginning, and that it is one that may lead eventually to greater intimacies, but neither as yet does anything which openly states this fact, so that there is still time for one to back out without hurting the other's feelings. Only when the growing relationship has been openly declared will the action of hand-holding or arm-holding become prolonged in duration. It then ceases to be a "supportive" or "guiding" act and becomes an undisguised intimacy.

5. *Arm to shoulder.* Up to this point the bodies have not come into close contact. When they do so, another important threshold has been passed. Whether sitting, standing, or walking, physical contact down the side of the body indicates a great advance in the relationship from its earlier hesitant touchings. The earliest method employed is the shoulder embrace, usually with the man's arm placed around the girl's shoulders to draw the two partners together. This is the simplest introduction to trunk contact because it is already used in other contexts between mere friends as an act of nonsexual companionship. It is therefore the smallest next step to take and the least likely to meet rebuff. Walking together in this posture can be given the air of slight ambiguity, halfway between close friendship and love.

6. *Arm to waist.* A slight advance on the last stage occurs with the wrapping of the arm around the waist. This is something the man will not have done to other men, no matter how friendly, so that it becomes more of a

direct statement of amorous intimacy. Futhermore, his hand will now be in much closer proximity to the genital region of the female.

7. *Mouth to mouth.* Kissing on the mouth, combined with a full frontal embrace, is a major step forward. For the first time there is a strong chance of physiological arousal, if the action is prolonged or repeated. The female may experience genital secretions and the male's penis may start to become erect.

8. *Hand to head.* As an extension of the last stage, the hands begin to caress the partner's head. Fingers stroke the face, neck and hair. Hands clasp the nape and the side of the head.

9. *Hand to body.* In the postkissing phase, the hands begin to explore the partner's body, squeezing, fondling, and stroking. The major advance here is the manipulation by the male of the female's breasts. Further physiological arousal occurs with these acts and reaches such a pitch that, for many young females, this is a point at which a temporary halt is called. Further developments mean increasing difficulty in breaking off the pattern without continuing to completion, and if the bond of attachment has not reached a sufficient level of mutual trust, more advanced sexual intimacies are postponed.

10. *Mouth to breast.* Here the threshold is passed in which the interactions become strictly private. For most couples this will also have applied to the last stage, especially where breast manipulations are concerned, but advanced kissing and body-fondling does occur frequently in public places under certain circumstances. Such actions may cause reactions of disapproval in other members of the public, but it is rare in most countries for serious steps to be taken against the embracing couple. With the advance to breast-kissing, however, the situation is entirely different, if only because it involves the exposure of the female breast. Mouth-to-breast contacts are the last of the pregenital intimacies and are the prelude to actions which are concerned not merely with arousal, but with arousal to climax.

11. *Hand to genitals.* If the manual exploration of the partner's body continues, it inevitably arrives at the genital region. After tentative caressing of the partner's genitals, the actions soon develop into gentle, rhythmic rubbing that stimulates the rhythm of pelvic thrusting. The male repeatedly strokes the labia or clitoris of the female and may insert his finger or fingers into the vagina, imitating the action of the penis. Manual stimulation of this kind can soon lead to orgasm for either sex and is a common form of culmination in advanced precopulatory encounters between lovers.

12. *Genitals to genitals.* Finally, the stage of full copulation is reached and, if the female is a virgin, the first irreversible act of the entire sequence

Sexual Intimacy

21

occurs with the rupture of the hymen. There is also, for the first time, the possibility of another irreversible act, namely that of fertilization. This irreversibility puts this concluding act in the sequence on to an entirely new plane. Each stage will have served to tighten the bond of attachment a little more, but, in a biological sense, this final copulatory action is clearly related to a phase where the earlier intimacies will already have done their job of cementing the bond, so that the pair will want to stay together after the sex drive has been reduced by the consummation of orgasm. If this bonding has failed, the female is liable to find herself pregnant in the absence of a stable family unit.

These, then, are twelve typical stages in the pair-formation process of a young male and female. To some extent they are, of course, culturally determined, but to a much greater extent they are determined by the anatomy and sexual physiology common to all members of our species.

THE SOCIAL CONSTRUCTION
OF THE SECOND SEX

Jo Freeman

Jo Freeman is critical of social science for "describing what" rather than "analyzing why," but she utilizes social science research insights to document her thesis that women are systematically trained to be dysfunctional in an achievement-oriented male-dominated society. Blaming what she calls "dependency training" of girls in our society, she calls attention to the low social status that accompanies being female; the minimal esteem accorded women by both sexes, including the phenomenon of women's collective self-hatred; the denigration of achievement by women; the identification of IQ increase with such "male" characteristics as assertiveness and dominance; and the resemblances between the experience of racial minorities in our culture, of colonial peoples abroad, and of women in the U.S.

This article is placed here rather than in the section on masculinity/femininity because it raises some interesting developmental questions regarding female sexuality. Are girls and women inherently nonachievers, or are they trained, subtly or overtly, in this behavior? If it is not an innate characteristic, why do women accept subordination in an essentially achievement-oriented society in which worth is often equated with productivity and assertiveness? What do the increasingly egalitarian family patterns cited here portend for future man-woman relationships and for growing up girlish or boyish?

The passivity that is the essential characteristic of the "feminine" woman is a trait that develops in her from the earliest years. But it is wrong to assert a biological datum is concerned; it is in fact a destiny imposed upon her by her teachers and by society.—SIMONE DE BEAUVOIR

During the last thirty years social science has paid scant attention to women, confining its explorations of humanity to the male. Research has generally reinforced the sex stereotypes of popular mythology that women are essentially nurturant/expressive/passive and men instrumental/active/aggressive. Social scientists have tended to justify these stereotypes rather than analyze their origins, their value, or their effect.

In part this is due to the general conservatism and reluctance to question the status quo which has characterized the social sciences during this era of the feminine mystique. In part it is attributable to the "pervasive permeation of psychoanalytic thinking throughout American society."[1] The result has been a social science which is more a mechanism of social control than of social inquiry. Rather than trying to analyze why, it has only described what. Rather than exploring how men and women came to be the way they are, it has taken their condition as an irremediable given and sought to justify it on the basis of "biological" differences.

Nonetheless, the assumption that psychology recapitulates physiology has begun to crack. Masters and Johnson shattered the myth of women's natural sexual passivity—on which her psychological passivity was claimed to rest. Research is just beginning in the other areas. Even without this new research, new interpretations of the old data are being explored. What these new interpretations say is that women are the way they are because they've been trained to be that way. As the Bems put it: "We overlook the fact that the society that has spent twenty years carefully marking the women's ballot for her has nothing to lose in that twenty-first year by pretending to let her cast it for the alternative of her choice. Society has controlled not her alternatives but her motivation to choose any but the one of those alternatives."[2]

This motivation is controlled through the socialization process. Women are raised to want to fill the social roles in which society needs them. They are trained to model themselves after the accepted image and to meet as individuals the expectations that are held for women as a group. Therefore, to understand how most women are socialized we must first understand how they see themselves and are seen by others. Several studies have been done on this. Quoting from one of them, McClelland stated that "the female image is characterized as small, weak, soft, and light. In the United States it is also dull, childish, helpless, sorry, timid, clumsy, stupid, silly, and domestic. On a study which asked men and women to choose out of a long list of adjectives those which most closely applied to themselves showed that women strongly felt themselves to be uncertain, anxious, nervous, hasty, careless, fearful, dull, childish, helpless, sorry, timid, clumsy, stupid, silly, and domestic. On a more positive side, women felt that they were understanding, tender, sympathetic, pure, generous, affectionate, loving, moral, kind, grateful, and patient.[4]

This is not a very favorable self-image, but it does correspond fairly well with the social myths about what women are like. The image has some nice qualities, but they are not the ones normally required for that kind of achievement to which society gives its highest social rewards. Now one can justifiably question both the idea of achievement and the qualities necessary for it, but this is not the place to do so. Rather, because the current standards are the ones which women have been told they do not meet, the purpose here will be to look at the socialization process as a mechanism to keep them from doing so. We will also need to analyze some of the social expectations about women and about what they define as a successful *woman* (not a successful person) because they are inextricably bound up with the socialization process. All people are socialized to meet the social expectations held for them, and it is only when this process fails to do so (as is currently happening on several fronts) that it is at all questioned.

Let us further examine the effects on women of minority group status. Here, an interesting parallel emerges, but it is one fraught with much heresy. When we look at the *results* of female socialization we find a strong similarity between what our society labels, even extols, as the typical "feminine" character structure and that of oppressed peoples in this country and elsewhere.

In his classic study on *The Nature of Prejudice,* Allport devotes a chapter to "Traits Due to Victimization." Included are such personality characteristics as sensitivity, submission, fantasies of power, desire for protection, indirectness, ingratiation, petty revenge and sabotage, sympathy, extremes of both self and group hatred and self and group glorification, display of flashy status symbols, compassion for the underprivileged, identification with the dominant group's norms, and passivity.[5] Allport was primarily concerned with Jews and Negroes, but compare his characterization with the very thorough review of the literature on sex differences among young children made by Terman and Tyler. For girls, they listed such traits as sensitivity, conformity to social pressures, response to environment, ease of social control, ingratiation, sympathy, low levels of aspiration, compassion for the underprivileged, and anxiety. They found that girls compared to boys were more nervous, unstable, neurotic, socially dependent, submissive, had less self-confidence, lower opinions of themselves and of girls in general, and were more timid, emotional, ministrative, fearful, and passive.[6]

Girls' perceptions of themselves were also distorted. Although girls make consistently better school grades than boys until late high school, their opinion of themselves grows progressively worse with age and their opinion of boys and boys' abilities grows better. Boys, however, have an increasingly better opinion of themselves and worse opinion of girls as they grow older.[7]

These distortions become so gross that, according to Goldberg, by the time girls reach college they have become prejudiced against women. He gave college girls sets of booklets containing six identical professional articles in traditional male, female, and neutral fields. The articles were identical, but the names of the authors were not. For example, an article in one set would bear the name John T. McKay and in another set the same article would be authored by Joan T. McKay. Each booklet contained three articles by "women" and three by "men." Questions at the end of each article asked the students to rate the articles on value, persuasiveness, and profundity and the authors on writing style and competence. The male authors fared better in every field, even such "feminine" areas as art history and dietetics. Goldberg concluded that "Women are prejudiced against female professionals and, regardless of the actual accomplishments of these professionals, will firmly refuse to recognize them as the equals of their male colleagues."[8]

This combination of group self-hate and distortion of perceptions to justify that group self-hate are precisely the traits typical of a "minority group character structure."[9] It has been noted time and time again. The Clarks' finding of this pattern in Negro children in segregated schools contributed to the 1954 Supreme Court decision that outlawed such schools. These traits, as well as the others typical of the "feminine" stereotype, have been found in the Indians under British rule,[10] in the Algerians under the French,[11] and in black Americans.[12] There seems to be a correlation between being "feminine" and experiencing status deprivation.

This pattern repeats itself even within cultures. In giving TATs to women in Japanese villages, De Vos discovered that those from fishing villages, where the status position of women was higher than in farming communities, were more assertive, not as guilt-ridden, and were more willing to ignore the traditional pattern of arranged marriages in favor of love marriages.[13]

Development and Sexuality

In Terman's famous 50-year study of the gifted, a comparison in adulthood of those men who conspicuously failed to fulfill their early promise with those who did fulfill it showed that the successful had more self-confidence, fewer background disabilities, and were less nervous and emotionally unstable. But, they concluded "the disadvantages associated with lower social and home status appeared to present the outstanding handicap."[14]

The fact that women do have lower social status than men in our society and that both sexes tend to value men and male characteristics, values, and activities more highly than those of women has been noted by many authorities.[15] What has not been done is to make the connection between this status and its accompanying personality.

The failure to extensively analyze the effects and the causes of lower social status is surprising in light of the many efforts that have been made to uncover distinct psychological differences between men and women to account for the tremendous disparity in their social production and creativity. The Goldberg study implies that even if women did achieve on a par with men it would not be perceived or accepted as such and that a woman's work must be of a much higher quality than that of a man to be given the same recognition. But these circumstances alone, or the fact that it is the male definition of achievement which is applied, are not sufficient to account for the lack of social production. So research has turned to male/female differences.

Most of this research, in the Freudian tradition, has focused on finding the psychological and developmental differences supposedly inherent in feminine nature and function. Despite all these efforts, the general findings of psychological testing indicate that: (1) Individual differences are greater than sex differences; i.e. sex is just one of the many characteristics which define a human being. (2) Most differences in ability in any field do not appear until elementary school age or later. "Sex differences become more apparent with increasing education even if it is coeducation."[16]

An examination of the literature of intellectual differences between the sexes discloses some interesting patterns. First, the statistics themselves show some regularity. Most conclusions of what is typical of one sex or the other are founded upon the performances of two-thirds of the subjects. For example, two-thirds of all boys do better on the math section of the College Board Exam than the verbal, and two-thirds of the girls do better on the verbal than the math. Bales' studies show a similar distribution when he concludes that in small groups men are the task-oriented leaders and women are the social-emotional leaders.[17] Not all tests show this two-thirds differential, but it is the mean about which most results of the ability test cluster. Sex is an easily visible, differentiable, and testable criterion on which to draw conclusions; but it doesn't explain the one-third that doesn't fit. The only characteristic virtually all women seem to have in common, besides their anatomy, is their lower social status.

Second, girls get off to a very good start. They begin speaking, reading and counting sooner. They articulate more clearly and put words into sentences earlier. They have fewer reading and stuttering problems. Girls are even better in math in the early school years. Consistent sex differences in favor of boys do not appear until high-school age.[18] Here another pattern begins to develop.

During high school, girls' performance in school and on ability tests begins to drop, sometimes drastically. Although well over half of all high-school graduates are girls, significantly less than half of all college students are girls. Presumably, this should mean that a higher percentage of the better female students go on to higher education, but their performance *vis-à-vis* boys' continues to decline.

Girls start off better than boys and end up worse. This change in their performance occurs at a very significant point in time. It occurs when their status changes, or to be more precise, when girls become aware of what their adult status is supposed to be. It is during adolescence that peer-group pressures to be "feminine" or "masculine" increase and the conceptions of what is "feminine" and "masculine" become more narrow.[19] It is also at this time that there is a personal drive for conformity.[20]

One of the norms of our culture to which a girl learns to conform is that only men excel. This was evident in Lipinski's study of "Sex-Role Conflict and Achievement Motivation in College Women," which showed that thematic pictures depicting males as central characters elicited significantly more achievement imagery than female pictures.[21] One need only recall Asch's experiments to see how peer-group pressures, armed only with our rigid ideas about "femininity" and "masculinity" could lead to a decline in girls' performance. Asch found that some 33 percent of his subjects would go contrary to the evidence of their own senses about something as tangible as the comparative length of two lines when their judgments were at variance with those made by the other group members.[22] All but a handful of the other 67 percent experienced tremendous trauma in trying to stick to their correct perceptions.

When we move to something as intangible as sex-role behavior and to social sanctions far greater than the displeasure of a group of unknown experimental stooges, we can get an idea of how stifling social expectations can be. It is not surprising, in light of our cultural norm that a girl should not appear too smart or surpass boys in anything, that those pressures to conform, so prevalent in adolescence, should prompt girls to believe that the development of their minds will have only negative results. The lowered self-esteem and the denigration of their own sex noted by Smith[23] and Goldberg[24] are a logical consequence. These pressures even affect the supposedly unchangeable IQ scores. Corresponding with the drive for social acceptance, girls' IQs drop below those of boys during high school, rise slightly if they go to college, and go into a steady and consistent decline when and if they become full-time housewives.[25]

These are not the only consequences. Negative self-conceptions have negative effects in a manner that can only be called a self-fulfilling prophecy. They stifle motivation and channel energies into those areas that are likely to get some positive social rewards. Then those subject to these pressures are condemned for not having strived for the highest social rewards society has to offer.

A good example of this double bind is what psychologists call the "need for achievement." Achievement motivation in male college sophomores has been studied extensively. In women it has barely been looked at; women didn't fit the model social scientists set up to explain achievement in men. Girls do not seem to demonstrate the same consistent correlation between achievement and scores on achievement tests that boys do. For example, Stivers found that "nonmotivated for college" girls scored higher on achievement motivation exams than "well-motivated for college" girls.[26] There has been little inquiry as to why this is so. The general policy followed by the researchers was that if girls didn't fit, leave them out. Nonetheless some theories have been put forward.

Pierce postulated that part of the confusion resulted from using the same criteria of achievement for girls that were used for boys—achievement in school. Therefore, he did a study of marriage vs. career orientation in high-school girls which did show a small but consistent correlation between high achievement motivation scores and marriage orientation.[27] In 1961 he did another study which showed a very strong correlation between high achievement scores and actual achievement of marriage within a year of high-school graduation. Those who went on to college and/or did not get married had low achievement scores.[28]

Although he unfortunately did not describe the class origins and other relevant characteristics of his study—it does seem clear that the real situation is not that women do not have achievement motivation but that this motivation is directed differently from that of men. In fact, the achievement orientation of both sexes goes precisely where it is socially directed—educational achievement for boys and marriage achievement for girls. Pierce suggested that "achievement motivation in girls attaches itself not to academic performance, but rather to more immediate adult status goals. This would be a logical assumption in that academic success is much less important to achievement status as a woman than it is for a man."[29]

He goes on to say that "girls see that to achieve in life as adult females they need to achieve in nonacademic ways, that is, attaining the social graces, achieving beauty in person and dress, finding a desirable social status, marrying the right man. This is the successful adult woman. . . . Their achievement motivations are directed toward realizing personal goals through their relationship with men. . . . Girls who are following the normal course of development are most likely to seek adult status through marriage at an early age."[30]

Achievement for women is adult status through marriage, not success in the usual use of the word. One might postulate that both kinds of success might be possible, particularly for the highly achievement-oriented woman. But in fact the two are more often perceived as contradictory; success in one is seen to preclude success in the other.

Horner just completed a study at the University of Michigan from which she postulated a psychological barrier to achievement in women. She administered a TAT word item to undergraduates that said "After first term finals Anne finds herself at the top of her medical school class." A similar one for a male control group used a masculine name. The results were scored for imagery of fear of success and Horner found that 65% of the women and only 10% of the men demonstrated a definite "motive to avoid success." She explained the results by hypothesizing that the prospect of success, or situations in which success or failure is a relevant dimension, are perceived as having, and in fact do have, negative consequences for women. Success in the normal sense is threatening to women. Further research confirmed that fear of social rejection and role conflict did generate a "motive to avoid success."[31]

Ability differences correlate strongly with interest differences,[32] and women have a definite interest in avoiding success. This is reinforced by peer and cultural pressures. However, many sex differences appear too early to be much affected by peer groups and are not directly related to sex-role attributes.

One such sex difference is spatial perception, or the ability to visualize objects out of their context. This is a test in which boys do better, though differences are usually not discernible before the early school years.[33] Other tests, such as the Embedded Figures and the Rod and Frame Tests, likewise favor boys. They indicate that boys perceive more analytically, while girls are more contextual. This ability to "break set" or be "field independent" also does not seem to appear until after the fourth or fifth year.[34]

According to Maccoby, this contextual mode of perception common to women is a distinct disadvantage for scientific production. "Girls on the average develop a somewhat different way of handling incoming information —their thinking is less analytic, more global, and more preservative—and this kind of thinking may serve very well for many kinds of functioning but it is not the kind of thinking most conducive to high-level intellectual productivity, especially in science."[35]

Several social psychologists have postulated that the key developmental characteristic of analytic thinking is what is called early "independence and mastery training," or "whether and how soon a child is encouraged to assume initiative, to take responsibility for himself, and to solve problems by himself, rather than rely on others for the direction of his activities."[36] In other words, analytically inclined children are those who have not been subect to what Bronfenbrenner calls "over-socialization,"[37] and there is a good deal of indirect evidence that such is the case. Levy has observed that "overprotected" boys tend to develop intellectually like girls.[38] Bing found that those girls who were good at spatial tasks were those whose mothers left them alone to solve the problems by themselves, while the mothers of verbally inclined daughters insisted on helping them.[39] Witkin similarly found that mothers of analytic children had encouraged their initiative, while mothers of nonanalytic children had encouraged dependence and discouraged self-assertion.[40] One writer commented on these studies that "this is to be expected, for the independent child is less likely to accept superficial appearances of objects without exploring them for himself, while the dependent child will be afraid to reach out on his own, and will accept appearances without question. In other words, the independent child is likely to be more *active,* not only psychologically but physically, and the physically active child will naturally have more kinesthetic experience with spatial relationships in his environment."[41]

The qualities associated with independence training also have an effect on IQ. Sontag did a longitudinal study in which he compared children whose IQs had improved with those whose IQs had declined with age. He discovered that the child with increasing IQ was competitive, self-assertive, independent, and dominant in interaction with other children. Children with declining IQs were passive, shy, and dependent.[42]

Maccoby commented on this study that "the characteristics associated with a rising IQ are not very feminine characteristics." When one of the people working on it was asked about what kind of developmental history was necessary to make a girl into an intellectual person, he replied, "The simplest way to put it is that she must be a tomboy at some point in her childhood."[43]

Likewise Kagan and Moss noted that "females who perform well on problems requiring analysis and complex reasoning tend to reject a traditional feminine identification."[44] They also observed that among the children involved in the Fels study "protection of girls was associated with the adoption of feminine interests during childhood and adulthood. Maternal protection apparently 'feminized' both the boys and the girls."[45]

However, analytic abilities are not the only ones that are valued in our society. Being person-oriented and contextual in perception are very valuable attributes for many fields where, nevertheless, very few women are found. Such characteristics are also valuable in the arts and some of the social sciences. But while women do succeed here more than in the sciences, their achievement is still not equivalent to that of men. One explanation of this, of course, is the Horner study that established a "motive to avoid success." But when one looks further it appears that there is an earlier cause here as well.

The very same early independence and mastery training that has such a beneficial effect on analytic thinking also determines the extent of one's achievement orientation.[46]

Although comparative studies of parental treatment of boys and girls are not extensive, those that have been made indicate that the traditional practices applied to girls are very different from those applied to boys. Girls receive more affection, more protectiveness, more control and more restrictions. Boys are subjected to more achievement demands and higher expectations.[47] In short, while girls are not always encouraged to be dependent *per se*, they are usually not encouraged to be *independent* and physically active. "Such findings indicate that the differential treatment of the two sexes seems to focus primarily on directing and constraining the boys' impact on the environment. With daughters, the aim is rather to protect the girl from the impact of environment. The boy is being prepared to mold his world, the girl to be molded by it."[48] The pattern is typical of girls, Bronfenbrenner maintains, and involves the risk of "oversocialization."

He doesn't discuss the possible negative effects such oversocialization has on girls, but he does express his concern about what would happen to the *Development* "qualities of independence, initiative, and self-sufficiency" of boys if such *and Sexuality* training were applied to them. "While an affectional context is important for the socialization of boys, it must evidently be accompanied by and be compatible with a strong component of parental discipline. Otherwise, the boy finds himself in the same situation as the girl, who, having received greater affection, is more sensitive to its withdrawal, with the result that a little discipline goes a long way and strong authority is constricting rather than constructive."[49]

That these variations in socialization result in variations in personality is corroborated by Schachter's studies of first and later-born children. Like girls, first children tend to be better socialized but also more anxious and dependent, whereas second children, like boys, are more aggressive and self-confident.[50]

Bronfenbrenner concludes that the crucial variable is the differential treatment by the father and "in fact, it is the father who is especially likely to treat children of the two sexes differently." His extremes of affection, and of authority, are both deleterious. Not only do his high degrees of nurturance and protectiveness toward girls result in "over-socialization," but "the presence of strong paternal power is particularly debilitating. In short, boys thrive in a patriarchal context, girls in a matriarchal one."[51]

His observations receive indirect support from Douvan who noted that "part-time jobs of mothers have a beneficial effect on adolescent children, particularly daughters. This reflects the fact that adolescents may receive too much mothering."[52]

The importance of mothers, as well as mothering, was pointed out by Kagan and Moss. In looking at the kinds of role models that mothers provide for developing daughters, they discovered that it is those women who are looked upon as unfeminine whose daughters tend to achieve intellectually. These mothers are "aggressive and competitive women who were critical of their daughters and presented themselves to their daughters as intellectually competitive and aggressive role models. It is reasonable to assume that the girls identified with these intellectually aggressive women who valued mastery behavior."[53]

There seems to be some evidence that the sexes have been differentially socialized with different training practices, for different goals, and with different results. If McClelland is right in all the relationships he finds between child-rearing practices (in particular independence and mastery training), achievement-motivation scores of individuals tested, actual achievement of individuals, and indeed, the economic growth of whole societies,[54] there is no longer much question as to why the historical achievement of women has been so low. In fact, with the dependency training they receive so early in life, the wonder is that they have achieved so much.

But this is not the whole story. Maccoby, in her discussion of the relationship of independence training to analytic abilities, notes that the girl who does not succumb to overprotection and develop the appropriate personality and behavior for her sex has a major price to pay: a price in anxiety. Or, as other observers have noted: "The universe of appropriate behavior for males and females is delineated early in development and it is difficult for the child to cross these culturally given frontiers without considerable conflict and tension."[55]

Some anxiety is beneficial to creative thinking, but high or sustained levels of it are damaging, "for it narrows the range of solution efforts, interferes with breaking set, and prevents scanning of the whole range of elements open to perception."[56] This anxiety is particularly manifest in college women,[57] and of course they are the ones who experience the most conflict between their current—intellectual—activities, and expectations about behavior in their future—unintellectual—careers.

Maccoby feels that "it is this anxiety which helps to account for the lack of productivity among those women who do make intellectual careers." The combination of social pressures, role-expectations, and parental training together tell "something of a horror story. It would appear that even when a woman is suitably endowed intellectually and develops the right temperament and habits of thought to make use of her endowment, she must be fleet of foot indeed to scale the hurdles society has erected for her and to remain a whole and happy person while continuing to follow her intellectual bent."[58]

The reasons for this horror story must by now be clearly evident. Traditionally, women have been defined as passive creatures, sexually, physically, and mentally. Their roles have been limited to the passive, dependent, auxiliary ones, and they have been trained from birth to fit these roles. However, those qualities by which one succeeds in this society are active ones. Achievement orientation, intellectuality, and analytic ability all require a certain amount of aggression.

As long as women were convinced that these qualities were beyond them, that they were inferior in their exercise and much happier if they stayed in their place, they remained quiescent under the paternalistic system of Western civilization. Paternalism was a preindustrial scheme of life, and its yoke was partially broken by the industrial revolution.[59] With this loosening up of the social order, the talents of women began to appear.

Development and Sexuality

In the 18th Century it was held that no women had ever produced anything worthwhile in literature with the possible exception of Sappho. But in the first half of the 19th Century, feminine writers of genius flooded the literary

34

scene.[60] It wasn't until the end of the 19th Century that women scientists of note appeared, and it was still later that women philosophers were found.

Only since the industrial revolution shook the whole social order have women been able to break some of the traditional bounds of society. In pre-industrial societies, the family was the basic unit of social and economic organization, and women held a significant and functional role within it. This, coupled with the high birth and death rates of those times, gave women more than enough to do within the home. It was the center of production and women could be both at home and in the world at the same time. But the industrial revolution, along with decreased infant mortality, increased life-span and changes in economic organization, have all but destroyed the family as the economic unit. Technological advances have taken men out of the home, and now those functions traditionally defined as female are being taken out also.[61] For the first time in human history women have had to devote themselves to being full-time mothers in order to have enough to do.[62]

Conceptions of society have also changed. At one time, authoritarian hierarchies were the norm and paternalism was reflective of a general social authoritarian attitude. While it is impossible to do retroactive studies on feudalistic society, we do know that authoritarianism as a personality trait does correlate strongly with a rigid conception of sex roles, and with ethnocentrism.[63] We also know from ethnological data that there is a "parallel between family relationships and the larger social hierarchy. Autocratic societies have autocratic families. As the king rules his subjects and the nobles subjugate and exploit the commoners, so does husband tend to lord it over wife, father rule over son."[64]

According to D'Andrade, "another variable that appears to affect the distribution of authority and deference between the sexes is the degree to which men rather than women control and mediate property."[65] He presented data which showed a direct correlation between the extent to which inheritance, succession, and descent-group membership were patrilineal and the degree of subjection of women.

Even today, the equality of the sexes in the family is often reflective of the economic equality of the partners. In a Detroit sample, Blood and Wolfe found that the relative power of the wife was low if she did not work and increased with her economic contribution to the family.[66] "The employment of women affects the power structure of the family by equalizing the resources of husband and wife. A working wife's husband listens to her more, and she listens to herself more. She expresses herself and has more opinions. Instead of looking up into her husband's eyes and worshipping him, she levels with him, compromising on the issues at hand. Thus her power increases and relatively speaking, the husband's falls."[67]

Goode also noted this pattern but said it varied inversely with class status. Toward the upper strata, wives are not only less likely to work but when they do they contribute a smaller percentage of the total family income than is true in the lower classes.[68] Hill went so far as to say "Money is a source of power that supports male dominance in the family. . . . Money belongs to him who earns it, not to her who spends it, since he who earns it may withhold it."[69] Hallenbeck feels more than just economic resources are involved but does conclude that there is a balance of power in every family which affects "every other aspect of the marriage—division of labor, amount of adaptation necessary for either spouse, methods used to resolve conflicts, and so forth."[70] Blood feels the economic situation affects the whole family structure. "Daughters of working mothers are more independent, more self-reliant, more aggressive, more dominant, and more disobedient. Such girls are no longer meek, mild, submissive, and feminine like 'little ladies' ought to be. They are rough and tough, actively express their ideas, and refuse to take anything from anybody else. . . . Because their mothers have set an example, the daughters get up the courage and the desire to earn money as well. They take more part-time jobs after school and more jobs during summer vacations."[71]

Barry, Bacon and Child did an ethnohistoriographic analysis that provides some further insights into the origins of male dominance. After examining the ethnographic reports of 110 cultures, they concluded that large sexual differentiation and male superiority occur concurrently and in "an economy that places a high premium on the superior strength and superior development of motor skills requiring strength, which characterize the male."[72] It is those societies in which great physical strength and mobility are required for survival, in which hunting and herding, or warfare, play an important role, that the male, as the physically stronger and more mobile sex, tends to dominate. This is supported by Spiro's analysis of sex roles in an Israeli kibbutz. There, the economy was largely unmechanized and the superior average strength of the men was needed on many jobs. Thus, despite a conscious attempt to break down traditional sex-roles, they began reasserting themselves, as women were assigned to the less strenuous jobs."[73]

Although there are a few tasks which virtually every society assigns only to men or women, there is a great deal of overlap for most jobs. Virtually every task, even in the most primitive societies, can be performed by either men or women. Equally important, what is defined as a man's task in one society may well be classified as a woman's job in another.[74] Nonetheless, the sexual division of labor is much more narrow than dictated by physical limitations, and what any one culture defines as a woman's job will seldom be performed by a man and vice versa. It seems that what originated as a division of labor based upon the necessities of survival has spilled over into many other areas and lasted long past the time of its social value. Where male strength and mobility has been crucial to social survival, male dominance and the aura of male superiority has been the strongest. The latter has been incorporated into the value structure and attained an existence of its own.

Thus, male superiority has not ceased with an end to the need for male strength. As Goode pointed out, there is one consistent element in the assignment of jobs to the sexes, even in modern societies: "Whatever the strictly male tasks are, they are defined as *more honorific* (emphasis his). . . . Moreover, the tasks of control, management, decision, appeals to the gods—in short the higher level jobs that typically do *not* require strength, speed or traveling far from home—are male jobs."[75]

He goes on to comment that "this element suggests that the sexual division of labor within family and society comes perilously close to the racial or caste restrictions in some modern countries. That is, the low-ranking race, caste, or sex is defined as not being *able* to do certain types of prestigious work, but it is also considered a violation of propriety if they do it. Obviously, if women really cannot do various kinds of male tasks, no moral or ethical prohibition would be necessary to keep them from it."[76]

Sex roles originated in economic necessities but the value attached to any one role has become a factor of sex alone. Even cross-culturally, these roles, and the attitudes associated with them, are ingrained by common socialization practices. Barry, Bacon, and Child discovered that "pressure toward nurturance, obedience and responsibility is most often stronger for girls, whereas pressure toward achievement and self-reliance is most often stronger for boys."[77] These are the same socialization practices traditionally found in Western society. As the Barry, Bacon, and Child study showed, these socializations serve to prepare children for roles as adults that require women to stay near the home and men to go out and achieve. The greater emphasis a society places on physical strength, the greater the sex-role differentiation and the sex differences in socialization.

These sex-role differences may have served a natural function at one time, but it is doubtful that they still do so. The characteristics we observe in women and men today are a result of socialization practices that were developed for survival of a primitive society. The value structure of male superiority is a reflection of the primitive orientations and values. But social and economic conditions have changed drastically since these values were developed. Technology has reduced to almost nothing the importance of muscular strength. In fact, the warlike attitude which goes along with an idealization of physical strength and dominance is proving to be positively destructive. The value of large families has also become a negative one. Now we are concerned with the population explosion and prefer that our society produce children of quality rather than quantity. The result of all these changes is that the traditional sex-roles and the traditional family structures have become dysfunctional.

To some extent, patterns of child-rearing have also changed. Bronfenbrenner reports that at least middle-class parents are raising both boys and girls much the same. He noted that over a 50-year period middle-class parents have been developing a "more acceptant, equalitarian relationship with their children."[78] With an increase in the family's social position, the patterns of parental treatment of children begin to converge.[79] He likewise noted that a similar phenomenon is beginning to develop in lower-class parents and that equality of treatment is slowly working its way down the social ladder.

These changes in patterns of child-rearing correlate with changes in relationships within the family. Both are moving toward a less hierarchical and more egalitarian pattern of living.

As Blood has pointed out, "today we may be on the verge of a new phase in American family history, when the companionship family is beginning to manifest itself. One distinguishing characteristic of this family is the dual employment of husband and wife. . . . Employment emancipates women from domination by their husbands and, secondarily, raises their daughters from inferiority to their brothers. . . . The classic differences between masculinity and femininity are disappearing as both sexes in the adult generation take on the same roles in the labor market. . . . The roles of men and women are converging for both adults and children. As a result the family will be far less segregated internally, far less stratified into different age generations and different sexes. The old asymmetry of male-dominated, female-serviced family life is being replaced by a new symmetry."[80]

All these data indicate that several trends are converging at about the same time. Our value structure has changed from an authoritarian one to a more democratic one, though our social structure has not yet caught up. Social attitudes begin in the family; only a democratic family can raise children to be citizens in a democratic society. The social and economic organization of society which kept women in the home has likewise changed. The home is no longer the center of society. The primary male and female functions have left it and there is no longer any major reason for maintaining the large sex-role differentiations which it supported. The value placed on physical strength which reinforced the dominance of men, and the male superiority attitudes that this generated, have also become dysfunctional. It is the mind, not the body, which must now prevail, and woman's mind is the equal of man's. The "pill" has liberated women from the uncertainty of childbearing, and with it the necessity of being attached to a man for economic support. But our attitudes toward women, and toward the family, have not changed concomitantly with the other developments. There is a distinct "cultural lag." Definitions of the family, conceptions of women and ideas about social function are left over from an era when they were necessary for social survival. They have persisted into an era in which they are no longer viable. The result can only be called severe role dysfunctionality for women.

The necessary relief for this dysfunctionality must come through changes in the social and economic organization of society and in social attitudes which will permit women to play a full and equal part in the social order. With this must come changes in the family, so that men and women are not only equal, but can raise their children in a democratic atmosphere. These changes will not come easily, nor will they come through the simple evolution of social trends. Trends do not move all in the same direction or at the same rate. To the extent that changes are dysfunctional with each other they create problems. These problems must be solved not by complacency but by conscious human direction. Only in this way can we have a real say in the shape of our future and the shape of our lives.

1. Rossi, A. Equality between the sexes: An immodest proposal. In Robert J. Lifton (Ed.), *The woman in America*. Boston: Beacon Press, 1965. Pp. 102–103.
2. Bem, S. & Bem, D. We're all nonconscious sexists. *Psychology Today,* 1970, 4(6), 26.
3. McClelland, D. Wanted: A new self-image for women. In Robert J. Lifton (Ed.), *The woman in America*. Boston: Beacon Press, 1965. P. 173.
4. Bennett, E. M. & Cohen, L. R. Men and women: Personality patterns and contrasts. *Genetics Psychology Monographs,* 1959, 59, 101–155.
5. Allport, G. *The nature of prejudice*. Reading, Mass.: Addison-Wesley, 1954. Pp. 142–161.
6. Terman, L. M. & Tyler, L. Psychological sex differences. In Leonard Carmichael (Ed.), *Manual of child psychology*. New York: Wiley & Sons, 1954. Pp. 1080–1100.
7. Smith, S. Age and sex differences in children's opinion concerning sex differences. *Journal of Genetic Psychology,* 1939, 54, 17–25.
8. Goldberg, P. Are women prejudiced against women? *Transaction,* April 1969, 28.
9. Clark, K. & Clark, M. Racial identification and preference in Negro children. In T. M. Newcomb and E. L. Hartley (Eds.), *Readings in social psychology*. New York: Holt, Rinehart & Winston, 1947.

10. Fisher, L. *Gandhi*. New York: Signet Key, 1954.
11. Fanon, F. *The wretched of the earth*. New York: Grove Press, 1963.
12. Myrdal, G. *An American dilemma*. New York: Harper, 1944.
13. De Vos, G. The relation of guilt toward parents to achievement and arranged marriage among the Japanese. *Psychiatry*, 1960, 23, 287–301.
14. Miles, C. C. Gifted children. In Carmichael, *op. cit.*, p. 1045.
15. See: Brown, R. *Social psychology*. New York: The Free Press. P. 162; Reuben Hill and Howard Becker (Eds.), *Family, marriage and parenthood*. Boston: D. C. Heath, 1955. P. 790; Goldberg, *op. cit.*, p. 28; Myrdal, *op. cit.*, Appendix V; and Goode, W. J., *The family*. Englewood Cliffs, New Jersey: Prentice-Hall, 1965. P. 70.
16. Tyler, L. Sex differences. Under "Individual differences" in the *International encyclopedia of the social sciences*, Vol. 7, 1968, New York: The Macmillan Co. Pp. 207–213.
17. Bales, R. F. Task roles and social roles in problem-solving groups. In T. M. Newcomb, E. Maccoby, and E. L. Hartly (Eds.), *Readings in social psychology* (3rd ed.). New York: Holt, Rinehart & Winston, 1958.
18. Maccoby, E. Sex differences in intellectual functioning. In E. Maccoby (Ed.), *The development of sex differences*. Stanford: Stanford University Press, 1966. Pp. 26 ff.
19. Neiman, L. J. The influence of peer groups upon attitudes toward the feminine role. *Social Problems*, 1954, 2, 104–111.
20. Milner, E. Effects of sex-role and social status on the early adolescent personality. *Genetic Psychological Monographs*, 40, 231–325.
21. Lipinski, B. *Sex-role conflict and achievement motivation in college women*. Unpublished doctoral dissertation, University of Cincinnati, 1965.
22. Asch, S. E. Studies of independence and conformity. A minority of one against a unanimous majority. *Psychological Monographs*, 1956, 70, No. 9.
23. Smith, *op. cit.*
24. Goldberg, *op. cit.*
25. Bradway, K. P. & Thompson, C. W. Intelligence at adulthood: A twenty-five year followup. *Journal of Educational Psychology*, 1962, 53, 1–14.
26. Stivers, E. N. *Motivation for college of high school boys and girls*. Unpublished doctoral dissertation, University of Chicago, 1959.
27. Pierce, J. V. & Bowman, P. H.: The educational motivation patterns of superior students who do and do not achieve in high school. U.S. Office of Education Project #208, *Co-operative Research Monograph No. 2*, U.S. Printing Office, Washington, 1960, 33–66.
28. Pierce, J. V. Sex differences in achievement motivation of able high school students, *Co-operative Research Project No. 1097*, University of Chicago, December 1961.
29. *Ibid.*, p. 23.
30. *Ibid.*, p. 42.
31. Horner, M. Femininity and successful achievement: A basic inconsistency. In Bardwick, et al., *Feminine personality and conflict*. Belmont: Brooks/Cole, 1970.
32. Terman & Tyler, *op. cit.*, p. 1104.
33. Maccoby, 1966, *op. cit.*, p. 26.
34. *Ibid.*, p. 27.
35. Maccoby, E. Woman's intellect. In Farber & Wilson (Eds.), *The potential of women*. New York: McGraw-Hill, 1963. P. 30.
36. *Ibid.*, p. 31. See also: Sherman, J. A. Problems of sex differences in space perception and aspects of intellectual functioning. *Psychological Review*, July 1967, 74, No. 4, 290–299; and Vernon, P. E. Ability factors and environmental influences. *American Psychologist*, Sept. 1965, 20, No. 9, 723–733.

37. Bronfenbrenner, U. Some familial antecedents of responsibility and leadership in adolescents. In Luigi Petrullo and Bernard M. Bass (Eds.), *Leadership and interpersonal behavior*. New York: Holt, Rinehart, & Winston, 1961. P. 260.
38. Levy, D. M. *Maternal overprotection*. New York: Columbia University Press, 1943.
39. Maccoby, 1963, *op. cit.*, p. 31.
40. Witkin, H. A., Dyk, R. B., Paterson, H. E., Goodenough, D. R., & Karp, S. A. *Psychological differentiation*. New York: Wiley, 1962.
41. Clapp, J. *Sex differences in mathematical reasoning ability*. Unpublished paper, 1968.
42 Sontag, I. W., Baker, C. T., & Nelson, V. A. Mental growth and personality development: A longitudinal study. *Monographs of the Society for Research in Child Development*, 1953, 23, No. 68.
43. Maccoby, 1963. *op. cit.*, p. 33.
44. Kagan, J. & Moss, H. A. *Birth to maturity: A study in psychological development*. New York and London: John Wiley and Sons, 1962. P. 275.
45. *Ibid.*, p. 225.
46. Winterbottom, M. The relation of need for achievement to learning experiences in independence and mastery. In Harold Proshansky and Bernard Seidenberg (Eds.), *Basic studies in social psychology*. New York: Holt, Rinehart & Winston, 1965. Pp. 294–307.
47. Sears, R. R., Maccoby, E., & Levin, H. *Patterns of child rearing*. Evanston, Ill.: Row, Peterson, 1957.
48. Bronfenbrenner, *op. cit.*, p. 260.
49. *Ibid.*
50. Schachter, S. *The psychology of affiliation*. Stanford: Stanford University Press, 1959.
51. Bronfenbrenner, *op. cit.*, p. 267.
52. Douvan, E. Employment and the adolescent. In F. Ivan Nye and Lois W. Hoffman (Eds.), *The employed mother in America*. Chicago: Rand McNally, 1963.
53. Kagan and Moss, *op. cit.*, p. 222.
54. McClelland, D. C. *The achieving society*. Princeton: Van Nostrand, 1961.
55. Kagan and Moss, *op. cit.*, p. 270.
56. Maccoby, 1963, *op. cit.*, p. 37.
57. Sinick, D. Two anxiety scales correlated and examined for sex differences. *Journal of Clinical Psychology*, 1956, 12, 394–395.
58. Maccoby, 1963, *op. cit.*, p. 37.
59. Myrdal, *op. cit.*, p. 1077.
60. Montagu, A. Anti-feminism and race prejudice, *Psychiatry*, 1946, 9, 60–71.
61. Keniston, E. & Keniston, K. An American anachronism: The image of women and work. *American Scholar*, Summer 1964, 33, No. 3, 355–375.
62. Rossi, *op. cit.*
63. Adorno, T. W., et al., *The authoritarian personality*. New York: Harper, 1950.
64. Stephens, W. N. *The family in cross-cultural perspective*. New York: Holt, Rinehart & Winston, 1963.
65. D'Andrade, R. Sex differences and cultural institutions. In Maccoby (Ed.), 1966, *op. cit.*, p. 189.
66. Blood, R. O., & Wolfe, D. M. *Husbands and wives*. Glencoe: The Free Press, 1960.
67. Blood, R. O. Long-range causes and consequences of the employment of married women. *Journal of Marriage and the Family*, 1965, 27, No. 1, 46.
68. Goode, *op. cit.*, p. 76.
69. Hill and Becker, *op. cit.*, p. 790.
70. Hallenbeck, P. N. An analysis of power dynamics in marriage. *Journal of Marriage and the Family*, May 1966, 28, No. 2, 203.
71. Blood, *op. cit.*, p. 47.

The Social
Construction
of the
Second Sex

72. Barry, H., Bacon, M. K., & Child, I. L. A cross-cultural survey of some sex differences in socialization. *Journal of Abnormal and Social Psychology*, 1957, 55, 330.
73. Spiro, M. E., *Kibbutz: Venture in utopia*. Cambridge: Harvard University Press, 1956.
74. D'Andrade, *op. cit.*, p. 191.
75. Goode, *op. cit.*, p. 70.
76. *Ibid.*
77. Barry, Bacon, & Child, *op. cit.*, p. 328.
78. Bronfenbrenner, U. Socialization and social class through time and space. In Maccoby, Newcomb and Hartly, *op. cit.*
79. Bronfenbrenner, U. The effects of social and cultural change on personality. *Journal of Social Issues*, 1969, 17, No. 1, 6–18.
80. Blood, *op. cit.*, p. 47.

Part 2

NEW DIRECTIONS IN FEMININITY/MASCULINITY

THERE IS A WOMAN

Tom F. Driver

There is a woman
    In every man, a man
in every woman. Let the four
    lie down together.
Four shall be two,
    two shall be one,
for a time.

There is an Arab
    in every Jew, a Jew
in every Arab. Let these four
    be one, for a time.

I am the honkey
    who lives in the black,
he is the nigger who dwells
    in me,
Not knowing that,
    we lay down for a time.

Oppression! he cried. He was right.
Two and two are only strangers.
But four may be one,
    for a time.

Reprinted from Grummon and Barclay, *Sexuality: A Search for Perspective*, Van Nostrand Reinhold Company, New York, 1971, by permission of the author.

NEW DIRECTIONS FOR WOMEN

Carol LeFevre

This selection summarizes years of scholarship and research on the problems and potentialities of women in our society. Taking issue with some of the views of Betty Freidan, pioneer of the women's movement, Carol LeFevre presents proposals of her own, indicating the variety of options possible for women. Men and women alike should consider whether men, reared in essentially hierarchical, male-oriented families and institutions, can accept a new egalitarianism without damage to their own self-image.

Suddenly women have escaped the oblivion of the women's page and become headline news. They are on the march, wearing witches' costumes, throwing away bras, and disrupting Senate hearings. The new feminists demand that women abandon traditional roles as man's servant, helper, sex object, and consumer, and finally gain full respect as human beings at work, at home, and at leisure. To them, being a housewife and staying at home to care for children is an age-old trap by which men have kept women in bondage. The new woman seeks to be free to work alongside men in equal jobs at equal pay with equal opportunity for promotion. She is no longer going to do man's typing, laundry, and dishes. The most extreme reject marriage and project women-only business enterprises. The moderates concentrate on job gains, seeking to desegregate want-ads and eliminate discrimination at work.

Depending upon the point of view, such ferment among women alarms or amuses those who hold more traditional beliefs about woman's proper role. For them, woman's primary function is determined by her biology—she is to bear and to care for children. The home and family are central to the wholesome development of the child and to the quality and stability of communal and national life. It is this which requires woman's full devotion, while man

New Directions in Femininity/ Masculinity

Reprinted from *The Chicago Theological Seminary Register*, Volume 40, Number 3, March 1970. Reprinted with permission of author and publisher.

works in the world to provide the necessary material support. Woman is expected to fulfill herself through caring, man through work.

Polarized Stereotypes

In the traditional view the one characteristic women have in common, their reproductive capacity, outweighs all individual differences in forming their character and determining their destiny. It is the sameness of all women that is emphasized, in contrast to the individual differences natural to men. From the fact that woman is dependent upon others for care and sustenance in the period surrounding childbirth and the nurture of her infant, lifelong dependency is postulated as part of woman's nature. Fully elaborated, this original difference in biology expands into a complete set of culturally prescribed "masculine" and "feminine" normative characteristics, behaviors, and occupations. Hence in our culture it is "feminine" to accept passively and to adjust and be sensitive to the expectations and needs of others, while it is "masculine" to assert oneself and aggressively master human and material circumstance. That the actual roles men and women in our society are called upon to play frequently equalize and even reverse this equation is ignored or deplored.

It is this rigid sex-typing of characteristics and behaviors far removed from the biological basis of "femininity" which rouses the ire of the feminists. They reject the determination of all of life by the fact of being female. Women are human beings with full individuality and capacity to act, think, and work. Because they are also female, they do have children, and the children must be cared for, but there is more than one way to provide proper care for children; each mother in her separate household devoting full time to her child is not necessarily the only or the best arrangement for either. Sex stereotypes, like all stereotypes, narrow the range of options available to persons and limit the development of full human possibility. Women too are born with varying temperaments and abilities, and the unique circumstances of each one's life experience and educational opportunities enhance these differences as she grows up. Is it really any more reasonable, they ask, to expect that every girl shall grow up to fit competently and joyfully into the single occupational role of housewife than it is to expect that all boys should grow up to be farmers? We need to distinguish between the natural desire to nurture one's infant and child, and the specific occupational role. The separation of the roles of parent and worker is clear enough in the case of men. But tradition and practice have long fused the two in our image of woman.

Both the feminist and the traditional views of woman oversimplify the actual complexity of woman's situation today. Those who feel woman's place is in the home do not fully appreciate the radical changes which have taken place in our society, while the feminists, in their anger at male chauvinism and discrimination, underestimate the enduring and unique role of women. Let us look more closely at the actual situation.

Biology No Longer Dictates

For women, probably the most radical change that has ever occurred in human history is the development of modern medicine, and especially of dependable contraceptive methods. These developments have, for the first time, freed woman to a very significant degree from her biology. Never before has she been able to choose the timing and number of her children. Never has she had such assurance that the child she bears will survive to adulthood nor run so little risk to her own life and health in the reproductive process.

In the 1880s the average married woman had little formal education but was thoroughly trained in the housewifely arts. Having survived the high mortality risk of childhood years, she could expect to bear her first child before she reached the age of 23, see her last child married by the time she was 56, and either bury her husband or die herself by the age of 57. There were children in the home throughout her entire marriage.

Not quite a century later the life span of woman looks very different. Her life expectancy at birth is 73 years. Now educated through high school and often through college, she marries at 21, bears her last child at 27, and send all her children off to school for much of the day by her early thirties. In another dozen years young people are leaving home, and she attends her last child's wedding at the age of 47. As the nest empties she finds herself a youthful, vigorous, often competent woman who can look forward to another 30 years of adult life—20 years with her husband and 10 years as a widow. There are children in the home during less than half of her adult life, and small children require her full-time care for only a few years. Child care is no longer a woman's whole life, but is one stage in that life. How does she, or might she, fill the long post-child period of her life?

In the 1950s many women sought to avoid this question by once again bearing the large families typical of an earlier era in our history. Since 1960 however, the birth rate has dropped a dramatic 29 per cent. As we become more aware of the specter of overpopulation, and as birth-control methods are further improved and more widely disseminated, responsible women wi no longer have more than two, or at most three, children. Even the most devoted mother will find only a fraction of her life filled by the care of children. It is high time that women, as well as men, gave careful thought to how they will spend the days of their lives.

The New Homemaker

Not only the timing but the quality and content of motherhood and home-making have changed. The housewife has probably retained the human, and humane, values in her role longer than most. But she, too, has found her work losing much of its former content and some of its meaning. The traditional, now rather nostalgic, view of woman's role derives from an era and place in which husband, wife, and children worked together as a viable economic and social unit on the family farm. Woman was a major contributor to the economic productivity of the family and to the education of her children for adult life. Cleaning routines and consumption activities were minimal. Life centered in the family, with school requiring a small fraction of the time it does today. Outside activities most often involved the whole family in a closely knit community life.

In America today the home is no longer the center of the family's economic, educational, and social life, but rather the base from which family members go forth to their separate destinations in the world outside. Father's work takes him away from home nine or more hours a day. Most children are in school by the age of five, and after school activities, dental appointments, music lessons, and all the rest take up much additional time. Even the home itself has been invaded by the outside world to an extent undreamed of a mere generation ago. Douglas Heath of Haverford College estimates that the average American child has watched from 12,000 to 16,000 hours of television by the time he graduates from high school—more hours than he has spent in school.

It is clear that the mother has lost much of her former productive role in the home, and that her educative and nurturant role is needed full time for only a few years. Instead, the middle-class woman has become the coordinator of the family's consumption of things and services, driving children here and buying there. At home constantly rising standards of consumption, entertainment, and cleanliness increase the routine work the family's heavy investment in machines was supposed to reduce. One result may be a somewhat driven, harried mother, another an overstrained bank account. At the same time, the educated, prosperous middle-class woman is likely to have varied interests and considerable competence, and may, if she chooses, eschew preoccupation with conformity and status to develop a satisfying, integrated individual style of life.

The working-class woman, on the other hand, is more relaxed about status and achievement. Though she, too, fills her days with household routines, she does not devote nearly so much energy to chauffering family members or to the purchase of things and services. Yet because her life is more narrowly circumscribed by home, family, and relatives, and her intellectual abilities less developed by education, she tends to be more deeply involved with her children, seeking her satisfaction in life through them, yet anxious and fearful of her ability to understand and control either them or the outside world. This anxious devotion puts a premium on rigid moralism, perpetuating a constricted life style into the next generation.[1]

Housework has a great tendency to expand to fill the time available, although the irreducible minimum, especially when there are children in the home, still requires many hours a week. French mothers who took full-time jobs reduced their housework time from 80 to 43 hours per week, increasing their total weekly work time by only three hours! Nor is there any convincing evidence that women are better mothers for limiting themselves to home and family; it is more than possible that they are worse. Until the last quarter-century motherhood was never a full-time occupation for women. Economic necessity has always required the great majority of women in all societies to spend their major energies on producing goods for the family's needs, while the minority of well-to-do delegated much of the responsibility for children to servants. The great increase in productivity attendant upon industrialization and the concomitant growth of a large and prosperous middle class have for the first time made it economically possible for large numbers of women to make mothering their primary business.

Rossi[2] attributes this unique phenomenon of full-time motherhood to two additional factors—the growth of the influence of child-care "experts" and the use of women to exhibit the family status. The rise of the expert has grown with the increasing isolation of the young mother from family and community support, and it seems rather ironic that only the rarest expert has ever attempted the full-time care of children, or has any real understanding of the situation of the mother. Experts, basing much of their advice on pathology, have emphasized the infant's need for total mothering, and considered women only as a kind of appendage for the child. Never before has a society placed mother and small child in a situation in which each is so totally dependent upon the other, and so completely at the other's mercy. The results have not always been benign, as Rheingold's monumental analysis of maternal destructiveness[3] or Keniston's study of overdependent sons attests.[4]

In one respect, however, the mother's role is more important today than it has ever been before. With schools and communities becoming ever larger and more impersonal, children's lives, like adults', become increasingly fragmented. The parent may be the only person who knows and responds to the child as a unique, valuable individual, cherished because he is, not for what he can do. With the encouragement of passivity and suppression of engagement with the human and material world induced especially by television, the mother can play a crucial role in promoting his active encounter with life, supporting his mastery of the physical environment, fostering his wonder and curiosity, and helping him to sort out his own feelings and to empathize with others.

When we turn from middle-class and working-class levels of society to those who live in poverty, however, the question of choice of life style loses most of its meaning. It is all the mother can do to survive. Two-thirds of the adult poor in this nation are women-headed households. Mothers subsisting on welfare or going out to do "day work" are at the mercy of circumstances beyond their control, their possibilities limited by ignorance, a narrow life experience, inadequate nutrition, neglected health, and a severely restricted and often unreliable income. If they must work, child care can be a severe problem. With licensed day-care facilities almost non-existent, 400,000 children under twelve are left without care while their mothers work, most of them in slum neighborhoods where children are most vulnerable.

"Atypical" Women Are Typical

Far too much of our thinking about women rests on the covert assumption that all women are married and have children, and that all families have a male adult or some societal substitute to provide their material needs. These assumptions appear quite naïve when we look at the facts.

There are more than 46 million married women in this country. Three-tenths, or 13 million, have no children. We do not know how many families there are in which the father is unable to provide an adequate income and mother goes to work for purely economic reasons—food and shoes are more urgently needed by her children than her full-time presence at home.

In addition, there are 18 million women age 20 and over who are single, widowed, or divorced. Most must earn their own living, and many also provide for dependent children or relatives. Often these women carry full responsibility for their children's care and education, and for housekeeping, budgeting, maintaining a car, and the family's social life in addition to full-time employment. Many single women support aging parents, and must bear the stigma of inadequacy for their singleness as well as exclusion from much of the family-dominated fabric of our society.

When 31 out of the 64 million adult women in this country cannot, in the nature of their circumstances, fill the traditional feminine role assignment because they do not have husbands or are childless, it seems worse than futile to maintain the myth of its universality. Indeed, the myth becomes even more absurd if we remember that a growing proportion of the mothers are older women whose children are all past the age of eighteen. It is here that the feminists score one of their most telling points. It is precisely the myth of the universality of woman's "proper" feminine role which underlies, often unconsciously, much of the continuing inequality in women's employment. Those who already carry an extra load as sole parent to their children are further burdened by limited work opportunities, lower pay, inflexible work schedules designed for men's, rather than women's, lives, and unequal promotion on the job. These inequities are justified by the overt or covert assumption that women do not really need the money and ought to be at home anyway.

Stereotypic Versus Actual Female Occupational Roles

Although employment statistics suggest that nearly half of our married female population is still maintaining the traditional homemaker pattern throughout most or all of their lives, while only a small minority are following the lifelong career pattern prescribed by the feminists, there are strong trends toward a new pattern of life, especially among younger women. The loss in the meaningful content of woman's homemaking role, the change in life-span pattern, and long-term inflation compounded by expectations for constantly rising standards of living, have led more and more women to seek paid employment during part or all of their lives. Between 1940 and 1968 the proportion of women in the labor force rose from 25 to 37 per cent. Every third worker is now a woman. Much of this increase resulted from the entry of married women into the labor market. In 1940 only 36 per cent of the female labor force was married; by 1968 the figure was 63 per cent.

While the number of women employed used to peak at the young adult, premarried stage of life and decline steadily thereafter, there is now a second employment peak for women in the middle years. Three-fourths of single women between the ages of 20 and 34 years are working, but only one-fourth of the women with preschool children. As children get older, however, the back-to-work trend rapidly accelerates, and there is now a larger percentage of women with school-age children employed than of post-child-stage women.[5] This unexpected development no doubt reflects differences in socialization of succeeding generations and the reduction of family expenses as children become self-supporting, but there is also reason to think that the higher level of education of younger women, enabling them to secure more attractive jobs, may be a significant factor. We do know that the employment rate of women rises steadily with the number of years of education.[6]

The Changing Employment Situation

Personal motives arising from woman's changed life situation may make her increasingly willing and ready to take a job, but there is a demand side to this employment equation which may be even more important. The children produced by the low depression birth rate became adult at the very time when the bumper crop of postwar babies entered the schools and a growing older population needed increased services. Thus the supply of employable young women dropped from 13 million to 9 million in the fifties and early sixties, creating a gap between the supply and the demand for workers in typical women's jobs which could be filled only by turning to the unemployed older women.

This employment situation, however, which attracted so many married women back into the labor market, will be reversed in the next decade when the entry of all those babies of the 1950s into the working world coincides with the decreased number of children produced by the falling birth rate of the sixties. Unless employers have had an unexpected basic change of attitude, the housewife will have an increasingly difficult time finding a job to finance the new living-room furniture or pay for the children's college tuition.

And this brings us to another significant aspect of women's employment. The great majority of women have worked for immediate financial gain, or because it is the thing to do until motherhood, rather than for long-term satisfaction in a committed career. They have filled a vast number of relatively unskilled, part-time and seasonal jobs, and few even in full-time work are protected by unions or tenure. Older women, especially, are in a highly vulnerable employment position, easily fired and last to be hired when the labor market shifts. At the same time, the number of unskilled jobs in the economy as a whole is steadily decreasing as mechanization and automation take over more and more lower level work. Thus it seems likely that women with no real vocational training or commitment will find it more difficult in the next decade than in the last to pick up a job to fill empty days or enrich the family exchequer.

At the higher work levels which require highly skilled technicians, training in new fields, or professional competence, however, there is a serious, growing shortage of personnel. Businesses compete greedily for both beginning and high-level executive talent, and the supply of doctors, nurses, mental health workers, and many others is far short of the need. At this level there will continue to be plenty of opportunity for employment. With the need acute in many areas of our national life, why are so many college-trained women competing to run the PTA? And why are so few women found at any of the higher occupational levels?

Limitations of The Feminist Position

The young feminists tend to blame the media image of women and educators' and employers' bias against the female sex for women's gross failure to equal men's achievement in the occupational world. They point, à la Betty Friedan, to the exploitation of women by advertisers, on the one hand, and to the reluctance of elementary schools to promote women to principalships, of colleges to make women full professors, and of businesses to develop women executives, on the other. While there is surely far more truth in this argument than in the conservative traditionalist's assumptions, still much with us, that women are less capable of achievement, and that they betray their femininity in seeking serious accomplishments, the fact remains that woman's life, concerns, and responsibilities in our present society make single-minded commitment to a career difficult and often unattractive to women. And because they will not or cannot devote most of their waking hours to their career, they cannot compete on equal terms with men who do.[7] That the total commitment to work is exacting a heavy toll from many men and from their families is unquestionably true, but the price it exacts from the woman whom all society, and almost all husbands, accord the major responsibility for family life even when she works, is much greater. It is a pattern which handicaps the advancement of women to more responsible levels of employment, and which restricts the full human development of men.

A variety of factors operate to prevent women from committing themselves to work as fully as men do. The most obvious, of course, is the fact that even the professional woman with a family (with the rare exception of the one with a completely responsible full-time housekeeper) goes home to get dinner, clean up the kitchen, attend to children, pick up the house, buy the family's clothes, take care of the laundry, and prepare for guests. She simply does not have the evening and week-end hours to spend on her professional development. Nor can she easily leave her family responsibilities for out-of-town professional activities, as the man with a wife at home can. As children get older, of course, this problem eases.

But there are value differences involved as well. Many women are not willing to sacrifice human concerns in order to play the promotion game. Just as they feel family needs are more important than getting the book written, so also they may choose to spend time helping students instead of concentrating on research or taking speaking engagements.

On a less conscious level, many women brought up in our culture find it difficult to compete with men. Brought up on a cultural norm which considers competition with males or any kind of aggressive behavior in women "unfeminine," if not a sign of emotional disturbance, many very able women become anxious in situations which call for assertion which might involve disagreement or confrontation with men.[8] Yet without a degree of firm assertiveness they can neither develop their own capacities, contribute to the full extent of their abilities professionally, or gain recognition for their achievement. There is still ample evidence of prejudice in evaluation of women's work; they must achieve at a higher level of performance against greater odds to reach the same professional levels as men, and frequently must cope with more intrapsychic conflict in the process.

There is still another factor which very significantly limits woman's ability to rise in her chosen vocation. One of the most powerful norms in our culture is that the wife shall follow her husband wherever the opportunities and exigencies of his vocation shall lead them. Even if husband and wife agree to consider both their careers in any move, it is difficult to synchronize moves with equal opportunity for both, and it is rare indeed for the wife's interests to take precedence over the husband's. Since the average family moves every five years this can be a serious obstacle for the career wife. A woman in a science field is especially likely to be hopelessly outdated if she must absent herself from work for five years. Then, too, many women who are qualified for college teaching and married to academic husbands are barred by nepotism rules from the only geographically available college.

Any woman's effort to commit herself to a role outside the home is critically affected by her husband's attitude. Probably a good many professional husbands, aware of the self-fulfillment they experience in work, are relatively understanding of a similar need in their wives. But many men who verbally support their wives subtly obstruct them in practice. High-status men in general are less enthusiastic about their wives' working than working-class husbands. For the former the inconvenience is more important, for the latter the money the wives earn.[9]

The pressure for mothers to stay at home with their children is so strong in our society that it is difficult for women who work out of choice not to feel guilty. A series of studies reported by Nye and Hoffman found that working mothers experienced more doubt about their maternal adequacy than non-working mothers, but their feelings about their relationships with their children were more positive than those of housewives. Virtually the only relationship which has been found between mother's working and children's adjustment is the mother's work satisfaction. If she is unhappy with her work she is likely to be more demanding and neglectful of her children, while if she is highly satisfied she may feel guilty and compensate by overindulgence.[10] Daughters identified more highly with working than with housewife mothers, although those with full-time working mothers appeared to remain more dependent on family ties and have fewer social activities, while those whose mothers worked part time were unusually outgoing, active, and independent. Both were highly autonomous and had more "masculine" (i.e., non-stereotyped feminine) interests. However, when studies focused on higher-status, college-educated mothers the negative effects of working were small or nonexistent.

There are, then, many factors in the lives of married women which make it difficult or undesirable for them to commit themselves to work roles with the same intensity men do. Rather, their genius lies in their ability to balance multiple roles and, at best, to enhance both their family and their work lives by combining the two. While unmarried women should be able to devote themselves more wholeheartedly to their work, in fact they often do not. It may be that in their early adult years their energies and self-confidence are too much consumed by the difficult position many single women find themselves in socially. It may actually be easier for the married woman who is secure in her emotional relationships and resourceful in her domestic arrangements to work up to her capacity. Both may make their greatest contribution a decade later than men, when their lives are more free of role or emotional conflict. Certainly women can make a much larger contribution to society if they will, and society can do a great deal more to make that contribution possible.

The Need for Multiple Options

Just as the traditional feminine ideal errs in assigning a single role to all women, so the feminists err in arguing that all women should work. They underestimate both the cost of full-time work, particularly at the professional level, for the mother with young children at home, and the very real joy women can find in their homes and children. Children *are* young for only a few years, and for most women those years are precious, provided their own lives are not too painfully constricted. While women who want to work full time during those years should be able to do so, others ought to be able to keep one foot in their field with part-time study or work, or to return as children grow up without severe penalty, although they may need additional training.

It is fallacious and constricting to universalize any one pattern of life for all. In a society as sophisticated and complex as ours it is absurd as well. Not all women are fitted for motherhood, let alone full-time motherhood, but neither are all women happier or more productive as workers. Rather, we need to increase the range of options for both women and men to include not only these two patterns but a virtually infinite number of variations and combinations of these and other possibilities. We need to free our thinking of stereotyped notions of what men and women ought to do. One woman of my acquaintance recently completed a doctoral degree so that she might work, at a profession she loves, and free her husband, miserable in his present job, for the creative writing he longs to do. Other young couples seek to find or create work situations in which both can work less than full time so both can be free to share family responsibilities and community work. Why should husbands in their forties and fifties literally die from work they cannot bear, while their perfectly healthy wives lead useless lives conspicuously consuming? Why not "collective houses" here, as well as in Europe, with cooked meals, day nurseries, laundry, and so on, available to families in which both parents work? Why not elegant simplicity, instead of an endless accretion of *things* whose care consumes us, in our homes?

Paid work is certainly not the only alternative to full-time housewifery. Women with strong interests in the arts may be able to be productive in our society only because they have the economic freedom not to work for money. Tremendously valuable roles in the community or social service or politics can be undertaken by committed women precisely because they do have leisure—though some come to feel limited by their volunteer status and become professional. There are women who are neighbors in the deepest biblical sense, nurturing and supporting others in simple, life-giving ways. But the common ingredient in all these rich and productive lives is the choice of commitment.

Too many women are committed only to themselves, or to their own little circle. They have ceased to grow, to be open and aware. Whether they seek virtuous complacency in the women's society, pseudo-self-realization in the fashion salon, distraction at the bridge table, or escape from the bottle, women can lead self-indulgent, useless, and ultimately empty and unhappy lives, scarcely aware that any world or need exists outside their silken cocoon. It is a life style that is unproductive at best, destructive of self and others at worst. Unfortunately, the culture supports women in such unsatisfying solutions. The mere fact of being married is justification enough for their existence. The feminine stereotype requires nothing more. In conservative circles it is the woman who is actively useful who must justify herself—especially if her usefulness carries a salary check—not the drone.

Stereotypes Constrict Life

Let us examine more carefully how sexual stereotypes actually affect men and women in our society. There is ample evidence that traditional sex-typed expectations for both boys and girls in our society limit development, rigidify thinking, and curtail even the perception of possibilities. Though superficially boys and girls appear to be treated in much the same way, closer investigation reveals significant differences which begin at a very early age. Middle-class fathers of nursery school children put quite different pressures on their sons than on their daughters, tolerating and encouraging even bullying aggression, pressuring for achievement, and censuring overconforming, tearful, or passive behavior. Girls, on the other hand, could cry, and cute, affectionate behavior brought the father's warm response. Being moral and popular was far more important than achieving. Thus the boy is being told that feelings, his own or others, are sissy ("non-masculine"), while girls are taught to give up doing in favor of pleasing.[11]

The results of such expectations, already so clearly spelled out for the three- and four-year-old, appear in a very interesting study by Tyler. She followed children from first grade through high school, and found significant differences in development between those children who conformed closely to the sexual stereotypes and those who did not. The girls who played more actively outside in first grade (a less "ladylike" behavior than staying in to help teacher) were more restless, talkative, and bossy, spent more time reading, and, obviously, were less well-liked in fourth grade. By eighth grade these same girls were rejecting statements like "Woman's work and man's work are fundamentally different," and in high school they were still open to changing interests and held career expectations in addition to typical "feminine" interests. And the fascinating finding is that as they matured in high school these girls became more confident and better adjusted than their more conventional peers. Apparently their continuing active engagement with the environment throughout childhood and adolescence enabled them to develop their own powers and interests more fully than the girls who early in life turned their energies toward pleasing others and restricted their activities and interests to those limited areas labeled "feminine." [12] In an excellent paper on differences in male and female intelligence Eleanor Maccoby concludes that a girl must be a tomboy at some time in her childhood if she is to develop her intelligence fully.[13]

A substantial number of young women do remain sufficiently open to develop intellectual and career interests and ambitions in high school or/and college, but as the full realization that they are rapidly approaching the time for marriage and motherhood hits them they tend to reduce their educational expectations and drop "non-feminine" career plans. The culture tells the girl that she must marry, and puts an intense premium on early marriage, but it prohibits her from direct action toward that goal. Finding herself in this vulnerable, passive, waiting position in a matter crucial to her future life, she withdraws from self-realization and seeks to fit the social stereotype of the feminine, desirable woman, shifting from medicine to teaching, and "hiding" her brains in deference to men. Many young women still do not look beyond the period of marriage and young children in thinking of their future lives.

It may be that the more human relationships which are said to be developing between the sexes in coed dorms, and the demise of the competitive dating pattern with all its dehumanizing stereotyping of both sexes on the basis of superficial qualities, will gradually break down this artificial denial of both men's and women's real being and allow them to relate as fully functioning persons. Or it may be that as young women come to have greater respect for themselves they will find men, too, enjoy real dialogue. A recent news item noted the cancellation of "men only" flights—executives preferred traveling with some interesting career women aboard!

Although the literature has generally agreed on the retrenchment of career plans in favor of temporary work expectations among young women, replies from 15,000 women graduates in the 1961 class suggest that we may need to distinguish between the short-range and the long-range goals of today's young college women. It is true that during the junior or senior year 31 per cent of the women who had planned to enter other fields shifted to the most popular "feminine" field, education,[14] and that in the two years following graduation the percentage planning to enter graduate school immediately dropped from 21 to 14 per cent. [15]

But this was not the whole story. An additional whopping 48 per cent hoped to go on to graduate school sometime in the future. Two years later 40 per cent still retained that ambition but were not enrolled. The major deterrents to immediate graduate school for women were lack of money and family responsibilities. In order to continue their education during this young married stage of their lives they needed excellent child-care facilities (57 per cent), part-time matriculation (52 per cent), their husband's approval (52 per cent), evening courses (43 per cent), and a stipend to cover school expenses (20 per cent).

Whether or not all these young women would in fact enter and complete graduate programs if these conditions were met is a moot question. But that there is a desire for graduate education, and presumably for a meaningful vocation later, evidently exists among far more college women today than we have generally realized. But they will not leave their children in makeshift baby-sitting arrangements, nor can they meet the demands of inflexible academic programs designed for men and non-family women. It is at least conceivable that women are ready to make a greater contribution to society, if society can begin to recognize and cope with their unique needs. These include not only child-care facilities and flexible academic and work arrangements, but also cooperation among universities so that women are less often penalized academically when their husbands move before their degree is completed.

Using other data on the 1961 graduates, Rossi sought to discover the difference between women who sought high professional degrees or entered traditionally masculine fields and those who made more conventionally feminine choices. The unconventional women, she found, came from less happy homes and saw less satisfaction in domestic life or intimate relationships. They were more interested in reading, study, and individual pursuits throughout childhood and adolescence. The "feminine" women, on the other hand, were strongly home- and person-oriented. They had not developed strong intellectual interests. Rossi concluded that our over-emphasis on social attractiveness in girls leaves them little time or interest for intellectual pursuits, an interesting feminist switch on the usual psychological explanation that intellectual women are only compensating for their lack of social attractiveness!

The fact that almost half the women with doctoral degrees do not marry appears to be less a matter of educating themselves out of the marriage market than one result of a life style which finds greater satisfaction and value in intellectual interests and work than in intimate personal relationships. Many women high school teachers have made a rather similar choice. Wright found that they tended to recall less happy relationships with their fathers and found their mother's example drab, while teachers had inspired a vision of a more exciting intellectual world.[16] For them, too, family life held little charm, and they were less likely to marry than elementary teachers.

For men, an interest in intellectual life or a preference for working with things rather than engaging in intimate relationships with people carries no opprobrium. It is considered quite natural that many men devote themselves to careers in physics or mathematics, spending little time in family life and in fact being rather uncomfortable with people. But, somehow, the woman who grows up in a home in which intimate personal relationships are unrewarding or painful, or mother a pretty unattractive role model, while learning and doing and finding out for oneself are exciting and satisfying and non-threatening, is damned as "masculine," or "maladjusted," as, in fact, a crippled human being. By whose standards, and why, we may ask? Why is she not allowed to be an individual, as a man is? The stereotype says she must be a *woman,* not a human being, and the only way to be a "genuine" woman in our society is to place primary value on intimate relationships. The woman who does not, or cannot, may spend her life pretending that she does, or ashamed that she does not. She is not valued as the person she is, in her own unique being.

A great deal of research confirms that certain personality profiles are typical of those engaged in certain kinds of work, and that these profiles vary widely between occupations. In fact, personality is often more predictable by occupation than it is by sex. Male and female engineers are very much more like each other than either are like their same-sex psychologists, elementary school teachers, or accountants. The wide variety of occupations in our society allows many, if not all, of its people to find a reasonably comfortable fit between personality and work. The narrow range of roles approved for women has given them less choice, and the prescription that all women should be housewives for a good many years can create much misery in both mother and child when women quite unfit for the role conscientiously force themselves to fill it.

So far we have distinguished three different life styles in the girl and the young woman—the conventional feminine style, with its emphasis on home-making and personal intimacy, the career-feminine style with its combination of family and work interests, and the career-non-feminine style, which pursues career and rejects strong interest in family roles. Let us turn now to what happens to women with these varied life styles as they continue through the life cycle.

Research has only begun in this area, but there are some very interesting findings. The most home-oriented young married women three years out of college reported great happiness and a transforming sense of fulfillment with their home and early motherhood role, while the most career-oriented women were having a difficult time, beset with problems and reporting (one-third of them) discrimination because of sex.[17] A small study investigating the effect of the first child's birth on parents found the adjustment difficult for most mothers, but especially traumatic for professional mothers, who had given up a very meaningful occupational role at the same time they had to learn to be mothers and full-time housewives.[18] A third study found lower self-esteem and greater self-blame among young women in their middle twenties (many of them mothers) than among men the same age or girls in their teens.[19]

Do these findings prove that those who say all women should be brought up to value homemaking and motherhood above all else are right, then? Certainly the most euphoric women at this stage of life are those who glory in motherhood, and the most miserable, whether or not they marry and have children, are those who have begun professional careers.

Those women whose personalities and interests are best suited to motherhood should, indeed, find the honeymoon stage of family life novel, fulfilling, and exciting. This is the time in their lives when their circumstances coincide most completely with their personal needs. We do not know how many young women are in this happy state, nor is there any way of assuring that all girls be brought up with this particular configuration of needs and aptitudes, despite their feminine hormones.

That many women do not find the same happiness in motherhood in our society as it is now organized, is also clear from these and other research findings. To scold them for being as they are, in the circumstances in which they find themselves as young mothers, or to attempt to turn the clock back a century, seems worse than useless. Rather, we need to explore the conditions which make their lives difficult at this stage, and to create more adequate means of meeting their needs. We need new social forms which will enable more women now to be happy, productive women and good mothers, to the benefit of themselves, their children, and the community.

That the professional women were having special problems is not surprising in a society which disapproves of them, although it may also be that the beginning stages of any professional career tend to be difficult and anxiety-producing. Certainly no one who has deeply invested himself or herself in meaningful work finds it easy to lose it suddenly. In many countries the professional woman is highly respected and quitting her profession to raise her children herself would be considered wasteful to society and unthinkable for her. They do not assume that only the biological mother can bring up a child properly, and they provide other resources for children's care. Indeed, less individualistic societies than our own would consider it madness to trust child care solely to an inexperienced, untrained, isolated mother.

In a rare and valuable study of the life career patterns of 475 mid-life women Mulvey found a much more complex combination of factors and greater variety of work patterns (homemaking is included as an occupation) than usually appear in men's career lines, as women varied between full-time committed careers, entered employment after a period of child-care, fluctuated in and out of jobs, or were active in volunteer activities.[20] In an effort to evaluate different life styles and patterns as well as to categorize them, she classified women as "productive" if they felt satisfied with their lives, reported a sense of fulfillment, and had a feeling of expansiveness rather than constriction of life in middle age, while those who were frustrated, felt defeated, and followed others' expectations regardless of personal satisfaction were labeled "unproductive."

At this stage in life she found that women of the conventional feminine orientation tended to center their lives on marriage and to be "unproductive" and not too well adjusted. Women who combined typical feminine interests with professional orientations were more likely to be career directed (often they were teaching) or active in volunteer activities, well adjusted, and "productive." The small number of least-feminine, strongly career-oriented women were highly adjusted and "productive." So it appears that women who limit their lives to family are happy when children fill their lives, but have few resources for later life, while the career women may have a difficult time in the beginning, but come into their own as they mature. The woman who combines both interests combines at least some of the pleasures of both worlds, though she may not reap quite the career result her more dedicated peer does.

Going back to high school records for these women, Mulvey found that socioeconomic background, scholastic achievement, and personality ratings were not related to later career patterns. Again we see that the feminine popularity and good adjustment so stressed for girls are not necessarily positively related to later development. The main factor in high school which distinguished the "productive" from the "unproductive" women in mid-life was the realism of their educational preparation before marriage for higher-level work. Many of the women who were dissatisfied with their lives at forty had fantasied a nursing or science career in high school, but had not attained the necessary education. At mid-life they were either at home or working in low-level jobs such as office work. Single women with an ego-sustaining work role, in contrast, were both satisfied and "productive." Mulvey points up the moral—"the folly of *too early* commitment to *marriage without* full exploration of *career*" (italics hers). Work, she concludes, is more central and internalized for women than we have generally thought.

Quite similar findings have come out of a recent study of a more specialized sample of women, the faculty wives of a college and university community. Arnott found that women who devoted themselves almost entirely to home and family put children first and husbands second in their value structure. When these women were faced with the empty nest, their satisfaction dropped. Only three out of ten of the older child-centered women engaged actively in activities outside the home, and it seems likely they also have less in common with their intellectual husbands after years of concentrated motherhood. Women who combined volunteer activities, degree work, or employment with family life ranked husband as high or higher than children, and sought a sense of usefulness or achievement and self-fulfillment as well. Seven out of ten mothers of elementary school children, and nine out of ten mothers of high school youth, carried these additional roles. Many of the younger women were consciously preparing for their future work roles, while older women who were active were more often in volunteer work. The most unhappy women were those who wished to work but felt they could not conscientiously leave their children.[21]

The implications seem quite clear. Child care no longer takes up all of a woman's adult life. If she is to lead a satisfying and productive life for herself and others in the quarter-century and more after children are grown, she needs to keep alive other interests and to develop other competences, whether these be in the arts, in volunteer activities, or in paid work. Yet, whether or not she herself works, it seems increasingly evident that work has become a central fact of life and of identity for women as well as men. Work that is intrinsically satisfying and recognized as worthwhile by the society is an important factor in self-esteem and mental health.[22] Girls and young women need to be helped to take a longer view and to realize that motherhood will fill no more than a stage in their lives. They, too, must *choose* their life style and commit themselves to it. A passive role which sacrifices personal development for the sake of children is no longer adequate even for the housewife and mother, and it often leads to emptiness and dissatisfaction in later years.

The younger educated women seem to be considering a long-range future in greater numbers than we have realized. But the woman who has not foreseen this need before motherhood, or whose education no longer can obtain for her the kind of work she wants, can also choose to act. In the last decade there has been a steadily increasing number of women going back to college and graduate school in their thirties, forties, and even fifties, and more and more colleges and universities are offering programs designed to fit their needs.[23] Though women who have long been housewives typically lack confidence and undervalue their ability when they apply, educators are finding that they bring a focus, excitement, and mature sense of responsibility to their course work which makes them a joy to teach. There is a need for many more programs that will admit women on a part-time basis, arrange classes at times women with children can attend, and give loans or scholarships for part-time study. Financing mother's education may be a wiser economic investment, and provide more emotional security, than an insurance policy. Even widowhood holds less terror for the woman who is actively engaged in a life of her own. An important added bonus may be a new dimension to the marital relationship. One need only experience the striking difference in the dinner party conversation when the women present are, in Arnott's phrase, "home-makers only," and when they are actively engaged in the world. A whole new dialogue between men and women as human beings becomes possible.

As women age the life style they have built up through the years determines the possibilities open to them.[24] The dismal picture of old age as lonely, failing, and often institutionalized is another of those myths built up from clinical and institutional populations. Only a tiny fraction of the aging population is ever institutionalized. About 80 per cent live near one or more children or other close relative whom they see at least once a week. The main keys to a satisfactory old age are educational and financial. The middle-class woman, for example, makes a much better adjustment to widowhood than her working-class counterpart, not only because she is more often financially secure but also because she has a greater variety of interests and social skills. Certainly the woman who has kept alive and developing is in a better position to enrich her husband's retirement or, if necessary, to make a life for herself, to relate to her own and others' children and grandchildren, and to live in a continually changing world.

To Bring Off A Life

Perhaps it is time we gave up the "sugar and spice and everything nice" theory of child-rearing for our girls and young women. Instead of worrying quite so much about cute dresses, obedience, popularity, and "good adjustment," we might begin looking instead at how we can keep their interests in "toads and snails and puppy-dog tails"—and mathematics and geology and politics and social problems—alive and curious and growing. It is high time we rid ourselves of that pervasive, almost unconscious assumption that *girls'* development does not really matter, that they need not become fully individual, competent, intelligent, concerned human beings, because they will "just" get married and have children.

In fact, a great many will not get married, and only a few will remain married for the rest of their lives. Millions of women will never have children, and the majority who do so will spend only a fraction of their lives in active mothering. Most women will need to earn a living during at least part of their lives. And all women will need meaningful, committed interests and work (whether or not the work is paid) in order to lead satisfying, human, productive lives.

By all means, let us teach our daughters the household arts (and our sons as well). Let us communicate—but not romanticize—the joy in caring for babies and living with the miracle of children's development. But let us not assume that our daughters *must* marry, or that marriage and children are going to fill their whole lives, or that women do not need to develop their intellectual and vocational capacities. Rather, let them bring to adult life and to marriage their own sense of identity and selfhood, not simply seek to clothe themselves in their husband's name. Let women, too, become fully functioning adults who can live *with* their husbands and children, rather than *through* them, who can create a family life in which each person can live and breathe and grow in encounter with other real persons, rather than exploit their children and goad their husbands to live out their needs and accomplish their goals.

Instead of stifling the young girl's development by teaching her to look only to what will please others, let us help her to develop a full and rich and sensitive and actively curious life style of her own which will enable her to continue growing and becoming throughout all her days, able to fulfill her own needs and to bless those whose lives are touched by her own. Let us help her to *choose* life, and to take the responsibility of commitment.

To bring off a life is neither simple or easy. Depth and direction are crucial.

> Implanted in the stuff of all life is one urge—*the drive of potential to become actual,* i.e., to take shape and realize its potential. This fundamental drive you cannot violate with impunity. But you can count on it. As a human being, you are to some degree in charge of it.
>
> A built-in goal of life then is that you actualize your potential in the heres and nows given you. You have been given the possibility of becoming fully personal. Do you importantly intend to do something about it?
>
> One of man's (woman's) grave sins is the sin of not being, of never having been born. Of being "a faceless one" with no boundaries, no distinctive contours, no mouth that speaks nor eyes that invite. Equally damnable is the life that refuses to be reborn. That regards itself as finished.[25]

Our attitudes toward girls and women have not helped them to bring off a life. They have made it difficult for them to realize a "face" of their own. They have militated against women's developing depth and direction. But the potential is richly there. It waits to be born, or to be reborn. Woman's life is not finished; it has only begun.

1. Lee Rainwater, Richard P. Coleman, and Gerald Handel, *Workingman's Wife* (New York: Oceania Publications, Inc., 1959).
2. Alice Rossi, "Case against Full-time Motherhood," *Redbook,* 125 (March 1965) 51.
3. Joseph C. Rheingold. *The Fear of Being a Woman: A Theory of Maternal Destructiveness* (New York: Grune & Stratton, 1964).
4. Kenneth Keniston, *The Uncommitted* (New York: Harcourt, Brace & World, 1965).
5. From 1950 to 1968 the percentage of employed women with children under 6 increased from 12 to 28, of women with children aged 6–17 only from 28 to 47, and of married women with no children under 18 from 30 to 40.
6. A 1967 survey found that 57 per cent of female college graduates were employed, compared to 47 per cent of high school graduates and 30 per cent of women with eighth-grade educations (*Continuing Education Programs and Services for Women* [U.S. Dept. of Labor, Wage and Labor Standards Administration, Women's Bureau, Pamphlet 10; revised January 1968], p. 5). Almost 70 per cent of women college graduates will work for part of the second half of their adult lives (*American Women: The Report of the President's Commission on the Status of Women and Other Publications of the Commission,* ed. Margaret Mead and Frances Balgley Kaplan [New York: Charles Scribner's Sons, 1965]).
7. Analyzing data from a recent University of Chicago study of the mental health professions, Jean Prebis found that women contribute less to their profession than men, if contribution is measured by hours worked, papers published, professional reading, and consulting jobs. Other studies indicate that women professors do less

publishing and research than men, although they spend more hours in helping students. Myrdal and Klein report that women have a higher level of absenteeism from work, but add that the surprising thing is that, carrying a double responsibility, they have so little (Alva Myrdal and Viola Klein, *Women's Two Roles: Home and Work* [2d ed.; London: Routledge & Kegan Paul, Ltd., 1968]).

8. In response to stories of girls' achievements, 65 per cent of a sample of college girls and less than 10 per cent of the boys showed evidence of the motive to avoid success. "A bright woman is caught in a double bind. . . . If she fails, she is not living up to her own standards of performance; if she succeeds she is not living up to societal expectations about the female role" (Matina Horner, "A Bright Woman Is Caught . . . ," *Psychology Today,* 3 [November, 1969], 36–38.

9. F. Ivan Nye and Lois W. Hoffman, *The Employed Mother in America* (Chicago: Rand McNally & Co., 1963).

10 *Ibid.*

11. David F. Aberle and Kaspar D. Naegele, " 'Middle-Class Fathers' Occupational Role and Attitudes toward Children," in M. S. Sussman (ed.), *Sourcebook in Marriage and the Family* (2d ed.; Boston: Houghton Mifflin, 1963).

12. The results for boys who strongly adopted the masculine stereotype were quite similar. They early confined themselves to sports and science, while their less "adjusted" classmates retained much wider interests and were later deciding their life work (Leona E. Tyler, "The Antecedents of Two Varieties of Vocational Interests," *Genetic Psychology Monographs,* 70 [November, 1964], 177–227).

13. Eleanor E. Maccoby, "Woman's Intellect," in Seymour M. Farber and Roger H. L. Wilson (eds.). *The Potential of Women* (New York: McGraw-Hill Book Co., Inc., 1963).

14. James A. Davis, *Undergraduate Career Decisions* (Chicago: Aldine Publishing Co., 1965).

15. *Special Report on Women and Graduate Study* (U.S. Dept. of Health, Education, and Welfare, Resources for Medical Research Report No. 13, June, 1968).

16. Benjamin D. Wright and Shirley A. Tuska, *From Dream to Life in the Psychology of Becoming a Teacher* (Office of Education Cooperative Reserch Project No. 1503, 1966).

17. Alice Rossi, "The Roots of Ambivalence in American Women" (paper delivered to the Continuing Education for Women Section of the Adult Education Association of the U.S.A., Chicago, November 15, 1966).

18. E. E. LeMasters, "Parenthood as Crisis," in M. S. Sussman (ed.), *op. cit.*

19. Ruth Granetz Lyell, *Self-Education as Related to Cultural Values* (doctoral dissertation, University of Chicago, 1968).

20. Mary C. Mulvey, "Psychological and Sociological Factors in Prediction of Career Patterns of Women," *Genetic Psychology Monographs,* 68 (November, 1963), 309–86.

21. Catherine Arnott, *Exchange Theory and the Role Choice of Married Women* (Master's thesis, University of Southern California, 1969).

22. A series of studies indicate the lower self-esteem, lower satisfaction, and greater number of mental health symptoms of housewives as compared to employed women (Nye and Hoffman, *op. cit.*).

23. Between 1960 and 1965 the University of Minnesota enrolled 2,600 older women in undergraduate and graduate programs. A program at Roosevelt University allows adults to test out of up to two years of college work on the assumption that adults have learned in many other settings than the formal classroom.

24. In a study of community-living older people Neugarten and her associates found that persons in their seventies did not seem to be at the mercy either of circumstances or of inexorable inner changes. Rather, the individual personality, developed through the choices and experiences of a lifetime, becomes even more central to the patterning of behavior and level of life satisfaction as people age. Bernice L. Neugarten, Robert J. Havighurst, and Shelden S. Tobin, "Personality and Patterns of Aging," in Bernice L. Neugarten (ed.), *Middle Age and Aging* (Chicago: University of Chicago Press, 1968).
25. Ross Snyder, *On Becoming Human* (Nashville, Tenn.: Abingdon Press, 1967), pp. 17, 21.

NEW WAYS TO MANLINESS

Myron Brenton

The impact of work (and the lack or loss of it) upon men and masculinity is analyzed in this male reflection on the implications of "liberation". Contradicting fears about role blurring, Brenton suggests that communication between men and women will improve when each accepts and adopts some of the other's characteristics.

Is it possible, as Brenton suggests, that the real sexuality of men and women may emerge if stereotyped roles diminish? What are the implications for marital accord or discord if dominance and leadership in the family shift or become flexible? If male and female roles are no longer clearly distinguishable on the basis of sex-linked characteristics, how will children's sex identity be established? Is the issue of sex identity a "red herring"? Do men and women differ in ways that necessitate the continuance in some form of sex-linked role distinctions?

"I don't think it's an accident that throughout history women have been subjugated. It almost seems as though man had a fair chance if women had their feet bound and no legal rights and were practically tied up. Now that they've been freed—have the same rights as men, the same opportunities—the question of the balance seems to be thrown off. And I begin to wonder if a woman doesn't perhaps have a wider range of tactics than a man has. Women have more flexibility, and in a fair encounter a man can't handle them. Men aren't able to handle weakness as women are, for example."—JAY HALEY, of the Mental Research Institute, in a conversation with the author.

"To me freedom involves the ability to participate in change, in having the flexibility to change, in the ability to perceive in new forms and manner, in being as self-critical as we are critical of others, of joining others to solve problems, being able to deal with crises, either individually or by social means, of creating institutions capable of meeting

New Directions in Femininity/ Masculinity

*both the needs of nurturance of our fellow men and the adaptive prob-
lems of man in his relationship to man and his environment."*—
DR. LEONARD J. DUHL.[1]

The Breadwinner

When sociologist Helena Lopata of Roosevelt University queried more than 600 women in the Chicago area to find out how they viewed their roles in life, in order of importance, she discovered that they considered themselves mothers first of all. When she asked them to do the same for their husbands, their replies were an even greater revelation. Did these women—suburban wives in their thirties, with a family income between $6,000 and $10,000; urban wives with a median age of forty-nine and a family income from $5,000 to more than $16,000—see their mates primarily as husbands? As fathers? Or as breadwinners? The answer, startling though it is, isn't difficult to guess. Nearly 65 percent of the wives in both groups stated unequivocally that the most important role of the man of the family is, in their eyes, his breadwinning one. Father came in second; husband, a poor third.[2]

These statistics lend themselves to a very plausible explanation. Since the American male bases his masculine identity so narrowly on the breadwinning role, since it occupies—both psychically and physically—the central position in his life, his wife naturally is inclined to see him in the same utilitarian way. If one leaves aside the implications this has for the emotional relationship between husband and wife, the fact is that by depending so heavily on his breadwinning role to validate his sense of himself as a man, instead of also letting his roles as husband, father, and citizen of the community count as validating sources, the American male treads on psychically dangerous ground. It's always dangerous to put all of one's psychic eggs into one basket.

This is not to deny the meaning and importance of work in a person's life. Ideally, work is an outlet for creative energy, a way of channeling aggression, a tie with reality, and what Erik H. Erikson has called the backbone of identity formation. What is suggested here is this: (1) The other roles a man plays in life may also be very valuable in these respects; (2) present-day working conditions do not permit fulfillment of the traditional psychological aims of work to any significant degree; and (3) a narrow concentration of work in terms of his identity does not allow the male enough scope and flexibility to deal with the complexities of the times.

The American male looks to his breadwinning role to confirm his manliness, but work itself is fraught with dehumanizing—*i.e.,* unmanning— influences. With the growing impact of automation, they're bound to increase.

*New
Ways to
Manliness*

The very fact that leisure time is already becoming a social problem in America, a problem getting a great deal of expert scrutiny (several major universities have centers for the study of leisure, and the American Psychiatric Association has a standing committee on leisure), is a manifestation of how an overemphasis on work in terms of identity has a boomeranging effect. Most factory workers don't want more free time; this is reflected in the fact that the majority of unions have stopped bargaining for a shorter workweek. It's the threat of being displaced, however, that makes automation a major threat for most people. That threat is felt not only by low-level workers but also by white-collar workers and junior executives. A contributor to *Mass Society in Crisis* observes in discussing the new computers:

> [They] combine high technical competence with just enough of an I.Q. to keep them tractable. They do precisely the kind of work to which junior executives and semi-skilled workers are usually assigned. . . . Many middle management people in automated companies now report that they are awaiting the ax, or if more fortunate, retirement.[3]

Scientists themselves are becoming obsolete in terms of their present skills. Many scientists—especially those in government defense work—are overtrained in one specialty. As their jobs are being eliminated, these Ph.D.'s and technicians face serious adjustment problems, for circumstances require them to retrain so as to put their expertise to work in a new field.

Eventually, automation is expected to make some profound changes in the work role. Depending on which expert you talk to and which crystal ball he uses, everybody will work, but only a few hours a day or week; or most people will only be occupied in research and services; or every person will acquire several different skills and jobs in his lifetime; or one-third of the population will always be in school; or the definition of work itself will undergo radical changes, encompassing some of the activities we now call leisure-time activities. Such changes, however, won't come about in the very near future. As for now, the man who invests his entire identity in the work role is rendered extremely vulnerable. Dr. Bressler summed it up this way:

Many people invest too much of their psyches in work. A wide variety of circumstances—limited native capacity, skills that become obsolescent, impersonal socio-economic forces, capricious judgments by superiors—make the prediction and control of occupational success very hazardous. Accordingly, a prudent man would do well to develop other sources of ego-gratification.

Dealing With Adversity

The more flexible a person is in terms of his life roles—that is, the greater his ability to commit himself to a wide repertoire of roles—the less vulnerable he is to temporary setbacks in the playing of any one of them. The more flexible a person is in his relationships with other people—that is, the fewer preconceived notions about appropriate male and female behavior he has—the greater his ability to deal with adversity.

A personal crisis—sudden unemployment, for example—demonstrates clearly and dramatically the stunting effects of inflexibility, of a rigidly patriarchal outlook. If further evidence is needed that for the majority of American males, work is at the center of their conception of themselves as men, their reaction to the abrupt loss of their jobs proves it amply. Often their immediate reactions are remarkably like those of war casualties or victims of sudden accidents. Almost everything on which they have based their inner security is shattered. They're bereft.

When the Packard automobile plant shut down in 1956, for instance, many of the workers showed "stupefaction, bewilderment, a feeling of being 'lost.' " One employee said, "I felt like a bomb hit me . . . no place to go." Another commented, "I felt like someone had hit me with a sledge hammer." And a third told an interviewer, "I felt like jumping off the Belle Island Bridge in the river—put that down, you put that down."[4] When news broke in the closing months of 1964 that the New York Naval Shipyard, in Brooklyn, would be shut down, one worker told a *Herald Tribune* marine reporter, expressing what many of the workers felt, "We've been bombed out." When sociologists looked at the dislocations caused by the Studebaker automobile plant shutdown a year earlier, they found a high number of suicides taking place among the former workers—a rate far higher than would be the case in the total population with people having the same characteristics.

According to Dr. Harold L. Sheppard, of the W. E. Upjohn Institute for Employment Research, many former workers shut themselves inside their houses after the Studebaker plant had closed down. They never went out. "It was," Dr. Sheppard told me, "like a sudden, unexpected death in the family." He pointed out that not only had these men banked so heavily on the breadwinning role in terms of their image of themselves, but they also had a unidimensional view of that role:

> When a man has been an auto worker or a miner for twenty or thirty years, he can't picture himself as being anything else. We need some

new counseling techniques to shake these men up, get them out of the rut, get them started thinking of new possibilities.

This pattern of a man who has lost his job shutting himself up in his house for days or weeks at a time, shutting out the world, is by no means an unusual one, It occurred in California when a Lockheed Aircraft Corporatio plant laid off 500 engineers. Many of the men—who had worked at Lockheed for eight years or more, who had nice houses, expensive furniture, and several cars, but who hadn't yet consolidated their gains—could not handle the stress situation. One man left his house and came back home at the normal times each day, just as though he were still working, but he spent those eight or nine hours sitting in the park. This went on for two weeks. As luck would have it, a friend of his learned of a fine opportunity, something the man was ideally suited for, but didn't tell him because he assumed from this going-to-work-as-usual pattern that he was in fact still working.

Dr. Gertrude Hengerer told me that financial counselors in her area, Palo Alto and Los Altos, California, become swamped with work when there are mass layoffs. One reason is that many of the people who lose their jobs are bogged down with debts, frequently in order to keep up, to buy the essentially unneeded homes, cars, expensive vacations, and the like that become very much needed as a result of an overemphasis on the fruits of work. Wives may have to go to work precipitously to bring in some money. The whole family, including the children, become anxiety-ridden. The man who was laid off watches others still on the job, and the overriding question in his mind becomes, "Why me?" The men still on the job become terribly anxious, too. Their fear is, "Will I be next?" Dr. Hengerer said, "You can't get away from that question, 'Why me?' It really hits at your sense of self-worth, of masculinity."

Dr. Sheppard pointed out that the loss of job or even a sharp cut in pay is apt to be far more traumatic today than it was in Depression times. Then, nobody was asking, "Why me?" It was happening to everyone, and this took some of the psychological sting out of the stress situation.

The loss of job is obviously never a cause of rejoicing. In a youth-oriented culture it's especially agonizing for a man over the age of forty, who not infrequently is made to feel as though he has reached the extremes of decrepitude as he goes job hunting. But men vary widely in their ability to deal with adversity, and it has been demonstrated time and again that men who see their identity in the narrowest of terms, see it based principally in their breadwinning role, are in the greatest psychological trouble when they are suddenly deprived of this role.

The Depression is a relevant phenomenon to explore in this connection, for a number of depth studies—both psychological and sociological—were made in those bleak times. In study after study what keeps showing up is that the experience of a sudden job loss was far more of a shock to the men than to the women, although the loss of income would affect both equally. It was the men who had been primarily making money. It was the men, now out of work, whose main role had disappeared, who lacked anything to involve themselves in, both physically and psychically. Revisiting Middletown during the Depression, about a decade after their initial trip there, sociologists Robert and Helen Lynd noticed that for women the reverse often held true. The women's roles didn't contract; they expanded. Not only did the wife have to go on with the household routine—cooking, cleaning, taking care of the children—but frequently the wife was also the one who held the family together when her husband was prone to go to pieces.[5]

Paul Lazarsfeld, another noted sociologist, found somewhat the same situation when, in 1931, he scrutinized a small Austrian village that two years earlier had lost its one and only industry, a textile plant. Of a population of 1,486, 80 percent were out of work. Again, it was the men who were hardest hit psychologically, the ones who now had nothing to do and nothing to invest themselves in. They drifted helplessly and apathetically in the streets, looking dully for some means of rescue. On the other hand, the woman's world—the world of cooking, cleaning, mending, and childrearing—remained intact.[6]

Since the women weren't deprived of their principal roles in life, it stands to reason that they would be less shattered than the men. Possibly if they were suddenly unable to fulfill their housewife-mother roles, they would also tend to fall apart, although I suspect that the very roles women concentrate on—the expressive, emotional ones, in terms of temperament—render them more adaptable. But there remains the point that a narrow concentration on role poses considerable psychological danger.

The subjects of the Lynd's study, and Lazarsfeld's, had strong patriarchal orientations. They conceived themselves as men principally in terms of being their families' breadwinners. When no bread was there to be won, they lacked the ability to make a shift, to obtain greater psychic rewards from their roles as husbands and fathers. On the contrary, since his supremacy was structured by externals, often an unemployed man's prestige as husband and father, as head of the household, deteriorated badly. "I still love him, but he doesn't seem as big a man," says a Depression wife about her husband in Dr. Komarovsky's classic study of *The Unemployed Man and His Family.*

Dr. Komarovsky gives a poignant description of such a man's loss of power and prestige at home:

> The general impression that the interviews make is that in addition to sheer economic anxiety the man suffers from deep humiliation. He experiences a sense of deep frustration because in his own estimation he fails to fulfill what is the central duty of his life, the very touchstone of his manhood—the role of family provider. The man appears bewildered and humiliated. It is as if the ground had gone out from under his feet. He must have derived a profound sense of stability from having the family dependent on him. Whether he had considerable authority within the family and was recognized as its head, or whether the wife's stronger personality had dominated the family, he nevertheless derived strength from his role as provider. Every purchase of the family—the radio, his wife's new hat, the children's skates, the meals set before him—all were symbols of their dependence on him. Unemployment changed it all. It is to the relief office, or to a relative, that the family now turns. It is to an uncle or a neighbor that the children now turn in expectation of a dime or a nickel for ice cream, or the larger beneficences such as a bicycle or an excursion to the amusement park.[7]

When there is prolonged unemployment, as in depressed areas, the erstwhile breadwinner's reaction can take a different turn. Witness what the unavailability of jobs over a protracted period has brought about in Appalachia. With unemployed miners unable to get other work—and unwilling to work in nearby textile mills because they considered what they would have to do woman's work—their wives have become the chief breadwinners in the family. But according to Dorothy Cohen, executive director of the Family Service Association of Wyoming Valley, Pennsylvania, there's no real role reversal:

> In many instances, the women are faced with carrying the responsibility for home and children in addition to their jobs. Often, the care of the children is haphazard. Sometimes, relatives help. Day-care facilities are almost completely lacking in Wyoming Valley.

Some of the unemployed miners have fallen victim to what observers in the area call the depressed-area syndrome. They no longer feel degraded by their lack of employment. They don't involve themselves in home responsibilities. They congregate and drink together, while their wives work.

But it doesn't take as traumatic and explosive an experience as sudden unemployment to demonstrate the hazards of a firm belief in rigid patriarchal standards. Retirement also proves the point. There are, in fact, some strong similarities between retirement and unemployment. Retirement too brings out different reactions in men and women. The woman has already had her functions reduced when the children left home, but she never really completely retires; she must still cook the meals, clean the house, and take care of her husband. It may have been a very difficult moment for her when the last child departed for a life of his own, but she still has a somewhat familiar routine to pursue.

> As she goes about her daily routines [observes Donald E. Super, an expert on the psychology of careers], the husband is occasionally in her way, and both of them become uncomfortably conscious of the fact that she belongs there, that—whereas she has a role to play and ideas as to how she should play it—he does not belong there, he has no role to play. His role has changed from that of breadwinner to that of do-nothing, while his wife is still a homemaker. The self-concept which goes with the role of do-nothing is not a comfortable one to try to adopt after thirty-five years of working and of being a good provider.[8]

Thus, the man who adjusts least well to retirement is the one who identifies himself—as a man—most closely with the breadwinning role. Conversely, the man who adjusts best is the one whose psychic investments have throughout the years been multidimensional:

> The physician-artist finds it easy to keep on painting, for he took up painting in the first place because of his interests; medical and artistic interests have been shown to tend to go together. Indulging these interests is purely avocational; it contributes nothing to his status as a physician; it brings him no fame or fees, merely satisfaction and friends. On the other hand, the executive does not find it easy to keep up his golf, his yachting or his cards, for he took these up originally not so much out of interest in the activities themselves as for the associations they would bring him. Mixing with the right people at the club brings clients, customers, contracts, and the right people are glad to mix with him for the same reasons. Once the business motivation is removed the association no longer has the same mutual appeal, and the activity itself loses point. There are exceptions, of course; businessmen have real friendships, as well as friendships of convenience, and some businessmen like golf, yachting or cards for their own sakes. But these are probably the exceptions.[9]

If avocations help the male adjust to retirement, it stands to reason that a flexible view of what it is that constitutes masculinity, a fundamentally equalitarian approach to the marital interaction, will also help enormously.

The husband who doesn't look at himself or his wife in terms of roles, who's neither demasculinized by doing the dishes or by having a working wife or by showing tenderness and love—the man who in his conception of himself finds genuine rewards in being a successful husband and father, as well as breadwinner—is hardly going to feel, after he retires, that he doesn't belong at home.

Equality, Flexibility, and Marital Happiness

The functional psychiatrists and sociologists don't quite see it like this. They don't approve of the loose-knit equalitarian marriage. Their way is to pigeon-hole men and women into neat categories. They envision the ideal family, from the mental-health viewpoint, operating on the basis of clear-cut role differentiation. The man is the instrumental or task leader, the breadwinner, the authority figure, the one who gets things done, the parent who offers conditional love. The woman is the emotional or expressive-integrative leader, the one who keeps house and raises the children, the one solely responsible for binding the family's psychic wounds, the parent who offers unconditional love.

Such an inflexible division of roles rides roughshod over any individual characteristics. Task division is sharp—people know exactly what their roles are and no mistake about it—but focus on the uniqueness of individual personality is very blurred.

Moreover, in today's world, it isn't even really functional. It isn't functional because the way the American pattern is going—especially in terms of ecological shifts—the American family absolutely needs strong, flexible men *and* strong, flexible women to get things done. Most middle-class people and a growing number of working-class families are fleeing the cities, establishing themselves in the suburban way of life. In the suburbs a great deal of reliance must be placed on the wife. If something goes wrong, who's to see that it's taken care of? The husband is fifteen or twenty miles away at his job and is possibly working late. As Dr. James A. Peterson points out, if the wife is weak, if she can't get things done, if she can't handle situations, the family is in real trouble. Of course, a city wife has to be strong, too: few husbands can take off from work to handle every domestic crisis that comes along.

Studies at the University of Southern California, Dr. Peterson's bailiwick, show that when marriages have a strict division of roles in the traditionally functional pattern—that is, when the husband is solely the task leader; the wife, solely the expressive leader—the family as a functioning unit ceases to function. He explains:

> Unless there's an interpenetration of roles, the whole thing doesn't work—that is, if the wife cannot play the instrumental role, can't do the tasks that previously the man would insist on doing, the family breaks down. But likewise, if the husband is not an expressive leader, emotional leader, and gives his wife these things, the family breaks down, so that the roles not only become confused, in our day, compared to earlier days, they've also shifted somewhat.

To be sure, society may insist that a man who responds emotionally enough to give this kind of leadership has a considerable feminine component in his personality. It may insist on a whole sequence of elaborate rules and standards for what constitutes appropriate masculine and feminine response, for the most part erroneously and arbitrarily connecting them to innate sex-linked traits. But to the extent to which such elaborations require demonstration as proof of sexual identity, to this extent many individuals will suppress portions of their personalities, or they will try to conform to the rules and standards but feel insecure because not all aspects of themselves really fit in with what is expected.

However, gaining a feeling of security about one's sexual identity doesn't really require such heavy reliance on any superficial or narrow set of standards or such great emphasis on the tasks one performs. Secure sexual identity depends far more on how fully one incorporates the notion that one is a male (or female)—how comfortable one feels in one's sex, how acceptant one is of it. This incorporation and this acceptance in turn depend very much on how fully the individual's family of origin accepted him, accepted his sex, and allowed him to develop at his own rate of speed.

Discussing this vital point at a symposium conducted by the Child Study Association of America, Dr. M. Robert Gomberg noted:

> We are moving towards an era when it will be progressively less important to distinguish between male and female on the basis of social activity and responsibility. When the emphasis is put on inner personal fulfillment, it will be less important whether the social roles are diametrically opposed or overlap than that the inner image of oneself be that of a person who is respected, loved, wanted. If a small child in his littleness feels wanted and respected, it is natural for him as he grows to know himself as a loved male child, protected by a family that supports his values, even if society is in transition and is confused in some of its dictates. He will find the strength from within, buttressed

by the family, to find his own way and to play out his own role. Conversely, an individual may learn the stereotypes of masculinity. But if he has acquired them in a family that is angry, frightened, and competitive, though he sounds assertive and male, he may be inwardly frightened and need the loud sound of yesterday's maleness to disguise an inner hollowness.[10]

The person who has grown up learning to accept himself and his sex—who learned this acceptance without pressure or compulsion—is the one best able to deal with the demands of a society that has worked out a whole sequence of sex-role elaborations. He's the one best able to take and leave it, to conform to sex-role demands when conformity is in accord with his personality or does no violence to it and to reject the rest without feeling threatened.

If a man is real—if he is fundamentally secure in his manhood—women do not threaten him; nor does he need to confirm his masculinity at their expense. If his manhood is secure, then, as one young woman writes, "there is nothing the destructive part of me can destroy or hurt, so I can relax and enjoy being a complete woman, revel in my femaleness and enjoy his complete maleness. If he's secure, he can live his equalitarian life and an equalitarian marriage without fear of having his sexual identity shattered because roles merge or overlap. The secure man is warm, expressive, tender, and creative, yet quite capable of showing a sufficient amount of assertiveness when assertiveness is called for. The secure man can wash a dish, diaper a baby, and throw the dirty clothes into the washing machine—or do anything else women used to do exclusively—without thinking twice about it.

It's only when a man depends on arbitrary mechanisms outside himself to determine whether he's appropriately masculine, when he uses the stereotypes as strict guidelines to his identity, that he comes to feel somewhat beleaguered by the changes taking place in the roles of men and women. He reacts by belittling the female or by surrendering his autonomy to her. It's true that the blurring of the roles creates a great deal of identity confusion in both men and women at present, but it's a confusion brought on by the fact that neither sex has actually been assimilating the continuing changes in the condition of—and relationship between—the sexes. Nor may this assimilation be expected to come easily. For centuries women's place was in the home, whereas her relative emancipation has existed for a comparatively small fraction of time.

Many people fear the phenomenon of role blurring because they earnestly believe that it will eventually spell the complete eradication of sex differentiation in role and in personality. This seems a needless fear. The biological differences between the sexes will, after all, remain. So will the psychological drives rooted in biological structure. In fact, sex differentiation may in one sense be more acute when it's not camouflaged by the stereotypes. Robert Sunley, assistant director of the Family Service Association of Nassau County, New York, noted:

> My impression is that the more the roles are blurred, the more the superficial functional differences are eliminated, actually the more essential sexual differentiation occurs. In other words, your more truly masculine and feminine attributes emerge. I think the artificial distinctions don't really fit the people's personalities, and they also don't fit the essential sexuality involved. It confuses it, if anything. I think if you eliminate the arbitrary kinds of role distinctions, then the real sexual attraction—if there is any—emerges.

We may . . . surmise that the wonderful human diversity in temperament and in total personality structure will itself ensure the maintenance of many traditional psychosocial patterns of masculinity and femininity, as well as the patterns truly grounded in biology. The breakdown of the stereotypes therefore doesn't necessarily mean that the patterns behind them will eventually disappear. What it means is that they will not pose a threat. They will exist for people, rather than have people existing for them. This would put sex differentiation on the basis of the individual, not an indiscriminate mass.

To be sure, sex differences are much narrower in the United States at present than they are—or have been—in patriarchal cultures. Although this may be seen as a loss by some people, it should be recognized that this narrowing enables the sexes to be more friendly and companionable with each other than in the past. Only when each sex accepts the fact that it has components of the other in its personality, only when each individual of either sex learns, in a sense, to act out the other's roles, can the two sexes really and essentially communicate with each other. In fact, identity is built up in part by one's ability to master not only one's own roles, whatever they may be, but the roles of others as well. Furthermore, the very process of learning the roles of the opposite sex enables a person, if he is not threatened by it, to be more comfortable with his own sex—hence, with himself. Dr. Reuben Hill, the prominent University of Minnesota sociologist, explained:

> I happen to think that a family functions best that is able to communicate rather fully. That does not deny the opportunity to communicate at all levels. This permits a much wider repertoire of roles because you can discover what it's like to be a woman from a communicating

mother, sister, and later, girl friend. If you're a young man growing up, it's not as much of a mystery. You make fewer *faux pas* in anticipating their responses and are known as a man who is at ease with women. And similarly, with respect to men, you feel more at home with men because the communication bars that would separate you from womankind are not up but down. Because you can understand what the other's roles are, you can better understand what your own may be.

So far this discussion has centered on the equalitarian relationship between male and female, husband and wife, in terms of its functional and psychological validity. What about it in terms of marital harmony? How harmonious can two people be in their marital union when both are strong and both are flexible and both adhere to equalitarian principles?

Dr. Elizabeth Bott, a social anthropologist working in Great Britain, examined a number of families in which there was a great deal of role sharing. They were for the most part in the professional and clerical categories insofar as the husbands' employment status was concerned. These role-sharing families derived a substantial amount of emotional satisfaction within the marital union, much more so than other families in which rigid role segregation predominated. Although they had to make some allowance for the fact that the husbands were primarily breadwinners and the wives were primarily mothers of young children (some also worked), in other respects they didn't view their activities within the context of appropriate roles for men and women. Division of labor was very flexible. Fathers participated quite actively in child care, and family finances were handled jointly. Most significant were Dr. Bott's observations of the way these successful couples—successful in terms of marital happiness—handled the instrumental and expressive tasks. Dr. Bott stated:

> As far as I could tell, these couples did not feel that fathers should be the final authorities and disciplinarians and that mothers should be more warmhearted. They thought husbands and wives should be more or less equal both in authority and warm-heartedness.[12]

However, Dr. Bott was forced to conclude:

> In some cases, so much stress was placed on shared interests and sexual equality (which was sometimes confused with identity, the notion of equality of complementary opposites being apparently a difficult idea to maintain consistently) that one sometimes felt the possibility of the existence of social and temperamental differences between the sexes was being denied.[13]

It's a big job that the equalitarian marriage is being asked to do: to be hospitable to the individual both as individual and as marriage partner; to encompass "complementary opposites," as well as to allow traits shared with members of the opposite sex to emerge; and to allow the expression of dependency needs, as well as to encourage independence. Yet it can be done; it is being done. What true equality means is the equal right to expression and growth, to be a person. It does not mean strict equality of leadership every time leadership is called for. It does not mean a rigid fifty-fifty kind of relationship between the marital partners, who place their lives, so to speak, on a scale to ensure undeviating equality. It does not mean a constant and dangerous tussle for authority, in which each member of the marital pair jealously guards his territorial rights and watches anxiously for any undermining of this authority. *True equality entails a shifting, fluid, dynamic kind of interaction, in which leadership changes from one partner to the other depending on their specific interests and areas of competence and on the specific contributions they're able to make in any given situation.* Leadership, dominance, and dependency—all shift with the particular needs and abilities of the marital partners and with the requirements of the situation.

This doesn't preclude a division of labor and of decision making, of course. Whenever any two persons of the same or opposite sex live together, such a division, based on interest and competence, comes into being. Without it, getting anything done may lead to chaos. But in the equalitarian marriage the divisions aren't frozen. Although it may be more logical, more practical, for one partner to take the responsibility in a given area most of the time, the other partner isn't inhibited from assuming or sharing in it on occasion.

A revealing picture of the shifting, dynamic kind of marital interaction is offered by Ernest W. Burgess and Leonard S. Cottrell, Jr., in their monumental study of marriage adjustment, *Predicting Success or Failure in Marriage.* Among the people the two behavioral scientists interviewed was one couple that rated extremely high in marital adjustment; in addition, a number of knowledgeable outsiders gave this husband and wife high marks for marital harmony. The marriage was equalitarian. Decision making was shared. Yet this was no fifty-fifty proposition. Dominance shifted spontaneously as "husband and wife were able to play superior, equalitarian and inferior parts, parental and dependent child roles, and a number of other roles in their marriage drama, with considerable facility." Significantly, the husband was much more rigid in the early stages of their marriage than he was at the time of the study. That was when he resisted his wife's suggestions and advice, even when he knew she was right ("I couldn't stand having her tell me what to do"), but he showed much more personality flexibility as the relationship progressed.[14]

The heart of the equalitarian marriage *is* personality flexibility. For this reason it provides the kind of marital structure best suited to individual growth: it allows each of the partners the freedom and the scope to expand, to unfold their personalities, to realize their particular potentials. In a worl that in many ways is becoming increasingly specialized, bureaucratized, anc conformist, it affords the one really fertile soil for the nurturing of the individual. Furthermore, it affords each partner recognition and acceptance of his or her particular strengths, weaknesses, and needs. This means that husband and wife can have from the marriage a much greater degree of mutua emotional support than is possible in other marital patterns. A highly patriarchal male may enjoy—or think he enjoys—a superior amount of power i the family. But it's the equalitarian male, not shackled by a convention that demands him to be *always* strong, who can turn to his wife for comfort at times. It's he who has a great deal of social interaction and the deepest com panionship with her. The equalitarian marriage, then, is both expedient and pragmatic.

But more than expediency and pragmatism are involved. The most impor tant thing to keep in mind is that people are first of all human beings—not members of a particular sex—and the initial concern of a highly complex, advanced society ought to be the stimulation of the human diversity that makes for a richness of culture. This means stimulating each individual to develop *all* aspects of his personality *and* affording him the opportunity of pursuing the tastes, attitudes, and occupational preferences most congenial to his particular person. In such a society the artistically gifted man and the man who is a gifted sportsman would be equally valued in terms of their maleness; the more nurturing type of male would not suffer by comparison with the more competitive one; each man and each woman would be given full opportunity to tread, without stigma, the paths temperamentally most suitable to them.

This is not what is generally being advocated now. The functionalists, con cerned about role confusion, would have us go back to traditional patriarcha patterns in which roles and personalities are rigidly differentiated. The angry neofeminists of the 1960s discount the possibility of any woman's finding a fulfillment in the homemaking-mothering role and demand a single societal pattern that would have all women, as well as all men, out pursuing meaningful careers. But why make one's life roles in American society an either-or proposition? Why not tap all our societal and temperamental resources to create an atmosphere in which all kinds of ways are possible and in which self-fulfillment becomes more than a pretty word? For most people this may well mean the more traditional pattern of the husband as breadwinner and the wife as homemaker. For others it would mean, as it already increasingly does, both partners engaging in outside work, whether for financial reasons or to meet creative challenges or both.[15] And if at some state in their unique family life cycle, the temperaments and circumstances of a particular couple dictate a complete reversal of roles—the husband taking care of the children, the wife earning the living—let them do so without hindrance or onus. All kinds of patterns are to be had. By all means, let us break down the stereotypes and have them.[16]

The American male in contemporary times, as part of the larger society, faces problems of enormous magnitude. The wonderful technology that he, along with other peoples in the world, is creating threatens to engulf him. The incredible machines he has developed are, in conjunction with the ever-increasing bureaucratization of his consumer society, threatening to turn him into a cipher. The conflict between the white and Negro races is anguished, and the wounds will need to be healed. There is the fouling of the air he breathes; there is the soiling of the water he needs for drink and sport. The daily headlines show no dearth of matters that demand—nay, that cry out for —solution. These are some of his new challenges.

The most important one of all concerns war and peace. Some fifty years ago, philosopher William James, reflecting on the "Moral Equivalent of War," saw in the fight against poverty and suffering one way of displaying masculinity, saw in this a constructive equivalent to militarism—man in combat against a different species of enemy.[17] His vision has even greater applicability today than it did then—as, on the one hand, more and more nations arm themselves with the weapons of total annihilation and as, on the other, the United States begins, if slowly, its offensive on this nation's rugged pockets of poverty. The fact that modern weaponry can destroy civilization— the very shock of it—acts as a deterrent to all-out war. Could it act as a catalyst to change the concept and direction of masculine aggression? Margaret Mead, taking stock of the contemporary human situation, sees ground for optimism, sees it especially in regard to the children of the times:

> Children today, growing up in a world able to destroy itself, do not have to pretend that they are not afraid of modern warfare. Nor do they have to feel that it is unmanly to work for peace. Their heroes need not be daredevils, but men who can soberly assess just how dangerous the new projects are that mankind must undertake—projects

that admittedly may not work out, that are subject to disastrous accidents. The children whose birthright is this new age will be saved from psychological disaster if they see around them men and women who estimate danger carefully and accurately, who work soberly to prevent war and who invent safer ways of keeping the peace.[18]

Masculinity and Choice   If the American male is not to become a neurotic weakling, as anthropologist H. R. Hays already accuses him of being, he has no recourse but to exercise his responsibility for choice on every level. The old roads are swiftly being closed to him, one by one. He can no longer surely and definitively confirm his masculinity in terms of unidimensional and sexually differentiated roles. He can no longer do so on the basis of female inferiority in the practical affairs of the world. Whether or not he knows how to fix the faucet, whether or not he takes to mowing the lawn, such matters are quite beside the point. So is physical configuration. It's remarkable how two men with the same physical conformation, even when they conform precisely to the stereotypes—tall, handsome, broadshouldered —can project such a different air. One conveys a feeling of confidence and ease, of a person who knows who he is; the other seems weak and easily led It's largely in the way he handles his choices—indeed, whether he has the autonomy to make them at all—that is at the crux of his manly stance. In this sense there's a merging of masculinity and individuality; in fact, they must be considered together. This also holds true, of course, for femininity. The person of either sex who has a sense of his own worth as an individual and who does not long to assume the mantle of the opposite sex doesn't worry about his sexual identity. It's there automatically, with or without reference to elaborate stereotypes.

Admittedly, the times are not conducive to this sense of self-worth. They're not conducive to the easy acceptance of one's sex, to individualism (except in a narrow, insular sense). As long as men feel that the equality of women will emasculate them, it is exactly what will happen. As long as men identify themselves so narrowly with the breadwinning role, with the competitive demands of their consumer society, with narrow and noncreative work, their psychic equilibrium will be shaky.

The question of identity in the larger sense, of individuality, has been viewed in many contexts and written about from many different points of view. David Riesman's *The Lonely Crowd* saw the American character changing from an inner-directed one to one in which Everyman *is* Everyman, whose outer-directed character is formed chiefly by the example of peers and contemporaries. William H. Whyte's *The Organization Man* saw the individual submerging himself wholly in the needs of the organization—be it corporate, governmental, or whatever—and leading the bureaucratized life in which adjustment becomes the greater good. Erich Fromm, in *The Sane Society*, wrote about the variety of conformist pressures on the individual who, in a democracy, supposedly has convictions and a will:

> The facts, however, are that the modern, alienated individual has opinions and prejudices but no convictions, has likes and dislikes, but no will. His opinions and prejudices, likes and dislikes, are manipulated in the same way as his taste is, by powerful propaganda machines—which might not be effective were he not already conditioned to such influences by advertising and by his whole alienated way of life.[19]

Implicit in each statement is the view that the technological society which man has created is taking over, is crushing man's ability to make his choices with any degree of autonomy. That is, he cannot stand back. He cannot weigh. He cannot pick and choose, cannot see the whole because of the economic and other pressures which manipulate him to see only the parts. Such books and the studies they reflect are immensely valuable in the perspective they give of the changing American society—a society whose greatness lies in the individual. But without in the least meaning to, they carry a built-in danger. . . . They seem to make the forces at work on the individual appear so powerful that an air of inevitability is somehow conveyed, that short of superhuman effort, short of really drastic economic or political change, the future will be like the present, only more so.

But is the individual really doomed to be a cipher—well fed, with creature comforts readily at hand—but a cipher all the same? The advertisers advertise, the manipulators manipulate, sex is single-mindedly extolled, a high degree of competitiveness fuels the individual and collective life of the nation, and man comes to see himself primarily as economic man; yet *although the scope and potential for autonomous choice have been drastically reduced, they have not disappeared.* Some people *are* making their choices in life on an individual, not mass, basis. . . . The American male has the choice of viewing his worth to his family and to himself mechanistically—by how much money he makes and how much status he garners or by how meaningful and broad-based is the relationship he establishes with them. He has the choice of making his marriage an either-or proposition—either he bosses his wife, or she bosses him—or of looking at himself and his spouse as persons with individual needs and temperaments. He has the choice of conveying his authority as father by the mere fact that he *is* a father or by not cheating on his income tax after talking to his kids about honesty, by not giving them a swat after conveying the importance of reasoning, and by following through on a promise after lecturing them on the value of a man's word. He has the choice of accepting the fact that he is becoming less hard and rough and that the female is becoming more competent and adventuresome as signs that the sexes are reversing roles or that both of them are becoming more civilized.

There is a new way to masculinity, a new concept of what it means to be a man. It has little to do with how strong the male is physically, how adept he is at ordering people around, how expensive his cars are, how versatile he is with a set of tools, or how closely he identifies with all the other stereotyped attitudes and acts. It has everything to do with the way he manages his life— the way he conducts himself as a human being in terms of his wife, his children, his business associates, his friends, his neighbors, and his compatriots in the community—and with his ability to make decisions, with his courage to say no, as well as yes, with his perception into the consequences of his actions and decisions. This isn't the easy way. It could hardly be called the path of least resistance. But there's no turning back the clock. With the equality of women an inexorable trend, with the traditional male patterns increasingly losing their significance for a variety of reasons, it is—at bottom —the only alternative to what may well become psychic castration.

What I am saying is that no matter how much American males may yearn for the simpler, more clearly defined times gone by, their yearnings are futile. They have the choice of remaining what collectively they are—a sex at bay —or of redefining themselves in the light of the changing culture. Historically, in the relationship between men and women and between men and men, this is a new approach. And it is the ultimate masculine challenge. It's the ultimate challenge because it does away with stereotypes, guidelines, and life plans. It simply requires a man to be more fully human, more fully responsive, and more fully functioning than he has ever before allowed himself to be. This is the freedom that equality of the sexes offers him.

If he's afraid to take this freedom, the American male will wind up enslaving himself all the more. If he grasps it, he may at last come to see that he's not really as fragile as his patriarchal concepts have made him out to be.

1. Leonard J. Duhl, "The American Character—Crisis, Change and Complexity," *The Journal of Nervous and Mental Disease*, Vol. 137, No. 2 (August, 1963).

2. Marya Mannes, "I, Mary, Take Thee, John, as . . . What?" *The New York Times Magazine* (November 14, 1965).
3. Ben B. Seligman, "Man, Work, and the Automated Feast," *Mass Society in Crisis,* Rosenberg, Gerver, and Howton, editors (New York: The Macmillan Co., 1964), pp.. 468 ff.
4. Harold L. Sheppard and others, *Too Old to Work—Too Young to Retire: A Case Study of a Permanent Plant Shutdown,* for the Special Committee on Unemployment Problems, 86th Congress, 1st Session (December 21, 1959).
5. Robert S. Lynd and Helen Merrell Lynd, *Middletown in Transition* (New York: Harcourt, Brace & Co., 1937), p. 178.
6. Paul Lazarsfeld, *Die Arbeitslosen von Marienthal* (Leipzig: Hirzel, 1933).
7. Mirra Komarovsky, *The Unemployed Man and His Family* (New York: Institute of Social Research, 1940), p. 74.
8. Donald E. Super, *The Psychology of Careers* (New York: Harper & Bros., 1957), p. 159.
9. *Ibid.*, p. 160.
10. M. Robert Gomberg, *Child Study* (Summer, 1957). It also helps if the parents don't reflect confusion in terms of what they expect of the child. But such confusion is often evident. In one study of an upper-middle-class group the following patterns were noted: (1) Mothers more often do the punishing; (2) both parents want both boys and girls to be bold and daring; (3) mothers more often than fathers prefer submissive boys; (4) fathers want their daughters to be traditionally feminine; (5) the mothers prefer their daughters to be more masculine in behavior than the fathers do and; (6) the children see the mother, not the father, as the more influential figure in their lives. M. Radke, *The Relation of Parental Authority to Children's Behavior and Attitudes* (Minneapolis: University of Minnesota Press, 1946).
11. Private communication to the author.
12. Elizabeth Bott, "Conjugal Roles and Social Networks," *Family and Social Network* (London: Tavistock Publications, Ltd., 1957), Ch. 3.
13. *Ibid.*
14. Ernest W. Burgess and Leonard S. Cottrell Jr., *Predicting Success or Failure in Marriage* (New York: Prentice-Hall, Inc., 1939), p. 182 f. Although happiness is a rather tenuous quality to measure, several other studies do show a high correlation between marital happiness and equalitarianism in marriage. Dr. Paul Popenoe told me of one such study his organization made. The results: of the marriages where the wife was dominant, 47 per cent were rated as happy; where the husband was dominant, 61 per cent were so rated; of the equalitarian marriages, 87 per cent were rated as happy.
15. But society would have to provide services to facilitate such an arrangement—for instance, day-care centers, educational institutions willing to provide part-time or discontinuous education to women, and part-time or half-day employment.
16. Dr. Emily Mudd sees many men who are "good cooks, and who love their gardens, and who are nurturing kinds of people" married to more competitive women. If they could reverse roles, she says, these couples "could be very happy," provided that society put no onus on this. Many experts would insist that such a drastic interchange of roles always produces identity problems for the children, if not for the adults. Problems invariably occur, of course, since at present society doesn't permit this kind of arrangement without considerable loss of status. It should be remembered, however, that identity problems also occur when the marriage partners play

the traditional roles but are unsuited to and ineffectual in them. This whole area is rife for more intensive and unprejudiced socioscientific study than it has been getting. For one man's experience in role reversal, see "Dilemmas of a Househusband," *Saturday Review* (January 2, 1965), p. 100.

17. William James, *Essays on Faith and Morals* (Cleveland: The World Publishing Co. 1962).
18. Margaret Mead, "Must Our Children Fear the Future," *Redbook* (March, 1962).
19. Erich Fromm, *The Sane Society* (New York: Holt, Rinehart, Winston, Inc., 1955), p. 339.

WHAT IT WOULD BE LIKE IF WOMEN WIN

Gloria Steinem

Gloria Steinem, sometimes described as a militant feminist, here specifies
the institutions, organizations, and patterns of life which, moving away
from restrictions on women, will enable all Americans to live more freely.
She points to specific changes that must occur if women are to be treated
as full human beings and seeks at the same time to allay fears that
"liberation" of women will threaten men.

Any change is fearful, especially one affecting both politics and sex roles, so
let me begin these utopian speculations with a fact. To break the ice.

Women don't want to exchange places with men. Male chauvinists, science-
fiction writers and comedians may favor that idea for its shock value, but
psychologists say it is a fantasy based on ruling-class ego and guilt. Men
assume that women want to imitate them, which is just what white people
assumed about blacks. An assumption so strong that it may convince the
second-class group of the need to imitate, but for both women and blacks
that stage has passed. Guilt produces the question: What if they could treat
us as we treated them?

That is not our goal. But we do want to change the economic system to
one more based on merit. In Women's Lib Utopia, there will be free access
to good jobs—and decent pay for the bad ones women have been performing
all along, including housework. Increased skilled labor might lead to a four-
hour workday, and higher wages would encourage further mechanization of
repetitive jobs now kept alive by cheap labor.

With women as half the country's elected representatives, and a woman
President once in a while, the country's *machismo* problems would be greatly
reduced. The old-fashioned idea that manhood depends on violence and
victory is, after all, an important part of our troubles in the streets, and in

Vietnam. I'm not saying that women leaders would eliminate violence. We are not more moral than men; we are only uncorrupted by power so far. When we do acquire power, we might turn out to have an equal impulse toward aggression. Even now, Margaret Mead believes that women fight less often but more fiercely than men, because women are not taught the rules of the war game and fight only when cornered. But for the next 50 years or so, women in politics will be very valuable by tempering the idea of manhood into something less aggressive and better suited to this crowded, post-atomic planet. Consumer protection and children's rights, for instance, might get more legislative attention.

Men will have to give up ruling-class privileges, but in return they will no longer be the only ones to support the family, get drafted, bear the strain of power and responsibility. Freud to the contrary, anatomy is not destiny, at least not for more than nine months at a time. In Israel, women are drafted, and some have gone to war. In England, more men type and run switchboards. In India and Israel, a woman rules. In Sweden, both parents take care of the children. In this country, come Utopia, men and women won't reverse roles; they will be free to choose according to individual talents and preferences.

If role reform sounds sexually unsettling, think how it will change the sexual hypocrisy we have now. No more sex arranged on the barter system, with women pretending interest, and men never sure whether they are loved for themselves or for the security few women can get any other way. (Married or not, for sexual reasons or social ones, most women still find it second nature to Uncle Tom.) No more men who are encouraged to spend a lifetime living with inferiors, with housekeepers, or dependent creatures who are still children. No more domineering wives, emasculating women, and "Jewish mothers," all of whom are simply human beings with all their normal ambition and drive confined to the home. No more unequal partnerships that eventually doom love and sex.

In order to produce that kind of confidence and individuality, child rearing will train according to talent. Little girls will no longer be surrounded by airtight, self-fulfilling prophecies of natural passivity, lack of ambition and objectivity, inability to exercise power, and dexterity (so long as special aptitude for jobs requiring patience and dexterity is confined to poorly paid jobs; brain surgery is for males).

Schools and universities will help to break down traditional sex roles, even when parents will not. Half the teachers will be men, a rarity now at preschool and elementary levels; girls will not necessarily serve cookies or boys hoist up the flag. Athletic teams will be picked only by strength and skill. Sexually segregated courses like auto mechanics and home economics will be taken by boys and girls together. New courses in sexual politics will explore female subjugation as the model for political oppression, and women's history will be an academic staple, along with black history, at least until the white-male-oriented textbooks are integrated and rewritten.

As for the American child's classic problems—too much mother, too little father—that would be cured by an equalization of parental responsibility. Free nurseries, school lunches, family cafeterias built into every housing complex, service companies that will do household cleaning chores in a regular, businesslike way, and more responsibility by the entire community for the children: all these will make it possible for both mother and father to work, and to have equal leisure time with the children at home. For parents of very young children, however, a special job category, created by Government and unions, would allow such parents a shorter work day.

The revolution would not take away the option of being a housewife. A woman who prefers to be her husband's housekeeper and/or hostess would receive a percentage of his pay determined by the domestic relations courts. If divorced, she might be eligible for a pension fund, and for a job-training allowance. Or a divorce could be treated the same way that the dissolution of a business partnership is now.

If these proposals seem farfetched, consider Sweden, where most of them are already in effect. Sweden is not yet a working Women's Lib model; most of the role-reform programs began less than a decade ago, and are just beginning to take hold. But that country is so far ahead of us in recognizing the problem that Swedish statements on sex and equality sound like bulletins from the moon.

Our marriage laws, for instance, are so reactionary that Women's Lib groups want couples to take a compulsory written exam on the law, as for a driver's license, before going through with the wedding. A man has alimony and wifely debts to worry about, but a woman may lose so many of her civil rights that in the U.S. now, in important legal ways, she becomes a child again. In some states, she cannot sign credit agreements, use her maiden name, incorporate a business, or establish a legal residence of her own. Being a wife, according to most social and legal definitions, is still a 19th century thing.

Assuming, however, that these blatantly sexist laws are abolished or reformed, that job discrimination is forbidden, that parents share financial responsibility for each other and the children, and that sexual relationships become partnerships of equal adults (some pretty big assumptions), then marriage will probably go right on. Men and women are, after all, physically complementary. When society stops encouraging men to be exploiters and women to be parasites, they may turn out to be more complementary in emotion as well. Women's Lib is not trying to destroy the American family. A look at the statistics on divorce—plus the way in which old people are farmed out with strangers and young people flee the home—shows the destruction that has already been done. Liberated women are just trying to point out the disaster, and build compassionate and practical alternatives from the ruins.

What will exist is a variety of alternative life-styles. Since the population explosion dictates that childbearing be kept to a minimum, parents-and-children will be only one of many "families": couples, age groups, working groups, mixed communes, blood-related clans, class groups, creative groups. Single women will have the right to stay single without ridicule, without the attitudes now betrayed by "spinster" and "bachelor." Lesbians or homosexuals will no longer be denied legally binding marriages, complete with mutual-support agreements and inheritance rights. Paradoxically, the number of homosexuals may get smaller. With fewer overpossessive mothers and fewer fathers who hold up an impossibly cruel or perfectionist idea of manhood, boys will be less likely to be denied or reject their identity as males.

Changes that now seem small may get bigger.

Men's Lib   Men now suffer from more disease due to stress, heart attacks, ulcers, a higher suicide rate, greater difficulty living alone, less adaptability to change and, in general, a shorter life span than women. There is some scientific evidence that what produces physical problems is not work itself, but the inability to choose which work, and how much. With women bearing half the financial responsibility, and with the idea of "masculine" jobs gone, men might well feel freer and live longer.

Religion   Protestant women are already becoming ordained ministers; radical nuns are carrying out liturgical functions that were once the exclusive property of priests; Jewish women are rewriting prayers—particularly those that Orthodox Jews recite every morning thanking God they are not female. In the future, the church will become an area of equal participation by women. This means, of course, that organized religion will have to give up one of its great historical weapons: sexual repression. In most structured faiths, from Hinduism through Roman Catholicism, the status of women went down as the position of priests ascended. Male clergy implied, if they did not teach, that women were unclean, unworthy and sources of ungodly temptation, in order to remove them as rivals for the emotional forces of men. Full participation of women in ecclesiastical life might involve certain changes in theology, such as, for instance, a radical redefinition of sin.

Literary Problems Revised sex roles will outdate more children's books than civil rights ever did. Only a few children had the problem of a *Little Black Sambo,* but most have the male-female stereotypes of "Dick and Jane." A boomlet of children's books about mothers who work has already begun, and liberated parents and editors are beginning to pressure for change in the textbook industry. Fiction writing will change more gradually, but romantic novels with wilting heroines and swashbuckling heroes will be reduced to historical value. Or perhaps to the sado-masochist trade.(*Marjorie Morningstar,* a romantic novel that took the '50s by storm, has already begun to seem as unreal as its '20s predecessor, *The Sheik.*) As for the literary plots that turn on forced marriages or horrific abortion, they will seem as dated as Prohibition stories. Free legal abortions and free birth control will force writers to give up pregnancy as the *deus ex machina.*

Manners and Fashion Dress will be more androgynous, with class symbols becoming more important than sexual ones. Pro- or anti-Establishment styles may already be more vital than who is wearing them. Hardhats are just as likely to rough up antiwar girls as antiwar men in the street, and police understand that women are just as likely to be pushers or bombers. Dances haven't required that one partner lead the other for years, anyway. Chivalry will transfer itself to those who need it, or deserve respect: old people, admired people, anyone with an armload of packages. Women with normal work identities will be less likely to attach their whole sense of self to youth and appearance; thus there will be fewer nervous breakdowns when the first wrinkles appear. Lighting cigarettes and other treasured niceties will become gestures of mutual affection. "I like to be helped on with my coat," says one Women's Lib worker, "but not if it costs me $2,000 a year in salary."

For those with nostalgia for a simpler past, here is a word of comfort. Anthropologist Geoffrey Gorer studied the few peaceful human tribes and discovered one common characteristic: sex roles were not polarized. Differences of dress and occupation were at a minimum. Society, in other words, was not using sexual blackmail as a way of getting women to do cheap labor, or men to be aggressive.

Thus Women's Lib may achieve a more peaceful society on the way toward its other goals. That is why the Swedish government considers reform to bring about greater equality in the sex roles one of its most important concerns. As Prime Minister Olof Palme explained in a widely ignored speech delivered in Washington this spring: "It is *human beings* we shall emancipate. In Sweden today, if a politician should declare that the woman ought to have a different role from man's, he would be regarded as something from the Stone Age." In other words, the most radical goal of the movement is egalitarianism.

If Women's Lib wins, perhaps we all do.

*New
Directions in
Femininity/
Masculinity*

THE CHANGING ROLE OF THE
BLACK WOMAN

Barbara Rhodes

According to Barbara Rhodes, the role of the Black woman can be defined by no force or individual outside herself—by neither the white woman, the white man, by white society, nor even by the Black man. Contradicting the view of some spokeswomen that the Black woman must step back in order to allow the Black man to step forward or that her role must be secondary to his, she believes that the Black woman's role must be worked out in conjunction with the Black man's destiny but not in subordination to him and that each woman must find her own answers.

This role has primarily to do with political awareness, with involvement in the Black people's struggle for liberation, and with building the necessary revolutionary consciousness for liberation to be accomplished. The Black woman cannot be identified, she says, with the "traditional" femininity that prevents her from dealing with ideas, especially political ideas.

As a mother, she must develop in her children a sense of "the realities of this society and the realities of involvement in a Black liberation struggle." This she accomplishes by inculcating in the child a deep self-love, self-knowledge, and self-acceptance, traits which the student of human sexuality will recognize as basic ingredients of psychological and sexual health.

In Nkhrumah's *Handbook of Revolutionary Warfare for Freedom Fighters in Africa*, he says, "The degree of a country's revolutionary awareness is measured by the political maturity of its women." This statement should provoke serious thought in America because of the Black people's intense struggle for liberation and the growing revolutionary spirit. Several years ago the prevalent philosophy toward Black women expressed by a militant Black organization was that the only position of the Black woman in the revolution was prone. That Black people have developed in terms of their revolutionary consciousness is evidenced by the fact that they have now reached the point of concern with the position of the Black woman in a revolution.

We are not now involved in a revolution. We are, however, involved in the building of a revolutionary consciousness. As a Black woman living in the United States today, I strongly feel that the necessity for a political maturity of Black women must be recognized. It must be recognized by Black men, and most importantly, by Black women themselves. Black women must examine the role that has been defined for them by this white society, a role that society has systematically used to elevate them above their Black men. The white society calls it the "matriarchy." That role shows the Black woman's adaptability to conditions imposed upon her Black man and upon her in this country. But when the white society defines the role of the Black woman as a matriarch, it is done in a negative way. It is not that a matriarch is to be criticized; many societies function very effectively under a matriarchal system. However, American society is traditionally patriarchal, and so the women's assumption of head of the household becomes a point from which to attack the male, who is not fulfilling his function in terms of this society's expectations.

The Black woman has often allowed herself to be confused because of the role which white society says she should play as a woman and the role they force her to play as a Black woman. In this confusion, Black women have attempted to act like white women. This is neither possible nor desirable. The white reality is not the Black reality. The role the white woman plays in this white world the Black woman cannot play. And she must not try. The Black woman must be involved in the struggle for the liberation of her people.

How is the Black woman to be involved? Many Black women in their new-found Black consciousness feel that they must look to the Black man to define their role, as they once accepted the role defined for women by the white man. But this is not necessary. There is no role for the Black woman that can be outlined and handed to her by someone else. Defining roles is expedient, but it is not always effective. Take the role historically assigned to Black women as a matriarch. This role defining allows for value judgments, judgments that elevate the Black woman at the expense of the Black man. The Black man cannot perform in the role assigned to man by white society because it is a role defined for white men. But the white man, he who stops the Black man from assuming this role, attacks the Black man on the basis o.

his not functioning in this role. Because the role is defined, if one does not carry out its definition, one can be attacked. This is expediency. An effective relationship in terms of the functions of Black men and women would be that distribution of functions which best relates to their Black reality. This is not expedient. But it is functional, and we as Black people are concerned with survival. It is the white man who is concerned with expediency. When it comes to Blacks, the white man's expediency keeps him on top.

The Black woman must act from a base of political awareness. This is the guiding principle in terms of her functioning. Then, as a mother, teacher, neighbor, or organization member, she is functioning in the building of the revolutionary consciousness of Black people.

How does a Black woman become politically aware? First, she must discard the myth of femininity that would effectively halt her progress. By femininity, I do not mean such superficial feminine traits as tone of voice and language. I am talking about the femininity that would prevent the Black woman from dealing seriously with ideas. The Black woman must free her mind from these restraints. She must open her mind to the ideologies of the Black struggle and allow it to consider total involvement in the effort to liberate Black people.

Black women must open their minds to all ideas that involve their survival. This is the education they must pass on to their Black children. They must continue to be effective counterparts of their Black men. The relationship between man and woman and the relationship between mother and child are extremely important for Black people. Black children must not be allowed to be conditioned by a white society, unaware of their Black reality. They must be conditioned by a Black mother, to the realities of this society and the realities of involvement in a Black liberation struggle.

No more will Black men submit to the emasculation inherent in the calling of their Black women matriarchs. They are determined to claim the total dignity of manhood at whatever cost. The role of the Black woman as it relates to that will be crucial. What is this role? Black women must supply the answers for themselves. Only they can determine how they will relate to these changing times. The suggestions that follow reflect the thoughts of one Black woman.

More than Empty Rhetoric for the Child

When the Black woman is faced with the multiple problems of raising a Black child in a white society, is it enough for her to say to the child, "Listen, my child, Black is beautiful"? Does the child understand what the mother is saying? Does this enable him to deal with the white environment as a proud, assured Black person? I say a resounding no! A child can understand when he is told. "You are beautiful." A child cannot understand when he is told, "Black is beautiful; you are Black and you are beautiful." The child does not understand the suffering and pain that has given significance to the phrase "Black is beautiful." The child does not understand the depths of darkness from which Black people have ascended, proudly lifting the darkness with them, glorifying in this darkness that is their Black selves, and proclaiming its beauty as innate and proud that it is manifest without. How can the child know all this? To the child, this phrase is empty rhetoric. As surely as he knows that darkness follows light in the passing of the days, he will come to know this. When he comes to this knowledge of his Blackness, he will willingly embrace it if he has been truly made to believe in his beauty as a person. "Child, you are beautiful. You are truly beautiful." This is what Black mothers must tell their children. In word and in deed, the Black mother must affirm all those qualities that make a person a total and beautiful person. She must affirm them from a conviction that she is beautiful. She must have no questions, no doubts. "Listen, my child, this fact let no one question; from it flows the strength of your existence. You are a beautiful person."

Not only must the Black mother affirm the beauty of her child, she must nurture it. It lies in the child like the seed of an oak tree with potential to develop into strength and endurance. But it must be nurtured. It must be cultivated carefully, for a seed has not yet taken root and lies vulnerable. Cultivate it; let its roots sink into the soil that is the child's very being, and it cannot be destroyed.

The child must be taught that there are those who would rob him of his beauty, that there are those who would deny its existence. The child must be taught that those who would so approach him are his enemies. He must be taught to identify his enemies. He must be taught to defend the beauty that is the wellspring of his being. This belief in his beauty is the foundation of his belief in all other things that make him a total person. From it flows the confidence that nurtures growth of intellect. From it flows the faith in self that nurtures courage to act. It is the very foundation from which springs courage to act. It is the very foundation from which springs the child's power to assert self. Love of self is a powerful weapon. It is man's best weapon in the war of survival. Black mothers must arm their every child with this weapon. When man loves self, he would rather be destroyed attempting to save self than let another destroy him. He will take whatever means necessary to assure the survival of the self he loves. Whatever means necessary. . . .

How is the Black mother to teach her child to identify his enemies? Who are those who would deny the beauty of the Black child, and why do they proceed systematically to do so? The answer to these questions is contained in the history of America. It is contained in a history based in large part on the denial of the beauty of the Black man and woman. This denial has robbed the Black man of one of his most essential weapons in the war of survival, love of self. By so robbing the Black man in America, this country has been able to keep him subjugated, to heap its frustrations upon him, and to use him to sustain the myth of white superiority.

The Black mother must open her mind to the facts of history, for these facts attest to the creation of the myth of white superiority largely at the expense of Black human beings. In its most recent pages, history attests to outrage after outrage being perpetrated on Black people because of the necessity of sustaining this myth. The outrage of little girls being bombed in a church in Alabama in 1964, of Black leaders being assassinated, Evers in Mississippi and King in Tennessee. Incident after incident of physical atrocities have been enacted against Black people. As many atrocities are being committed today as 150 years ago.

However, the Black mother must look further than a review of the physical inhumanity of white America to the Black man. She must look closely at the psychological atrocities perpetrated against Black human beings. These psychological atrocities had their birth during slavery and have survived to this very day, attaining, as they age, a higher degree of sophistication. It is these psychological atrocities that must be combatted because they work to destroy the Black man's love of self. These psychological atrocities have no compassion for the child, for it is the child that offers the most fertile ground. How should the Black mother begin in this effort to unveil the psychological networks devised to destroy her children? She must first begin with the knowledge that she has been a victim of this design. She must first begin with a real knowledge of self, no matter how painful this knowledge may be.

*The
Changing
Role of
the
Black Woman*

101

Part 3

HETEROSEXUAL INTERACTION — MARITAL AND NONMARITAL

LOVE MAKES IT RIGHT

Richard F. Hettlinger

Several recent studies indicate a growing acceptance of premarital sex by the young, if not by society as a whole. A 1970 study of Robert Bell and J. Chaskes that compared two samples of coeds who attended the same university ten years apart found that the girls of the first sample who had had premarital coitus had experienced it during engagement, while the girls of 1968 had had frequent sexual experience while dating or going steady.

Mr. Hettlinger, men's counselor at Kenyon College, addresses himself mainly to males and asks the young man to consider the depth of his commitment to any girl he wishes to involve in sexual experience. In spite of high divorce rates and the general instability of the family today, he stresses the "permanence" of the marriage bond and encourages commitment before sex.

This selection has been included principally because many students are concerned about their sexual feelings and inadequacies, real or imagined. Girls, especially, report that they are importuned to "go to bed" at virtually the outset of a relationship. Men are feeling the pressure of "performance" as measured by their ability to "satisfy" women. There may be fewer guilt anxieties about premarital sex, but there is still concern about meaning (the meaning of "affection," for example) and about options of free choice in decision making regarding their sexual lives.

Mr. Hettlinger explores both sides of the question: "Does love make it right to go to bed unwed?" He leans heavily on the Judeo-Christian ethic of reserving sex for marriage but gives no prescriptive answers.

The crux of the sexual dilemma, for most students, was succinctly formulated as long ago as 1721 in a debate held that year at Harvard: "Whether it be

---

Reprinted from Richard F. Hettlinger, *Living with Sex: The Student's Dilemma*, Chapter 10, Seabury Press, 1966. Reprinted with permission of publisher.

Fornication to lye with one's Sweetheart before Marriage." Any responsible man is likely, whatever his actual practice may be, to acknowledge to himself that sexual satisfaction divorced from affection and respect for the other person is debased and unnatural in a human being. The use of a prostitute to satisfy mere curiosity or for the release of sexual tension is frequently reported, even among the small number of contemporary students who resort to it, to be unsatisfying, revolting, or humiliating.

Again, few men of maturity are happy with themselves if they achieve a "quick lay" with a casual date, however easily they may be carried away by urgent desire. Lester A. Kirkendall, in a study of two hundred college-level men with sexual experience, found that only a small percentage of those who had engaged in this type of liaison declared themselves satisfied with the exploitive use of a girl for physical pleasure or the demonstration of masculine prowess. Most men of integrity who are aware of the harm they may do to a sensitive girl will try to avoid overriding her scruples by placing her under emotional pressure or by taking advantage of her eagerness for a permanent relationship. Yet it is generally taken for granted that such hesitations are irrelevant once a serious mutual attachment has been achieved.

"So long as nobody gets hurt," runs the argument, "love makes it right."

> *If we deeply love one another*, and we find in sex a way of showing its deepest levels; if we find that during and after and because of it we are straining to grow in stature in the other's eyes; if we find that because it is loving, the release of the sex energy also releases, rather than uses up, our deepest creative energies; if each time there is a sexual interlude, we find we love and respect and admire each other more afterwards, then, and only then, but so sensitively and wonderfully then, *it is right.*

Traditional Objections Re-examined

... I have no sympathy with the traditional religious and social dismissal of all sexual activity outside marriage as immoral, or with the too-simple labeling of all premarital intercourse as "fornication." Many of the intimacies which our society condones or encourages, such as petting, may be more reprehensible when indulged in for purely physical pleasure than intercourse between a boy and a girl deeply in love. Moreover, there is no evidence to support the view that when an engaged couple sleep together, some harm is always necessarily done to their future marriage. Kirkendall found that when intercourse was accepted freely by both parties and on the basis of a long-standing mutual commitment, it sometimes did no damage to the relationship. On the other hand, he also found that in some cases considerable harm resulted, sometimes quite unexpectedly, and any young man who ignores the complexity of the factors involved can hardly settle the dilemma of sex with any confidence of success.

The two chief weapons in the armory of those who would (surely quite immorally) frighten young men and women into chastity are almost entirely ineffective as deterrents today. Nevertheless, the facts cannot be ignored. Kinsey's statement, as recently as 1953, that "present methods of simple and rapid cure for both syphilis and gonorrhea make their spread through premarital coitus a relatively unimportant matter" has proved to be entirely premature. The overoptimistic assumption that penicillin and other drugs would eliminate these twin curses has led to a false sense of security, and at present venereal diseases are rampant in epidemic proportions in thirty major American cities. Cases of syphilis in persons under twenty years old are estimated to have increased by 200 per cent between 1960 and 1965. And in January, 1964, the chief of the Ohio Health Department's Communicable Diseases Division warned: "More, and more, . . . it is appearing among middle and upper economic class people—business people, professional people. And it used to be almost exclusively a disease that occurred in large cities. It still does, but it is appearing more and more in small communities and rural areas." According to the Surgeon General of the United States, 1,500 young Americans contract venereal disease *every day in the year.* Much of this horrifying increase is due to homosexual activity. It is obviously irrelevant to engaged couples who never have coitus except with each other. But, without again elevating the threat of VD to the status of a decisive deterrent, it is clearly a fact of which every one should take account.

The possibility of pregnancy is also largely ignored in the thinking of most male students, although Gael Greene reported that it is one of the most common factors (though not frequently the decisive factor) quoted when girls analyze what keeps them from accepting intercourse. And the fear is by no means as ill-founded as is commonly supposed. The magical pill has not solved the problem: it is not even generally understood by male students that it has to be used throughout the whole menstrual cycle to be effective. Girls, except those who feel themselves committed to uninhibited promiscuity, neither take the pill as a regular safeguard nor wear a diaphragm for all occasions. The majority take the entirely superstitious view, "It can't happen to me"—and the result is that *one out of every five girls who have intercourse before marriage becomes pregnant.* Despite all the increased knowl-

edge and discussion of birth control, the number of illegitimate births amon
teenagers doubled between 1940 and 1961, and in the same period the number for the twenty to twenty-five age group nearly quadrupled.

Moreover, it must be remembered that unwanted pregnancies are most
likely to occur among those who are least promiscuous. Those who plan
consciously to go all the way normally take the necessary precautions. But
many students, of both sexes, who really want to avoid intercourse, fail to
plan for the eventuality because such premeditation runs contrary to their
best intentions. They are then carried away by high passion after an enjoyable evening together and take a risk which proves disastrous. Even when a
attempt at contraception is made, college students are notoriously ill-informe
and inefficient. It is also true that the very people who emphasize the romantic element in sexual relationships frequently regard any mechanical contraceptive device as an interference with the spontaneity of the fact, or as a
debasement. Although they may be the last to yield to the urge to engage in
coitus, they are the mosts likely to reap the consequences in conception.

Of course, the consequences of extramarital pregnancy are by no means a
serious as they were even a few decades ago. Yet, once again, it is as stupid
to minimize them as it is unconvincing to exaggerate them. Abortion is the
most common solution. Despite the fact that it is illegal, it can be readily
arranged in the United States, and the report of the Institute for Sex Researc
makes it clear that neither the cost nor the risk to health is as serious as
many imagine. They found that some unfavorable consequences were
reported by one-third of the girls interviewed, but in most cases these were
minor, and significant psychological effects occurred in less than 10 per cen
of the cases. Gael Greene found that although horror stories of abortion
were widespread among college girls, "the girls who described their *own*
experiences with illegal abortions rarely spoke in terms of horror or strong
repulsion." Yet profound psychological trauma, serious physical harm, and
occasionally death do result from induced abortions, and it would seem that
the man who really loves a girl will hardly take comfort from the statistical
fact she is not *likely* to suffer seriously. The more concerned he is, the less
he is likely to be prepared to allow her to undergo an abortion that involves
even a slight risk to her life.

The consequence is that the majority of responsible and mature couples
who engage in premarital intercourse accept the fact that they are parents o
a child and get married. Although this is certainly undesirable if there is no
real bond of love and no prior thought of marriage, an early wedding under
duress can be the prelude to permanent happiness. The social stigma attache

to childbirth within nine months of marriage is relatively slight today, and there is even one State in the Union which will provide an antedated marriage certificate to prevent embarrassment to the baby in later years.

But the possible threats to the success of a marriage occasioned by its beginning under the cloud of necessity are not to be ignored. Instead of the couple having a number of years in which to cement their relationship and prepare for the challenge of children, they start their marriage with the additional demands of parenthood. Consciously or unconsciously, there may be hostility against the child or the partner for interrupting a career. When the inevitable later strains develop, there may be an unexpressed feeling that *if* there had been no baby on the way, one or other would have broken the engagement before marriage. These reactions may often be avoided or overcome, but they are significant possibilities to be weighed against the attractions of premarital intercourse.

The Test of Suitability

Having put the traditional objections in some balanced light, we must now take an equally honest look at the supposed advantages of going to bed unwed. One widely accepted argument is that intercourse is a final necessary test of the suitability of the couple for each other. There is a certain contradiction between this approach and the romantic declaration, "I love her and I'm going to marry her anyway, so why not?" But perhaps nobody uses both arguments at the same time. The question I would put is, "What do you expect to find out about each other through intercourse before marriage that you do not already know, or that you cannot better find out when you are already married and embarked on the discipline of life together?" Let us assume (rather optimistically, perhaps) that a couple know each other in the [following] terms . . .

> I think I do love her; that is, if love means: that you want to see the girl every day, that you enjoy spending time with her, that you always want to do favors for her, that you are able to talk of marriage and can somehow visualize being married to her, that we are happy and satisfied sexually, that we sometimes have arguments which we both admit to having started, that we go out of our way to please each other, that we say that we love each other, and that we have planned marriage.

What more do they need to know, or can they know, that is necessary as a preliminary to marriage? What, given this degree of mutual understanding and honesty between two people, could be a good reason for failing to get married? What, in particular, is intercourse going to prove or disprove?

Well, one possible answer is that they might discover whether one or the other is sterile, and whether they will be able to have children; but quite apa from the fact that several years continuous experimentation would be neces- sary to prove anything, the experiment is usually conducted in such a way that the primary objective is *not* to become pregnant! In our culture, again, it is hardly necessary to have intercourse to discover whether you arouse some sexual response in each other. From the first sexual encounter—and remember that this begins when you first hold hands—you become aware of mutual erotic stimulation, which is fully tested in necking and petting activi- ties. *Pace* Helen Gurley Brown, very few girls and even fewer boys need to go as far as bed to discover whether the partner is homosexual.

In Mary McCarthy's novel *The Group*, Dottie Renfrew and her mother agreed that an engaged couple ought to have intercourse once to make sure of a happy adjustment, because her mother "knew of some very sad cases within her own circle of friends where the man and the woman just didn't fit down there and ought never to have been married." If the reference is to the man's inability to achieve erection, this is certainly a matter for profes- sional counsel; but it can hardly be unknown to him in the course of heavy petting activities. If the reference is to the purely physical proportions of the male and female sex organs, instances of serious or permanent difficulty are almost unknown. There may be physical factors, such as an unusually tough hymen, which make intercourse temporarily impossible. But suppose a couple attempts intercourse before marriage and are unsuccessful; what are they going to do? Decide that despite their love for each other they are not suited, and break up over a problem which, if discovered after marriage, would almost certainly be cleared up by medical treatment? They may, of course, find that the girl has difficulty reaching orgasm during intercourse; but despite what the marriage handbooks say, this is a common experience which only patient attention—perhaps for several years—will overcome. Opportunities for intercourse before marriage, especially when they are rushed or threatened with interruption (as many still are, despite the con- venience of motels), frequently make the necessary relaxation impossible fo the girl. To part company then, because they cannot reach a mutual climax after one or two or many attempts may be to break up a wonderful relation- ship which could have blossomed into perfect sexual accord within marriage. In other words, as a test of suitability premarital intercourse tells us nothing of significance that cannot be discovered in other ways. And what it may appear to tell us is more likely to be misleading than helpful.

Premarital Intercourse and Marriage

A second popular argument in favor of premarital intercourse is to the effect that it makes for better and happier marital relationships. The "Playboy Forum," for example, recently affirmed that, in the Kinsey studies, "a significant correlation was found between premarital sexual experience and successful marriage." But this widespread impression is not justified by the facts, and Kinsey drew no such conclusion. What he did find was that there was a market correlation between the experience of orgasm in coitus by a girl before marriage and her capacity to reach orgasm in coitus during the early years of marriage. But, whereas there is no doubt that in the long run the achievement of mutual physical satisfaction in coitus is a significant factor in the permanence and success of marriage, there is no reason to suppose that the achievement of orgasm early in marriage is an indicator of a mature marriage relationship. Indeed, in view of Kinsey's own findings that women often do not reach their orgasmic peak until their late twenties, and in view of the recent recognition that this is not, for them, the significant criterion of sexuality that it is for the male, orgasm in early marriage may be largely an irrelevant criterion of success for the woman.

There are many women who do respond earlier to physical sexual arousal, and achieve coital orgasm both before marriage and in the early years of marriage. It may be that the earlier experience of satisfying coitus is the cause of quicker adjustment within marriage, and Kinsey believed this to be the case. But it may also be simply that girls with earlier sexual interests (in the male sense of the term) and fewer inhibitions are more ready to engage in premarital intercourse, and that if they had not done so they would still have responded early in marriage. Kinsey acknowledged this possibility:

> The most responsive females may have been the ones who had had the largest amount of premarital experience and, because they were responsive, they were the ones who had most often reached orgasm in marriage. The females who had abstained before marriage may have been the physiologically less responsive individuals who, therefore, were the ones who had most often remained chaste, both before and after marriage.

But, in either case, evidence is lacking to show that girls of this type, or girls with this experience, make the most successful marriage partners, as distinct from the most enjoyable bed partners on the honeymoon. Hamblin and Blood argued that a more careful analysis of the Kinsey data showed that experience or inexperience in premarital intercourse shows no consistent causal relationship to sexual adjustment in marriage. Burgess and Wallin, in an independent study, *Engagement and Marriage*, concluded that on the whole a husband and wife *without* experience of premarital intercourse have a higher chance of marital success.

Furthermore, Kinsey noted two negative considerations which should make the advocate of premarital intercourse hesitate. In the first place, it is quite clear that unsatisfactory or unsuccessful experience in coitus before marriage is very likely to make sexual adjustment after marriage more difficult for the woman. Kinsey wrote:

> It should be emphasized that premarital coital experience which had not led to orgasm (perhaps because of moral or religious doubts about the practice) had not correlated with successful sexual relations in marriage. On the contrary *it showed a high correlation with failure in the marital coitus. . . .* a girl who becomes involved in premarital coitus in which she does not respond may be traumatically affected by such experience, and thus be handicapped in her later adjustments in marriage.

In the second place, Kinsey found a marked correlation between premarital intercourse and extramarital intercourse. To put it bluntly, the girl who goes to bed before marriage is about twice as likely, according to Kinsey's figures, to go to bed with someone other than her husband after marriage. Once again, whether the premarital intercourse is the cause or the effect cannot be established. But Kinsey recognized that "it is not impossible that nonmarital coital experience before marriage had persuaded those females that nonmarital coitus might be acceptable after marriage." I would not want to put any great weight on this correlation, nor to question that in many cases a couple who have engaged in coitus before marriage remain faithful to each other afterward. But I do want to point out that these various qualifications greatly reduce the value of Kinsey's statistics as *evidence* for the view that premarital intercourse increases the prospects for a full and meaningful relationship in marriage.

On the contrary, there is reason to believe that moving into intercourse has a contrary effect upon engagement and eventual marriage in many instances. Kirkendall found that one-third of the engaged men he interviewed had feelings of guilt or regret following intercourse. Many reported tensions between them and their fiancées, and there was frequently a breakdown in mutual communication and understanding. Of twenty-eight men who had engaged in coitus with fiancées, five had given up intercourse (mostly because they felt it endangered their relationship), and seven had broken the engagement. When we remember that the breaking of an engagement is, especially for the girl, much more difficult after coitus, the latter figure is extremely significant. It indicates that at least one man in four finds that the girl he thought he loved, and with whom he had intercourse on this "moral" basis, proved in fact not to be the girl he eventually married. We can hardly avoid considering the effects of such broken engagements upon the status of the girl who has agreed, or been persuaded, to "lose it" for the man she thought she would marry. Kinsey found that one out of every two upper-level males under twenty-five stated that he intended to marry a virgin, or at least a girl who had only slept with him before marriage. Although this double standard is probably less rigorously applied today, it still has many advocates. "It's okay for me to sleep with your sister, but it's not okay for you to sleep with mine," said a Harvard graduate student recently. This means that the man who persuades his girl to have intercourse, and doesn't eventually marry her, often puts her out of the market for the kind of marriage he thinks most desirable. Of course, he may not love her enough to worry about that prospect; but in that case does he love her enough to justify intercourse on the basis from which this discussion started?

The Religious Objection

At this point we must reconsider the position of those who believe that pre-marital intercourse is altogether undesirable. I am not thinking of the traditional religious view, which settles the issue simply by appeal to the biblical or ecclesiastical condemnation of fornication. That approach, now that it has little support from the threat of pregnancy or VD, carries weight with few students, in my experience. However, it is worth pointing out that anybody who has serious religious objections to premarital intercourse and allows himself to be seduced or pressured into it by his peers or his emotions is courting trouble. "For a person who believes that premarital intercourse is morally wrong," wrote Kinsey, "there may be, as the specific histories show, conflicts which do damage not only to marital adjustments, but to the entire personality of the individual." And it must be recognized that the possibility that such harm will be done to the girl with deep religious objections is much greater.

There are, however, more rational and convincing arguments, based upon the connection between sex and personal relationships, in favor of preserving the experience of intercourse until marriage. The first of these can be illustrated from that touching and beautiful story, *A Taste of Honey.* In the course of discussion about the relations with men, the extremely promiscuous Ellen tells her daughter, Jo, "You always remember the first time"—and it is quite clear from the development of the drama that Jo will indeed remember the first time with a mixture of joy and sorrow. Otto Piper has argued that the first experience of coitus involves a critical discovery of the self and of the other person—of the essence of masculinity and femininity—which should be experienced only with the woman with whom one is to share one's life. "The sexual act leads to a new and deepened understanding of oneself which is characterized by three features: it is an intuitive knowledge given in and with the sexual experience; it discloses what was thus far hidden from the individual; and its subject matter is one's Self seen in the mutual relationship in which it stands with the partner's Self."

In this view, therefore, to engage in coitus with any girl other than the one the man marries is to deny to her and to himself the privilege of sharing together in a unique experience—an experience which no future act of intercourse can embody. William Hamilton has put the point effectively:

> If it is true that sexual intercourse mediates a unique kind of personal knowledge, it is clear that a very special status must be given to the first experience of the sexual act. While, in a marriage, new things are always being learned about the other by a couple truly in love, it is also true that a decisive importance must be attached to the first time this mutual and intimate knowledge was ever shared. . . . The first sexual experience is so overwhelming and so different from any other experience that it is better reserved as a means of symbolizing and giving meaning to marriage.

Another rather metaphysical approach has been cogently presented by Sherwin Bailey. . . . He suggests that, man being a unity of body and spirit, sexual intercourse is "a personal encounter between man and woman in which each does something to the other for good or for ill, which can never be obliterated." When a couple lie together (other than in cases of rape or the seduction of the young or feeble-minded), he believes that they truly become "one flesh," whether they realize it or not. However much their future actions may deny it, this union, or *henosis,* remains a profoundly significant reality which affects their very being. If they are married, it provides the basis for ever-deepening community between them. If they are not "they merely enact a hollow, ephemeral, diabolical parody of marriage, which works disintegration in the personality and leaves a deeply seated sense of frustration and dissatisfaction—though this may never be brought to the surface of consciousness and realized." This understanding of the significance of intercourse, like that of Piper, has firm roots in the biblical idea of man's nature and sexuality. Obviously, the man to whom it is convincing, and who wants to enjoy all the richness of personal union, will avoid establishing empty and superficial relationships with women other than the one he marries.

The Final Intimacy and the Final Commitment

Both these approaches, although they avoid any purely dogmatic appeal to authority, are likely to seem highly doctrinaire and idealistic to many readers of this book. I think that two other considerations may be more relevant and persuasive. First, I would ask whether the act of intercourse, with all its unique quality and intimacy, can be rightly or meaningfully experienced apart from the permanent commitment of marriage. Does not love, in any profound sense, remain unfulfilled until the couple are actually responsible for each other? And if so, can the act which expresses and seals the unity of love be justified in advance of that moment? Should the man who has not yet taken the decisive step of committing his future to a girl ask of her this risk to her future? If he does not yet share his economic and domestic life with her, is he ready to share this unity of body with her? There is, after all, a real difference between the relationship of a couple before and after marriage. Before, even in the most sincere and honest engagement, neither is fully and objectively responsible for the other. After the wedding they are legally, socially, and personally committed beyond recall, no longer independent centers of action but "one flesh." Even trial marriage is an entirely different relationship, because in this experiment people are trying each other out, rather than committed to each other. Indeed, a trial marriage is a contradiction of terms, because the essence of marriage is that (at least in intention) it is not a trial at all but a permanent bond. And if the full meaning of sex is discovered in personal relationships, the ultimate intimacy of intercourse should be preserved until the ultimate commitment to another person, which is represented by marriage.

A man who really loves a girl he is dating or engaged to cannot ignore the fact that at the moment she is not his wife, that she has not yet left father and mother and become one flesh with him. She is still a member of her parental family, not of his. Although he may not feel any special obligation to that family, she does; and although he may be quite ready to act as if they were already married, she may have serious reservations. If he is a responsible human being, he will at least take account of the possibility that in persuading or allowing her to act contrary to the judgment of her family, he may be treating her as a thing rather than as a person—using her and her love in order to satisfy his own urgent need of sexual release.

Second, I think that the radical dissociation of coitus and reproduction involves a distortion of human sexuality. . . . I dissent vigorously from the traditional ecclesiastical view that reproduction is the only, or even the primary, justification for sexual intercourse. But I would argue that it is one of the proper and fundamental implications of any true sexual union. I do not mean that it is necessary in every instance, or even in most instances, that procreation must be an open possibility to justify or fulfill sexuality. I do not mean that the childless couple are incapable of a deep and satisfying union: they already have a family in themselves, and their hope for children is frustrated by factors beyond their control. On the other hand, the unmarried couple approach intercourse with an anxious repudiation of the possibility of parenthood. The balance, meaning, and unity of human sexuality is therefore distorted because one of its natural consequences and joys—as well as one of its challenges and costs—is rejected and feared as utterly inappropriate in the circumstances. To enjoy coitus in the safe period, or with the safeguard of contraception, within the context of a married relationship in which the responsibility and privilege of parenthood are accepted (whether or not it has already been achieved) is one thing. To clutch at the immediate pleasure of intercourse while one of its natural ends is absolutely renounced is quite another. Particularly for many girls, the total isolation of intercourse from reproduction involves a kind of sexual anarchy. If the man feels little of this complication, he should at least ask himself whether, for her sake, the argument should run: "I love her—that makes it wrong until we're married." Under the emotion of physical stimulation, it is extremely difficult for a girl to refuse intercourse to a man she loves, and this places a special responsibility on the man, who is more likely to be the advocate of "going all the way." Love surely requires of us that we respect the actual (and not merely the expressed) sensibilities and interests of the other person.

So much can be said not only in defense but in honor of waiting until marriage. But I would wish to avoid elevating a principle and an ideal, however sound, into an absolute law—especially since experience suggests that no absolute and clear-cut application of the principle is possible. In our culture, as we have seen, the young couple are often trapped between the premature arousal of their sexual instincts and economic barriers that society places in the way of early marriage. In the circumstances it is almost inevitable that they will sometimes justifiably anticipate that union which should, ideally and perfectly, be consummated only after the commitment of marriage. If intercourse is accepted mutually after full and free discussion by a couple planning to be married, if there is a clear acceptance of the possibility of pregnancy and a readiness for the sacrifices it will involve, and if they are mature and established in their respect and love for each other, it is quite possible that the act will be little different in its significance for them if it precedes marriage. Certainly, it need not be inconsistent with eventual marital success and happiness. Even those adults who are most ready to cluck their tongues when they hear of a premarital pregnancy, or those clergy who are most prone to inveigh against the sinfulness of anticipating the wedding night can usually, if they examine their own experiences or those of their friends, discover at least one happily married couple who engaged in premarital intercourse.

I have always been impressed by the advice of Canon Bryan Green, of Birmingham, England, who tells students that when an engaged couple who are in love find themselves engaging in intercourse they should thank God for the experience and ask forgiveness for the lack of discipline. This dictum, on at least one occasion, produced in the newspaper of a town where Canon Green was conducting a preaching mission the headline: GREEN GIVES GREEN LIGHT TO SIN. Sin it may be, in technical terms, insofar as it falls short of perfection; but it is at least a very warm-hearted sin compared with some of the cold sins of pride, exploitation, and indifference to humanity upon which the churches and society have always looked with much greater patience and sympathy.

I would have to go further than this, and say that in some circumstances, intercourse before marriage may be an alternative to something worse—the withering and death of a meaningful and valuable relationship which cannot yet, for completely good reasons, be consummated in marriage. The too-easy assumption by moralists that the act will always be expressive of lust or selfishness is simply not true to the facts. Kirkendall records a number of occasions on which intercourse had definitely enabled a couple to gain in understanding, trust, and love for each other. And what is most striking about these accounts is the fact that far from becoming an obsession and pandering to merely physical desire, coitus, once it had been accepted, fell into proper proportion in relation to the wider interests and mutual comfort of engagement. One example is worth quoting:

We had held strongly all during our courtship to what we regarded as a Christian pattern of sexual conduct, that is, avoidance of premarital intercourse. We had been going together for over a year and were wanting to get married. I was eighteen and my fiancé the same age. My parents were opposed to our marriage, and we were just "spinning our wheels." . . . It was at this point that we went into intercourse. As I look back at it—it was about a year ago that this happened—I think I can see several reasons for what we did. We were so frustrated and blocked that intercourse did two things for us. First, we needed to be close to each other, and this was the way we could get the closeness we wanted. Second, it helped me feel that in spite of the objection of my parents, we were moving toward marriage. Actually, in a certain Christian sense, we were already married after intercourse. Then, perhaps here was an element of spite against our parents in what we did. It is all very complex.

One friend of mine who read the original lectures upon which this book is based remarked: "It won't make any difference whether they go to bed before marriage or not. And why don't you tell them so honestly?" My answer is twofold. First, I do not conceive it to be my responsibility to tell the reader anything so dogmatic and oversimplified. Most students will not determine their conduct by any authoritative statement, ecclesiastical or otherwise, and this is as it should be. Those few who are looking for a dogmatic pronouncement in favor of premarital intercourse should certainly be denied the immature satisfaction of supposing that this author has settled the issue for them. But, second, it does make *some* difference, and I do not know whether the difference it makes for any particular couple will be for their mutual good or ill.

What I have tried to do is to show what the score is, if the expression can be pardoned. I have argued, in brief, that there is no evidence to show that premarital intercourse is either necessary for a successful marriage or more probable to lead to it, that there are some considerations to show that intercourse is best engaged in within the marriage commitment, but that in certain circumstances exceptions may be justifiable or even beneficial. Whether any individual can or should claim such circumstances, and whether in his case it will prove to be a valid claim, I do not know—and indeed he will not either until long after. Kirkendall concluded that unless the relationship was of long-standing and the couple of more than average maturity premarital intercourse was more likely to be damaging than beneficial. Indeed, he made the striking point that "in practically all instances 'nondamaging' intercourse [a phrase he prefers to the more positive 'strengthening'] occurred in rela-

Heterosexual Interaction— Marital and Nonmarital

118

tionships which were already so strong in their own right that intercourse did not have much to offer toward strengthening them."

Here are three considerations which must be weighed before any couple can reasonably conclude that premarital intercourse is likely to be the right solution to their dilemma. First, once moral absolutes are abandoned—as they already are in this field among most students—there is a danger of complete chaos and untold disaster unless those who claim to order their actions by love rather than by law are absolutely honest in examining their motives critically. If it is followed with real integrity, the principle, "love makes it right," will not be less but more demanding than the legalism it has replaced. Second, it is exceptionally difficult to be objective about one's own sexual life. There is no field of human activity in which it is so easy to deceive oneself and to be convinced by arguments which are in fact nothing but rationalizations of clamant desires. Joseph Conrad's dictum, "No man fully understands his own artful dodges to escape from the grim shadow of self-knowledge," is particularly relevant to the sphere of sex. One woman college senior admitted frankly to Gael Greene that "some of us manage to fall in love two or three times a week." And the man who is seriously convinced that intercourse is the appropriate expression of mutual love may in fact be seeking merely to bolster his own sense of inadequacy or to stifle some inner loneliness. He may only be looking for a mother image or a status symbol. He may be using sex merely as an expression of his power over another person. Finally, the added criterion, "so long as nobody gets hurt," is extremely difficult to apply with any consistency. The decision must surely take account of the effect not only upon the girl and any possible child but also upon the parents and friends and classmates of both parties. I think there may be occasions on which the relative pain caused to others is justified by the much greater benefit to the engaged couple, as in the case cited above (which eventually worked out well). But the private needs of one couple must also be assessed in the light of the possible effect upon society as a whole. . . .

SEX IN MARRIAGE

William J. Lederer and Don D. Jackson

Many couples have fallacious romantic notions about sex which break down under the reality of daily married life. In the selection that follows Lederer and Jackson criticize "experts" who lead people to believe that "good sex" is the only basic key to marital success, contending that this is too simplistic a concept to apply to the complexities of married life.

There is no standard, they claim, against which a couple can measure marital "success"; each couple must determine its own standards of intimacy, satisfaction, and sexual relationship without excessive concern for spurious "norms" set by society. A viable marriage is possible without the romanticized sex relationship imaged by the mass media. Although the concept of a satisfactory marriage without passion is often rejected by the young, Lederer and Jackson say that sex is only *"one* of the cements which holds the bricks of married life together."

What is the role of sex in marriage?

Like every other element in the marital relationship, sex involves behavior between individuals. The response of each partner varies with his mood, his physical state, and the oscillations of the relationship.

Given adequate physiological and anatomical equipment (which Nature rarely fails to provide) and a modicum of knowledge of sexual techniques, the spouses will enjoy sexual union *when both are in a collaborative mood.* The collaborative mood exists when each is adding something to the sexual act, not just submitting. When the spouses are not in a loving mood, they still may find in sex a release from tension and thus derive another type of pleasure from it, especially if they are in agreement about what they expect,

Heterosexual Interaction— Marital and Nonmarital

120

but it is likely to be less fulfilling and often may be frustrating, because one partner has contrary needs which are left unmet.

This sex act—a comparably simple matter—has become the most written about, the most talked of, and the most muddled aspect of marriage. There are several reasons why the role of sex in marriage has become excessively emphasized and distorted.

A cultural fear of sex's losing its effective status in the social structure. This fear is as ancient at least as the Old Testament dictum that "a man . . . shall cleave unto his wife." The expectation is that if this pronouncement is violated the species will not fulfill its obligation to procreate in a familial or nurturing setting.

The fear of desertion and abandonment. In our culture, this fear is stronger in women than in men. Women are tied down by the processes of childbearing and childbirth and require assistance physically and emotionally. In response to this fear, and to provide a weapon for fighting it, the belief has developed in our culture that if one is "sexy" enough, one's mate will *not* desert. The result has been an exaggerated consciousness of sexual performance as a ritual to increase personal security in marriage or to induce marriage. Yet if one is "sexy" enough there is the danger of being *too* "sexy" and violating the ancient commandments.

The female's simulation of sexiness. The male requires an erection to enter into the sex act. If he is uninterested in sex, or afraid of it, he will not have an erection. However, a woman does not have any obvious physiological indications of spontaneous readiness. She can fake sexual spontaneity, and the male (at least for a time) may not be aware of the deceit. The female extends this stimulation of sexual interest into parasexual areas by means of hair dyes, falsies, girdles, cosmetics, perfumes, and high heels. These parasexual devices scream, "Look, I'm sexy. I'm desirable." This may or may not be true, but it is probable that women resent their need to advertise and would prefer to be accepted as they really are; men resent the necessity for sexual deception even though they foster it.

The economic forces in our culture sustain and stimulate these hypocritical actions. Any attempt to alter the pattern involves resisting the advertising and other merchandising techniques used by multibillion-dollar businesses to peddle false female sexuality. The women who attempt to retain a "natural" appearance, with undoctored hair, no makeup, and so forth, are few in number, and they may (because of cultural conditioning) be regarded by both men and women as deviates. Most of the people who might be inclined to rebel against this type of sexual mores are intimidated by cultural pressure and mass value judgments.

Furthermore, the emphasis upon female sexual paraphernalia is an inherited social custom which long has been associated with the elite. In past ages, makeup, breast accentuators, and the like were worn mainly by the ruling classes, and the tendency to show upward social mobility by imitating the elite still exists. Even today, the wealthier the spouses, the more they exaggerate the differences between the sexes. The wife wears elegant gowns, elaborate hairdos, scintillating jewelry, and expensive furs and perfumes. Her husband may favor dark conservative suits, homburgs, and thick-soled, handmade English Shoes.

The erroneous belief that unsatisfactory sexual relations are the major cause of bad marriages. The speciousness here is clear. Unsatisfactory sexual relations are a symptom of marital discord, not the cause of it. It is difficult for the victims to see this because of the mass of propaganda about sex that attacks them day and night, on the street, in the home, in the office. We are such an absurd culture that even mouthwashes and Lysol are related to the sexual aspects of marriage.

John Jones, for example, is dissatisfied with his marriage. On his way to work he may look up and see a billboard with a picture of a nearly nude, beautiful woman, advertising a brand of stockings. John is stimulated sexually and says to himself, "Boy, I'd like to have an affair with something like that." He knows this is wishful thinking, and may even recognize that the beautiful model might be incompatible with him. Next he retreats from the daydream and his thoughts turn toward his wife. But the sexual fantasy he has had about the girl in the ad colors his reflections about his marriage relationship, and he thinks, "Golly, Mary's legs might look better in that kind of hosiery." What he means is, "If Mary were a better sexpot we'd both have a happier marriage." He is caught in a double error: the appearance of Mary's legs has nothing to do with the couple's sexual satisfaction, *and* he has forgotten his *own* function in achieving a successful union.

Such a process may be repeated frequently during the day, for John is never permitted to escape advertisements which suggest that sexuality is the key to happiness. Yet there is considerable evidence that an individual's *perception* of the sexual relationship is more related to marital satisfaction than the sexual act itself.

In a survey conducted at an Ohio university, interviews of several hundred couples showed that by and large those who reported their marriages as "satisfactory" gave the frequency of their intercourse as twice a week. Those who reported their marriages as "unsatisfactory" also reported a frequency of twice a week, yet among the unhappy couples the husbands said that twice a week was more than their wives wished but satisfactory from their point of view, and the wives said it was less than their husbands wished but just right for them personally. The "happy" husbands and wives said the frequency of twice a week was satisfying to both themselves *and* their spouses. In other words, the problem was in the couples' communication and not in the actual frequency of their sexual relations.

While sexual problems are often blamed for marital difficulties, one is seldom made aware of the other side of the coin: sexual relations may keep some marriages going, providing virtually the only kind of contact which the spouses have. Psychiatrists and other professionals who treat marital problems are aware that some individuals have been able to establish successful sexual relations with each other although they cannot get together in any other context. Many of these couples have the experience of waking at night to discover themselves involved in sex, with neither partner aware of who took the initiative.

The differences between male and female. The physical differences between male and female contribute to the novelty and adventure of sex. Heterosexuality is extrafascinating and carries with it the illusion of intrigue. At the same time, the differences make understanding one another more difficult. Also, the excessive emphasis on sex as the major factor in marriage results in a distorted viewpoint. The natural differences between male and female are made to appear crucial for the success of a marriage. Actually, a woman will not improve her marriage by achieving a voluptuous bust, legs like a model, and an aura of exotic perfume. If her marriage is an unhappy one, her husband may develop a preference for small-breasted women who dress plainly and do not wear perfumes.

Having reviewed some reasons for mistaken attitudes toward sexual intercourse, let us now take a look at its actual role in marriage. What is special about sexual intercourse, a highly satisfying male-female symbiosis, is that it requires a higher degree of collaborative communication than any other kind of behavior exchanged between the spouses. Sex is consequently precious, but also perilous. It is the only relationship act which must have mutual spontaneity for mutual satisfaction. It can only be a conjoint union, and it represents a common goal which is clear and understood by both.

The reason people keep asking where sex fits into marriage is that they have been hoodwinked, bamboozled, pressured, conned, and persuaded that the sexual act is compulsory in their lives and *must be performed alike by everyone*; the "standards" are established by advertisers, publicity for sexpot motion-picture stars, literature, movies, plays, television, and so on. But these are standards of fantasy. Therefore people ask silly questions: How often should we have sex? What is the best position? How intense should it be? Should we scratch and bite each other? What time of day should it be done? The questions sound like inquiries about the type of gymnastic procedures to be followed for attaining muscles like Mr. America's or a rear end or bust like Miss America's. Perhaps even worse off are the myriads of couples who don't dare ask questions and just assume they *must* be abnormal because their own practice differs from some so-called standard.

The problem is obvious. In sex, trying to keep up with the Joneses is the road to disaster. To decide where sex fits into their particular marriage, a couple must look inward at the marriage, not outward at the deceptive advice and make-believe standards set by others. There are no standards, and most "advice" from friends or family is misleading, for few people can speak honestly about their own sex life. Rather than admit their own sex problems and misgivings, friends often let one assume that their sex experiences are indeed superior; otherwise, the implication is, they wouldn't be giving advice.

Can women and men live without sex and still stay healthy?

Yes, they can. People cast away on isolated islands have gone for years without sex and have not experienced any physiological or psychological breakdowns or deficiencies as a result. Priests, nuns, and many mystics, such as the great Mahatma Gandhi have eschewed sexual union and not damaged their health or decreased their longevity.

Sex, of course, is necessary for propagation; nature has provided this instinctual drive so that the species will survive. The drive is effective because of the variety of intense pleasures derived from its fulfillment. But no harm will occur to the normal individual to whom sex is denied.

Almost all adult human beings somehow have the feeling that experiencing sex frequently is a requirement for good physical and mental health, even if intellectually they know better. Both men and women who have enjoyed sex at regular intervals become frustrated, sometimes desperate, when it is withheld for (what seems to them) a long time. The sex aggressions of men at war in foreign lands and of sailors who have been at sea for months are well known. Such behavior stems more from a feeling of deprivation than from pure physical necessity. A person who voluntarily renounces or limits sexual intercourse—as priests, nuns, and others do for varied reasons—suffers no ill health or mental anguish as long as the renunciation corresponds to his emotional needs. If, however, a person desires sexual union and has deep, unmet needs for this form of human intimacy, yet is unable for some reason to meet the need, the resulting sense of deprivation and frustration may create emotional problems.

Sometimes unusual sex actions are stimulated by nonsexual deficiencies. For example, male children with a dread of being abandoned by their mother often will masturbate excessively. Men who have repressed homosexual tendencies (frequently the result of having a passive—or dead—father and a dominant mother) often are inclined to act oversexed in order to "prove their manhood."

The *beliefs* (most of them specious) which most individuals have on "what kind" of sex is desirable, and "how much," have several sources:

1. So-called "scientific" information obtained from books, articles, and lectures.

2. Customs, traditions, and advice conveyed by relatives and friends.

3. Customs, traditions, and examples transmitted by literature, radio, television, movies, and advertising.

Tradition molds many beliefs and habits having to do with sex in marriage. For example, consider the barbaric custom of the honeymoon—particularly in past centuries, when the girl's chastity was treasured and important. In those days the bride and groom, who hardly knew each other, departed to a strange geographical area and into sexual intimacy. Usually the bride possessed only hearsay information on sexual matters and the husband's sexual experience had not necessarily prepared him to understand the needs of a virginal bride. They hurried away from the courtship milieu of jollity, gregariousness, and traditional optimism into a new sexual environment of their own, and were expected to emerge a week or ten days later with all the tenderness, love, and devotion needed to create a successful, happy marriage —whether or not the sexual experience had been traumatic for one or both of them.

A modern version of the same ritual occurs today, with an additional cultural expectation introduced: the newlyweds are expected to achieve *mutual* sexual satisfaction during the honeymoon. The young couple usually is launched with a lavish wedding and a tremendous amount of effort and expense on the part of both their families. The newlyweds are under pressure to "have fun" on their honeymoon and to return looking radiant and serene. Frequently the opposite happens. We estimate that most honeymoons are periods of frustrating sexual disappointment. The honeymoon may be an exciting novelty, but usually it results in confusion even when there has been premarital sexual experience. The situation of the bride who cried all through her honeymoon is a common one. Sex, like anything else, has to be learned; and even if the two have had relations before marriage, the marriage state places them in a new psychological milieu to which they must adjust. Now they are "legitimate," and they believe that their sexual experience will therefore be better. Now they are legally tied; they cannot walk away from each other. They feel the sex act *must* be a success every time; otherwise, the marriage is disintegrating.

This situation is aggravated by the pronouncements of most sex consultants, books, and articles on marriage. They usually indicate that sex is the keystone of marital success. We disagree. Sex is significant; and good sex is satisfying and emotionally nourishing. Sex is highly desirable, but it is not the only vital force in marriage, either during the honeymoon or later.

The situation is muddied further by the conflicting views of "experts" who give "scientific" information on sex. It is important that all "expert" opinions on sex be taken with a grain of skepticism.

Most "scientific" information on sex comes from two sources: psychiatrists and other physicians writing about data obtained from the experiences of their patients, and social scientists generalizing from data obtained in surveys conducted by means of some type of questionnaire.

In point of fact, conclusions based upon the medical data obtained from patients are not necessarily applicable to most people. Patients go to doctors for the treatment of one or more problems. If they have come for psychiatric therapy, they expect to spend many hours discussing sex and exploring the negative aspects of themselves, their spouses, their friends, and so on. Few (if any) will pay twenty-five or thirty dollars an hour and then spend the time discussing pleasant and satisfactory experiences. The gynecologist or the family physician who writes a sex book is scientific only in regard to anatomy. The nonanatomical aspects of the text are based upon his own personal sex experiences plus whatever his ailing patients have told him.

Some of the most popular tracts on sex and marriage are written by gynecologists whose practices consist to a great extent of women who *spontaneously and voluntarily* talk freely to the physician in their efforts to describe their personal discords. The fact that a person talks and answers questions in a doctor's office (instead of in a public bar or a living room) does not prove that the individual is accurate or objective, and certainly does not indicate that his conclusions are generally applicable. Almost all patients' views on sex are subjective and weighted, especially since those who feel the need to discuss their sex lives usually have special problems.

The same difficulty causes the flaws in the Kinsey reports (and in most other studies whose data comes from question-and-answer procedures). Although Kinsey made an important study, one that required courage to initiate, we cannot overlook one important fact: he depended primarily on *volunteers* to answer his questions. Can we be sure that the people who volunteer to answer sex questions are representative? Some of the Kinsey interviewees talked two or three hours about their experiences—evidently revealing intimacies was fun for some.

Also, there were considerable differences in experience and ability among Kinsey's interviewers. Only recently, the work of the Department of Psychiatry at Harvard has demonstrated that the nature of an interviewing context (including the interviewer's attitude) has a tremendous influence on the interviewee's response. An interviewer who strongly believes that, say, many wives have intercourse with other men when their husbands are on trips, will come up with much more evidence to support this view than will an interviewer who holds the opposite opinion at the start of the investigation.

Nevertheless, the Kinsey material provides the most complete and reliable data we have on the sexual practices of middle- and upper-class Americans. It reveals that increasingly in our culture, sexual intercourse is not confined to married people; and it is certainly not limited to sexual congress between men and women.

The bulk of the Kinsey material and of other surveys (which primarily relate to college students) concerns homosexuality, masturbation, premarital intercourse, perversion, post-divorce sexual activities, the activities of spinsters and bachelors, and adultery. To our knowledge, *no one has studied a sample of normogenic (average) married couples in significant numbers* and scientifically determined what married people think and do in relation to sex. Little is known about socio-economic class differences, let alone ethnic idiosyncrasies.

Where does sex fit into marriage? It is almost impossible to estimate (except with respect to a specific married couple, after many hours of interviews) because so few studies have been made on the subject, and those which do exist are limited in scope and objectivity.

The answer to this question also depends upon time and circumstances, for sexual needs are fundamentally psychological. Middle-income spouses who have been married for a year and have no children, but want some, may have different sexual needs from the husband and wife without jobs, so poor they can't pay the rent, who therefore are afraid to have children. A couple married for thirty years, with four children in college, may have different sexual needs from a couple married for five years, with only one child. Such differences are not merely due to age. Boredom plays a more significant role in decreasing the frequency of intercourse than do withering sex glands. Also, a couple whose sex experience is beautiful and satisfying may engage in sex less frequently than an unhappy pair frantically experimenting for a solution to their discord.

There is no accurate sex information which gives exact answers for everyone, since there are so many variables. Yet in the United States, the sex ethic has become all important. As we have already stressed, the fallacious concept that sex determines our lives is spread far and wide by those promoting the tremendous sales of products supposed to enhance sexual attractiveness. Also, "authorities" on sex lecture, write, and give sexual advice *for a fee*. Naturally, they exaggerate the importance of sex in marriage. Offering complicated sex techniques is a profitable profession, and the more difficult the techniques, the longer the expensive counseling will last. The most popular sex manual has been through countless revisions and has outsold all other books except the Bible!

The myth that perfect and heavenly sex must be experienced by an individual before he can consider himself normal has become the foundation for a national mania. Sex success is the theme of social instruction and of almost all advertising, even for products not in any way associated with the sex act.

Spouses who are disappointed in sex are profoundly concerned about their difficulty. This is a reasonable reaction, if the disappointment is well founded. Men often wonder about their manhood or suspect that their wives are frigid or malicious. Wives wonder about their frigidity and suspect that perhaps their husbands are having affairs or that they are effeminate or at least inconsiderate or ignorant of satisfying sexual techniques.

Spouses will try anything to bring about a happier union, *one closer to the sex-success image* which is our national demigod. Many a man and wife have spent a small fortune to go to a posh luxury lodge where they hoped they would miraculously achieve a sexual congress they couldn't bring about in their own bedroom. If the weather is nice and the view is good, something may come of the weekend, but it is not apt to result in unusual sexual satisfaction. People frequently buy new houses, hire interior decorators—with the hope that a fresh environment will improve sexual relations.

If the various manifestations of sex were accepted as natural, and if people could abandon the view that there is a single absolute standard to be reached by all who are normal, the unhappiness of many couples would decrease—*and their performance would automatically improve.*

Our concern in this chapter has been with the problem: Is great, *great,* GREAT sex necessary for a satisfactory marriage, for a workable marriage? If sex is not up to culturally created expectations, is the marriage a failure?

It need not be a failure. It can be a good marriage even if the partners don't find heaven in bed.

Next, is a less-than-heavenly sex performance "normal"?

No one knows the answer, neither clergymen nor doctors. No one knows what normogenic sex performances are in marriage. Scientists have studied pathological marriages, but not normal ones. Small-sample research (such as that by Epstein and Westley at McGill University) supports our contention that sex is not essential; it has been found that some apparently well-adjusted spouses have "given up" sex after a few years of marriage.

In summary, the important thing to remember is that there is no absolute standard against which the success of married sex can be measured as one would clock a hundred-yard dash. Occasionally, there are medical abnormalities (such as disfigured or diseased genitals, impotence, a pathological fear of sex), but assuming that these are not present, there is only one important question: Is sex a source of pleasure—in the spouses' own judgment?

What is a satisfying sex experience for two people may well be undesirable for two others, and vice versa. For example, it is estimated by most physicians that more than half of all women married an average of ten years and having three children have never experienced an orgasm. In a sampling made of such cases most of the women were not aware that they had not had a full sex act. They derived varying degrees of pleasure from the physical intimacy with their husbands. Equally interesting is the fact that the husbands frequently did not know that their wives voluntarily made the same noises and motions which they *had heard or read* were performed by passionate women; the husbands had accepted these as spontaneous and derived satisfaction from them as evidence of the wives' pleasure.

Spouses should not permit their satisfactions to be influenced by authority figures (such as actors and actresses), advertising, art, literature, and social customs and traditions. Personal sex values concern the two people involved. For example, we know a couple in their seventies. Every evening they bathe and dress elegantly for dinner. They treat each other with the dignity and courtesy of a blossoming courtship. At night when they go to bed they hold each other throughout the night, even though they have not exercised their genitalia for years. The elderly gentleman has described their experience as "having a ten-hour orgasm every night." For these two, it is a complete and wonderful sex act, and a very satisfying and nourishing one. Who is to differ with them?

Is sex important in married life? Yes, it is. It is *one* of the cements which hold the bricks of married life together. But the when, the how, the how often, and the quality can only be determined by the people involved.

TECHNIQUES IN SEXUAL AROUSAL

James L. McCary

While excessive attention to sexual technique may lead to depersonalization and mechanization, there is advantage in knowing the physiology of the sexes, especially the erogenous areas. Disregard of such basic knowledge often brings unfulfilling sexual encounter. In the following selection, Dr. McCary offers a primer of arousal techniques for both sexes. Building on the primer, each couple may explore their own unique preferences and repertoire of intimacy.

The Erogenous Zones

Erogenous zones are those parts of the body possessing a great concentration of nerve endings (sometimes termed "sexual nerves") that, when stimulated, cause sexual arousal. These areas are numerous, and they are basically the same in man and woman—although there are, of course, individual variations in the areas producing excitement and in the degree of arousal.

The French physician Ernest Chambard became in 1881 the first person to make a thorough scientific investigation into the erogenous areas of the human body, subsequently issuing a report of his findings. Since the time of Chambard, various studies have demonstrated that the surfaces of mucous membranes are important erogenous zones, and that many of these are capable of erection and tumescence. The most sensitive erogenous areas are the genitals and the areas surrounding them: the inner and outer regions of the thighs, the buttocks, and the abdomen. The nongenital erogenous zones extend over a large portion of the body, some areas being more sensitive than others. The breasts (particularly the nipples), armpits, small of the back, shoulders, neck, earlobes, scalp, eyelids, and especially the mouth, tongue, eyes, and nose are all areas rich in nerve endings.

Sexual arousal takes place when messages are sent by the stimulated sexual nerve endings to the brain, and the brain then transmits them to the centers of the lower spinal column controlling sexual impulses. These center can also receive messages directly from the genital area without the intermediary transmission and relay of the impulses by the brain.

A psychological or physical block at some point can deter or even prevent sexual excitement. For example, messages of disapproval, unpleasantness, fear, pain, or injury can and often do delay or obstruct altogether the channel to sexual centers, thus preventing arousal. On the other hand, . . . pleasant messages such as a lovely sight, a gentle word, a soft touch, an exotic scent, or a harmonious sound, can easily evoke sexual feelings. Pleasing sensory stimuli may produce erotic thoughts, which in turn may cause penile erection; women, however, are apparently less responsive to this type of psychological stimulus than men are.

The erogenous zones appear to be a matter of heredity and, in general, are common to all people. However, individual differences are wide, and are largely the result of conditioning. Present scientific data indicate that there are no abnormal erogenous regions, and those that are uncommon are so simply as the result of individual background and experience. For example, if a man were to tickle the sole of his wife's foot preceding each pleasant act of coitus, sooner or later foot-tickling would come to be associated with pleasurable intercourse, and the sole of the foot would become a conditioned erogenous zone for that particular woman. Should she later marry another person, however, the conditioned erogenous zone on the sole of the foot might well appear to be abnormal to her new husband.

As with psychological factors which serve as potent erotic stimuli, mutual experimentation and frank discussion are the best ways to discover which physiological areas of stimulation are the most effective for individual sexual arousal. To repeat, the erogenous parts of the bodies of both men and women are, by and large, the same. There is, however, a marked degree of difference among members of the same sex, as well as between the sexes, in the method of, and time required for bringing about sexual arousal. A man frequently becomes sexually excited with minimal tactile stimulation, while a woman very often needs loving foreplay prior to the caressing of the erogenous areas of her body.

Heterosexual Interaction— Marital and Nonmarital

The genitals, which are the part of the body most responsive to stimulative techniques, contain millions of nerve endings concentrated in small regions of erectile-type tissue. A man's glans or head of the penis, particularly the lower surface at the corona (ring) and frenum, is the most sensitive part

132

of the genitalia, while the skin covering the shaft of the penis is somewhat insensitive to the touch. A woman's clitoris and its glans contain a delicate network of nerve endings in erectile-type tissue that is covered with mucous membrane. Although a woman's clitoris is the catalyst for sexual excitation and orgasm, the entire vulval region, especially the vestibule and labia minora, are rich in nerve endings and are highly responsive to stimulation. The walls of the vagina, with the exception of the upper front area where the roots of the clitoris are located, are somewhat insensitive because they contain only a few nerve endings. The cervix, furthermore, is so insensitive that it can be cauterized or surgically cut without the aid of anesthesia.

The perineum of both man and woman is sensitive to manipulation. This area includes the anus and inner portion of the thighs, and extends from the anus to the lower region of the sexual organs. About a half of all men and women, in fact, report that they experience erotic reactions to some form of anal stimulation. While the mouth, lips, and nose are widely recognized as highly erogenous areas, there is nonetheless considerable variation in the degree of their sensitivity, because of personal differences resulting, primarily, from conditioning and, secondarily, from differences in supplies of nerve endings, the latter condition being a matter of individual heredity. The breasts are another important erogenous zone common to both men and women. The nipples and areolae are especially responsive to several stimuli.

Methods of Sexual Arousal

One should be reminded occasionally that any act within the marital bed that enhances sexual pleasure, that hurts no one, and that is out of sight and sound of an unwilling observer, is permissible and should be engaged in freely. This reminder appears especially relevant in view of the persistent presence in bookstores of erroneous and misleading writings on human sexuality. Such books state outright, or at least imply, that petting, for instance (which includes any form of sexual foreplay and afterplay), more particularly petting to orgasm, may be harmful at the time, or may interfere with future pleasure and fulfillment in sexual intercourse. To the contrary, the evidence is that those people who enjoy petting and are capable of responding freely to it are those most capable of responding freely to sexual intercourse and of deriving much pleasure from it. The only problems liable to arise from petting are unjustified feelings of guilt, and congestion of the tissue in the sexual region resulting in physical distress when the petting is protracted but does not culminate in orgasmic relief.

Wives and husbands who are reluctant to involve themselves in sex play are often simply fearful that their spouses will consider them too bold in their manner of sexual stimulation or response. The less inhibited of the two should start the amatory foreplay, and then at the appropriate time should gently but firmly put the partner's hands and lips at the spots where they are most desired.

Sexual excitement is most easily heightened when a maneuver of advance and retreat is adopted. Stimulation is instigated, then after a brief buildup, the stimuli are withdrawn in a slightly teasing, tantalizing manner. Stimulation is begun again, carried to a more advanced point of excitement, and once more withdrawn. Quite naturally, timing is of the essence: knowing just how long to continue advancing and retreating, recognizing when these efforts have produced an optimal level of sexual excitement, and then ceasing the teasing are the keys to success in this lovemaking strategy. To continue beyond this point may very well be interpreted as rejection by the recipient, and what started out to be a promising adventure ends in stress and unhappiness.

Hands play an indispensable role in successful lovemaking. The hands—especially the fingers—should be used to caress, stroke, message, squeeze, and otherwise manipulate the erogenous zones of the body to bring as great pleasure as possible to both lovers. With proper use of the hands, not only can be brought to and maintained at the response level of the spouse. As can sexual excitement be built up in one's partner, but one's own excitement an example: light stroking and caressing by the husband of his wife's body with his fingertips will build her sexual excitement faster than his own; but when he uses the palms of his hands, as well as his fingertips (along with other excitements such as darting tongue-kissing), his own excitement usually develops at about the same tempo as his wife's. With this in mind, a husband may pace the development of mutual excitement to achieve a synchronized crescendo.

Initial sexual excitement is brought about by light touch—not pressure—and the more intense and prolonged the sexual buildup, the greater the orgasmic response. While at first the bodies of both the man and woman are stimulated with gentle, slow, generalized stroking, the caressing should gradually become more specific as sex play progresses. The general orientation of the stroking should be toward the erogenous zones, particularly the genitalia, the caresses taking place in the teasing advance-retreat-advance manner already described. It is of special importance that the genitals be stimulated lightly at first because of the sensitivity and tenderness of the area; as excitement increases, the wife may wish the pressure to be heavier.

A woman's skin is considerably more sensitive to the touch than a man's is, and care should be taken, especially during the early part of marriage, to avoid overstimulation. Exceptionally gentle caressing will gradually "awaken" the nerve endings of the genital region, and will condition the bride to welcome this manner of lovemaking as something pleasant and exciting during the following years of marriage. Fingertip stroking of the abdomen and inner thighs—with general movement in the direction of the genitals—will usually prepare a woman for more direct stimulation of the genitalia.

Breast manipulation is usually thought to be one of the most effective sexual stimulants for a woman. An interesting point, however, is that only about 50% of women are sexually aroused by having their breasts stimulated, while about 75% of men who view and stimulate women's breasts become themselves sexually excited. This is yet another instance of the superiority of psychological over physiological factors in sexual matters. Surprising to many is the fact that men can become as sexually exited from having their breasts stimulated as women become. That men enjoy this stimulation is a normal response, and the pleasure has a sound physiological basis.

In his lovemaking, a man should gently massage his wife's breasts, interspersing the manipulation with a light brushing of the nipple and an occasional tweak of its sensitive tip. Caressing with the hands can very pleasurably be alternated with soft, moist kisses and an exploring tongue. To erotic advantage, the tongue may change its tempo occasionally, and dart back and forth across the nipple in a tense, rapid-fire, impertinent manner, then resume once more the soft, moist tongue stimulation, together with manual caressing of the breasts. Research evidence shows that a small percentage of women can actually achieve orgasm from breast stimulation alone.

The erogenous nerve endings in men's breasts are limited to the nipples and areas immediately surrounding them. When a man's breast is stimulated by gently rolling the nipple between the thumb and finger, or by the sort of oral contact described in the previous paragraph, he quite likely will experience the same sort of sexual desire and excitement that women do from the same techniques.

Kissing, like hand-fingertip caressing, should be varied in a teasing manner: open mouth, closed mouth; light lip pressure, heavy lip pressure; moist lips, dry lips; soft lips, nibbling teeth and lips; a darting, teasing tongue, a soft, sensuous tongue. The lover's face and body should be covered with kisses as the point of action varies quickly, then slowly, from the lips to the eyes, hairline, earlobes, to the mouth again, to the breast, the neck, to the abdomen, back to the lips, and all the while, the tongue should also be participating in this exploration of the lover's body. The kissing maneuver should be repeated again and again with increasing passion and delicate timing. Ordinarily, kissing of the mouth should precede kissing of other parts of the body, except perhaps the hand. In the latter instance, it should be noted that having the palms of her hands kissed is a particularly exciting and stimulating experience for a woman. There is also the psychological element of its being a rather courtly and tender gesture on the part of the man.

No matter what approach the husband takes, his hands should seldom be motionless during the entire period of sex play. They should dart and slide over his wife's body—stroking, holding, caressing boldly and lightly, squeezing, and massaging—alternating strong palmar movements with light, silky stroking of the fingertips. As he brings his wife to successive levels of arousal, he must take heed of the very thin and delicate tissue of the vulva and vagina. These areas should not be manually stimulated unless the husband's fingernails are clipped and smooth, and the vulval region well moistened with either bodily secretions or with a commercial product, such as K-Y jelly. The clitoris, furthermore, is often too sensitive to accommodate direct and uninterrupted manipulation comfortably. The regions to the side and around the clitoris are the sites of stimulation preferred by most women who masturbate, and this knowledge can wisely be incorporated by a husband into his love play.

As mentioned earlier, sex play should be a gradual, slowly unfolding experience, especially for the woman. It has been suggested that kissing and manual stimulation of erogenous areas should be carried on for at least fifteen minutes before intercourse itself commences, although some couples prefer longer, others shorter, periods of stimulation. Couples should be warned, however, that an overly protracted period of sex play can actually interfere with maximum pleasure. Kinsey and his associates report that many couples prefer sexual intercourse itself as a method of stimulation. Communication and good timing are once more essential, and when both lovers are ready to proceed with coitus, they should let one another know.

Sexual stimulation is not a one-way street, and the wife should reciprocate with the same sort of fervor that the husband extends to her, not only because she wishes to excite and please him, but because the act of exciting one's lover should be a highly pleasurable and fulfilling experience for the bestower. There are many things a wife can do by way of lovemaking that will bring delight to her husband. She should initiate kissing or return his kisses passionately, stimulate his nipples orally and by fingertip and palmar manipulation, lightly rake her fingers over his bare back, gently stimulate the scrotum and perineal area, and manipulate the penis with alternating light and heavy stroking (particularly at the glans and frenum). The wife, too, should remember the importance of the teasing game of advance and retreat in the art of building up sexual excitement.

In her efforts to determine what sort of lovemaking brings the greatest pleasure to her husband, the new wife should bear in mind individual differences. For example, while some men prefer a gentle stroking of the penis, others may desire heavy pressure and squeezing in such a manner that there is tugging at the scrotum and perineal area. The wife should not hesitate to use her hands, mouth, thighs, legs, toes (even eyelashes, if it comes to that) to stimulate her husband. She should employ a variety of methods of arousal, and by all means she should let it be known that she thoroughly enjoys giving, as well as receiving, such pleasurable stimulation.

In attempting to discover a pleasurable means of stimulating her husband's genitalia, a bride can often obtain a helpful guideline from any masturbatory techniques he may have used prior to marriage. If, for instance, a man stimulated himself with light, slow stroking of his penis, it is quite likely that he will welcome the same sort of caressing from his wife.

Women who masturbate will frequently insert their fingers into the vagina to aid their fantasy during self-stimulation. Since they are so conditioned, these women will probably find it pleasurable if their husbands arouse them in the same manner during sex play. Another method of masturbation for women, one which is far more common than many suspect, is to direct a stream of water over the genitals while bathing. The running water provides a continuous pressure, with just enough variation in constancy to satisfy the physiological requirements involved in producing an orgasm. Women describe the sensation received from this method of self-arousal as being somewhat similar to (although less intense than) that received from the application of an electric vibrator.

Concerning the vibrator, couples would do well to make note of its value in heightening the pleasure of their sexual interaction. Some women apparently cannot achieve orgasm with penile penetration, nor indeed can some reach it through any of the techniques of stimulation already discussed. But direct clitoral and vulval arousal through the husband's application of a vibrator as he fondles and kisses her seldom fails to bring a woman to orgasm.

A few women prefer the type of vibrator that the husband attaches to the back of his hand. It allows him free movement of his fingers, to be sure, but most of the vibration is absorbed by his hand. Most women, therefore, find greater stimulation and gratification from the application of a rubber-knobbed vibrator directly on or to the side of the clitoris. Use of this vibrator meets with great success in producing single or multiple orgasms in women who might otherwise be incapable of reaching such an intense sexual response level. Furthermore, using a vibrator is much less tiring to husbands who otherwise might attempt arousal of their wives' genitals for prolonged periods of time before bringing about an orgasm, if it occurs at all. The husband also remains free to kiss, caress, and stimulate his wife in any other way he chooses. Marriage counselors frequently recommend vibrator stimulation for women who are "frigid," or who experience difficulty in reaching orgasm; and to women who are widowed, yet need sexual release.

Some couples find the vibrator too "mechanical" for their tastes, and others are afraid that their orgasmic response to this sort of stimulation will be so intense that other methods will be pleasurable only to a lesser degree. Some husbands feel threatened by the machine, and object to using it. None of these arguments against the vibrator is strictly sound, and any such objections to it as a method of sexual arousal are psychological in nature.

Another form of sexual activity that is far more popular than many know is oral-genital stimulation. Kinsey's research shows that oral-genital contact is experienced by at least 60% of those married couples who have gone to college, by about 20% of those who have gone through high school, and by about 10% of those who have gone only through grade school. That the first figure is so high may come as a surprise to some people, because of the traditional taboo society has placed on this sort of sexual behavior. Many marriage counselors believe that considerably more than 60% of the higher educational-level group indulge in oral-genital sexual expression, but that they are reluctant to admit it because they fear the disapproval of others

The prevailing negative attitude toward genital kissing is primarily an outgrowth of the fact that many people regard the genital region as "dirty." The proximity in the woman of the anus and the urethra to the genitals, and the fact that the male penis is both a seminal and a urinary outlet, are the physiological factors that have given rise to the "dirtiness" concept, but these do not constitute a logical objection to the act. Certainly if one allows his body to become unclean and malodorous, especially in the anal-genital region, any type of sexual contact is likely to become objectionable. However, with the myriad supply of cosmetic and hygienic products currently on the market, there is really no excuse for an offensive odor emanating from any part of the body—including the anal-genital area.

People seldom enjoy even kissing someone when his or her breath is reeking, to say nothing of entering into more intimate physical contact with someone who needs a bath. If one has recently eaten, or suspects that the mouth might otherwise be offensive, then one is well advised to tackle the problem with toothbrush and mouthwash. The same sensible precautions should be taken with the genitals. Because the folds of skin that partially cover the surface of the genitals are natural receptacles for a collection of smegma and secretions, the region should be cleansed in such a way that there is no chance that any of the offensive material or odor lingers. In the same fashion used in cleaning the ear, a finger should move in and around the folds of the genitalia to cleanse them. If a couple give this sort of attention to keeping themselves clean and pleasant-smelling, making whatever use is indicated of "personal hygiene" and cosmetic products, the objection to oral-genital contact on the grounds of "dirtiness" is less than valid.

Oral-genital sexual behavior is considered perverted by many and is, in fact, illegal in many states, even if performed between husband and wife. Nonetheless, most people of the upper educational level (*i.e.*, those who have attended college) find this act to be a normal, highly exciting, valuable means of sexual stimulation, and it constitutes a regular part of their repertoire of sexual activity.

It is generally agreed by couples who engage in oral-genital contact that it is an act to be enjoyed by both husband and wife, whether giving or receiving. It is an accepted fact that the mouth and lips are erogenous zones common to nearly all people, and there is, in addition, an abundance of nerve endings in the tip of the nose. That these two areas of sensitivity universally exist no doubt accounts for mouth contact and nose-rubbing being the chief methods of "kissing" in our world, and for the fact that oral stimulation of the genitals is so pleasurable for many people. Furthermore, recent neurophysiological studies have shown that there is a close relationship between the parts of the brain concerned with oral functions (amygdala) and those parts concerned with sexual functions (septum and rostral diencephalon). Stimulation of an area of the brain affecting oral activity will readily produce a "spillover" into areas related to genital function.

A couple may engage in mutual oral-genital contact during the early part of stimulation, but to continue the mutual act for any length of time, or to the point of climax, usually requires more acrobatic agility than most couples possess. Furthermore, simultaneous orgasms resulting from oral-genital stimulation—or even prolonged simultaneous oral-genital contact—present some of the same problems discussed under simultaneous coital orgasm: that is, neither partner can properly concentrate at the same time on himself and the spouse to the fullest satisfaction of either while receiving such intense stimulation.

The clitoris usually receives the greatest measure of the husband's attention during *cunnilingus* (Latin: *cunnus*, vulva; and *lingere*, to lick). Its sensitive glans can be stimulated in much the same manner as the nipples of the breasts are in mouth-tongue-breast contact. The tongue-stroking begins in a light, teasing manner with intermittent heavy, moist, bold tongue-stroking; the technique is varied to keep pace with the heightening sexual excitement. As the climax nears, and if the couple wishes to bring it about in this manner, the husband should put into action the findings of Masters and Johnson, which demonstrate that orgasm is best produced by a steady, constant stroking of the clitoral *area*; at the height of sexual tension the clitoris withdraws under its prepuce, and direct contact can no longer be maintained in any case. Other parts of the vulva, particularly the labia minora, are also sensitive to oral stimulation. Women who have experienced oral-genital stimulation report that the method is overwhelmingly pleasurable and effective, both as sex foreplay and as the primary avenue to achieving orgasm.

Kinsey has shown that women are less inclined to engage in *fellatio* (Latin: *fellare*, to suck) with their husbands than their husbands are to engage in cunnilingus with them. Any such reluctance is almost always based on psychological blocks. If a wife will talk over carefully the matter of fellatio with her husband, she can usually overcome this reticence, and eventually the act may become quite pleasurable for her.

The glans of the penis, especially at the frenum and contiguous areas, is highly sensitive to the wife's kisses and sucking, and to her warm, moist, now darting, now soft tongue. All the while, she should also stroke the corpus of the penis with an up and down movement, and occasionally fondle the testicles and the scrotum. This technique of lovemaking can quickly bring the husband to sexual heights that can easily terminate in orgasm. Van de Velde, who has written one of the classics among marriage manuals, gives unqualified endorsement to mouth-genital stimulation as a vastly pleasurable form of sexual behavior. So also have many other authorities in the field of sex and marriage.

Whether climax occurs as a result of manual stimulation, oral activity, or sexual intercourse is a matter each couple must decide individually. The method that is best suited for a particular occasion should readily be adopted, with each participant expending his best effort to bring about maximum satisfaction for his partner.

Many variations of the sex act, together with special techniques for heightening pleasure during the various phases of increasing sexual response, have been proposed in marriage manuals and other writings on sexual matters. However, each couple because of their individual and combined personalities and preferences must decide—through open discussion and uninhibited experimentation—just what brings them the greatest erotic pleasure. What one couple finds exciting, another might find dull or even repulsive. One person, for instance, might find highly pleasurable the applition of crushed ice wrapped in a cloth to the perineal area at the time the paroxysms of orgasm commence, whereas another might find it a rather ludicrous (if not chilling) experience. Some couples have found that applying certain mild chemicals, such as Mentholatum, to the glans of the penis or to the vulval region (or even the use of the salve as a lubricant during coitus) enhances their sexual pleasure, while others find such a practice physically painful. Some desire anal stimulation, or the insertion of fingers or small objects into the rectum, during certain phases of the sexual response cycle; but others consider such techniques unnecessary, repugnant, or even barbaric. Whatever the sexual variation, it should be introduced spontaneously and with obvious desire by one participant, and received pleasantly and happily by the other.

Sex relations do not, or rather should not, end with orgasm. Many couples find the interval after the sexual act to be as pleasant and emotionally fulfilling as any other part of marriage. To hold each other in a close and lingering embrace, to discuss softly the delights of the experience they have just shared, to caress the lover's body with tender, sweeping movements of the hands, to doze and relax with intertwined bodies, all serve to aid in the emotional fulfillment. Other couples are completely overcome by the release of physical and emotional tension, and are ready to drop off into a deep and restful sleep after a brief expression of love and appreciation. Partners must give as careful attention to the spouse's wishes concerning the period of resolution of sexual tensions as they do to each other's preferences in the matter of sexual foreplay.

The sum and substance of this chapter is that sex is a pleasurable, significant part of marriage, and that both husband and wife should do everything in their power to make it as joyous and satisfying as possible. Lovemaking can fulfill both the psychological and physiological needs of human beings in a way that nothing else in marriage is capable of doing. It can be approached and executed in a variety of ways, any one of which may be highly pleasurable to one couple, undesirable to a second, and simply dull to a third. Sex may be a rather grim business in a marriage, especially when it is unsatisfactory. But it can also be fun. A well-known and respected psychologist, A. H. Maslow, with great perception summarized a healthy love relationship when he wrote in *Motivation and Personality:*

> It is quite characteristic of self-actualizing people that they can enjoy themselves in love and in sex. Sex very frequently becomes a kind of game in which laughter is quite as common as panting. It is not the welfare of the species, or the task of reproduction, or the future development of mankind that attracts people to each other. The sex life of healthy people, in spite of the fact that it frequently reaches great peaks of ecstasy, is nevertheless also easily compared to the game of children and puppies, it is cheerful, humorous, and playful.

IS MONOGAMY OUTDATED?

Rustum and Della Roy

The question of whether traditional marriage is an outdated institution has engaged critics of the American marriage and family for several decades. The Roys, writing from the viewpoint of Christian humanism, believe that "man was meant to live in community" and that monogamous marriage may be less viable or reasonable today. They suggest that other humane and fulfilling relationships between the sexes are possible, encompassing a wider range of relationship than is now patterned in the monogamous structure. Among other modifications and reforms, they recommend marriage education courses, easier access to a more equitable divorce policy, and a "marriage-of-community," either in a legally structured relationship of bigamy or acceptance of significant others in extramarital relationships with or without sexual involvement.

The problem lies in finding a favorable social climate and commitment to effect changes. Although we call ourselves a pluralistic society, tolerant of variable value systems expressed through modes of lifestyle, dress, beliefs, and behavior, radically new marriage patterns are extremely slow to be legitimatized by the larger society. Forty years ago, for example, Bertrand Russell, Walter Lippmann, and Judge Benjamin Lindsay triggered widespread public controversy by promoting trial marriages with liberal options for "divorce" when a relationship failed to satisfy a couple's needs. Today we are beginning, with varying degrees of support, to accept such arrangements.

Monogamy: Where We Stand Today

The total institution of marriage in American society is gravely ill. This statement does not apply to the millions of sound marriages where two people have found companionship, love, concern, and have brought up

This article first appeared in *The Humanist*, March/April 1970 and is reprinted by permission.

children in love. But it is necessary in 1970 to point to the need for *institutional* reforms, even when the personal or immediate environment ma not (appear to) need it. Yet many refuse to think about the area as a whole because of personal involvement—either their marriage is so successful that they think the claims of disease exaggerated, or theirs is so shaky that all advice is a threat. Is the institution then so sick? For example:

> Year after year in the United States, marriage has been discussed in public print and private session with undiminished confusion and increasing pessimism. Calamity always attracts attention, and in the United States the state of marriage is a calamity.

These are the words with which W. J. Lederer and D. Jackson open their new book *The Mirages of Marriage.* Vance Packard in *The Sexual Wilderness* summarizes the most recent major survey thus: "In other words, a marriage made in the United States in the late 1960s has about a 50:50 chance of remaining even nominally intact."

Clifford Adams concludes from an Identity Research Institute study of 60 couples that while numerically at 40 per cent in this nation, and in some West Coast highly-populated counties the *real* divorce rate is running at 70 per cent, that in fact "75 per cent of marriages are a 'bust.' " And Lederer and Jackson report that 80 per cent of those interviewed had at some time seriously considered divorce. So much for the statistics. Qualitatively the picture painted by these and 100 others is even bleaker but needs no repeating here.

There is no doubt then about the diagnosis of the sickness of marriage taken as a whole. Yet no person, group, magazine, or newspaper creates an awareness of the problems; no activist band takes up the cause to *do* something about it. Some years ago, we participated in a three-year-long group study and development of a sex ethic for contemporary Americans, and we found this same phenomenon: that serious group study and group work for change in the area of sex behavior is remarkably difficult and threatening, and hence rare. Thus, we find an institution such as monogamous marriage enveloped by deterioration and decay, and unbelievably little is being done about it on either a theoretical basis or detailed pragmatic basis.

For this there is a second major reason: marriage as an institution is partly governed by warring churches, a society without a soul, a legal system designed for lawyers, and a helping system for psychiatrists who almost by their very mode of operation in the marriage field guarantee its failure.

Consequently, marriage is rapidly losing its schizophrenic mind, oscillating between tyrannical repression and equally tyrannical expression.

By the term "traditional monogamy," we refer to the public's association with the word, i.e., marriage to one person at a time, the centrality of the nuclear family and the restriction of all overt sexual acts, nearly all sexually-tinged relationships and heterosexual relations of any depth to this one person before and after marriage, expectation of a lifetime contract and a vivid sense of failure if termination is necessary. John Cuber and Peggy Harroff in *The Significant Americans* have called this "the monolithic code," and it is based on precepts from the Judaic and Christian traditions. All working societies are structured around such codes or ideals, no matter how far individuals may depart from the norms and whether or not they accept the source of such "ideals."

How does change in a code or ideal come about? When the proportion of the populace living in conflict with their own interpretation of the monolithic code, and "getting away with it," reaches nearly a majority, then *new* ideals must evolve for the social system to remain in equilibrium. We are convinced that although no *discontinuous* change in the ideals of a culture is possible, "traditional monogamy" as an ideal may be altered *in a continuous fashion* in order to respond to the needs of men and women today.

Traditional monogamy was *one* interpretation of the Judaeo-Christian tradition. We are convinced that for widespread acceptability any *new* ideals must be interpretable in terms of Judaeo-Christian humanism, the basic framework of mainstream "Americanism," and the most explicit humanism so far developed. Such an interpretation is neither difficult nor likely to encounter much resistance from the many other contemporary American humanisms which have not swung far from the parent Protestant humanism. But the importance of such an interpretation for "continental" middle-class America is crucial, as the tenor and very existence of the Nixon administration bring home to those who live in the more rarified climes of East or West Coast. If a new monogamous ideal is to evolve, it must be acceptable to middle America, liberated, affluent, but waspish at heart.

Causes of the Crisis

Social institutions are the products of particular social environments, and there must be a finite time lag when an institution appropriate for one situation survives into a new era in which the situation has changed drastically. It is clear that "traditional monogamy" is caught precisely in this "overlap" of two radically different situations. It is important to identify precisely the particular problem-causing elements of change in the environment.

The sexual revolution has made it infinitely more difficult to retain monogamy's monopoly on sex.

We live in an eroticized environment which is profoundly affecting many institutions. The change towards greater permissiveness and its effect on the sexual climate can be summed up in the aphorism, "What was a temptation for the last generation is an opportunity for this." Underneath it all are the measurable, real physical changes: the advent of prosperity, mobility, and completely controlled conception.

Parallel to physical changes are vast social changes. The eroticization of our culture oozes from its every pore, so much so that it becomes essentially absurd to expect that all physical sexual expression for a 50-year period will be confined to the marriage partner. Moreover, this eroticization escalator shows no sign of slowing down, and its effect on various institutions will be even more drastic in the future. Following are some illustrations.

The influence of the literature, the arts, the media, and the press on the climate for any institution is profound, and marriage is no exception. Caught between the jaws of consumer economics in a free-enterprise system and the allegedly objective purveyors of accurate information (or culturally representative entertainment), human sexuality has become the most salable commodity of all. Perform, if you will, the following simple tests: examine the magazine fare available to tens of millions of Americans; spend a few hours browsing through *Look*, and *Life*, and try *Playboy*, work up to something like *Cosmopolitan*. If you are serious, visit a typical downtown book shop in a big city and count the number of pictorial publications whose sole purpose is sexual titillation. Next try the paperbacks available to at least 100,000,000 Americans—in every drugstore: *Candy*, Henry Miller, *Fanny Hill*, the complaining Portnoy, valleys of dolls, and menchild in promised lands, carpetbaggers at airports, couples and groups. Does *one* speak of the beauty and wonder of uniting sex to marriage? Go see 10 movies at random. Will *The Graduate, I Am Curious*, or *La Ronde* rail against sexual license? Thus the mass media have had a profound effect on the American people's marriage ideals. They especially confuse those to whom their "traditions" speaking through emasculated school, bewildered Church, and confused home still try to affirm a traditionally monogamous system. Yet some have mistakenly denied that there is a causal relation between the media and our rapidly changing value systems. Worst of all, very few of those who urge the freedom of access to more and more sexual stimuli work to legitimize, socially and ethically, a scheme for increased sexual outlets.

There is a vast increase in the number and variety of men-women contacts after marriage, and no guidelines are available for behavior in these new situations.

Of the sexual dilemmas which our present-day culture forces upon the "ailing" institutions of traditional monogamy, premarital sexual questions now appear very minor. For all intents and purposes premarital sexual play (including the *possibility* of intercourse) has been absorbed into the social canon. We foresee in the immediate future a much more serious psychological quandary with respect to extra- or co-marital sexual relations of all levels of intensity. The conflict here is so basic and so little is being done to alleviate it, that it is only surprising that it has not loomed larger already. Traditional monogamy as practiced has meant not only one spouse and sex partner at a time but essentially only one heterosexual *relationship*, of any depth at all, at a time. We have shown above that our environment suggests through various media the desirability of nonmarital sex. Further, our culture is now abundant in opportunity: time, travel, meetings, committees, causes, and group encounters of every stripe bringing men and women together in all kinds of relationship-producing situations. Our age is characterized by not only the opportunity but by the necessity for simultaneous multiple-relationships. One of the most widely experienced examples is that chosen by Cuber and Harroff in their study of the sex lives of some "leaders" of our society. They noted the obviously close relationship of such men with their secretaries with whom they work for several hours a day. But the same opportunity now occurs to millions of middle-class housewives returning to work after children are grown. They too are establishing new heterosexual friendships and being treated as separate individuals (not to mention as sex-objects) after 10 or 15 years.

Traditional monogamy is in trouble because it has not adjusted itself to find a less hurtful way to terminate a marriage.

From the viewpoint of any philosophy that puts a high value on response to human need and the alleviation of human suffering the mechanisms available for terminating marriage are utterly unacceptable. Traditional monogamy involves a lifetime commitment. Anything that would necessitate termination short of this must, therefore, be a major failure. "Divorce, American Style" demands so much hurt and pain and devastation of personalities that it is imperative that we attempt to temper the hurt caused to human beings. We must take as inescapable fact that about half of all the marriages now existing will, and probably should, be terminated. The question is how best this can be done to minimize total human suffering, while avoiding the pitfall that the relief of immediate pain of one or two persons is the greatest and single good. Full consideration must always be given to all the "significant others"—children, parents, friends—and to the long-range effects on society. The institution of traditional monogamy will increasingly come under attack while it is unable to provide a better means to terminate a contract than those now in use.

Traditional monogamy does not deal humanely with its have-nots—the adult singles, the widowed, the divorced.

Statistically speaking we in America have more involuntarily single persons above age 25 or 30 than those who had no choice about a disadvantageous color for their skin. The latter have had to bear enormous legal and social affronts and suffered the subtler and possibly more debilitating psychological climate of being unacceptable in much of their natural surroundings. But this disability they share with voiceless single persons in a marriage-oriented society. Our society proclaims monogamy's virtue at every point of law and custom and practice, as much as it says white is right. Biases, from income tax to adoption requirements, subtle advertisements, and Emily Post etiquette all point to the "traditional monogamist" as the acceptable form of society. Unbelievably, this barrage goes on unopposed in the face of some tens of millions of persons outside the blessed estate. Monogamy decrees that the price of admission into the complex network of supportive relationships of society is a wedding band. Yet it turns a blind eye to the inexorable statistical fact that of those women who are single at 35 only 1/3, at 45 only 1/10, AND at 50 only 1/20 will *ever* find that price. Is access to regular physical sexual satisfaction a basic human right on a plane with freedom or shelter or right to worship? For effective living in our world every human being needs individuals as close friends and a community of which he or she is a part. Traditionally, monogamous society has ruled, ipso facto, that tens of millions of its members shall have no societally approved way of obtaining sexual satisfaction. Much worse, because sexual intimacy is potentially associated with all heterosexual relationships of any depth, they must also be denied such relationships.

Here, surely, every humanist must protest. For it is *his* social ideal—that the greatest good of human existence is deep interpersonal relationships and as many of these as is compatible with depth—that is contravened by traditional monogamy's practice. Moreover, there is less provision today for single women to develop fulfilling relationships than there was a generation or two ago. The "larger-family" then incorporated these losers in the marital stakes into at least a minimal framework of acceptance and responsibility.

A Theory for Change

Any vision of a better future for society presupposes, consciously or unconsciously, a value system and basic assumptions about the nature of man. A theory of man and life must precede a theory of monogamy. Our view of the nature of man is the Judaeo-Christian one. Man was meant to live *in community*. The normative ideal for every man is that he live fully known, accepted, and loved by a community of significant others. In this environment his individual creativity and his creative individuality will be realized to the maximum extent, and he can serve society best.

Man—Community—Society In this spectrum we have, as yet, not even mentioned marriage, and instructively so. There is a crucially important hierarchy of values, in which the individual's needs and the community's good are vastly more important than the "laws" or preferred patterns of marital behavior. Indeed, these "laws" must be tested empirically by the criterion of how well they have been found to meet the individual-community-society needs most effectively. It is important to see that the humanist is not committed, prima facie, to *any* particular pattern of men-women relationships.

Marriage, monogamous or polygamous, fits somewhere between the individual and community levels of social organization. Unfortunately, in many cultures the institution of marriage and the stress on the family has generally militated against, and sometimes destroyed, the community level of relationship.

This has not always been so—not even in America. The "larger family" of maiden aunts and uncles and grandparents, and occasional waifs and strays, has been a part of many cultures including that of the rigidly structured joint-family system in India and the plantation system of the American South.

Tribal cultures abound. In the Swiss canton or settled New England town the sinews of community are strong enough to make them fall in between the extremes represented above and lying, perhaps, closer to the former. There is an inverse correlation between the complexity of a highly-developed society and the strength of community channels and bonds. It is in the technology-ruled society where we find men and women turning to the intimacy of marriage to shield them from further impersonalization when the second level of defense—the community level—has disintegrated through neglect. But monogamous marriage is altogether too frail an institution to carry that load also. A typical marriage is built frequently of brittle and weak members held together by a glue of tradition rapidly deteriorating under the onslaught of a half-dozen corroding acids—mobility, prosperity, permissiveness, completely controlled conception, and continuously escalating eroticization.

There is no question that the first and essential step in the evolution of monogamy is the recovery of the role of community in our lives. It appears to us, however strange a conclusion it seems, that precisely because our world has become so complex, depersonalization is an essential, ineradicable fact of our lives in the many public spheres. This requires then a radical restructuring of the private sphere to provide the supports we have found missing in the "traditional-monogamy" pattern. To know and accept ourselves deeply we need to be known and accepted. And most of us are many-sided polyhedra needing several people to reflect back to ourselves the different portions of our personality. With changing years and training and jobs this need grows instead of diminishing. Thus, it comes about that the humanist has a great deal to contribute to his fellows.

Our proposed modification of monogamy, then, has the reemphasis of community as one of its primary goals. This is hardly novel, but it has been the conclusion of every group of radical Christian humanists trying to reform society for hundreds of years. And it was the New World which provided for them a unique opportunity to attempt the radical solutions. Hence, we have dotted across America the record and/or the remnants of hundreds of experiments in radical community living.

Today we believe that society's hope lies in working at both ends of the game—the basic research and the development. We need to become much more active in optimizing or improving present marriage in an imperfect society: changing laws, improving training, providing better recovery systems, etc. But alongside of that, we need to continue genuine research in radically new patterns of marriage. This can only be carried out by groups or communities. Further, we need not only those groups that seek solutions with-

drawn from the day-to-day world, but those that are willing to devise
potential solutions which can serve as models, for its eventual reform within
the bourgeois urban culture.

Basic Research in Marriage Patterns

We cannot here do justice to a discussion of possible models for radical new
patterns of marriage-in-community. Instead, we wish only to emphasize the
importance of such experimentation and its neglect, in our supposedly
research-oriented culture, by serious groups concerned for society. It is
hardly a coincidence that the yearning for community should figure so
prominently in all utopian schemes for remaking society. The contemporary
resurgence is described in B. F. Skinner's *Walden Two* or Erich Fromm's
Revolution of Hope and Robert Rimmer's *Harrad Experiment*. It is being
attempted in groping unformed ways in the "hippie" or other city-living
communes, and is being lived out in amazingly fruitful (yet unpublicized)
models in the Bruderhof communities in the United States and Europe, and
the Ecumenical Institute in Chicago. And in rereading the details of the
organization of the hundreds of religious communities we find that they have
an enormous amount to teach us, on many subjects from psychotherapy to
patterns for sexual intercourse.

Probably the most important lesson for contemporary America, however,
is that communities survive and thrive and provide a creative framework for
realizing the human potential if their central purpose is outside themselves
and their own existence. The second lesson is one taught by the complex
technology: wherever many persons are involved, *some* discipline and order
are absolutely essential.

Were it not for the sheer prejudice introduced by a misreading of Judeao-
Christian tradition, and its bolstering by the unholy alliance of state-and-
church Establishment, we may well have learned to separate potential from
pitfall in various patterns of communal living. The Mormon experience with
polygamy is not without its value for us, and Bettelheim has helped shake the
prejudice against nonparent child rearing drawing on data from the kib-
butzim. Rimmer, perhaps, through his novels *The Rebellion of Yale Marratt*
and *Proposition 31*, has reached the widest audience in his crusade for a
variety of new marital patterns. He has dealt sensitively, and in depth, with
the subtle questions of ongoing sexual relations with more than one partner—
the threat of which is perhaps the most difficult taboo against communal life
for most educated Americans. From some dozens of histories in personal and

"marathon" encounter situations, we believe that Rimmer's portrayal of typical reactions is remarkably accurate. Most middle-class, educated Americans above 35 have been so schooled into both exclusivity and possessiveness that no more than perhaps 10 percent could make the transition into any kind of structured nonexclusivity in marriage. But for the younger group, especially those now in college, the potential for attempting the highly demanding, idealistic, disciplined group living of some sort is both great, and a great challenge. It is here perhaps by setting up contemporary-style communities of concern and responsibility that young humanists can make one of their greatest contributions to society at large.

Modifying Traditional Monogamy

No company survives on its fundamental research laboratory alone, although many cannot survive long without one. Each needs also a development group that keeps making the minor changes to its existing products in order to eliminate defects in design and to meet the competition or the change in customer needs. So too with marriage. While "far-out" research *must* proceed on new patterns, we must simultaneously be concerned with the changes that can modify traditional monogamy to meet its present customer-needs much more effectively—that is to say humanely.

Our society is pluralist in many of its ideals. The first and most important change in society's view of marriage must also be the acceptance of the validity of a range of patterns of behavior. The education of our children and of society must point to ways and points at which, *depending on the situation*, it is right and proper to make this or that change. Indeed, we can doubtless describe the era we are entering as one of "situational monogamy" —that is traditional monogamy can still be upheld as the ideal in many circumstances, but, in specific situations, modifications are not only permitted but required.

Institutionalizing Premarital Sex   Premarital sexual experience is now rather widely accepted, covertly if not overtly, throughout our society. Especially when we use the word "experience" instead of "intercourse," the studies from Kinsey to Packard support a very substantial increase in necking and petting including petting to orgasm. The new rise in "keeping-house-together" arrangements in college and beyond is spreading like wildfire. We see an opportunity here for a simple evolution of the monogamous ideal within relatively easy reach. Almost all analysts believe that postponing marriage by two or three years and making it more difficult—with some required period of waiting or even waiting and instruction—would be very beneficial. Traditional marriage in its classical form enjoined a "decent" (six months to two years) engagement period partly for the same reason. One of the main drives toward early marriage is that there is no other way to obtain regular sexual gratification in a publicly acceptable manner. By one simple swish of tradition, we can incorporate all the recent suggestions for trial marriages, "baby" marriages, etc., and cover them all under the decent rug of the "engagement." Engagements with a minor difference: that in today's society they entitle a couple to live together if they desire, and sleep together—*but not to have children*. Thus, engagement would become the first step that entitles one to legal sex—publicly known sex with contraceptive devices. By no means need this become the universal norm. Pluralism of marital patterns should start here, however, Many parents and various social groups may still urge their members to restrict engagements to a noncoital or nonsexual level of intimacy; but even here they would do well to legitimize some advanced level of sexual activity and by so doing they would probably protect their marriage-institution more effectively. Our very spotty feedback from student groups would suggest that "everything-but-coitus"—which is a lot more sex than the last generation's "little-but-coitus"—has some value as a premarital maxim. The humanist must also affirm that quintessential humaneness is choice against one's immediate desires. He must point to the loss by this generation of perhaps the most exquisite sexual pleasures when it comes as the culmination of long-deferred desire of the loved one. We mourn the loss of Eros in a day when Venus reminds us that we are *human* animals. Well may we paraphrase the Frenchman and say: "In America we tend to eat the fruit of coital sex, green."

Along with the engagement-including-sex concept could be introduced the idea of "training" for marriage. Everyone falls for the training gimmick. Driver education, often taken after three years of driving, is still useful, and is induced by the lowered insurance rates. Similarly if society required a "marriage-education" course before granting a license, another important step in improving the quality of marriage would have been achieved.

Expanding the Erotic Community in the Post-Marital Years

With the engagement-including-sex, we have broken the pre-marital half of monogamy's monopoly on sex. It is our judgment that for the health of the institution it will become necessary in America in the next decade to break the second half also—post-marital sexual expression. (Recall that our theory demands that we seek to maximize the number of deep relationships and to develop marriages to fit in with a framework of community.) To do this we are certain that the monopolistic tendencies of relationships must be broken, and hence the question of sexual relations cannot be bypassed. We believe that in the coming generation a spectrum of sexual expression with persons other than the spouse are certain to occur for at least the large majority, and possibly most persons. If monogamy is tied inextricably with post-marital restriction of all sexual expression to the spouse, it will ultimately be monogamy which suffers. Instead, monogamy should be tied to the much more basic concepts of fidelity, honesty, and openness, which are concomitants of love of the spouse, but which do not necessarily exclude deep relationships and possibly including various degrees of sexual intimacy with others. In the studies and counseling experience of many, including ourselves, there is no evidence that all extra-marital sexual experience is destructive of the marriage. Indeed, more and more persons testify that creative co-marital relationships and sexual experience can and do exist. But most persons need guidelines to help steer them from the dangerous to the potentially creative *relationships*, and to provide help on the appropriateness of various sexual expressions for various relationships. A few practices are crucial:

> *Openness:* Contrary to folklore, frank and honest discussions at every stage of a developing relationship between all parties is the best guarantee against trouble. We know of husbands who have discussed with their wives possible coitus with a third person, some to conclude it would be wrong, others, unwise; others to drop earlier objections, and still others to say it was necessary and beautiful. We know of wives who have said a reasoned "no" to such possibilities for their husbands and kept their love and respect; and many who have said "yes" in uncertainty and have found the pain subside. Openness is not impossible.

> *Other-centeredness:* Concern for *all* the others—the other woman or man, the other husband or wife, the children—must be front and center in reaching decisions on any such matters.

> *Proportionality:* Sexual expressions should be proportional to the depth of a relationship. This leads, of course, to the conclusion that most coitus and other intimate expressions should only occur with very close friends: a conclusion questioned by many, but essential for our theory.

> *Gradualism:* Only a stepwise escalation of intimacy allows for the open discussion referred to above. Otherwise such openness becomes only a series of confessions.

It is important to discover the value of self-denial and restraint. It is incumbent on them to demonstrate, while accepting other patterns, their ability to maintain loving, warm relationships with both single and married persons of the opposite sex and of limiting the sexual expression therein in order, for example, to conserve psychic energy for other causes.

Providing a Relationship Network for the Single   It is principally because of the fear of sexual involvement that the single are excluded from married-society. In the new dispensation, a much more active and aggressive policy should be encouraged to incorporate single persons within the total life of a family and a community. She or he should be a part of the family, always invited—but not always coming—to dinner, theaters, and vacations. The single person should feel free enough to make demands and accept responsibility as an additional family member would. The single woman, thus loved and accepted by two or three families, may find herself perhaps not sleeping with any of the husbands but vastly more fulfilled as a woman. No couple should enter such relationships unless the marriage is secure and the sexual monopoly not crucially important: yet all concerned couples should be caused to wonder about their values if their fear of sexual involvement keeps them from ministering to such obvious need. The guidelines for decisions, of course, are the same as those above. We know of several such relationships, many but not all involving complete sexual intimacy that have been most important in the lives of the single persons. Recently, we have observed that our present society makes it very difficult for even the best of these relationships to continue for a lifetime. And we see the need for developing acceptable patterns for altering such relationships creatively after the two-to-five-year period which often brings about sufficient changes to suggest reappraisal in any case. The dependent woman often becomes confident and no longer needs the same kind of support: the independent one becomes too attached and becomes possessive enough to want exclusivity. The mechanisms we discuss under divorce should no doubt operate here as well.

Legalizing Bigamy   It may appear as a paradox, but in keeping with the theory above and the pluralist trend of society, it is almost certainly true that contemporary-style monogamy would be greatly strengthened if bigamy (perhaps polygamy-polyandry) were legalized. This would provide a *partial* solution to the problems dealt with in the last two sections; moreover, it would do it in a way that is least disturbing to the monogamous tenor of society. The entire style—contract and living arrangements of most persons —would be unaffected if one woman in 20 had two husbands in the house; or one man in 10 had two wives—sometimes in different cities and frequently in different houses. There is a substantial unthinking emotional resistance to legalizing bigamy based partly on a supposed, but incorrect, backing from Christian doctrine. There is, however, no Biblical injunction sanctifying monogamy: the Christian humanist is not only free to, but may be required to, call for other patterns. Indeed, after World War II the Finnish Church is reported to have been on the verge of legalizing bigamy, when the great disparity in women:men ratio, which stimulated the inquiry, was found to have improved beyond their expectations.

In the next decade, this ratio is expected to get as high as 7:5 in this country, and it is higher in the highest age brackets. Various gerontologists have suggested the legalization of bigamy for the aged, and the capacity for social change in our society is so weak that perhaps bigamy will have to be legalized first under Medicare! It is indeed difficult to see why bigamy should not be legalized, once the doctrinal smoke screen were to be exposed for what it is.

Making Difficulties and Divorce Less Destructive of Personalities

A reform of the total system of marriage *must* provide for a much less destructive method for terminating one. The first change required in our present ideal is to recognize that a good divorce can be better than a poor marriage. We can continue to affirm the importance of the intention of the lifelong commitment, but we must begin to stress the quality of the commitment and the actual relationship as a higher good than mere longevity. Early detection of trouble makes repair easier and surgery less likely. If we take our automobiles to be inspected twice a year to be safe on the highways, is it too much to expect that the complex machinery of a marriage could be sympathetically "inspected" periodically to keep it in the best working condition? Here the church and the university can help by showing the need for, and providing such "inspections." Conceivably a biennial or triennial marriage-marathon or weeklong retreat utilizing the newest insights of encounter groups could be made normative for all marriages. Such check-up would in some cases catch the cancer early enough, and in others indicate the need for surgery. In any case, a failing marriage needs to be treated by a person or persons who are neutral on the value of divorce itself, committed to the goal of maximizing human potential, and not determined to preserve marriage for its own sake. We believe that a team of a marriage counselor and, where appropriate, younger clergymen or another couple who are close friends can, over a period of several months, help the husband and wife arrive at a wise decision most effectively. The use of a fixed-length trial period for either separation or continuance, after specific changes, with an agreed-upon evaluation at the end of the period has proved its real value in all cases where we have seen it used. Our own experience has been that many of the worst situations are avoided if the couple can keep channels open to their closest friends—always working with them together. Two helpful changes need to occur here. First, it should be made much more acceptable to talk openly and seriously about marital tensions with close friends; and second, we should all learn the principle of never giving any personal information about absent *third* parties except when we think it can specifically do some positive good.

For ordinary divorce, it is difficult to see what the professional psychiatrist or lawyer-as-adviser can contribute; indeed it appears axiomatic that with traditional Freudian psychiatry there can be no compromise—it is simply incompatible with the rational approaches to helping even irrational persons. In most instances, its result is the introduction of wholly unnecessary polarization (instead of a reconciling attitude, even while separating) between two persons who were the most important in the world to each other. This we find tends to undercut the faith that such persons can ever have in any other person or cause. The price of so-called self-understanding is the mild cynicism which extinguishes the fire of the unlimited liability of love and drains the warmth and color from two lives. Neither paid psychiatrist nor loving friend can avoid the tragedy in the kind of situation when John married to Mary has become deeply attached to Alice. But this tragedy need not be compounded by bitterness, anger, and self-justification in the name of helping. We do know of couples, divorcing and parting as friends; persons who *love* each other to the best of their ability and yet, after sober agonizing months of consideration, decide to separate. We know that that is the way it must happen in the future.

Conserving Ideals: Changing the Marriage Service Because our psychological conditioning is affected, even by every minor input, we can help preserve the monogamous *ideal* by bringing in honesty at the high points in its symbol-life. This would mean, for instance, minor alteration of the traditional-marriage service, and not necessarily to "water-down" its commitments. Thus, everyone recognizes the value of a lifelong commitment. But to what should that commitment be? To preserving a marriage when we know that half will fail and make all involved guilty over it? Why not, rather, a lifelong commitment to loving and speaking the truth in love? One can be true to this even if separation occurs. Why should not the marriage service make the closest friends—best man, maid of honor, etc., who have essentially trivial roles in the ceremony—take on a real commitment to become the loving community for the couple, covenanting to communicate regularly, stand by them always, but also to speak admonition in love whenever they see it needed. Even such a small beginning would symbolize the fact that each couple enters not only into a marriage but also into a much-needed community.

Disease Diagnosed, Prognosis: Poor

The rebellion of the young reflects only intuitively their alienation from a science-technology dominated world which they have not the discipline to understand. The need for new and revitalized institutions that would provide every kind of support to individuals could not be greater. Inexorable logic points to the centrality of community in any such attempts. Yet no American, indeed Western, sociologist or psychologist of any stature (always excepting Skinner) has paid any serious attention to their structuring. We attribute this largely to their ignorance of the primitive Christian roots of their own heritage, and see in it the great loss to contemporary humanism of the insight and *experimental data* from those bold humanist experimenters of the last century. However, it is unlikely that in the permissive society it will be possible to demand the minimum discipline required for a community to cohere. What changes can we really hope for on the basis of present observations? On the basis of emotional reactions and capacity for change in attitudes to men-women relationships, sexual patterns, or marriage, which we have observed even in the most secure and highly motivated persons, we can only be discouraged and pessimistic. Always here and there the exception stands out: concerned persons acting out love in new ways demanded by new situations. We agree with Victor Ferkiss when he says in *Technological Man:*

There is no new man emerging to replace the economic man of industrial society or the liberal democratic man of the bourgeois political order. The new Technology has not produced a new human type provided with a technological world view adequate to give cultural meaning to the existential revolution. Bourgeois man continues dominant just as his social order persists while his political and cultural orders disintegrate.

Bourgeois man will persist and along with him, traditional monogamy. But for humanists, there is no release from the mandate to try to alter traditional monogamy to make it better serve human needs for "we are called upon to be faithful, not to succeed."

ADULTERY: REALITY VERSUS STEREOTYPE

John F. Cuber

Based largely on a moralistic view of the narrowly sexual aspects of adultery, too many writings in the family field have overemphasized the "deleterious" effects of adultery on its participants and on the marriage relationship as well. The following paper, which upsets some of the myths that people hold about extramarital relations, is based on a research study of a number of middle- and upper-class marriages described in *The Significant Americans*. The subjects were not "clinical" patients, on whom too many of our stereotypes are based, but "normal" people, and the paper is restricted to a consideration of the effect of adultery upon the marriage itself.

Three types of adulterous relations stand out: (1) adultery that compensates for a defective marriage (as perceived by the participant); (2) adultery that is the result of a discontinuous marriage in point of contact (separations due to military service, career commitments, etc.); and (3) adultery that proceeds when "true Bohemian" men and women do not accept a monogamous commitment. Much of the data obtained ran counter to certain enduring assumptions about adultery, the most important being "the tremendous variations that exist in practice of adultery." How valid, then, are society's stereotypes in this matter?

Although there has been concern about adulterous relationships throughout history, this concern has been more moralistic than empirical, more hortatory than analytic. And even today, despite a pronounced verbal stance at being objective, there is still, even among the more scientific, a clear tendency to

Heterosexual Interaction— Marital and Nonmarital

concentrate on negative aspects and to present them more vividly. At the same time, most analysts tend to underestimate the incidence of adulterous behavior and, perhaps worst of all, to overlook the enormous variations in adulterous experience with respect to its function in the lives of the participants, its relationship to marriage, and its impact on the mental health of the participants. Insofar as these dimensions have been given attention, that attention has been focused overwhelmingly on the narrowly sexual aspects of adultery; the effects on the marriage of the adulterous spouse have been presumed always to be destructive, and the effects on the mental health of all participants have been assumed to be deleterious. Probably the most categorical exception to the foregoing generalization has occurred among the literary artists who have at least sometimes portrayed the adulterous situation in holistic terms.

The chief basis for this paper has been a study of 437 distinguished white Americans between the ages of thirty-five and fifty-five who were studied through an intensive and unstructured depth interview technique. These people constituted a completely nonclinical sample, none having had psychotherapy in any form, or, in the opinion of the interviewers, clearly requiring it at the time of interview. It should be understandable that the use of such a "normal" population would show results quite different from the results taken from studies of adulterous behavior among persons in clinical situations or caught in life crises.[1]

Throughout this study we did not concern ourselves with a *count* of the incidence of adulterous episodes. We were more concerned with context than with number. This was partly by intent and partly a result of the procedure which we chose to follow. We learned early that a mere count of adulterous behavior yields a useless, if not a seriously spurious, statistic because the concept of *adultery* is a moralistic-legalistic-theological one which lumps together heterogeneous and contradictory dimensions of behavior which, when treated together, can lead only to error. In such a category we would have the person who has had "one too many" at the office party, the one who "lives off the land" at every opportunity, the lecher in the literal sense of the word, as well as the one who feels mismated but trapped and finds warmth and comfort where he can, and the one whose marriage is so seriously destructive that he desperately seeks and clings to another meaningful relationship which sustains him. Such an encompassing category contributes nothing but a moralistic label which obscures more discriminating understanding of behavior.

I

Several important distinctions regarding adulterous behavior came to our attention. The first of these, which should have been anticipated from the more general studies of sexual deviation by Kirkendall,[2] Reiss,[3] and others, is to the general effect that there is an important qualitative difference between the sexual act which constitutes virtually the sum total of the interaction and coital behavior which takes place in the course of a more or less continuous, affectionately meaningful, totally companionable relationship. Despite a lifetime of attention to marital triangles in counseling situations, I have been surprised at the relatively high incidence of this latter type of relationship, sometimes lasting a decade or two, in the lives of these relatively self-actualized people. Aside from this latter comment, our study merely validates what other students have pointed out, namely, that this dichotomy is apparently a true one and that the behavioral dimensions of these two types are utterly different.

Since *The Significant Americans* was concerned with the whole man-woman world and only incidentally with the question of nonmarital sex, we were soon alerted to the relationship between adulterous behavior and marriage itself. Our data seemed to us to suggest strongly that there are at least three types of relationships between adulterous behavior and the marriage of one or both of the participants. In Type I the adulterous relationship simply compensates or substitutes for a defective marriage. By a defective marriage we mean that, *for the partner involved*, a judgment has been reached that the marriage is seriously frustrating or at least not fulfilling in some important dimensions, and that the adulterous relationship compensates for whatever is missing, lacking, annoying, or hurtful in the marriage. We learned again the hard lesson, which behavior analysts always say they have learned and which their judgment often betrays they have not learned very well; namely, that reality is subjective to the actor. This is a very old point in behavior science, but, apparently, it has to be learned over and over again. For example, if a man says that his wife is frigid, it is of little practical use to point out to him that by technical definition she may not be so at all. As Cooley says, "The imaginations which people have of one another are the solid facts of human life." Another formulation of the same idea is that even mistaken judgment is real in its consequences. The standardizing principle for this type of adulterous relationship, then, is that the relationship with the spouse has some serious lack but not serious enough to terminate the marriage and that the other person compensates for the lack in a satisfactory manner. In a society which places so much emphasis upon the mere maintenance of an established marriage and exacts for so many people such serious sanctions for its termination, it is small wonder that so many maintain essentially loveless marriages and find their sexual and affectional fulfillments somewhere else. Qualitative analysis of long-term extramarital relationships shows that they are strikingly similar to good marriages in their psychological dimensions. There are strong emotional and sexual bonds, continuity in the relationship, monogamous sentiments, intense sharing of a variety of ideas and activities, and mutual emotional supports.

Type II is fairly well understood and probably constitutes a set of circumstances which people are most likely to "forgive." This is the behavioral configuration in which a married person of either sex experiences a discontinuous marriage in its face-to-face aspects. Discontinuities in our society typically result from long absence for military duty or extended periods of residence away from home in connection with career or profession. It is startling to realize how many millions of Americans live for prolonged periods in foreign countries in connection with their professional and occupational roles. And, of course, there are the periods of travel for recreational purposes—particularly where both husband and wife are employed and, sometimes by intent, extended vacations are taken separately. Under these conditions, we found that substantial numbers of contemporary Americans of the upper middle class consider themselves freed from the bonds of monogamy for the duration of their absence from home, although the expectation in such a case is that the encounter be a relatively brief one and not a sustained, meaningful relationship which may threaten the marriage.

In Type III we find the true Bohemians. These are people who simply do not accept the monogamous commitment with respect to their personal lives, although they still feel committed to and fulfilled in marriage and parenthood.[4] If this sounds like the old double standard, it should quickly be added that we found that *if* there is a double standard in the upper middle class today, it is not so much between men and women as between the more Bohemian men and women and the other men and women.

II

A prevailing preoccupation, again rooted in folklore but also present among professionals with a primarily clinical experience, is with the effects of adulterous behavior on the spousal relationship. Here again, some distinctions must be made at the outset. It matters enormously (a) in the first place, whether the adultery is carried on furtively or is known to the spouse; (b) whether the married partners agree to the propriety or expediency of such behavior; (c) whether one or both participates; and (d) whether the condonement is genuine and based on principle or is simply the result of an ultimatum by one of the two parties. Despite all the possible permutations, a few generalizations from our data appear to be defensible. These are mostly counter-generalizations in the sense that they call into question some almost universally assumed propositions about the effects of adulterous behavior on marriage. The first of these is that the assumption that such behavior is necessarily furtive does not square with the facts. A considerable number of spouses have "levelled" with their mates, who cooperate in maintaining a public pretense of monogamous marriage. We have found a number of truly empathic spouses of this sort, and others, as would be expected, who merely reluctantly go along and say that they are surprised at how good their marital relations continue to be, even though there is involvement with another person. This leads to a second generalization counter to the notion that such triangles are *necessarily* destructive of the marriage. Not so. Both for cases in which the spouse knew about the affair and where the affair was secret, we can document with a long list instances in which the spousal relationship remains at least as good qualitatively as within the average pair without adultery. It is a common mistake, when a couple with a poor sex life is seen clinically, to assume that if one or the other had not been adulterous the sex relationship would have been better. Yet, it is widely known among professionals that abysmally poor sexual adjustment can exist and endure in the completely monogamous marriage. Our study, incidentally, richly documents the latter point.

A different comparison involves the sexual relationships between the married partners before the adultery and afterward. Here again, we found all three theoretical possibilities—sometimes the marital sexual relationship deteriorated, sometimes it improved, and sometimes it remained unchanged. Differences among these three categories seemed not great enough to warrant any comparisons other than making the important point that adultery does not *necessarily* result in deteriorated spousal relations. We found the same for the more total aspects of the spousal relationship—all three possible outcomes occur in fact and none is rare.

A related concern has to do with the effect of adulterous behavior upon the mental health and functioning of either or both of the participants, as well as upon the spouse concerned. Here again, we have inherited a morbid legacy which vigorously asserts that because of the guilt and deception involved for the participants and the feelings of humiliation and rejection experienced by the spouse, the net effect is necessarily negative to mental health. The evidence presented is invariably from clinical cases and here is probably the source of the stereotype. People who have the same experiences as the clinical cases but who don't come to "bad ends" aren't included in the sample under surveillance. Our non-clinical sample would justify almost the opposite conclusion, although not without exception by any means. Overwhelmingly, these people expressed no *guilt* with respect to what they were doing, although sometimes they acknowledged *regret* over practical consequences. The "offended" spouses were often not offended at all; sometimes they were even relieved to be "out from under" a relationship which was personally frustrating and, because of the adultery, they were able to maintain the marriage for other reasons. We were struck by the sizeable group of people who were involved in adulterous relationships of many years standing, who were enriched and fulfilled through the relationship in much the same way that intrinsically married people are, whose health, efficiency, and creativity remain excellent—many of these pairings are in effect *de facto* marriages.

The dynamics of adulterous relationships also break with conventional stereotypes about them which generally run to assertions that such relationships typically follow a cycle which begins in infatuation, has a relatively short decline, ends in disillusionment, a new partner is found, and the cycle is repeated. We found examples fitting this model, to be sure, but typically the cases were otherwise. The most conspicuous contrast is, of course, the brief, emotionally uninvolved "sexcapade," commonly known as the "pickup." There is no cycle; partners are typically relative strangers, even names may not be known; neither expects any continuity or wants it. And even in the prolonged adulterous relationships, there is often no more a "cycle" than there is to marriage—the relationship often is monogamous, continuous "until death . . ." Where there is a cycle in any real sense, it tends to be like the cycle in a goodly number of marriages. In both cases relationships move from vitality and a strong erotic accent to a more matter-of-fact, comfortable kind of interaction. Surprisingly enough, many "affairs" have settled into a kind of apathy which makes one wonder why they go on, since there are no institutional obligations involved. But perhaps sentiment and a quiescent kind of attachment may be stronger bonds than external social sanctions.

It is a moot question to what extent the long standing adulterous relationships are vulnerable because one or the other may find a new partner. We certainly would be disinclined to make any sweeping generalizations other than to point out that such a conclusion from our data would indeed be riskful. When speaking about quality rather than the mere fact of continuity, all relationships, marital or otherwise, are vulnerable. To assert that either is more susceptible than the other is to go beyond the data.

III

Perhaps the most important theoretical overall generalization which our study supports is the great heterogeneity masked in the monolithic word "adultery." A companion generalization points up the strong parallels between the structure, the functions, the fulfillments and the frustrations of enduring adulterous relationships on the one hand and married relationships on the other. While there are differences, to be sure—if nothing else the grudging public tolerance of the former—still the basis for attraction, the satisfactions derived, the rewards and punishments involved are remarkably parallel.

Yet adulterous relationships in this culture at this time must operate within a network of obvious threat. Even if there is tolerance as far as spouses and friends are concerned, such relationships are still illegal and, although the law is rarely invoked, no one knows when some freak of fate may force an exposure which no one intended. Then there is the risk of pregnancy which, even with present contraceptive know-how, is not completely eliminated. Persons who are quite tolerant of sexual freedom may not be tolerant with respect to reproduction outside the limits of marriage. While we found much less evidence of the double standard than we expected, one aspect showed up importantly in the adulterous relationship, namely, the feelings of "second-class" status on the part of the "other woman." Social sanctions are still more austere where women are concerned and, of course, women bear the brunt of the burden of illicit pregnancy. It is not wholly clear from our data whether this sensitivity on the part of women derives from the differential pregnancy risk and more austere social sanctions or whether .it runs more deeply into female psychology, but unless she has satisfactory extrinsic gratifications in her legal and open status, it seems difficult for her to be totally satisfied by the intrinsic aspects of her clandestine relationship.

Because of the absence of institutional buttressing of the long-term adulterous relationship, it is more easily terminated, on the average, than is marriage. This may be comforting to the moralist, but the person with a concern for mental health should take little comfort from it. Other aspects of our study have documented the enormously high incidence of psychologically destructive relationships in enduring marriages and the intrusion of utilitarian motives in the establishment and perpetuation of conspicuously unfulfilling relationships in which people many times feel trapped and helpless to escape. So, while the adulterous relationships are, on the average, less enduring than the marriages, this is counter-balanced by the fact that the long-term ones are, on the average, more psychologically fulfilling than marriage. This is not because there is any strange alchemy involved in adulterous mating for any but a few romantics. Rather, it results from the fact that spousal relationships are maintained in homage to monolithic expectations, because society values mere *endurance* of marriages, even if they are psychologically unsatisfying, frustrating, and destructive. Adulterous relationships carry no such burden of expectation; when they endure, they do so for reasons intrinsic to the pair.

References

CUBER, JOHN F. and HARROFF, PEGGY B. *The Significant Americans: A Study of Sexual Behavior among the Affluent.* New York: Appleton-Century-Crofts, Inc., 1965, (especially Chapter 8, "Other Involvements").

KIRKENDALL, LESTER A. *Premarital Intercourse and Interpersonal Relationships.* New York: The Julian Press, 1961.

REISS, IRA L. *Premarital Standards in America.* Glencoe, Ill.: The Free Press, 1960.

WILSON, J. B., with MEYERS, EVERETT. *Wife Swapping: A Complete Eight-year Survey of Morals in North America.* New York: Counterpoint, Inc., 1965.

JOIE DE VIVRE

Simone de Beauvoir

As Simone de Beauvoir points out in her recent book *The Coming of Age,* the treatment accorded aging citizens by Western society is depressing. Unwilling to acknowledge the existence of sex among the aged, we either idealize the serenity we imagine they have achieved in their freedom from carnal desire or we denigrate old-age sexuality in such expressions as "dirty old man."

In the following selection, Mme de Beauvoir describes the vicissitudes which the old (and aging women especially) endure in coming to terms with their diminishing sexual powers. At the same time, however, she entitles the article "zest for life" and provides accounts of several literary and political figures who maintained much of their youthful libido into very old age. To the author, "sexuality, vitality, and activity are indissolubly linked" and together keep human beings involved in life instead of shelved away out of sight.

This reading offers some discerning comments about sexuality in the aged, a subject rarely treated in the professional literature, and also offers the young a glimpse into their future. She observes gently that to find sex of "positive value" to the total personailty in youth may well be to augur satisfaction and zest in the older years as well.

On Sexuality and Old Age

Those moralists who vindicate old age claim that it sets the individual free from his body. The purification of which the moralists speak consists for them essentially in the extinction of sexual desires: they are happy to think that the elderly man escapes from this slavery and thereby achieves serenity. In his well-known poem, "John Anderson My Jo," Robert Burns described the ideal old couple in whom carnal passion has died quite away. The pair

Heterosexual Interaction— Marital and Nonmarital

Reprinted from the January, 1972 issue of *Harper's Magazine* by permission of the author.

has climbed the hill of life side by side; once they tasted blissful hours; now with trembling steps but still hand in hand they must go together along the road that leads to the end of the journey. This stereotype is deeply imprinted upon the hearts of young and middle-aged people because they met it countless times in the books of their childhood and because their respect for their grandparents persuades them of its truth. The idea of sexual relations or violent scenes between elderly people is deeply shocking.

Yet there also exists an entirely different tradition. The expression, "dirty old man," is a commonplace of popular speech. Through literature and even more through painting, the story of Susanna and the Elders has taken on the value of a myth. The comic theater has endlessly repeated the theme of the ancient lover. As we shall see, this satirical tradition is closer to the truth than the edifying speeches of idealists who are concerned with showing old age as it ought to be.

In childhood, sexuality is polymorphous: it is not centered upon the genital organs. "Only at the end of a complex and hazardous evolution does the sexual drive assume a preeminently genital aspect; at this point it takes on the apparent fixity and finality of an instinct."[1] From this we may at once draw the conclusion that a person whose genital functions have diminished or become nonexistent is not therefore sexless: he is a sexed being—even eunuchs and impotent men remain sexed—and one who must work out his sexuality in spite of a given mutilation.

An inquiry into the sexuality of the aged amounts to asking what happens to a man's relationship with himself, with others, and with the outside world when the preeminence of the genital aspect of the sexual pattern has vanished. Obviously it would be absurd to imagine that there is a simple return to infantile sexuality. Never, on any plane, does the aged person lapse into "a second childhood," since childhood is by definition a forward, upward movement. And then again, infantile sexuality is in search of itself, whereas the aged man retains the memory of what it was in his maturity. Lastly, there is a radical difference between the social factors affecting the two ages.

The enjoyment the individual derives from his sexual activities is rich and manifold to a very high degree. It is understandable that a man or woman should be bitterly unwilling to give it up, whether the chief aim is pleasure, or the transfiguration of the world by desire, or the realization of a certain image of oneself, or all this at the same time. Those moralists who condemn old age to chastity say that one cannot long for pleasures one no longer desires. This is a very short-sighted view of the matter. It is true that normally desire does not arise as desire in itself: it is desire for a particular pleasure or a particular body. But when it no longer rises spontaneously, reflection may very well regret its disappearance. The old person retains his longing for experiences that can never be replaced and is still attached to the erotic world he built up in his youth or maturity. Desire will enable him to renew its fading colors. And again it is by means of desire that he will have an awareness of his own integrity. We wish for eternal youth, and this youth implies the survival of the libido.

Its presence is found only among those who have looked upon their sexuality as something of positive value. Those who, because of complexes rooted in their childhood, took part in sexual activities only with aversion eagerly seize upon the excuse of age to withdraw. I knew an old woman who got her doctor to supply her with certificates so that she could avoid her disagreeable "conjugal duties": as she grew older, the number of her years provided her with a more convenient alibi. A man, if he is half impotent, or indifferent, or if the sexual act worries him badly, will be relieved when age allows refuge in a continence that will seem normal for that time onward.

People who have had a happy sexual life may have reasons for not wishing to prolong it. One of these is their narcissistic relationship with themselves. Disgust at one's own body takes various forms among men and women; but in either, age may provoke it, and if this happens they will refuse to make their body exist for another. Yet there exists a reciprocal influence between the image of oneself and one's sexual activity: the beloved individual feels that he is worthy of love and gives himself to it unreservedly; but very often he is loved only if he makes a conscious effort to be attractive, and an unfavorable image of himself stands in the way of his doing this. In this event a vicious circle is created, preventing sexual relations.

Another obstacle is the pressure of public opinion. The elderly person usually conforms to the conventional ideal. He is afraid of scandal or quite simply of ridicule, and inwardly accepts the watchwords of propriety and continence imposed by the community. He is ashamed of his own desires, and he denies having them; he refuses to be a lecherous old man in his own eyes, or a shameless old woman. He fights against his sexual drives to the point of thrusting them back into his unconscious mind.

As we might on the face of it suppose, seeing that there is so great a difference between them in their biological destiny and their social status, the case of men is quite unlike that of women. Biologically men are at the greater disadvantage; socially, it is the women who are worse off, because of their condition as erotic objects. In neither case is their behavior thoroughly understood. A certain number of inquiries into it have been carried out, and these have provided the basis for something in the way of statistics. The replies obtained are always of dubious value, and in this field the notion of an average has little meaning.

The Fear of Ridicule

As far as men are concerned, the statistics, as it so often happens, merely confirm what everybody knows —sexual intercourse diminishes in frequency with age. This fact is connected with the degeneration of the sexual organs, a degeneration that brings about a weakening of the libido. But the physiological is not the only factor that comes into play. There are considerable differences between the behavior patterns of individuals, some being impotent at sixty and others very sexually active at over eighty. We must try to see how these differences are to be explained.

The first factor, and one of perfectly obvious importance, is the subjects' marital status. Sexual intercourse is much more frequent among married men than among bachelors or widowers. Married life encourages erotic stimulus; habit and "togetherness" favor its appeasement. The "psychological barriers" are far easier to overcome. The wall of private life protects the elderly husband from public opinion, which in any case looks more favorably upon legitimate love than upon unlawful connections. He feels that his image is less endangered. The word image in this context must be thoroughly understood. Whereas the woman object identifies herself with the total image of her body from childhood on, the little boy sees his penis as an alter ego; it is in his penis that his whole life as a man finds its image, and it is here that he feels himself in peril. The narcissistic trauma that he dreads is the failure of his sexual organ—the impossibility of reaching an erection, or maintaining it, and of satisfying his partner. This fear is less haunting in married life. The subject is more or less free to choose the moment for making love. A failure is easily passed over in silence. His familiarity with his partner makes him dread her opinion less. Since he is less anxious, the married man is less inhibited than another. That is why many aged couples continue sexual activities.

The loss of his wife will often cause a trauma that shuts a man off from all sexual activities, either for a long or short period or forever. Widowers and elderly bachelors obviously have much more difficulty in finding an outlet for their libido than married men. Most have lost their charm; if they try to have an affair, their attempts come to nothing. All that remains is venal love; many men have shrunk from it all their lives, and it would seem to them a kind of giving-in, an acquiescence in the decline of age. Yet some do turn to it: they either go with prostitutes or they have a liaison with a woman they help financially. Their choice, continence or activity, depends on the balance between the urgency of their drive and the strength of their resistance.

Many find an answer in masturbation. A quarter of the subjects questioned by *Sexology* magazine said they had indulged in it either for many years or since the age of sixty: the latter were therefore brought back to it by aging. Statistical cross-checks show that even among married men, many turn to this practice. No doubt many elderly men prefer their fantasies to their wife's age-worn body. Or it may happen that either because deep-rooted complexes or awareness of age turn her against physical love, the companion refuses. Masturbation is then the most convenient outlet.

The subject's sexual activities are also influenced by his social condition. They go on far longer among manual workers, among men with a low standard of living than among those who are well to do. Workers and peasants have more straightforward desires, less dominated by erotic myths, than the middle classes; their wives' bodies wear out early, but they do not stop making love to them. When a working man's wife is old, she seems to him less spoiled than would be the case with a richer husband. Then again he has less idea of himself than the white-collar worker. And he does not take so much notice of public opinion, which has less and less force as one goes down the social scale. Old men and women who live almost entirely outside convention—tramps of both sexes, and inmates of institutions—lie together without any shame, even in front of others.

Finally, the happier and richer sexual life has been, the longer it goes on. If the subject has valued it because of the narcissistic satisfaction it gives him, he will break it off as soon as he can no longer see a flattering reflection of himself in his partner's eyes. If he has intended to assert his virility, his skill, or the power of his charm, or if he has meant to triumph over rivals, then he may sometimes be glad of the excuse of age to relax. But if his sexual activities have been spontaneous and happy, he will be strongly inclined to carry them on as long as his strength lasts.

Yet the elderly man does not take so vehement a pleasure in intercourse as a youth does, and this is because the two stages of ejaculation are reduced to one; he no longer has that piercing sensation of imminence which marks the passage from the first to the second, nor yet the triumphant feeling of a jet, an explosion—this is one of the myths that gives the male sexual act its value. Even when the aged man is still capable of normal sexual activity, he often seeks indirect forms of satisfaction; even more so if he is impotent. He takes pleasure in erotic literature, licentious works of art, dirty stories, the company of young women, and furtive contacts; he indulges in fetishism, sadomasochism, various forms of perversion, and, particularly after the age of eighty, in voyeurism. These deviations are readily comprehensible. The fact is, Freud has established that there is no such thing as a "normal" sexuality: it is always "perverted" insofar as it does not break away from its origins, which required it to look for satisfaction not in any specific activity but in the "increase of pleasure" attached to functions dependent upon other drives. Infantile sexuality is polymorphically perverse. The sexual act is considered "normal" when the partial activities are merely preparatory to the genital act. But the subject has only to attach too much importance to these preliminary pleasures to slip into perversion. Normally, seeing and caressing one's partner plays an important part in sexual intercourse. It is accompanied by fantasy; sadomasochistic elements appear; and often fetishism, clothes, and ornaments evoking the presence of the body. When genital pleasure is weak or nonexistent, all these elements rise to the first place. And frequently the elderly man prizes them very highly because they are manifestations of that erotic world that is still of the greatest value to him. He continues to live in a certain climate, his body still existing in a world filled with other bodies. Here again it is often timidity, shame, or difficulties from the outside that prevent him from indulging in what are called his vices.

We have a fair amount of evidence about elderly men's sexual life. It depends on their past and also upon their attitude toward their old age as a whole and toward their image in particular. Chateaubriand so loathed his aged face that he refused to sit for his portrait. In the first part of *Amour et vieillesse—chants de tristesse*, which he wrote when he was sixty-one, he rejects the amorous advances of a young woman: "If you tell me you love me as a father, you will fill me with horror; if you claim to love me as a lover, I shall not believe you. I shall see a happy rival in every young man. Your deference will make me feel my age, your caresses will give me over to the most furious jealousy. . . . Old age makes a man as ugly as can be wished. If he is unhappy, it is even worse . . ." He was cruelly sensitive to the "insult of the years" and his refusal was dictated by a kind of inverted narcissism.

Old men's loves are not always doomed to failure: far from it. Many of them have a sexual life that goes on very late. The Duc de Bouillon was sixty-six when his son Turenne was born. The famous Duc de Richelieu's father married for the third time in 1702, at the age of seventy. When his son was sixty-two and governor of Guienne, he led a life of debauchery. In his old age he seduced a great many young women. At seventy-eight, bewigged, made-up, and very thin, he was said to look like a tortoise thrusting its head out of its shell; this did not prevent him from having affairs with the actresses of the *Comédie française*. He had an acknowledged mistress, and he spent his evenings with whores; sometimes he used to bring them home—he liked listening to their confidences. He married when he was eighty-four and had recourse to aphrodisiacs: he made his wife pregnant. Furthermore, he deceived her too. He continued his sexual activities right up until his death, at the age of ninety-two.

Tolstoy is a well-known example of sexual vitality. Toward the end of his life he preached total continence both for men and for women. Nevertheless, when he was sixty-nine or seventy he would come back from a very long ride and make love to his wife. All the next day he would walk about the house looking pleased with himself.

Sexuality was of great importance in Victor Hugo's youth and during his middle years. The image of old age that he had always set up for himself allowed him to accept his sexual desires until he was very old: no doubt he thought of Boaz when a young woman offered herself to him. In his view, age was by no means a blemish, but rather an honor; it brought one nearer to God and it was in harmony with everything that is sublime, with beauty and innocence. The aged Hugo certainly suffered from no feeling of inferiority whatsoever. In his opinion he was answerable to no one but himself: at no time in his life did he ever yield to public opinion—if he had desires, he satisfied them.

There are many other examples to show that an elderly man may be importuned by the most urgent sexual desires. H. G. Wells was sixty when he fell in love with Dolores after they had corresponded; he fell passionately in love and found himself possessed of unsuspected sexual powers. "For the first time in my life it was revealed to me that I was an astonishing fellow, an extraordinary chap, an outstanding virtuoso. Casanova certainly could never have held a candle to me," he wrote with a smile. The affair turned sour; there were ugly scenes; in the end he could no longer bear Dolores and when he was sixty-six he broke with her. Having done so he met the girl he called Brylhil; this was the most violent passion of his life, a mutual passion that lasted many years.

Among our contemporaries there are a very great many examples of elderly men married or attached to young women: Charlie Chaplin, Picasso, Casals, Henry Miller. These examples confirm the notion that if it has been rich, sexual life goes on for a long time. But it may also happen that a man who has been indifferent to women for most of his life discovers the delights of sex in his later years. Trotsky had looked upon himself as old since the age of fifty-five, but at fifty-eight he had an odd outburst of eroticism. Bernard Berenson, who died at ninety-four, wrote, "I only really became aware of sex and of women's physical, animal life at the period that might be called my old age."

Many elderly men look for younger partners. Those subjects for whom sex continues to play an important part are gifted with excellent health and lead an active life. Impotence does not exclude desire; desire is most often satisfied through deviations in which the fantasies of middle age are accentuated.

L'Après-midi d'un Faune

We have one most remarkable piece of evidence concerning an old man's relationship with his body, his image, and his sex: this is Paul Léautaud's *Journal*.[2] He provides us with a living synthesis of the various points of view we have considered in this study.

Léautaud always looked at himself with a certain approval. It was from the outside that he learned he was aging, and it made him very angry. In 1923, when he was fifty-three, a railway official referred to him as "a little old gentleman." Furious, Léautaud wrote in his *Journal*, "Little old man! Old gentleman? What the devil—am I as blind as all that? I cannot see that I am either a little or an old gentleman. I see myself as a fifty-year-old, certainly, but an exceedingly well preserved fifty-year-old. I am slim and I move easily. Just let them show me an *old gentleman* in such good shape!" At fifty-nine he looked at himself with a critical eye: "Mentally and physically I am a man of forty. What a pity my face does not match! Above all my lack of teeth! I really am remarkable for my age: slim, supple, quick, active. It is my lack of teeth that spoils everything; I shall never dare to make love to a woman again."

In him we see with remarkable clarity how impossible it is for an old man to realize his age. On his birthday he wrote: "Today I begin my sixty-fourth year. In no way do I feel an old man." The old man is Another, and this Other belongs to a certain category that is objectively defined; in his inner experience Léautaud found no such person. There were moments, however, when his age weighed upon him. On April 12, 1936, he wrote, "I do not feel happy about my health nor about my state of mind; and then there is the sorrow of aging, too. Aging above all!" But at sixty-nine he wrote, "During my seventieth year I am still as lively, active, nimble and alert as a man can be."

Léautaud had every reason to be pleased with himself: he looked after his house and cared for his animals; he did all the shopping on foot, carrying heavy baskets of provisions; wrote his *Journal*; and he did not know what it was to be tired. "It is only my sight that is failing. I am exactly as I was at twenty. My memory is as good as ever and my mind as quick and sharp."

This made him all the more irritable when other people's reactions brought the truth home to him. He was seventy when a young woman lost her balance as an underground train started off with a jerk; she cried out, "I'm so sorry, Grandpa, I nearly fell on you." He wrote angrily, "Damn it all! My age must show clearly in my face. How impossible it is to see oneself as one really is!"

The paradox lies in the fact that he did not really dislike being old. He was one of those exceptional cases I have mentioned, where old age coincides with childhood fantasy: he had always been interested in old people. On March 7, 1942, when he was seventy-two, he wrote, "A kind of vanity comes over you when you reach old age—you take a pride in remaining healthy, slim, supple and alert, with an unaltered complexion, your joints in good order, no illness and no diminution in your physical and mental powers."

But his vanity demanded that his age be invisible to others: he liked to imagine that he had stayed young in spite of the burden of his years.

He only gave way to discouragement at the very end of his life, when his health failed. On February 25, 1945, he wrote, "I am very low indeed. My eyesight. The horrible marks of age I see on my face. My *Journal* behindhand. The mediocrity of my life, I have lost my energy and all my illusions. Pleasure, even five minutes of pleasure, is over for me." He was then seventy-five, and his sexual life had come to an end. But except in his very last years one of the reasons for his pride was that he still felt desire and was still capable of satisfying it. We can follow his sexual evolution in his *Journal*.

Heterosexual Interaction— Marital and Nonmarital

Léautaud only became fully aware of women when he was approaching his fiftieth year. At thirty-five he wrote, "I am beginning to regret that my temperament allows me to enjoy women so little." He lacked the "sacred fire." "I always think too much of other things—of myself, for example." He was afraid of impotence and his lovemaking was over very quickly: "I give women no pleasure since I have finished in five minutes and can never start again. . . . Shamelessness is all I really like in love. .. . There are some things not every woman can be asked to do." He had a lasting affair with a woman called Bl——. He says he loved her very much, but he also says that living with her was hell. When he was about forty, although he was still rather indifferent, since he could give his partner no pleasure, he delighted in looking at pictures of naked women. Yet a few years later he speaks sadly of the "rare love-scenes in my life which I really enjoyed." He reproaches himself for being "timid, awkward, brusque, oversensitive, always hesitant, never able to take advantage of even the best opportunities" with women. All this changed when at fifty he met "a really passionate woman, wonderfully equipped for pleasure and exactly to my taste in these matters," and he showed himself to be "almost brilliant," although up until then he had thought that he was not very good—as he had only known women who did not suit him. From this time on, sex became an obsession to him: on December 1, 1923, he wrote, "Perhaps Madame [one of the names he gave to his mistress] is right: my perpetual desire to make love may be somewhat pathological. . . . I put it down to a lifetime's moderation—it lasted until I was over forty—and also to my intense feeling for her, which makes me want to make love to her when I see so much as a square inch of her body. . . . I think it is also because I have been deprived of so many things, such as that female nakedness for which I have acquired such a liking. I am quite amazed when I think of what has happened to me in all this. . . . Never have I caressed any other woman as I caress Madame." In the summer they parted, and abstinence lay heavy upon him: he masturbated, thinking of her. "Of course I am delighted to be such an ardent lover at my age, but God knows it can be troublesome."

Madame was a little older than he: all his life he had loved only mature women. A twenty-three-year-old virgin threw herself at his head, and he agreed to have an affair with her; but it did not give him the least pleasure and he broke immediately. Except for this one fling he was faithful to Madame for years. He liked watching himself and her in a mirror during their lovemaking. From 1927—age fifty-seven—on, he was forced to take care not to make love too often; he found consolation in bawdy talk with the Panther (another name he gave to his mistress). He did not get on well with her; "we are attached to each other only by our senses—by vice—and what remains is so utterly tenuous!" But in 1938 he did recall with great satisfaction the "seventeen years of pleasure between two creatures the one as passionate and daring as the other in amorous words and deeds." When he was fifty-nine his affair with the Scourge, as he now called her, was still going on, though she was already sixty-four. He was shocked by couples where the woman was much younger than the man. "I myself at fifty-nine would never dare to make any sort of advance to a woman of thirty."

He was still very much attracted to the Scourge, and he took great pleasure in his "sessions" with her. Yet he did complain, "What a feeble ejaculation when I make love: little better than water!" Later he wrote, "I am certainly better when I do not make love at all. Not that it comes hard—far from it—but it is always a great effort, and I do not get over it as quickly as I did a few years ago. . . . What I miss most is female nakedness, licentious attitudes, and playing amorous games."

"Until I was sixty-six or sixty-seven I could make love two or three times a week." Now he complained that his brain was tired for three or four days after making love, but he still went on, and he corresponded with three of his former mistresses.

When he was seventy Léautaud wrote, "I miss women and love terribly. He remembered how he used to make passionate love to the Scourge from the age of forty-seven to sixty-three, and then for two years with CN [another mistress].

"It was only three years ago that I noticed I was slowing down. I can still make love, and indeed I quite often feel sad at being deprived of it; though at the same time I tell myself that it is certainly much better for me to abstain."

At seventy-two he was still planning idylls that never came to anything, and he had erotic dreams that gave him an erection. "At night I still feel ready for anything." But that same year he observed that his sexual powers were declining. "It is no use giving yourself over to lovemaking when the physical side is dead or nearly so. Even the pleasure of seeing and fondling is soon over, and there is not the least eagerness to begin again. For a real appreciation of all these things, there must be the heat of physical passion." It is clear that Léautaud's greatest pleasure was visual. He retained it longer than any other form of sensual enjoyment, and after the age of forty he prized it very highly indeed. When he lost it he considered that his sexual life was over. It is also clear how a man's image of himself is bound up with sexual activity. He was "in the depths of sorrow" when he could no longer experience these pleasures. Still, his narcissism did survive his sexual decline at least for some time.

The Feminine Disadvantage

Biologically women's sexuality is less affected by age than men's. Brantôme
bears this out in the chapter of his *Vies des dames galantes* that he dedicates
to "certain old ladies who take as much pleasure in love as the young ones."
Whereas a man of a certain age is no longer capable of erection, a woman
"at no matter what age is endowed with as it were a furnace . . . all fire and
fuel within." Popular tradition bears witness to this contrast. In one of the
songs in the Merry Muses of Caledonia an old woman laments her elderly
husband's impotence. She longs for "the wild embraces of their younger
days" that are now no more than a ghostly memory, since he no longer
thinks of doing anything in bed except sleeping, while she is eaten up with
desire. Today scientific research confirms the validity of this evidence.
According to Kinsey, throughout their lives women are sexually more stable
than men; when they are sixty their potential for pleasure and desire is the
same as it was at thirty. According to Masters and Johnson, the strength of
the sexual reaction diminishes with age; yet a woman can still reach orgasm,
above all if she is regularly and properly stimulated. Those who do not often
have physical relations sometimes find coition painful, either during the act
or after, and sometimes suffer from dyspareunia or dysuria; it is not known
whether these troubles are physical or psychological in origin. I may add
that a woman can take great pleasure in making love even though she may
not reach orgasm. The "preliminary pleasures" count even more perhaps for
her than they do for a man. She is usually less sensitive to the appearance of
her partner and therefore less worried by his growing old. Even though her
part in lovemaking is not as passive as people sometimes make out, she has
no fear of a particular failure. There is nothing to prevent her from going on
with her sexual activities until the end of her life.

Still, all research shows that women have a less active sexual life than
men. Kinsey says that at fifty, 97 per cent of men are still sexually active
compared with 93 per cent of women. At sixty it is 94 per cent of men and
only 80 per cent of women. This comes from the fact that socially men,
whatever their age, are subjects, and women are objects, relative beings.
When she marries, a woman's future is determined by her husband's; he is
usually about four years older than she, and his desire progressively lessens.
Or if it does continue to exist, he takes to younger women. An old woman,
on the other hand, finds it extremely difficult to have extramarital relations.
She is even less attractive to men than old men are to women. And in her
case gerontophilia does not exist. A young man may desire a woman old

enough to be his mother but not his grandmother. A woman of seventy is no longer regarded by anyone as an erotic object. Venal love is very difficult for her to find. It would be most exceptional for an old woman to have both the means and the opportunity of getting herself a partner; and then again sham and fear of what people might say would generally prevent her from doing so. This frustration is painful to many old women, for they are still tormented by desire. They usually find their relief in masturbation; a gynecologist told me of the case of one woman of seventy who begged him to cure her of this practice—she was indulging in it night and day.

When Andrée Martinerie was conducting an inquiry for *Elle* magazine (March 1969) she gathered some interesting confidences from elderly women. Madame F., a rich middle-class sixty-eight-year-old, a militant Catholic, mother of five and grandmother of ten, told her, "I was already sixty-four. . . . Now just listen: four months after my husband's death I went down into the street just like someone who is going to commit suicide. I had made up my mind to give myself to the very first man who would have me. Nobody wanted me. So I went home again." When she was asked whether she had thought of remarrying, she answered, "That is all I ever do think of. If I dared I would put an advertisement in *Le Chasseur français*. . . . I would rather have a decrepit invalid of a man than no man at all!" Talking of desire, Madame R., sixty years old and living with her sick husband, said, "It is quite true that you don't get over it." She sometimes felt like beating her head against the wall. A woman reader of this inquiry wrote to the magazine, "I must tell you that a woman remains a woman for a very long time in spite of growing older. I know what I am talking about, because I am seventy-one. I was a widow at sixty; my husband died suddenly and it took me at least two years to realize fully what had happened. Then I started to answer advertisements in the matrimonial column. I admit that I did miss having a man—or rather I should say I do miss it: this aimless existence is terrifying, without affection or any outlet for one's own feeling. I even began wondering whether I was quite normal. Your inquiry was a great relief. . . ." This correspondent speaks modestly of "affection," an "outlet for one's own feelings." But the context shows that her frustration had a sexual dimension. The reaction of a young woman who wrote to *Elle* is typical: "In our group of young people we laughed heartily about the passionate widow (the member of the Action Catholique) who cannot 'get over it.' I wish you would now hold an inquiry on love as it appears to the fourth age of women, in other words those between eighty and a hundred and twenty." Young people are very shocked if the old, especially old women, are still sexually active.

A woman, then, continues in her state as erotic object right up to the end. Chastity is not imposed upon her by a physiological destiny but by her position as a relative being. Nevertheless it may happen that women condemn themselves to chastity because of the "psychological barriers" that I have mentioned, which are even more inhibiting for them than for men. A woman is usually more narcissistic in love than a man; her narcissism is directed at her body as a whole. She has a delightful awareness of her body as something desirable, and this awareness comes to her through her partner's caresses and his gaze. If he goes on desiring her she easily puts up with her body's aging. But at the first sign of coldness she feels her ugliness in all its horror; she is disgusted with her image and cannot bear to expose her poor person to others. This lack of assurance strengthens her fear of other people's opinions: she knows how censorious they are toward old women who do not play their proper role of serene and passion-free grandmothers.

Even if her husband wants to make love with her again later, a deeply rooted feeling of shame may make her refuse him. Women make less use of diversion than men. Those who enjoyed a very active and uninhibited sexual life before do sometimes compensate for their enforced abstinence by extreme freedom in conversation and the use of obscene words. They become something very like bawds, or at least they spy upon the sexual life of their young women friends with a most unhealthy curiosity, and do all they can to make them confide their secrets. But generally speaking their language is as repressed as their lovemaking. Elderly women like to appear as restrained in their conversation as they are in their way of life. Their sexuality now shows only in their dress, their jewelry and ornaments, and in the pleasure they take in male society. They like to flirt discreetly with men younger than themselves and they are touched by attentions that show they are still women in men's eyes.

However, it is clear from pathology that in women, too, the sexual drive is repressed but not extinguished. Psychiatrists have observed that in asylums female patients' eroticism often increases with age. Senile dementia brings with it a state of erotic delirium arising from lack of cerebral control. Repressions are also discarded in some other forms of psychosis. Dr. Georges Mahé recorded twenty cases of extreme eroticism out of 110 sixty-year-old female patients in an institution; the symptoms included public masturbation, make-believe coition, obscene talk, and exhibitionism. Unfortunately he gives no idea of the meaning of these displays: he puts them into no context and we do not know *who* the patients were who indulged in these practices.

Many of the inmates suffer from genital hallucinations such as rape and physical contact. Women of over seventy-one are convinced that they are pregnant. Madame C., seventy and a grandmother, sings barrack-room songs and walks about the hospital half-naked, looking for a man. Eroticism is the most important factor in many delirious states; it also triggers off some cases of melancholia. E. Gehu speaks of an eighty-three-year-old grandmother who was looked after in a convent. She was an exhibitionist, showing both homosexual and heterosexual tendencies. She fell upon the younger nuns who brought her meals; during these crises she was perfectly lucid. Later she became mentally confused. She ended up by regaining her mental health and behaving normally once more. Here again, we should like a more exact, detailed account of her case. All the observations that I have just quoted are most inadequate; but at least they do show that old women are no more "purified of their bodies" than old men.

Neither history nor literature has left us any worthwhile evidence on the sexuality of old women. It is an even more strictly forbidden subject than the sexuality of old men.

There are many cases of the libido disappearing entirely in old people. Ought they to rejoice in it, as the moralists say? Nothing is less certain. It is a mutilation that brings other mutilations with it: sexuality, vitality, and activity are indissolubly linked. When desire is completely dead, emotional response itself may grow loose at its edge. At sixty-three Rétif de La Bretonne wrote, "My heart died at the same time as my senses, and if sometimes a tender impulse stirs me, it is as erroneous as that of a savage or a eunuch: it leaves me with a profound feeling of sorrow." It seemed to Bernard Shaw that when he lost interest in women he lost interest in living. "I am aging very quickly. I have lost all interest in women, and the interest they have in me is greater than ever and it bores me. The time has probably come for me to die."

Even Schopenhauer admitted, "It could be said that once the sexual urge is over life's true centre is burnt out, leaving a mere shell." Or again, "life is like a play acted at first by live actors and then finished by automata wearing the same costumes." Yet at the same time he says that the sexual instinct produces a "benign dementia." The only choice left to men is that between madness and sclerosis. In fact what he calls "dementia" is the spring of life itself. When it is broken or destroyed a man is no longer truly alive.

The link that exists between sexuality and creativity is striking: it is obvious in Hugo and Picasso and in many others. In order to create there must be some degree of aggression—"a certain readiness," says Flaubert—and this aggressivity has its biological source in the libido. It is also necessary to feel united with the world by an emotional warmth; this disappears at the same time as carnal desire, as Gide understood very clearly when on April 10, 1942, he wrote, "There was a time when I was cruelly tormented, indeed obsessed by desire, and I prayed, 'Oh let the moment come when my subjugated flesh will allow me to give myself entirely to . . .' But to what? To art? To pure thought? To God? How ignorant I was! How mad! It was the same as believing that the flame would burn brighter in a lamp with no oil left. If it were abstract, my thought would go out; even today it is my carnal self that feeds the flame, and now I pray that I may retain carnal desire until I die."

It would not be truthful to state that sexual indifference necessarily brings inertia and impotence. There are many examples to prove the contrary. Let us merely say there is one dimension of life that disappears when there is no more carnal relationship with the world; those who keep this treasure to an advanced age are privileged indeed.

Part 4

HOMOSEXUALITY

THE ROOTS OF HOMOSEXUALITY

Martin Hoffman

The 1960s marked a "coming out" period for homosexuality in the United States. Organizations such as the Mattachine Society are now demanding freedom of choice in social contacts as well as equal rights and fair treatment under law against discrimination in employment. The Gay Liberation movement has centers on campuses across the country to discuss mutual problems and to educate the "straights".

Despite some softening of attitudes in many parts of the country, however, there are still taboos against, and much misinformation, misunderstanding, and biased dicta about, homosexuality. Part of the problem lies in the split between medical-psychiatric "experts," who believe that homosexuality is an illness, and the behavioral scientists, who believe that homosexual behavior is a learned phenomenon in a particular social milieu.

Martin Hoffman's *The Gay World* brings light instead of heat to the subject. In the excerpt reprinted here, he suggests how gender-role training in early childhood and the culturally prescribed repression by males of any conscious homosexual feelings pave the way for adult heterosexuality. Of particular interest to the student are the case studies illustrating the kinds of family interactions, distorted interpersonal experiences both within the family and among peers, and parental patterns of behavior that recur in the histories of male homosexuals.

The evidence presently available to students of human sexuality points strongly to the conclusion that sexual object-choice is basically a learned phenomenon. It is therefore related to many factors which act upon the individual's development during all phases of his life. With such a complexity of interacting relationships, it would, of course, be impossible to identify a single cause for homosexual preference. Nonetheless, I think we can point

Reprinted from Martin Hoffman, *The Gay World*, Chapter 8; © 1968 by Basic Books, Inc., Publishers, New York. Reprinted by permission of publisher.

out *some* of the possible meanings which homosexual behavior has for different persons. One of the clear points of agreement among disparate schools in modern psychiatry and social science is—to put the matter in its simplest form—that the same things have different meanings for different people. For example, if a patient in analysis tells a dream about being driven through a countryside in a red car and then being taken to an old gothic house for a dinner party which includes his grandmother, his child, and an old sweetheart, we cannot immediately know what this dream means. Patients often imagine that the analyst can simply read the dream as if he had a secret code which will tell him immediately what a red car means, what a dinner party means, and so on. On the contrary, the only one who can "tell us" what this dream means is the patient himself, who can elaborate on his associations to the various elements of the dream. He would find that a red car, for instance has a particular meaning in his life, and that the gothic house reminded him of some especially significant past event, and so forth. Thus, the meanings of the same dream elements for one person are usually quite different than for another.

The same rule of the variability of meanings holds for sexual preference. Two different men may engage in the same kind of sexual act, but this does not indicate that this behavior has the same meaning for both of them. Fellatio, for example, performed under the very same circumstances, e.g., in the baths, may have wholly different meanings for two different 30-year-old men who are performing it. In order to find out what this behavior does mean we would have to investigate the particular life history of the individual, ascertain his fantasies during the sexual act, and find out the present life circumstance that led him to the baths on this particular night.

What can we say, then, about homosexual behavior in general? Can we say anything at all about it? In spite of the caution I have proposed here, I think it is quite possible to say a good deal that is significant about the roots of homosexual behavior, for we find that when we do investigate individual lives, there are certain patterns which recur, and some of these we shall describe in the present chapter.

But we must insert yet another caution, one that is not sufficiently stressed when the psychodynamics of homosexual behavior are discussed in the literature. This is that it is much easier to explain pathological manifestations of a particular category of behavior than normal manifestations, and the more pathological the cases become, the easier they are to explain. If sexual behavior is learned, then all sexual object-choices can be explained in psychological and/or sociological terms. This would include normal heterosexual behavior as well as the most bizarre perversions. While . . . I do not want to get into the controversy about whether homosexuality is an illness . . . I do at least want to emphasize that because those types of homosexual object-choice which are connected with some kind of trauma or unhappiness in childhood are the easiest to explain, the following pages may give the erroneous impression that all homosexual behavior can be explained in "symbolic" terms. Let me try to clarify this.

"Normal" Sexual Behavior

How can we explain heterosexual behavior if this too is a learned phenomenon? And if there is homosexual behavior which can be called nonpathological, can it be explained along the same lines? The answer to these questions becomes much more obvious when we reflect upon the reason why heterosexual behavior is the most common form of sexual behavior in our present society. The reason, I think, is very clear. It is because heterosexuality is encouraged and because homosexual behavior is discouraged. Consequently, it is the "natural" thing for young men to prefer girls as sexual objects. One need only reflect upon the content of the popular media to realize that the cues are all around us and that they exist in the most subtle as well as the most gross forms. Men learn heterosexual object-choice because no other object-choice is considered possible for them; that is, they are not allowed to conceive of the possibility that there can be another kind of sexual object other than the opposite sex. This starts at the earliest age when, for example, they play "house," a game in which roles are segregated according to sex; it continues throughout the development of the child and adolescent. The boy is given innumerable messages, both overt and covert, by his parents, his peers, and the culture at large, that relationships with girls are considered very desirable. But not only is he told that he should have relationships with girls, he is also *not given the alternative possibility*, that homosexual relationships are possible. This possibility is withheld from him by a combination of omission and prohibition. In other words, he is not taught that such things are possible, and so *he does not even conceive of it.*

If a conception of homosexual sex does, however, somehow manage to find its way into his consciousness, it is quickly obliterated by severe sanctions. The culture tells him that if he prefers men as sexual objects, he is not himself a real man; there is something wrong with him; he is queer. This message is given to him in such a way that it evokes uncanny feelings, what Sullivan describes as the "not-me." In other words . . . the male child is trained so that his self-esteem will suffer a severe drop if he conceptualizes intimate relations with another male. His self-concept is not permitted to entertain the notion of himself as a paramour of another male. This is forbidden. Any such notions are subject to immediate repression. If the thought of homosexual relations should happen to arise in his mind, about all the normal male has is a sort of uncanny feeling that these things are not part of his world. Although it is possible that he is not threatened by the thought of other men engaging in homosexual relations, even this tolerance has its limits. Non-homosexual men who come into contact with homosexual males who are together *as homosexuals*, e.g., at a gay dance club, often find that their lack of rational objection to homosexual behavior and their liberal tolerance for other styles of life simply do not go deep enough to prevent them from feeling acutely uncomfortable in the presence of men who are dancing together or embracing. I think we know enough about different mental states from psychoanalytic investigation to be fairly certain that this distaste— which the experiencing individual often himself believes to be "irrational"— is a product of his own unconscious identification with the other persons, specifically the homosexual males who are dancing together, and the consequent repression this emphatic feeling needs to undergo as it meets the adverse definition of homosexual feelings present within the individual's conception of himself.

There are, of course, some men who are less subject to this kind of self-condemnation of homosexual feelings than are others. There is almost an infinite variation among families in the degree to which homosexual and heterosexual feelings are permitted or encouraged. In some families, as a number of psychoanalysts have pointed out, *heterosexual* feelings are explicitly discouraged as being wicked, while nothing is said about homosexual impulses, so that the child gets the message, even if covertly, that homosexual behavior may be less undesirable than heterosexual behavior.

We will not, of course, have a really satisfactory understanding of homosexuality until we understand what psycho-physiological mechanisms are involved in the development of sexual excitation. We know why a man may be attracted to a certain kind of woman, but we don't actually know why he gets an erection when he is with her. In order to know this, we would have to know the relationship between the psychological factors involved in his attraction and the physiological mechanisms involved in the sexual response itself. About all we can say at this point in our knowledge of human sexuality is that sexual feelings seem to have their origin in the interpersonal relations that go on between the child and other people in his world, particularly his parents, but also other adults, his siblings, and his peers. We know that factors which affect the relations between individuals in the child's interpersonal world will also have profound effects on later sexual development. Evidence from animal studies, such as Harlow's, and from studies of other cultures, strongly supports this belief.

For a case in point, let me quote from Frank Beach's account of Davenport's report of gender-role training in a primitive society:

> From very early childhood boys and girls are physically segregated, trained in distinctly separate social roles, and prevented insofar as possible from learning anything about the opposite sex including even the details of physical appearance. Adult males and females intermingle only on special occasions and even then the forms of social exchange are highly constrained and narrowly limited. The combination of these factors has powerful effects on all forms of heterosexual interaction not excluding marital relationships. Young men and women find the first stage of marriage to be, "one of the most excruciating periods of their entire life." The initial problem is not to achieve mutually satisfying genital union, but to overcome the shame and embarrassment of merely speaking to one another, even in privacy. A bride and groom often actively avoid each other whenever possible, and one or two years may elapse before they are sufficiently at ease to take joint residence in the dwelling which the husband has constructed.

If it is true that adult sexuality is an outgrowth of early interpersonal relations, as studies of both other species and other societies, as well as our own, seem clearly to indicate, then what I have called the undifferential sexual potential may be directed in a number of different ways depending upon the interactions which occurred during childhood and youth. For most children, the close feelings they had toward their mother and father are prohibited from taking sexual form by the incest taboo, a taboo which is practically universal and which is probably necessary for the maintenance of society because it, in effect, socializes the child *out* of the family into the larger group. The homosexual feelings which might develop toward the father or, after the father is prohibited as a sexual object by the incest taboo, toward other males, are—in our culture—removed by the general stricture which society places on homosexual desires. Thus, the child is left with heterosexual feelings directed toward those women who are outside his own immediate family. This is the "normal" pattern of sexual object-choice in our own society. However, in a complex pluralistic society such as our own, social norms are not learned uniformly, and the individual's family may, for one reason or another, not socialize him as the culture would desire. Thus, the heterosexual feelings which persist into adulthood may be accompanied by homosexual feelings which have arisen in the same way, i.e., in relation to the parents. Even with the fact of the incest taboo, homosexual feelings may still be present in conscious form and may be directed to other boys in the child's environment. In some cases, as has been indicated, the family may find these less "wicked" than the boy's heterosexual feelings and may unwittingly encourage the homosexual component by suppressing the other.

What I am trying to present here is an explanation of how homosexual feelings may arise in the child, in the absence of the very definite symbolic meanings which one would think they universally carry if one reads psychoanalytic writings on the matter. It is, of course, simpler to describe the "symbolic" forms of homosexual behavior, as we are now going to do, but it should not be thought that all homosexual behavior arises from such sources. One only has to reflect that normal *hetero*sexual behavior has itself to be accounted for as a product of learning in social interaction during the early years, and then one sees that all sexual behavior can be explained in terms of very obvious "symbolic" patterns.

. . . Many homosexual men do not develop an awareness of their homosexuality until they are many years past puberty. For example, I interviewed a psychologist who, looking back, realizes that he has always been gay, has never had any sexual interest in women, and has had sporadic overt homosexual contacts since childhood. Nevertheless, he did not realize he was homosexual until he was 27 and did not come out, in the sense of defining himself as such and entering the gay world, until after his 28th birthday. (He regrets this delay very much, as these were quite lonely years for him, and although he does not entirely escape loneliness now—since, like so many others, he too is searching for a stable relationship with another man—he feels he is much better off than when he was in his early 20's and did not know he was gay, yet had no heterosexual interests.)

I think this phenomenon can only be explained as being due to a combination of the two factors we have been discussing, namely, the failure of society to make people aware of homosexuality as an existent way of life (and of the existence of the gay world), and the strong repressive forces that prevent people from knowing what their real sexual feelings are. One might consider this phenomenon a psychological conspiracy of silence, which society insists upon imposing because of its belief that it thereby safeguards existent sexual norms.

A Case of Homosexuality

Let me now describe a patient whom I saw in clinical practice some years ago. . . . This individual was a young man in his 20's who came to see me about some neurotic problems, including sexual ones. He was an extremely promiscuous homosexual, who had had literally hundreds of sexual encounters. The figure 1,003 given for Don Giovanni might well have been surpassed by this individual in his constant search for sexual partners. One day, early in the treatment, on his way to my office, he saw what he regarded as an especially attractive young man. When he got into the office he made the statement that there must be something wrong with him, since he wanted to perform fellatio on every adolescent he saw.

His feeling was that his behavior was "sick," as he put it. At first I thought this was simply a feeling of guilt, and there is no question that he did have a great deal of guilt over his sexual activities. Later in the therapy, however, it became clear that something else was causing this feeling. When he saw a young man he found attractive, he did feel distressed, but he covered up this feeling right away by overlaying it with a feeling of sexual desire and then planning the conquest. The distressing feeling, which was his very first reaction to the person, and which actually got him interested in the young man in the first place, underwent a very quick repression.

What was this feeling about? My patient's reaction to an attractive male adolescent was one of acute bewilderment in the face of a painful situation. He saw the individual, and the individual's presence disturbed, confused, annoyed him in some inexplicable fashion. The young man's presence somehow made a call to action necessary in order to gain some form of mastery over the situation. What appeared superficially as merely a desire for a great deal of sexual pleasure was in reality a need to master a predicament which followed upon any chance encounter with a certain kind of individual.

This patient has suffered through a very trying childhood, in which his older brother had received all the attention and glory he felt he needed for himself. The result was that the patient developed a very low sense of self-value in relation to his brother. Somehow this crystallized in adolescence, when his brother's superiority seemed to overwhelm him. In reacting to the young men whom he desired sexually, he was transferring feelings from an earlier period of his life into the current situation. He was reacting to these young men as if they were his brother, and he was therefore faced with the same bewilderment, confusion, and sense of extremely low self-esteem in relation to them that he had earlier experienced in relation to the brother. The feeling was so acute that he needed to repress it immediately. His ego had found that a sexualized response was a way of solving the dilemma and so the promiscuous homosexual pattern was begun.

It is important to ask the crucial question: why was this unconscious problem sexualized? The answer is that by sexualizing the problem, our patient transformed a distressing situation into a pleasurable one. He had found no other way to deal with his feelings of envy, hostility, depression, all stemming from his sense of low self-value, which were developed in relation to his brother. Whenever he saw a young man who brought these feelings close to the surface he found himself in a psychological quandary. By transforming this distressing creature (the young man) into a creature from whom pleasure could be derived, he was able to transform the minus situation into a plus.

Our patient's sexual promiscuity was probably related to at least four factors. First, his hostility to the sexual partner could only stand repression through one sexual encounter. This meant that after the act was over, he wanted to get away from his partner as soon as possible. Second, he felt very guilty about his homosexuality and this also led to the desire to forget the individual with whom he had just had sex. Third, almost every new adolescent was a challenge to him: could he eliminate this particular individual as a constant reminder of his distress by permanently grouping him with the givers of pleasure—the young men who had made it possible for him to convince himself that his ego was able to handle the unconscious distress? Therefore, of course, virtually every young man he encountered became a candidate for seduction. Fourth, as was to be expected with such an unhappy background, his skill in interpersonal relationships was poor. A close, long-lasting relationship with another man was too much for him. He simply was not able to conceptualize such a complex interpersonal role. This was, of course, intimately tied up with his low self-esteem.

We see in this case the use of homosexual behavior as a way of handling a severe, problematic situation in one's life. It is a "reparative" device which the individual uses to solve particular life problems. Psychoanalytic literature contains many examples of homosexual behavior as a symbolic means for solving particular existential problems. It would be well worth our time if we considered a few of the other meanings which certain kinds of homosexual behavior might have for some individuals.

Fellatio

Some homosexuals engage in behavior which is so irrational that it virtually requires a psychodynamic explanation. A good example of this is the case of the compulsive fellator who finds himself actually driven to engage in fellatio under what are sometimes situations of radical danger. This person frequently picks up rough-looking young men, e.g., hitchhikers and servicemen, and tries to persuade them to let him bring them to orgasm by fellatio. He is often a typical client of hustlers. As a result of his efforts, this individual frequently is assaulted and is occasionally murdered, although very often it is not clear from reading the press reports that there was a sexual basis to the crime.

What is the reason for this compulsive desire for fellatio? It seems that this particular manifestation of fellatio is very much like the Biblical historian W. Robertson Smith referred to as a sacramental feast, in which the participant eats the flesh and drinks the blood of the divine animal during a primitive religious ceremony, in order to get the *mana* or vital power which is present within the animal. As Gilbert Murray noted,

> The classical instance is the sacramental eating of a camel by an Arab tribe, recorded in the works of St. Nilus. The camel was devoured on a particular day at the rising of the morning star. He was cut to pieces alive, and every fragment of him had to be consumed before the sun rose. If the life had gone out of the flesh and blood the sacrifice would have been spoilt; it was the spirit, the vitality, of the camel that the tribesmen wanted.

The compulsive fellator is unwittingly re-enacting an ancient religious rite. By sucking the penis of what he believes to be an especially masculine male, he feels he is incorporating some of this masculinity and vitality into his own person. Obviously his sense of his own masculinity must be at a chronically low ebb in order for him to engage in this kind of magical behavior. This would account for the inexplicable nature of his search for sexual partners. He himself feels bewildered by the phenomenon and cannot explain why, during certain times, he feels an acute restlessness and needs to go out cruising in the car, looking for hitchhikers, sailors, or hustlers. In many cases where such individuals have been analyzed, it is found that this acute sense of sexual longing is preceded by some kind of blow to the self-esteem, so that the individual's sense of his own value has been pushed to a new low. His search for a sexual partner is therefore a search for a replenishment of his own vitality, and it is uncannily like the primitive search for the sacred animal whom he must consume in order to engage in a renewal of his own powers. For reasons which vary from case to case, such homosexual males have fixed upon the penis as being an especially powerful object and believe, at an unconscious level, that by taking the penis into their mouth, they can incorporate some of this power into themselves.

This explanation fits in very well with the well-known emphasis on penis size among male homosexuals. Any student of gay life can attest to the fact that very many male homosexuals are particularly fetishized on the size of the penis, and that this forms a recurrent topic of discussion among them. While this can partly be attributed to reasons no more pathological than the heterosexual male's interest in his partner's breast size, such an interest on the part of the homosexual male very often results in his going to great lengths to secure a partner with the largest possible penis. Often, this results in his taking risks which would be unnecessary if he were merely searching for a male sexual partner. A good deal of this behavior is so dangerous that it demands a psychoanalytic explanation, and the viewing of fellatio as a sacramental feast provides this kind of understanding of an otherwise inexplicable phenomenon.

Perhaps the reader may wonder why a "masculine" male would want to be the divine animal in a sacramental feast, i.e., be fellated (or take the inserter role in anal intercourse—for the receptor may prefer to incorporate the penis in this way). Obviously, many reasons would be involved. The individual may get a feeling of power from assuming what he feels is a "dominant" role with another male. Or he may be sexually excited by another man and wish to consummate that excitement by being physically stimulated to the point of orgasm. (These two possible explanations are not, of course, mutually exclusive.)

Since the receptor in a homosexual encounter may not achieve ejaculation, it is somewhat easier to explain insertion than its converse when considering homosexual sexual relations. Men, generally, like to have their penises stimulated to the point of orgasm. (These two possible explanations are not sexual preferences for multiple acts. The fellator may get an erection because he is sexually aroused by sucking his partner's penis. He may then wish his partner to reciprocate the fellation, or, alternately, may masturbate himself to orgasm. Sometimes receptors do not achieve orgasm, e.g., during anal intercourse. But they may, after their partner's orgasm, then achieve ejaculation themselves—and the ways in which they might do this include all those which are physically possible.

Castration Anxiety

A classic psychoanalytic explanation used to account for the existence of homosexual behavior is "castration anxiety," the fear, by the male homosexual, of the female genitals. For example, Fenichel writes that homosexual men are terrified of the sight of a partner without a penis because of their own unconscious fear that they might be subject to castration. This is connected with the Oedipus complex, in which the boy is said to be frightened away from his incestuous feelings toward his mother by a feeling that the father will castrate him if he persists in this desire toward his maternal parent. Fenichel writes,

> The sight of female genitals may arouse anxiety in a boy in two ways: (1) The recognition of the fact that there are actually human beings without a penis leads to the conclusion that one might also become such a being; such an observation lends effectiveness to old threats of castration. Or (2) the female genitals, through the connection of castration anxiety with old oral anxieties, may be perceived as a castrating instrument capable of biting or tearing off the penis. Quite frequently a combination of both types of fear is encountered.

The possibility that an individual may not desire sex with women because of castration anxiety cannot be discounted. The notion that all male homosexuals suffer from castration anxiety is patently false, however, because there are a large number of males with an extensive homosexual history—the majority, in fact—who during the same time engage in considerable heterosexual intercourse. That there are many men who are subject to the kind of fear which Fenichel describes is not to be gainsaid here. But we see that this hypothesis, if carried too far, can lead to false conclusions. For example, on the next page, Fenichel states that what these men really want is a "girl with a penis," i.e., they are naturally attracted to women but they are afraid of a penisless object, so they are really looking for a woman who has a penis. Since there are no such creatures, they choose boys. But the boys must have a maximum of girlish and feminine traits. Thus they are attracted to the feminine homosexual who is the closest approximation to a girl with a penis.

Actually, as a description of homosexual preferences this is simply false. Male homosexuals are most attracted by *masculine* partners and not by effeminate ones. It is clear to any student of the homosexual world that effeminate men are held in much lower esteem than are masculine-looking homosexuals, and it is masculinity rather than girlishness which is most desired in the sexual partners of most male homosexuals.

A complete catalogue of the psychological reasons lying behind homosexual object-choice would take us very far afield, for each individual is different, and the constellation of factors which lead to homosexuality in each particular man is quite diverse. Nevertheless, I would like to mention several other elements in the causation of a homosexual orientation.

One of the most frequently cited is the boy's identification with his mother. According to this explanation, the boy models certain aspects of his behavior after those of the mother (with whom he is usually in closer proximity as a child) rather than the father. One of the results of this may be a desire to enjoy sexual intercourse in the way in which the child imagines the mother does. He wants to play the mother's role in relation to a man. In some cases this leads to the desire to take the receptor role in anal intercourse. If the identification with the mother is strong enough, the boy may develop effeminate traits.

Another result of identification with the mother is that the homosexual male takes as his sexual object younger partners, e.g., adolescent boys, and behaves in some respects toward them as he would have liked his mother to behave toward him. This is what analysts refer to as a narcissistic type of sexual object-choice. In this case, the individual, while choosing the object on the basis of maternal identification, is also identifying with the partner, whom in some sense he regards as a representation of himself. He takes care of the partner and shows tenderness toward him, in some respects like the way in which he imagined or would have liked his mother to behave toward him. Obviously, this latter type of homosexual object-choice can also result from a paternal identification with a desire to behave toward a young man as he would have liked his father to behave toward him. Actually there is virtually no end to the possible combinations of psychodynamics involved in any given case of sexual object-choice, and this statement holds for heterosexual as well as homosexual behavior.

Another type of homosexual orientation results from factors very similar to those involved in the case of the young man we presented earlier. . . . In this instance the individual has strong angry feelings toward another male, e.g., the father or brother. However, this anger is not very easy to live with since it means making a member of his immediate environment, or someone very close to him, a continual object of hatred, and thus results in introducing a dangerous figure into his interpersonal world. In what is technically known as a reaction formation, he handles this problem by developing "love" for

he other person and thus neutralizes the hostility. If this other person is
male this may result in a homosexual orientation, which may persist in
ater years. This may have other psychological advantages besides the
limination of a hostile figure from the environment. For example, if the
ndividual feels guilt from heterosexual behavior, he can enjoy heterosexual
onquest on the part of his brother in a vicarious way. When his love
bject is successful with women, he not only avoids the competition with
im, but also does not have to deal with his own feelings of guilt about
eterosexuality.

To some extent, these examples of the psychodynamics of homosexuality
re presented only as illustrative. They are certainly not intended to be
omprehensive, for we can see that when many factors are involved—as
hey usually are—there are a large number of possible combinations.

Family Dynamics

A number of writers, among whom Irving Bieber is eminent, have empha-
ized a particular family constellation present in male homosexuals. In some
ense this is a stereotype, for it clearly applies to some and not to all male
omosexuals. And yet it is not without value in understanding the origins of
omosexuality, for it points to the fact that the psychodynamics that we
ave been discussing must have originated in relation to particular kinds of
amilial patterns present during the early years of the future homosexual.

Bieber's characteristic homosexual-producing mother is over-close and
ver-intimate with her son. She is very much afraid of losing the son and thus
s possessive, and this possessiveness results in a kind of demasculinization
f him. She favors that son who is later to become a homosexual over her other
children and often over the husband as well, and encourages an alliance with
im against the father, so that the son is alienated from masculine identi-
ication. She is herself puritanically sexually frigid but, on the other hand,
er closeness stimulates the son sexually so that he is aroused and *at the
same time* inhibited in the presence of a woman. This is a crucial factor in
is later inability to relate sexually to women, for as a child he has to
everely repress his overaroused heterosexual feelings. The son develops a
ubmissiveness and a tendency to worry about displeasing his mother. Often
he sleeping arrangements are atypical and the son and mother sleep together
until well into adolescence—if not in the same bed, at least in the same
oom. The result of all this is a severe inhibition of masculinity and assertive-
ess on the part of the son. This, Bieber feels, is due in large part to an

unconscious attempt on the part of the mother to extinguish the son's heterosexuality. Certainly, if this is done, the mother does not lose the boy to other women but retains him as an unconscious incestuous object. If this is, in fact, her psychodynamics, she would also want to desexualize him since, if she has unconscious sexual feelings toward her son, she would not want him to respond sexually to those feelings, because they would be too threatening to her. Even if one does not postulate an unconscious incestuous wish on the part of the mother toward her son, it is clear that there are a lot of women who find in their children the only meaningful relationships in their lives and they often hold the children much too close, well past the time when the child should be going out in the world and making his own new attachments. The "mama's boy" is obviously that kind of boy in large part because the mama wants her boy to stay with her as an interpersonal, if not a sexual, object.

Latent Homosexuality

A term which is used very widely, in fact often bandied about, is "latent homosexuality." If all males have feelings toward both sexes, as Freud held, then all exclusive heterosexuals are latent homosexuals and all exclusive homosexuals are latent heterosexuals. Bisexual men would be the only ones who presumably do not have these two general types of "latent" sexual feelings (although they may have latent incestuous and otherwise sexually repressed feelings). . . . We have felt it wise to reject the notion of constitutional bisexuality. What, then, of the concept of latent homosexuality? It seems that while this notion has been subject to abuse, it is one which cannot be discarded, for it *does* point to an obvious factor in the sexual lives of many persons. If it is true that sexual feelings develop in relation to the parents, on a learned basis, and that conscious homosexual feelings do not exist in the majority of adult males because society causes its males to repress them, then they exist, in some sense, in the unconscious. If this is so, as we believe, then very many males have latent homosexual feelings, although we would not want to state unequivocally that 100 percent of all non-homosexual males have unconscious homosexual feelings. Still, there must be a considerable fraction who do, for it is hard to account for a good deal of the hostility toward homosexuals which many heterosexuals display without postulating that they find homosexual males very threatening because of something *within themselves*. If homosexual feelings arise in the way we have hypothesized and then are subject to repression because of social pressure, then Freud was a good deal more correct than we might otherwise believe when we discarded his theory of constitutional bisexuality. What is very clear is that there are a great many men who are struggling with homosexual problems. We will try to show in a later chapter how this struggle may lead to clinical mental illness, and also we want to implicate it in some of the crucial difficulties that overt homosexuals themselves have in the gay world.

Adolescent Peer Relationships: A Vignette

Walter is a 47-year-old business executive. His view of his homosexuality (with which I agree) is that a crucial factor in its development was the problems he had during adolescence with his schoolmates, especially his male peers. He came from a family *not* like those described by Bieber as typical for homosexuality. His mother was the passive parent and was quite devoted to her husband. Walter's relationship with his father was close and, he feels, quite satisfactory. He says his childhood was very happy.

When he entered high school, however, he began to have troubles. He was rather clumsy and never good at athletics, in which he had no interest anyway. (It might be added that neither did his father, so even if his father was a good role model, Walter certainly wouldn't have picked up any such interests from him.) As a result of this disinterest and inability at sports, he became isolated from his age-mates, who all considered athletic interest a *sine qua non* for social acceptance and gave the greatest prestige to athletic stars. As a complicating factor, Walter had a fairly severe case of acne during his early teens, and so was considered unattractive by the good-looking girls at school.

As a result of all this, he began to feel that maybe there was something amiss in his masculinity. He formed a friendship with another outcast who, unlike Walter, had effeminate mannerisms. They finally engaged in some homosexual experiences, which were not at first defined as such, but which they later came to regard as gay. (Unlike most of their classmates, both were interested in reading, and they eventually discovered that there was such a thing as homosexuality. They then had to admit to themselves that they were engaging in homosexual acts.)

From this point in his life, Walter's sexual development took a definitely homosexual course. By the time he got to college he was ready and eager to enter the gay world. He feels that if he had been accepted socially by his high school peers he might have developed in a more "normal" direction. While this cannot be proved, it is hard to imagine that his adolescent problems did not have a profound effect on his sexual orientation.

Social Factors in the Genesis of Homosexuality

In the bulk of this chapter we have been trying to account for homosexual object-choice, the desire for members of one's own sex as sexual partners. There are, however, reasons other than those which are explicitly sexual that cause young men to enter the gay world and participate in homosexual activity. Certainly the phenomenon of male prostitution would indicate that money alone may be a significant factor. Although certain psychoanalysts have claimed that all male prostitutes whose clients are men are "really" homosexual, it appears that most contemporary students of the subject have concluded that there exists a significant number of these male prostitutes who are not basically gay, but who are nevertheless capable of achieving an erection and orgasm if sufficient physical stimulus is applied to the genitals. We do not want to consider hustling at this time; what we want to do is point out certain factors in the modern urban world which lead young men into a homosexual way of life in the relative absence of a strong sexual desire for other men. In discussing these factors, we don't wish to imply that they are somehow mutually exclusive to psychogenic sexual factors, for the two very often combine, especially in those who are bisexually oriented, to produce a homosexual way of life which lasts for a period of at least a few years.

A number of observers, such as Kenneth Keniston, have pointed out the damaging effects of modern urbanized, technological society in producing a serious alienation between persons, especially in the larger cities. This decline in a sense of community between urban Americans has created a powerful impetus toward deviant behavior, for one of the positive virtues to be gained from being deviant is that one gains both a sense of identity and a community of fellows. Being heterosexual does not provide an identity for an alienated, confused modern individual, since everybody is expected to be heterosexual, and this provides about as much of a clue to *who one is* as liking ice cream. To be a homosexual, however, is quite a different matter, for the individual can define himself as a homosexual and can make this identity the center of his own self-concept and of his behavior. At the same time, it makes him a member of a deviant community, and wherever he goes he can find a small group of individuals who will have something in common with him which is very real and very intrinsic to their own being. This is true, of course, for a number of other forms of deviant behavior as well, such as "bohemian" or "hippie" life-styles.

Especially if one is young and attractive, being homosexual means belonging to an underground community of fellows which provides one with not only a sense of one's identity, but also with places to go and things to do, even in an otherwise foreign location. In this sense, if the analogy may be pardoned, the homosexual community is like the early Christian communities during the time when Christianity was persecuted by the Romans. When a Christian ventured from his own city to another town, he would immediately look up the Christians in that new locale and would find camaraderie, food, and a place to stay. It is the same for the young homosexual. Before he ventures from his own town to a different city, he will be provided by his home-town friends with a list of gay bars and perhaps with the names of a number of homosexuals whom he can look up. He feels that he belongs to a fraternity of individuals like himself, with whom he has something very basic in common. He feels they will care about him, and in a very real sense he is right. The analogy, of course, ends very abruptly, because unlike the early Christians, who cared for their brothers as persons, the young homosexual will find that his homosexual brothers usually only care for him as a sexual object. Although they may invite him out to dinner and give him a place to stay, when they have satisfied their sexual interest in him, they will likely forget about his existence and his own personal needs.

Still, something is better than nothing, and a shallow community is better than no community at all. Furthermore, there is a very seductive quality about gay life in the large cities which is extremely attractive to the kind of young man who wants to be admired and sought after by other individuals. For in that gay community he can find a kind of attention, from a large number of individuals, which he simply cannot get from a large number of women—certainly not without great effort on his part. Among the individuals who will actively court him, take him out to dinner, buy him presents, and otherwise indicate that to them he is (at least temporarily) a very special person, are people of prominence and wealth. There is no question that, to a number of young men, homosexuality is a way of rising in the socioeconomic scale. The social mobility which is offered to a young man by the homosexual world is much greater than he would find in the heterosexual world, unless he was very lucky indeed. The garage attendant or laundry man will find himself attending elegant cocktail parties in San Francisco's Nob Hill or Pacific Heights. If he is lucky, he will find himself living there, perhaps driving a new sports car or having his way paid through college. These are very powerful inducements, and there are plenty of handsome boys who find themselves caught up in the gay world and engaging in frequent homosexual acts who would otherwise not have a compelling interest in sexual relations with other males. Of course, this is often a form of hustling, and like the street hustler, such a career may end in a commitment to a homosexual way of life, but it may also end by a return to heterosexuality once the young man has achieved the material goals he is after. There is no question, however, that aims which our society considers quite laudable, such as obtaining a higher education, may only be made possible for some persons by their willingness to engage in a homosexual relationship.

The most serious problem which many young men face today is the problem of what to do with their time and how to make their actions meaningful. One of the most attractive features of the gay world, especially in large cities, is that it provides a constant round of activities. There are always bars to visit and parties to go to; there are always new people to meet and go to bed with. There is a certain routine about settling down with one sexual partner which can be entirely obviated by taking up a promiscuous homosexual life. In spite of the increasing availability of girls as sexual partners, there is nothing to compare with the ready availability of other males to the attractive young homosexual. The whole scene is very seductive and glamorous, especially when one has first entered it. It is a constant source of meaning and one's self-esteem is continually buoyed up.

Since virtually the sole criterion of value in the homosexual world is physical attractiveness, being young and handsome in gay life is like being a millionaire in a community where wealth is the only criterion of value.

WHAT IS HOMOSEXUALITY?

I am going to use the term "homosexual" in this book to refer to those individuals who have a sexual attraction toward partners of the same sex, over at least a few years of their lives. It should, however, be made clear that there is no definition of "homosexual" or "homosexuality" which is going to be agreed to by 100 percent of the scientists working in this field. Kinsey, for example, objects to using the term "homosexual" or "heterosexual" even as an adjective to describe persons, and prefers to reserve these words to describe the nature of the overt sexual relations or of the stimulae to which the individual erotically responds. Yet, a few pages later in this same book, he sets up a heterosexual-homosexual rating scale, which includes both psychological reactions and overt experience and in which individuals are rated, for example, as "predominantly homosexual, but more than incidentally heterosexual." So we see that Kinsey himself is forced into using the term as an adjective to describe persons. I think that there is no way that we can talk intelligently about the subject without speaking of individuals as homosexuals. To avoid doing so would be to sacrifice any attempt at a common understanding of the subject to a merely quantified study of overt behavior. Even Kinsey, who was himself most sympathetic to a taxonomic approach to sexuality, does not quite do this. It would certainly behoove those of us who wish to arrive at a broad socio-psychological understanding of the phenomenon to adhere to the common-sense use of the terms, at least insofar as they can be made serviceable.

When I use the term "homosexual" to describe a man, by this I do not mean that he may not also be heterosexual, for I think there are a significant number of people, such as Tom, who are sexually attracted to and seek out sexual partners of both sexes. These people we could very conveniently call bisexual, and I will do so, providing only that it is understood that the nature of the sexual attraction to men may not be the same as the sexual attraction to women. In other words, just because we say that Tom is sexually attracted to both men and women does not imply that his feelings on seeing a man and his feelings on seeing a woman are the same. In both cases he may be sexually stimulated, but his entire perception of the situation may be quite different, and his behavior with men—both in bed and out—may be of an altogether different kind than his behavior with women. We saw in the last chapter how Tom's sexual interest in men was almost entirely directed toward performing fellatio and that he engaged in foreplay and other sexual acts with his partner simply in order to satisfy the partner. When Tom goes to bed with his wife, on the other hand, he *is* interested in extensive foreplay and *is* interested in having conventional sexual intercourse with her. His feeling toward women is much more of a warm and enveloping kind in which he ultimately (in fantasy) wants to mingle his body with that of his partner. With men, on the other hand, he feels as if sucking his partner's penis will be very exciting and he can somehow derive a peculiar kind of satisfaction from this activity, the nature of which is not entirely clear to him. I think, therefore, that when we use the term "homosexual" to describe Tom, we must be clear that he is also heterosexual, and when we use the term "bisexual" to describe him we must be completely clear, as many writers are not, that we are talking about two very different kinds of feeling and behavioral states.

What I am saying here, in effect, is that there are many different kinds of homosexuals and many different kinds of bisexuals. We might also add that there are many different kinds of heterosexuals. This will hopefully become clearer when we come to the discussion of the genesis of homosexuality. In asking the question "Why is a man homosexual?" We do not wish to imply by any means that this is to be regarded as a basically different kind of question from "Why is a man heterosexual?" Virtually all the literature on homosexuality is marred by the failure of its authors to take account of the fact that heterosexuality is just as much a problematic situation for the student of human behavior as is homosexuality. The only reason it does not seem to us a problem is because we take its existence for granted. However, we should know enough about science by now to realize that it is just those questions we take for granted that are the ones, when properly asked, which would open up new areas of scientific exploration. The question should really be put as follows: "Why does a person become sexually excited (i.e., in the case of a man, why does he get an erection) when confronted with a particular kind of stimulus?" If the question is asked in this way it can be seen that heterosexuality is just as much of a problem as homosexuality, in the scientific if not in the social sense.

The fact is that there are almost as many different kinds of homosexual, bisexual, and heterosexual responses as there are individuals. On the other hand, there *are* a number of common features which characterize large groups of individuals, so that we *can* make generalizations about particular kinds of response. Obviously, Tom's wish for fellatio and David's wish to hold another man close to him are not unique, but are shared by a sufficient number of other men so that in fact they have already been described and very convincing explanations of them have already been given in the psychiatric literature.

Incidence

Homosexuality is a social problem of enormous proportions. . . . The incidence figures on male homosexual behavior from the 1948 Kinsey report . . . that I think are particularly significant are the following: "4 percent of the white males are exclusively homosexual throughout their lives, after the onset of adolescence." This figure, which refers to at least 4,000,000 American males, tells us that there is a very significant number of men who are exclusively homosexual, both in regard to their overt experience and their psychic reactions. These are people like David, who never have any interest in having sexual relations with a woman. They constitute a considerable part of those individuals who make up the most visible portion of the gay world. However, because 10 percent of the American male population is more or less exclusively homosexual for *at least* three years between the ages of 16 and 55, a significant number of those men who are to be seen in the visible sector of the gay world, e.g., in the bars, are not exclusively homosexual for their whole lives. This added 6 percent includes those individuals who, at the very least, have three years during their late adolescent or adult lives in which, although they may have incidental experience with the opposite sex, and sometimes react psychically to members of the opposite sex, are almost entirely homosexual in their overt activities and/or their reactions. This 6 percent includes a substantial number of men who have had some trial heterosexual experience but who have then become exclusively gay. It is probably this figure which deserves the most emphasis, because it indicates how very widespread male homosexuality is. Kinsey pointed out that those who are more or less exclusively gay for at least three years represent approximately one male in ten in the white male population. The journalist Jess Stearn once wrote a book called *The Sixth Man,* which gave the idea that one out of every six American men was gay. This, of course, was pooh-poohed and I remember that when I first saw the book's title I reacted very skeptically. But, as a matter of fact, if one looks at Kinsey's figures, one finds that 18 percent of the males have at least as much homosexual as heterosexual experience in their lives for at least three years between the ages of sixteen and fifty-five. This is more than one in six of the white male population.

Individual Types

What kind of men are these homosexuals? What do they look like? How do they act? To these questions one can only give the most general (and unsatisfactory) answer, namely, that these people run the entire gamut from the swishy faggot who can be identified a block away, to the husband, son, or brother whom even the fairly sophisticated person would not suspect of any homosexual interest. They include people who are handsome, clever, and rich, those who are ugly, stupid, and poor, and all combinations and gradations in between. Homosexuality penetrates into every conceivable socioeconomic, religious, and geographical classification. There *are* some slight differences, however. For example, Kinsey found that the highest rate of homosexual behavior occurs among those males who go to high school but not beyond. It is also quite true that homosexuals migrate to large urban centers, so that there is probably a higher percentage of practicing homosexuals in Los Angeles than in Bakersfield, California. But these minor differences do not obviate the more significant fact that homosexuals are to be found throughout the entire nation in all social strata.

A great deal of nonsense has been written in the scientific literature about "active" and "passive," "masculine" and "feminine" homosexuals. The implication is often made that there is a sharp difference between these two kinds of individuals. It is certainly true that there is a minority of homosexual men who can be classified both from the point of view of their own conscious definition of themselves as masculine or feminine and from the point of view of what they will do or not do in bed. But this is true only for a minority. The fact is that most homosexuals cannot be so classified and, in fact, will generally take a great variety of roles in sexual performance. Evelyn Hooker has arrived at the same conclusion from her detailed study of 30 predominantly or exclusively homosexual males whom she has intensively interviewed over a period of eight years. She found that the consciousness of masculinity or femininity on the part of her research subjects appeared to bear no clear relation to particular sexual patterns, and that for the majority of individuals in her sample, there was no apparent correspondence between a conscious sense of identity as masculine or feminine and a preferred or predominant role during the sexual act. This does not mean that these men don't have preferred sexual patterns. They do. But these patterns do not, with a very few exceptions, bear any relationship to their conscious sense of themselves as "masculine" or "feminine."

Granted, then, that homosexuals do a lot of different things in bed, just what exactly do they do? Most American investigators have found that there are four "classic" positions in which an individual might find himself engaged when he is in bed with another male. These can be divided into oral and anal and then again into insertor or receptor roles, so that an individual may be an oral insertor, an anal insertor, an oral receptor, or an anal receptor. He can also engage in mutual fellatio and can engage in a great deal of alternation among these roles.

Curiously enough, the English social psychologist, Michael Schofield, found that the largest proportion of homosexuals who were members of the English homosexual community which he studied (using roughly the same kind of ethnographic methods which Hooker and I have used) prefer "genital apposition," or very close body contact without penetration of a body orifice as the means to ejaculation. The term "rub-off" is sometimes used to refer to this method of achieving orgasm. The individual simply rubs his penis against his partner's body, for example, against his belly or his leg. Schofield's finding is in quite sharp contrast to what all investigators would agree is the sexual preference of American male homosexuals, who by and large think of this technique as rather adolescent and generally prefer one or more variations of either oral or anal insertion. Why this curious national contrast exists has never been explained, and, as a matter of fact, it has not really even been noticed. I am not going to attempt an explanation of it here, but I think it is certainly something which is at least very curious and might even be an indicator, especially if it can be verified by other English investigators, of a quite different attitude toward sexuality across the ocean.

In classifying homosexual sex behavior in this way, we cannot , of course, really give the reader a feeling for the immense variation that exists in sexual practices, both among individuals and, to a lesser but significant extent, within the *same* individual over a period of time. It must be emphasized that people *learn* sexual behavior just as they learn any other form of complex activity. Thus, the sexual preferences and sexual repertory of an individual who has been "out" for five years is going to be quite different from that which he had at the time of his first experience. Or perhaps this statement might be qualified: these factors may very well be quite different, but they are not necessarily different. For some people stick to the very same preference that they began with. Some people find out right away what they "really" like, but with others it takes much more time. Some of them are never sure. Both Bieber and Hooker have reported that there is a substantial number of homosexuals who express no sexual preference. That is, they do not prefer one sexual act to another. My own interviews have yielded a different result and I have been somewhat at a loss to explain this. I have never encountered a male homosexual who did not express a preference for a particular kind of sexual act. It seems to me that this discrepancy can be explained in the following way: Hooker and Bieber, in classifying sexual behavior, have stuck pretty close to the four "classic" types of sexual activity, i.e., oral and anal insertion, and they have not included as objects of preference those kinds of activities which fall outside these four types. In other words, because the four "classic" types are so standard among American male homosexuals, some men have been at a loss to explain what they really like to do in terms of them, since they really do not like to do one of those four things best of all. I would guess that when Hooker or Bieber asked them about this they were somewhat unsure of what to say, so they said that they didn't know what they liked to do or said that they really had no preference—that anything would do. My own interviews indicate that they actually do have a specific preference but they don't know how to express it. When they say that they will do anything or that they like to do anything, what they really mean is that they are quite willing to go along with their partner's desires, and thus they will engage in one or more of these four "classic" kinds of sexual activity. Very often, however, such individuals might actually prefer simply to go to bed with another man, engage in necking and petting and close body contact, and might not really be interested in either achieving orgasm themselves or in inducing their partner's orgasm. One might say that, for these individuals, *simply going to bed with another male* is the thing they really want. Obviously, this can be described as sexual, provided it is understood that an ejaculation is not the thing that is most desired. Among these people, one would probably find a number of those whom Schofield has described in his English studies to which we have referred above. Although this does not explain the discrepancy in numbers between the English and American homosexual populations, it does serve, to some extent, to include these individuals in the American figures. In other words, it may be that the American investigators have simply included as "expressing no preference" those whom Schofield would have classified as preferring "genital apposition." (Schofield reports that 42 percent of his sample prefer genital apposition. Hooker reports that 23 percent of her sample express no preference; and Bieber reports that 24 percent of his sample express no preference.)

Two Roommates

The story of Bob and Danny, who have been living together for about nine months, is a good example of the varied (and sometimes non-preferred) sexual role homosexuals will utilize in order to achieve different kinds of sexual and non-sexual goals. Bob is 26 years old. He first began engaging in homosexual behavior when he was in college, at the age of 20. He had had substantial heterosexual experience and considered himself as heterosexual, but he was willing to go along with homosexual behavior for reasons which he did not entirely understand. He was willing to do anything in bed in order to please his partner. But he didn't particularly like any form of sexual activity in any special sense. He said that he liked a close relationship with another man, especially an older one, and he was willing to go to bed with him in order to get this kind of relationship. He had a number of affairs with older men, and then he became a male prostitute. By the time he was

22, after he had been hustling for about a year, he realized that he actually liked having fellatio performed on him and he definitely enjoyed the experience of having another man's mouth on his penis. His hustling has continued off and on until the present time. During all this time he has engaged in considerable heterosexual experience and it would appear that in a strictly sexual sense his interest has always been more directed toward women than toward men. However, for psychological reasons, he has had great difficulty in his relationships with women. He is more emotionally comfortable with men, so that he has been continually attracted into homosexual practices, until the point was reached at which he actually began to enjoy them. He really only enjoys the insertor role and prefers being fellated, although if his partner enjoys being screwed, he can work up a certain amount of enthusiasm for this activity as well.

Danny is one of those individuals who always knew what he liked. He began having homosexual experiences at the age of 24. He is now 28. For about ten years prior to his first homosexual experience he had the fantasy, which was especially clear during masturbation, that he wanted to be screwed by another man and he has always adhered to this desire. He found that the practice of this activity was at least as satisfying as the fantasy and he has made no secret of his preference to all his sexual partners. When he and Bob have sex together, which is about once every two weeks, there is no question about what they are going to do in bed. They do not engage in very many preliminaries.

It should be added that by no means do these two men limit their sexual relationships to each other. Bob is still having heterosexual relations and Danny has numerous other homosexual partners. Danny is quite willing to do other things in bed besides taking the receptor role in anal intercourse, but it is clear what his real preference is. As a matter of fact, he feels that he has become more interested in this kind of activity and less interested in any other type in the four years since he has been out. It should probably be added here that Bob has a great deal of difficulty in coming to terms with the self-concept of himself as homosexual. . . . Danny has not really shown much conscious guilt about his homosexual interests, nor has he let considerations of prudence interfere with his very vigorous search for sexual partners. He has been known to engage in his favorite form of sexual activity in public places, especially parks. It remains to be asked, however, why Danny waited a full ten years after he knew he was gay and knew what he wanted sexually before he engaged in his first homosexual experience. And while this is a question that cannot definitely be answered, it is our opinion that he has in fact been struggling with some of the same kinds of problems on an unconscious level that Bob has been struggling with consciously. Just why he was finally able to throw off what he described as "hesitancy" in approaching other men and develop instead what psychiatrists might call a counter-phobic attitude toward homosexuality, i.e., an over-reaction to his previous shyness, is not at all clear. This is, however, a not uncommon thing to find in the biographies of male homosexuals, for quite a considerable number of them have waited a very long time before they engaged in their first sexual act.

Also, for a remarkable number of individuals, including many people who have gone into professions concerned with the study of human behavior, and who are both bright and sensitive, a number of years have elapsed between puberty and the time when they began to become *aware* of their homosexual interests. Although Danny was aware of his homosexual feelings practically since puberty, other individuals who have shown the same overt pattern of behavior, that is, who have not engaged in their first homosexual act until they were well into their 20's, have gone those ten years without ever realizing that they had any interest in other men. A lot of them simply did not feel that they had any interest in girls, but they were never able to feel an active sexual interest in their male schoolmates, nor were they able to define themselves in any way as sexually deviant. . . .

THE REALITIES OF LESBIANISM

Phyllis Lyon and Del Martin

A welcome addition to the sparse literature on female homosexuality, this article offers a candid, nonsensational insight into some aspects of the Lesbian lifestyle in the United States today and suggests that stereotyped role definition and particular personality types are not inevitable accoutrements of homosexual preference. Like most participants in the gay movement, the authors declare that a Lesbian is a human being first, a woman second, and a homosexual third, that sexual preference is only a part of her personal identity, not the key to it. The words "homosexual" and "Lesbian" should, in fairness, be used as adjectives instead of as nouns, so that sexual preference becomes only one descriptive element among others (such as American, white, female, urban, etc.) rather than a categorical definition.

For men and women alike, and for teenagers especially, the social, economic and emotional cost of homosexual preference is high, but the authors link the Lesbian's difficulties with the general problematic status of women in our society as well. They deny that gay women endure less legal and social stigma and repressive action than men but believe that, costs notwithstanding, homosexual women are more likely than homosexual men to affirm their lifestyle unreservedly.

For a longer work by the same authors, the interested student should see Del Martin and Phyllis Lyon, *Lesbian Woman* (New York: Bantam Books, 1972).

The Lesbian minority in America, which may run as high as ten million women, is probably the least understood of all minorities and the most down-trodden. She has two strikes on her from the start; she is a woman and she

From *The New Women* by Joanne Cooke, Charlotte Bunch-Weeks, Robin Morgan, copyright © 1970 by The Bobbs-Merrill Company, Inc., reprinted by permission of the publisher.

is a homosexual, a minority scorned by the vast majority of people in our country. If, in addition, she is a member of a racial minority, it is hard sometimes to understand how she survives.

A Lesbian is a woman who prefers another woman as a sexual partner; a woman who is drawn erotically to women rather than to men. This definition includes women who have never experienced overt sexual relations with a woman—the key word is "prefers." There is really no other valid way to define the Lesbian, for outside of the sexual area she is as different in her actions, dress, status and behavior as anyone else. Just as there is no typical heterosexual woman, neither is there any typical Lesbian.

However, there is a popular misconception, or stereotype, of the Lesbian. She is believed to embody all the worst masculine attributes of toughness, aggressiveness, lack of emotion, lack of sentiment, overemphasis on sex, lack of stability—the need and desire to dress as a man or, at least, as much like a man as possible.

At some time in her life the Lesbian may fit this stereotype—usually when she is very young and just finding out about herself. After all, the Lesbian is a product of her heterosexual environment and all she has to go on, at her first awareness of Lesbian feeling in herself, is society's image. Part of the reason for her over-masculinization is the sexual identity of being attracted to women. At this point the Lesbian feels that in order to be attractive to another woman she must appear masculine. Another reason is for identification purposes. How will she meet other Lesbians? How will they know her to be one of them unless she indicates herself in her outward appearance? A third reason is one of releasing her hostility against society, of defying the mores which she finds stifling to what she considers her very being. A fourth reason is comfort. Any woman who says that girdles and high heels are comfortable is simply lying.

While it is true that occasionally a Lesbian gets trapped in this way of life (emulation of the male) and never finds her way to being a person rather than a symbol, the vast majority pass through this phase and learn to accept their femininity. As a Lesbian she comes to realize she is a human being first, a woman second, and a Lesbian only third. Unfortunately, however, society places the emphasis on the third—sexual identification—and does not acknowledge the Lesbian as a woman or a person.

But the average Lesbian (if there can be anything approaching "average" in our very complex world) is indistinguishable from other women in dress, in manner, in goals and desires, in actions and in interests. The difference lies only in that she looks to women for her emotional and sexual fulfillment.

She is a member of the family—a distant cousin, or perhaps, a maiden aunt. But more than likely she's closer to home—maybe a daughter, a wife and mother, a grandmother or a sister. She may work in an office, in a factory production line, in the public school system, at the corner grocery. She is not bound by lines of class distinction or educational level, race or religion.

What causes a woman to become a Lesbian? How can it be that two sisters, raised by the same parents in the same home, can turn in two different directions—one toward heterosexuality, the other toward homosexuality? Very simply, the answer is that no one knows. A great deal of research and study has been done in this country on the male homosexual, but very little has been done on the Lesbian. The reason for this, we suspect, lies in the status of women in our country. Because the male—masculinity—is so highly valued, it has been deemed to be imperative to search out the reasons for any deviation from this American norm. Also, the majority of persons working in research are men. Research on the Lesbian has, for the most part, been confined to women who were either psychiatric patients or in prison—which hasn't made for a very full or accurate picture.

Nevertheless, if you begin reading about the "causes" of homosexuality you will find that, as in the Bible, the answer you want to find will be somewhere. Each "expert" on the subject presents a different "cause." Our feeling, which is supported by a growing number of professional persons, is that homosexuality (in both men and women) is merely one dimension of the vastly complicated and varied spectrum of human sexuality. There has always been homosexuality; it has appeared in almost every culture in recorded history; it occurs in every species of animal.

Perhaps the most logical and least hysterical of all statements about homosexuality is the following made by Dr. Joel Fort, psychiatrist and public health specialist; Dr. Evelyn G. Hooker, research psychologist at the University of California at Los Angeles; Dr. Joe K. Adams, psychologist and former mental health officer in California. The statement, made in August of 1966, is as follows:

> Homosexuals, like heterosexuals, should be treated as individual human beings, not as a special group, either by law or social agencies or employers.

> Laws governing sexual behavior should be reformed to deal only with clearly antisocial behavior, such as behavior involving violence or youth. The sexual behavior of individual adults by mutual consent in private should not be a matter of public concern.

Some homosexuals, like some heterosexuals, are ill; some homosexual like some heterosexuals, are preoccupied with sex as a way of life. But probably for a majority of adults their sexual orientation constitutes only one component of a much more complicated life style.

Why then, if the Lesbian is by and large indistinguishable from other women and if her sexuality is not abnormal, does she face such genuine problems in her search for self-fulfillment? For struggle she does against myriad obstacles presented to her by a hostile society. Through our work with the Daughters of Bilitis, Inc., a Lesbian organization started in San Francisco in 1955, we have talked to literally thousands of Lesbians (and almost as many male homosexuals). And, although each case is different, each person individual, through it all is a searching for self-identity and self-fulfillment to the utmost of the person's ability.

Consider the stereotyped "box" most women in this country are placed in from birth: that of becoming wife and mother, nothing else. Consider then, the girl brought up in this box who finds her sexual identification to be Lesbian. How then express the "wife-and-mother" role? This conflict often starts the process of self-searching which goes on for years and which, for some, is never resolved.

Toward a Quaker View of Sex, which came out of England and is more enlightened than most religious treatises on male homosexuality, fails utterly in its chapter on the female homosexual. The only statement with which we can agree is the first sentence: "Homosexuality is probably as common in women as it is in men." The Quaker view of the Lesbian is apparently th of the wishy-washy, namby-pamby old maid who holds hands with another old maid (or preferably an adoring younger girl, if available) because she never was able to catch a man and fulfill her deep yearnings for the rewards of the pangs of childbirth. At least the American stereotype of the predatory aggressive masculine woman has a little more color!

The Quaker view indicates that woman's prime requisite is her "maternal tenderness," that her only reason for being is to have babies, and that the Lesbian is warped and frustrated because she isn't doing her fair share toward the population explosion. To this question of maternity we must poi out that the mere possession of biological machinery to produce babies has no correlation whatever with the attributes of motherhood. Let's face it— many women can have babies but make lousy mothers.

The art of motherhood in the human species is not instinctual. It is learne We have courses in the care of the baby, and there are countless books on the market to help the young mother with the problems she may encounter during the course of her child's growth and development. In some cultures, babies are taken from the mothers and raised by the community without any apparent psychically traumatic results for the biological mothers or their offspring. In other cultures it is the male who tends the young.

It simply does not follow, then, that every Lesbian is suffering untold qualms because she is frustrating her "natural" birthright for giving birth. There are many other ways for women to contribute creatively to society, and at this particular point in the history of the population of our globe, they may also be highly desirable. The Lesbian who does feel frustrated because she doesn't have any children of her own may work in the teaching profession, she may be a playground director or a social worker who comes in contact with families and children. But the majority of Lesbians we have known have not expressed in any way the "void" they feel because they have no children. To the contrary, the expression, "I would prefer to lead a heterosexual life if I could," is much more apt to come from the male homosexual than from the female.

It must be said, however, that there are many Lesbians who are raising children—some successfully, some not so successfully. The rate of success is of course, determined by the degree of self-acceptance and self-assurance of the mother, and the permanence and stability of her relationship to her Lesbian partner. It takes guts, grit and determination. For if a mother is determined to be a Lesbian the courts will assume she is an "unfit mother" on the face of it and take her children away from her. It seems children must have the protection of heterosexuals, regardless. The fact that *all homo-sexuals are products of heterosexuality* seems to escape those who would judge the homosexual relationship.

The teenage Lesbian has a particular problem which has not been met. Homophile organizations, like the Daughters of Bilitis, have had to refuse membership to those under 21 for fear that they will be charged with "contributing to the delinquency of a minor." The teenager has no one to turn to. Society thinks only in terms of counseling of the variety that would tend toward reestablishing the sexual identity in heterosexual vein, and the teenage Lesbian is whisked off by her parents to the family doctor or clergy-man to put a stop to this nonsense. However, in the cases that have come to our attention, the teenager has no doubt about her sexual orientation. What she wants to know is what to do about it. She wants to meet others like herself; she wants to socialize and to discuss the problems she faces. She is looking for Lesbian models, those who have worked out their problems and have established long-term relationships.

When she is denied this social outlet, she very often winds up in unsavory areas of a city like the Tenderloin in San Francisco. There she may find other youth, but she also finds herself in the company of prostitutes, pimps, drug addicts and dope peddlers. There have been several attempts in various cities to set up coffee houses where there is dancing for the teenage homosexual. But they have lacked the influential backing of, say, the church, to provide protection against police harassment while creating a wholesome social fabric for the teenage homosexual.

Because of the absence of role models in working out her way of life, and because the only marriage she has known is that of Mom and Dad, the young Lesbian usually gets hung up in the "butch-femme" syndrome in her early relationships. It is only with painful experience that she learns the Lesbian is attracted to a woman—not a cheap imitation of a man. The lasting Lesbian liaison (and there are many) is one based on mutuality of concern, love, companionship, responsibility, household chores, outside interests and sex.

The successful Lesbian relationship cannot be based on society's exaggerated male-female, dominant-passive roles, as depicted in the flood of Lesbian novels on the newsstands which are, for the most part, written by men for heterosexual male consumption. It is the realization that, contrary to cultural myths, all human beings have both feminine and masculine traits and that a person has to find her own identity as a woman and as a partner in this love relationship that makes for success. The fact that Lesbian relationships are generally long-lasting without benefit of religious ceremony or legal sanction is indicative of a strong bond of love and respect which sees the couple through all the obstacles society places in their way.

Fortunately for all women, there is a growing awareness in this country that woman needs and is more openly demanding an identity for herself as a human being, an identity over and beyond the societal role of housewife and mother. This awareness, coupled with more openness about sexuality and homosexuality, is making it easier now for the young girl, newly aware of her Lesbianism, to cope with the negative sanctions of society. But it is still true that in most areas of our country she has no place to turn for counsel, no one with whom she can talk about her feelings without running the very real risk that the counselor will turn away from her with horror and revulsion.

The Quakers state: "Female homosexuality is free from the legal and, to a large extent, the social sanctions which are so important in the problems of male homosexuals." This is a myth that even the male homosexual has come to believe. It is true that in England there were never any laws pertaining to female homosexuality. But this is not true in the U.S.A. The Lesbian is just as subject to the sanctions of certain laws as the male homosexual; she is just as subject to arrest when she sets foot in a "gay bar"; she is just as subject to blackmail and police harassment. The stigma attached to homosexuality has just as much effect on the Lesbian as she tries to deal with fear and society-imposed guilt in the problem areas of employment, family relationships and religion. Just because the record of arrests is so much smaller is no indication that the Lesbian is relatively free from legal or social sanction. It only means that she is less obvious and less promiscuous. She has done a better job of covering up.

Lesbian problems we have dealt with over the years include the 20-year-old driven to thoughts of suicide because she could not resolve the conflict between her identity as a Lesbian and as a Christian. Or the 40-year-old mother who telephoned Daughters of Bilitis 3,000 miles across the country to break "18 years of silence" after reading a book called *The Grapevine* by Jess Stearn. Then there was the nurse with a "perfect work record" in a federal hospital who was interrogated by a government investigator, flown from Washington, D.C., at the taxpayers' expense, because someone wrote, to a Congressman accusing her of being a Lesbian.

There was the 19-year-old who was trying to find out what homosexuality was all about because she was drummed out of the armed services on a charge she didn't understand. The daughter who receives a monthly allowance from her wealthy family in the Midwest to stay on the coast lest her district attorney father be threatened with a "family skeleton" by his political foes. And the 25-year-old who, after five years of psychiatric therapy, decides she must make the best of herself as herself—a Lesbian.

The most serious problem a Lesbian faces in life is that of self-acceptance. Like everyone else, she has been taught the cultural folklore that a Lesbian is something less than human—a sick, perverted, illegal, immoral animal to be shunned and despised. Needless to say, with the first glimmering of self-knowledge, of awareness that she has Lesbian tendencies, she becomes bogged down in doubt, fear, guilt and hostility.

Some Lesbians claim they have been aware of their Lesbianism since early childhood. Others first become aware during adolescence. Yet there are some women who make this discovery about themselves much later in life—after they have been married and have had children. Still others, either by choice or lack of opportunity, never admit or act out their Lesbianism.

It isn't easy for a woman to say to herself, let alone anyone else, "I am a Lesbian." But once the words are said, has she really changed? Isn't she still the same person she was—the dear friend, the competent employee, the loving sister? And yet the words become a barrier in her personal and working relationships. To protect her family and her job, she is forced to live a lie, to take on a dual life. No wonder many Lesbians seek out some type of psychiatric or therapeutic help. The miracle is that so many are able to function so well and to contribute so much to society.

The Lesbian is thus a secretive, chameleon creature. She is not easily recognized. The old adage, "It takes one to know one," is not true. Not being distinguishable from other women, she has difficulty meeting others like herself. The "gay bar" is still a meeting place, but there are few such bars which cater to women exclusively because they do not constitute a steady clientele. Besides, a Lesbian, as a woman, has no doubt heard many times the old saw "nice girls don't go into bars," or "no lady would ever go into a bar alone." The Lesbian goes out on the town only occasionally and is more apt to settle down with a partner, to build a home and a lasting relationship, and to develop a small circle of friends—usually both homosexual and heterosexual. Another social outlet for the Lesbian can be homophile organizations throughout the country (if she knows about them), such as Daughters of Bilitis, which has chapters in New York and San Francisco.

The Lesbian, being a woman, comes out of the same cultural pool as do heterosexual women. Therefore, on top of everything else, she may have the same hangups and inhibitions about sex, dress, work, actions, etc., as do her heterosexual sisters. Since women have been taught to be passive, to shun the role of the aggressor, the Lesbian finds herself without the slightest idea of how to approach another woman for a date, for a conversation, for sex. It is a rarity for a heterosexual woman to be approached by a Lesbian unless she has given much indication that such advances are welcome.

Even when the Lesbian accepts her sexual identity and herself as a person, she still faces very real discrimination from society. If she has educated herself to a profession (a role doubly difficult for any woman), she can lose her professional status merely because someone points a finger. This is especially true of teachers, attorneys, doctors, social workers and other professionals licensed by the state. But it can also be true for file clerks and secretaries. Very few employers are aware enough to realize that in the Lesbian he has an employee who must work, who will not get married or pregnant, who will devote her energies and capabilities to her job because she will always have to support herself.

As Rabbi Elliot Grafman has stated, "People fear that which they do not understand, and what they fear they despise." It is only through more knowledge and more personal confrontation that the stereotype of the Lesbian can be dispelled. However, to accomplish this feat is to overcome the vicious circle that now envelops the Lesbian who tries to be honest.

If she divulges her identity, she automatically becomes vulnerable. She faces loss of job, family and friends. Yet, until she opens herself to such possibilities, no one will have the opportunity to come to know and to understand her as the whole person she is.

Through The Council on Religion and the Homosexual, which was formed in San Francisco in 1964 after a three-day retreat attended by clergymen and male and female representatives of the homophile community, such a dialogue began in earnest. Avenues of communication have been opened up not only with the religious community (seminaries and other church groups), but with government agencies, the police, business and professional groups, college and high school students. But the task of demythologizing, of education and redefinition of the homosexual is a long and arduous one.

COMING OUT IN THE GAY WORLD

Barry M. Dank

In the following article—which, like much sexual research, concentrates exclusively on the male experience—Dank explores the identity change that accompanies "coming out" (the time of self-designation as a homosexual) and the various settings in which this occurs.

One issue raised by Mr. Dank involves the continuing conflict concerning whether homosexuality is a way of life, a personal sexual preference, as it is regarded by the gay community and many researchers, or whether it is a mental or emotional illness, as some counselors and psychologists see it. (Much professional literature still categorizes homosexuality as "deviant," with all the stigma attached with that term.)

The issue of the relationship between homosexual identity and behavior is also raised. Is a man homosexual because he feels and says he is and/or because he associates with gay people? Or is he homosexual only when he participates in homoerotic behavior? To the question of whether homosexuality is reversible (leaving aside bisexual persons), Dank suggests that once a gay person has "found himself" and "comes out," his identity is established.

Another issue concerns the effect of societal attitudes on the incidence of homosexuality. In Dank's view, the cognitive change now required for a person to see himself as acceptable and human, though homosexual, may be facilitated as society becomes more accepting of homosexuality, but this does not necessarily mean that the number of self-identified homosexuals will increase. Why is this so?

In spite of the recent sociological interest in the study of the transition from primary to secondary deviance, few empirical studies have been addressed to this question. It is in essence posited that at one point in time the actor

Reprinted by special permission of The William Alanson White Psychiatric Foundation, Inc., and by permission of the author, from *Psychiatry*, Journal for the Study of Interpersonal Processes, (1971) 34; 180–97. Copyright © by The William Alanson White Psychiatric Foundation, Inc.

can be described as being at the "primary stage," in which he engages in rule-breaking behavior and still regards himself as "normal"; at a later point in time he may reach the secondary stage, in which he may engage in overtly the same behavior but regard himself as "deviant," or at least in some way different from the average, ordinary person. For example, at one point in time a person may furtively take goods from a store and regard himself as a borrower, but at a later time he may take similar goods and regard himself as a thief (Cameron). This paper is devoted to exploring the emergencies of a particular deviant identity—the male homosexual identity.

There is almost no sociological literature on "becoming" homosexual. There is a vast literature on the etiology of homosexuality—that is, the family background of homosexuals—but little is known concerning how the actor learns that he is a homosexual. In terms of identity and behavior, this paper is concerned with the transition to a homosexual identity, not in the learning of homosexual behavior per se, or the antecedent or situational conditions that may permit an actor to engage in a homosexual act. One may engage in a homosexual act and think of oneself as being homosexual, heterosexual, or bisexual. One may engage in a heterosexual act and think of oneself as being heterosexual, homosexual, or bisexual, or one may engage in no sexual acts and still have a sexual identity of heterosexual, homosexual, or bisexual. This study is directed toward determining what conditions permit a person to say, "I am a homosexual."

Research Method

This report is part of a study that has been ongoing for over two years in a large metropolitan area in the United States. The analysis is based on data obtained from lengthy interviews with 55 self-admitted homosexuals, on observations of and conversations with hundreds of homosexuals, and on the results of a one-page questionnaire distributed to 300 self-admitted homosexuals attending a meeting of a homophile organization. The statistical data are based on the 182 questionnaires that were returned.

The 4- to 5-hour interviews with the 55 self-admitted homosexuals were generally conducted in the subject's home, and in the context of a "participant-observation" study in which the researcher as researcher became integrated into friendship networks of homosexuals. The researcher was introduced to this group by a homosexual student who presented him correctly as being a heterosexual who was interested in doing a study of homosexuals as they exist in the "outside world." He was able to gain the trust of the most prestigious person in the group, which enabled him, on the whole, to gain the trust of the rest of the group. The guidelines employed in the study were based on those outlined by Polsky for participant-observation studies.

There is no way of determining whether the sample groups studied here, or any similar sample, would be representative of the homosexual population. Thus it remains problematic whether the findings of this study can be applied to the homosexual population in general or to other samples of homosexuals. Since age is a critical variable in this study, the questionnaire sample was used in the hope that the replies to a questionnaire would represent a fairly wide age range. The age distribution of the questionnaire sample is shown on Table 1.

Table 1   AGE CHARACTERISTICS OF SAMPLE

Age	Age distribution		Age of first sexual desire toward same sex		Age at which decision was made that respondent was a homosexual	
	N	(%)	N	(%)	N	%
0-4	0	(0)	1	(0.5)	0	(0)
5-9	0	(0)	28	(15)	1	(0.5)
10-14	0	(0)	83	(46)	27	(15)
15-19	13	(7)	54	(29)	79	(44)
20-24	36	(20)	14	(8)	52	(29)
25-29	39	(22)	1	(0.5)	11	(6)
30-34	28	(16)	1	(0.5)	4	(2)
35-39	21	(12)	0	(0)	3	(2)
40-44	18	(10)	0	(0)	1	(0.5)
45-49	6	(3)	0	(0)	0	(0)
50-59	11	(6)	0	(0)	0	(0)
60-69	8	(4)	0	(0)	1	(0.5)
Total	180	(100)	182	(99.5)	179	(99.5)
	$\overline{X} = 32.5, S = 11.3$		$\overline{X} = 13.5, S = 4.3$		$\overline{X} = 19.3, S = 6.4$	

Coming Out

The term "coming out" is frequently used by homosexuals to refer to the identity change to homosexual. Hooker states: "Very often, the debut, referred to by homosexuals as the coming out, of a person who believes himself to be homosexual but who has struggled against it will occur when he identifies himself publicly for the first time as a homosexual in the presence of other homosexuals by his appearance in a bar." Gagnon and Simon refer to coming out as that ". . . point in time when there is self-recognition by the individual of his identity as a homosexual and the first major exploration of the homosexual community."

In this study it was found that the meaning that the informant attached to his expression was usually directly related to his own experiences concerning how he met other gay people and how and when he decided he was homosexual. For purposes of this study the term "coming out" will mean identifying oneself as being homosexual. This self-identification as being homosexual may or may not occur in a social context in which other gay people are present. One of the tasks of this paper is to identify the social contexts in which the self-definition of homosexual occurs.

The Social Contexts of Coming Out

The child who is eventually to become homosexual in no sense goes through a period of anticipatory socialization (Merton); if he does go through such a period, it is in reference to heterosexuality, not homosexuality. It is sometimes said that the homosexual minority is just like any other minority group (Cory; Westwood); but in the sense of early childhood socialization it is not, for the parents of a Negro can communicate to their child that he is a Negro and what it is like to be a Negro, but the parents of a person who is to become homosexual do not prepare their child to be homosexual—they are not homosexual themselves, and they do not communicate to him what it is like to be a homosexual.

The person who has sexual feelings or desires toward persons of the same sex has no vocabulary to explain to himself what these feelings mean. Subjects who had homosexual feelings during childhood were asked how they would have honestly responded to the question, "Are you a homosexual?," at the time just prior to their graduation from high school. Some typical responses follow:

> SUBJECT 1: I had guilt feelings about this being attracted to men. Because I couldn't understand why all the other boys were dating, and I didn't have any real desire to date.
>
> INTERVIEWER: Were you thinking of yourself as homosexual?

SUBJECT 1: I think I did but I didn't know how to put it into words. I didn't know it existed. I guess I was like everybody else and thought I was the only one in the world. . . . I probably would have said I didn't know. I don't think I really knew what one was. I would have probably asked you to explain what one was.

SUBJECT 2: I would have said, "No, I don't know what you are talking about." If you had said "queer," I would have thought something about it; this was the slang term that was used, although I didn't know what the term meant.

SUBJECT 3: I don't think I would have known then. I know now. Then I wasn't even thinking about the word. I wasn't reading up on it.

Respondents were asked the age at which they first became aware of any desire or sexual feeling toward persons of the same sex; subsequently they were asked when they decided they were homosexual. Results are presented in Table 1. On the average, there was a six-year interval between time of first sexual feeling toward persons of the same sex and the decision that one was a homosexual. The distribution of the differing time intervals between a person's awareness of homosexual feelings and the decision that he is homosexual is presented in Table 2. As Table 2 indicates, there is considerable variation in this factor.[4]

Table 2   TIME INTERVAL BETWEEN FIRST HOMOSEXUAL DESIRE AND THE DECISION THAT ONE IS A HOMOSEXUAL

Time interval (years)	Distribution	
	N	%
0	29	(16)
1-4	66	(37)
5-9	49	(27)
10-14	21	(12)
15-19	7	(4)
20-29	5	(3)
30-39	1	(0.5)
40-49	0	(0)
50-59	1	(0.5)
Total	179	(100)

$$\overline{X} = 5.7, S = 6.4$$

The fact that an actor continues to have homosexual feelings and to engage in homosexual behavior does not mean that he views himself as being homosexual. In order for a person to view himself as homosexual he must be placed in a new social context, in which knowledge of homosexuals and homosexuality can be found; in such a context he learns a new vocabulary of motives, a vocabulary that will allow him to identify himself as being a homosexual. This can occur in any number of social contexts—through meeting self-admitted homosexuals, by meeting knowledgeable straight persons, or by reading about homosexuals and homosexuality. Knowledge of homosexuals and homosexuality can be found in numerous types of physical settings: a bar, a park, a private home, a psychiatrist's office, a mental hospital, and so on (see Table 3). It is in contexts where such knowledge tends to be concentrated that the actor will be most likely to come out. It is therefore to be expected that an actor is likely to come out in a

Table 3 SOCIAL CONTEXTS IN WHICH RESPONDENTS CAME OUT

Social Contexts	N^*	(%)
Frequenting gay bars	35	(19)
Frequenting gay parties and other gatherings	46	(26)
Frequenting parks	43	(24)
Frequenting men's rooms	37	(21)
Having a love affair with a homosexual man	54	(30)
Having a love affair with a heterosexual man	21	(12)
In the military	34	(19)
Living in a YMCA	2	(1)
Living in all-male quarters at a boarding school or college	12	(7)
In prison	2	(1)
Patient in a mental hospital	3	(2)
Seeing a psychiatrist or professional counselor	11	(6)
Read for the first time about homosexuals and/or homosexuality	27	(15)
Just fired from a job because of homosexual behavior	2	(1)
Just arrested on a charge involving homosexuality	7	(4)
Was not having any homosexual relations	36	(20)

* Total N of social contexts is greater than 180 (number of respondents) because there was overlap in contexts.

context in which other gay people are present; they are usually a ready and willing source of knowledge concerning homosexuals and homosexuality. In the questionnaire sample, 50 percent came out while associating with gay people.

It is also to be expected that a likely place for an actor to come out would be in one-sex situations or institutions . Sexually segregated environments provide convenient locales for knowledge of homosexuality and homosexual behavior. Examples of these one-sex environments are mental institutions, YMCAs, prisons, the military, men's rooms, gay bars, and school dormitories. The first six case histories below illustrate the influence of such milieux.

The first example of an actor coming out in the context of interacting with gay persons concerns a subject who came out in a mental hospital. The subject was committed to a mental hospital at age 20; his commitment did not involve homosexuality and the hospital authorities had no knowledge that the subject had a history of homosexual behavior. Prior to commitment he had a history of heterosexual and homosexual behavior, thought of himself as bisexual, had had no contact with self-admitted homosexuals, was engaged to marry, and was indulging in heavy petting with his fiancée. In the following interview excerpt the subject reports on his first reaction to meeting gay persons in the hospital:

> SUBJECT: I didn't know there were so many gay people, and I wasn't used to the actions of gay people or anything, and it was quite shocking walking down the halls, going up to the ward, and the whistles and flirting and everything else that went on with the new fish, as they called it.
>
> And there was this one kid who was a patient escort and he asked me if I was interested in going to church, and I said yes . . . and he started escorting me to church and then he pulled a little sneaky to see whether I'd be shocked at him being gay. There was this queen[5] on the ward, and him and her, he was looking out the hall to see when I'd walk by the door and they kissed when I walked by the door and this was to check my reaction. And I didn't say a word. So he then escorted me to the show, and we were sitting there and about half-way through the movie he reaches over and started holding my hand, and when he saw I didn't jerk away, which I was kind of upset and wondering exactly what he had in mind and then when we got back to the ward he wrote me a long love letter and gave it to me; before we knew it we were going together, and went together for about six months.

[After 3 weeks] he had gotten me to the point where I'd gotten around the hospital, where I picked up things from the other queens and learned how to really swish and carry on and got to be one of the most popular queens in the whole place. [About that same time] I'd gotten to consider myself—I didn't consider myself a queen, I just considered myself a gay boy; we sat down, a bunch of us got together and made out the rules about what was what as far as the joint was concerned, drew definitions of every little thing . . . if someone was completely feminine, wanted to take the female role all the time, then they were a "queen," if they were feminine but butchy, then they were a "nellie-butch," and I was considered a "gay boy" because I could take any role, I was versatile.

INTERVIEWER: Before this bull session were you considering yourself gay?

SUBJECT: Yes, I had definitely gotten to be by this time; after three months my folks came down to see me and I told them the whole thing point blank.

INTERVIEWER: What would you say was the most important effect the hospital had on you?

SUBJECT: It let me find out it wasn't so terrible. . . . I met a lot of gay people that I liked and I figured it can't be all wrong. If so and so's a good Joe, and he's still gay, he can't be all that bad. . . . I figured it couldn't be all wrong, and that's one of the things I learned. I learned to accept myself for what I am—homosexual.

This subject spent a year and a half in the mental hospital. After release he did not engage in heterosexual relations, and has been actively involved in the gay subculture for the past four years.

The above example clearly demonstrates how a one-sex environment can facilitate the development of a homosexual identity. Although some one-sex environments are created for homosexuals, such as gay bars, any one-sex environment can serve as a meeting and recruiting place for homosexuals, whether or not the environment was created with that purpose in mind.

The YMCA is a one-sex environment that inadvertently functions as a meeting place for homosexuals in most large urban areas in the United States.[6] The following subject came out while living and working at a YMCA. He was 24 when he first visited a Y, never had had a homosexual experience, and had just been separated from his wife.

I became separated from my wife, I then decided to go to Eastern City. I had read of the Walter Jenkins case and the name of the YMCA happened to come up, but when I got to the city it was the only place I knew of to stay. I had just $15.00 in my pocket to stay at the Y, and I don't think I ever had the experience before of taking a group shower. So I went into the shower room, that was the first time I remember looking at a man's body and finding it sexually enticing.[7] So I started wondering to myself—that guy is good-looking. I walked back to my room and left the door open and the guy came in, and I happened to fall in love with that guy.

After this first experience, the subject became homosexually active while living and working at the Y and became part of the gay subculture that existed within the Y.

.... I found that the kids who were working for me, some of them I had been to bed with and some of them I hadn't, had some horrible problems and trying to decide the right and wrong of homosexuality .... and they would feel blunt enough or that I had the experience enough to counsel them along the lines of homosexuality or anything else. .... Part of this helped me realize that one of the greatest things that you can do is to accept what you are and if you want to change it, you can go ahead and do it. ....

This subject spent six months living in this Y; by the end of three months he had accepted himself as being homosexual and has been exclusively homosexual for the last two years.

The prison is another one-sex environment in which homosexual behavior is concentrated. Although there have been studies of situational homosexuality in prison (Giallombardo; Sykes; Tittle; Ward and Kassebaum), and of how homosexual activities are structured in prison, there have been no studies that have looked at the possible change of the sexual identity of the prisoner. In the following case the subject was sentenced to prison on a charge of sodomy at the age of 32, and spent five years in prison. He had been homosexually active for 22 years, and before his arrest he had been engaging predominantly in homosexual behavior, but he had not defined himself as being a homosexual. He had had only peripheral contacts with the gay subculture before his arrest, largely because he was married and held a high socioeconomic position.

INTERVIEWER: In prison did you meet homosexuals?
SUBJECT: Yes.
INTERVIEWER: I'm not talking about people who are just homosexua while in prison.
SUBJECT: People who are homosexual, period. I became educated about the gay world, how you can meet people and not lay yourself

open to censure, and how to keep from going to prison again. And still go on being homosexual. . . . I had frequent meetings with psychiatrists, various social workers. We were all pretty much in tacit agreement that the best thing to do would be to learn to live with yourself. Up until then, I rationalized and disillusioned myself about a lot of things. As I look back on it, I was probably homosexual from ten years on.

After his release from prison, this subject became involved in the gay sub-culture and has been exclusively homosexual for the last eight years.

The military is a one-sex environment that is a most conducive setting for homosexual behavior. In the military, a large number of young men live in close contact with one another and are deprived of heterosexual contacts for varying periods of time; it is not surprising that a homosexual subculture would arise. Given the young age of the military population, it should also be expected that a certain proportion of men be entering military service with homosexual desires and/or a history of homosexual behavior, but without a clearly formulated homosexual identity. Approximately 19 percent of the sample came out while in military service. The following subject had a history of homosexual desires and behavior previous to joining the Navy, but came out while in military service.

INTERVIEWER: How did you happen to have homosexual relations while in the Navy?

SUBJECT: We were out at sea and I had heard that one of the dental technicians was a homosexual, and he had made advances toward me, and I felt like masturbation really wouldn't solve the problem so I visited him one night. He started talking about sex and everything. I told him I had never kissed a boy before. And he asked me what would you do if a guy kissed you, and I said you mean like this and I began kissing him. Naturally he took over then. . . . There were other people on the ship that were homosexual and they talked about me. A yeoman aboard ship liked me quite a bit, was attracted to me; so he started making advances toward me, and I found him attractive, so we got together, and in a short period of time, we became lovers. He started to take me to the gay bars and explain what homosexuality was all about. He took me to gay bars when we were in port.

INTERVIEWER: Did you start to meet other gay people aboard ship?

SUBJECT: The first real contact with gay people was aboard ship. . . .

INTERVIEWER: Was it while you were in the Navy that you decided you were a homosexual?

SUBJECT: Yes. Once I was introduced to gay life, I made the decision that I was a homosexual.

Public restrooms, another part of society which is sexually segregated, are known in the gay world as T-rooms, and some T-rooms become known as meeting places for gay persons and others who are looking for homosexual contacts (Humphreys). Sex in T-rooms tends to be anonymous, but since some nonsexual social interaction also occurs in this locale, some homosexuals do come out in T-rooms. In the sample studied here 21 percent came out while frequenting T-rooms for sexual purposes. The following subject came out in the context of going to T-rooms when he was 15. Previously he had been homosexually active, but had not thought of himself as being a homosexual.

> I really didn't know what a homosexual was. In the back of my mind, my definition of a homosexual or queer was someone who wore girls' clothes and women's shoes, 'cause my brothers said this was so, and I knew I wasn't.

At the age of 15 this subject had a sexual relationship with a gay man.

> And he took me out and introduced me to the gay world. I opened the door and I went out and it was a beautiful day and I accepted this whole world, and I've never had any guilt feelings or hang-ups or regrets. . . . I was young and fairly attractive and I had men chasing me all the time. . . . He didn't take me to bars. We went to restrooms, that was my outlet. He started taking me to all the places they refer to in the gay world as T-rooms, and I met other people and I went back there myself and so on.

After meeting other gay persons by going to T-rooms, this subject quickly discovered other segments of the gay world and has been exclusively homosexual for the last nine years.

Gay bars are probably the most widespread and well-known gay institutions (Achilles; Hooker, 1965). For many persons who become homosexual, gay bars are the first contact with organized gay society and therefore a likely place to come out. In this sample 19 percent came out while going to gay bars. Since gay bars apparently are widespread throughout the nation, this could be viewed as a surprisingly low percentage. However, it should be remembered that generally the legal age limit for entering bars is 21. If the age limit is enforced, this would reduce the percentage of persons coming out in gay bars. T-rooms and gay private parties and other gatherings perform the same function as gay bars, but are not hampered by any age limit. Thus, it is not really surprising that the percentages of persons who came out in several other ways are higher than the percentage coming out in gay bars.

The following subject came out in the context of going to gay bars. He had been predominantly homosexual for a number of years and was 23 at the time he came out.

> SUBJECT: I knew that there were homosexuals, queers and what not; I had read some books, and I was resigned to the fact that I was a foul, dirty person, but I wasn't actually calling myself a homosexual yet. . . . I went to this guy's house and there was nothing going on, and I asked him, "Where is some action?," and he said, "There is a bar down the way." And the time I really caught myself coming out is the time I walked into this bar and saw a whole crowd of groovy, groovy guys. And I said to myself, there was the realization, that not all gay men are dirty old men or idiots, silly queens, but there are some just normal-looking and acting people, as far as I could see, I saw gay society and I said, "Wow, I'm home."
>
> INTERVIEWER: This was the first time that you walked into this gay bar that you felt this way?
>
> SUBJECT: That's right. It was that night in the bar. I think it saved my sanity. I'm sure it saved my sanity.

This subject has been exclusively homosexually active for the last 13 years.

Even after an introduction to gay bars, labeling oneself as homosexual does not always occur as rapidly as it did in the previous example. Some persons can still, for varying periods of time, differentiate themselves from the people they are meeting in gay bars. The following subject came out when he was 22; he had been predominantly homosexual before coming out. He interacted with gay people in gay bars for several months before he decided he was a homosexual. He attempted to differentiate himself from the other homosexuals by saying to himself, "I am not really homosexual since I am not as feminine as they are."

> Finally after hanging around there for so long, some guy came up to me and tried to take me for some money, and I knew it, and he said, "You know, you're very nellie."[8] And I said I wasn't, and he said, "Yes, you are, and you might as well face facts and that's the way it is, and you're never going to change." And I said, "If that's the case, then that's the way it's going to be." So I finally capitulated.

This subject has been predominantly homosexually active for the last 21 years.

I should be made clear that such a change in sexual identity need not be accompanied by any change in sexual behavior or any participation in homosexual behavior. It is theoretically possible for someone to view himself as being homosexual but not engage in homosexual relations just as it is possible for someone to view himself as heterosexual but not engage in heterosexual relations. Approximately 20 percent of this sample came out while having no homosexual relations. The following subject is one of this group; he came out during his late twenties even though he had had his last homosexual experience at age 20.

> I picked up a copy of this underground newspaper one day just for the fun of it. . . . and I saw an ad in there for this theatre, and after thinking about it I got up enough nerve to go over there. . . . I knew that they had pictures of boys and I had always liked boys, and I looked at the neighborhood and then I came home without going in. . . . I went back to the neighborhood again and this time I slunk, and I do mean slunk through the door. . . . and I was shocked to see what I saw on the screen, but I found it interesting and stimulating and so I went back several more times.

Eventually this subject bought a copy of a gay publication, and subsequently he went to the publication's office.

> I visited with the fellows in the office and I had time on my hands and I volunteered to help and they were glad to have me. And I have been a member of the staff ever since and it was that way that I got my education of what gay life is like. . . . For the last ten years, I had been struggling against it. Back then if I knew what homosexuality was, if I had been exposed to the community . . . and seen the better parts, I probably would have admitted it then.

This subject has been very active socially but not sexually in the gay subculture for the last year.

In contrast to the previous examples, there are cases in which the subject has no direct contact with any gay persons, but yet comes out in that context. Fifteen percent (27) of the sample came out upon first reading about homosexuals or homosexuality in a book, pamphlet, etc.; ten of these (about 6 percent of the sample) were not associating with gay people at the time they came out. The following subject came out in this context. He was 14 at the time, had just ended a homosexual relationship with a person who considered himself to be straight, and had had no contact with gay society.

> I had always heard like kids do about homosexuals and things, but that never really entered my mind, but when I read this article, when I was in the 8th grade, and it had everything in it about them sexually, not how they looked and acted and where they go. It was about me and

that was what I was thinking. I just happen one day to see a picture of a guy, and thought he was kind of cute, so I'll read the article about him. But before that I didn't realize what was happening. I didn't even realize I wasn't right as far as heterosexuals were concerned. I didn't realize that what I was thinking wasn't kosher. . . . If people don't like it I'll keep my mouth shut. The article said people wouldn't like it, so I decided to keep my mouth shut. That's the way I was, so I accepted it.

This subject has been active sexually and socially in the gay subculture for the last five years.

Another context in which a subject can come out is that of having a homosexual relationship with a person who defines himself as being heterosexual; 12 percent (21) of the sample came out in such a context. Of these, 12 (about 7 percent of the sample) had never met any self-admitted homosexuals and had never read any material on homosexuality. The following case involves a subject who came out in such a context. At the age of 21 he was having an intense love affair with a serviceman who defined himself as straight. The subject also became involved in a triangular relationship with the serviceman's female lover.

This got very serious. I told him I loved him. . . . He wanted me for a sex release; I didn't admit it then, but now I see, through much heartbreak. He liked me as a person. . . . At the same time he was dating a married woman; he was dating her and having sex with her. . . . She couldn't admit to having a relationship with him 'cause she was married, but he told me and I was extremely jealous of her. [We worked together] and privately she was a very good friend of mine. So I started feeling hatred toward her because she was coming between he and I, competition. I was strong competition, 'cause I frankly dominated it, and she sensed this; so one day she said, "I bet he'd be very good in bed." So I said, "You know he is." She said, "What did you say?" and I said, "Oh, I guess he would be." And I wanted to tell her; so I finally acted like I just broke down and I told her everything in order to make her not like him. So she got on his tail and told him to stop seeing me or she wouldn't have anything to do with him. . . . I taped all their phone conversations and told her if she wouldn't leave him alone, I'd play them for her husband. She got furious, so she said if I tried to blackmail her she would go to the police with the whole thing . . . it all backfired on me and I really didn't want to hurt her, but my love for him was so strong; I'd hurt anybody to keep him, so I erased the tape. And later I bawled and bawled and cried about it to her because I was very sensitive at this time and I told her I was sorry, didn't want to hurt her, but I loved him so much. . . . After I fell in love with him I knew I was homosexual. I talked to my brother about it and he said I wasn't really in love. He said you're just doing it cause you want to; it's not right, boys don't fall in love with boys. He wasn't nasty about it . . . I really loved him; he was my first love; I even dream about him once in a while to this very day. . . . It was during this time that I came out, and I was extremely feminine, not masculine in any way. I wore male clothing, but dressed in a feminine way, in the way I carried myself, the way I spoke. . . . I realized that I was homosexual because I loved him. I was afraid of gay people; heard they did all kinds of weird things from straight people talking about them.

Before this relationship, the subject had engaged in both homosexual and heterosexual petting. Shortly after the relationship terminated the subject became involved in the gay subculture and has been almost exclusively homosexual since that time.

Cognitive Change

What is common to all the cases discussed is that the subject placed himself in a new cognitive category (McCall and Simmons), the category of homosexual. In some cases, such placement can occur as soon as the person learns of the existence of the category; an example of this is the boy who placed himself in that category after reading about homosexuals in a magazine. However, probably most persons who eventually identify themselves as homosexuals require a change in the meaning of the cognitive category *homosexual* before they can place themselves in the category.

The meaning of the category must be changed because the subject has learned the negative stereotype of the homosexual held by most heterosexuals, and he knows that he is no queer, pervert, dirty old man, and so on (Simmons). He differentiates himself from the homosexual image that straight society has presented to him. Direct or indirect contact with the gay subculture provides the subject with information about homosexuals that will challenge the "straight" image of the homosexual. The subject will quite often see himself in other homosexuals, homosexuals he finds to be socially acceptable. He now knows who and what he is because the meaning of the cognitive category has changed to include himself. As one subject said: "Wow, I'm home"; at times that is literally the case since the homosexual now feels that he knows where he really belongs.

A person's identification of himself as being homosexual is often accompanied by a sense of relief, of freedom from tension. In the words of one subject:

> I had this feeling of relief; there was no more tension. I had this feeling of relief. I guess the fact that I had accepted myself as being homosexual had taken a lot of tensions off me.

Coming out, in essence, often signifies to the subject the end of a search for his identity.

Identification and Self-Acceptance

Identifying oneself as being homosexual and accepting oneself as being homosexual usually come together, but this is not necessarily the case. It can be hypothesized that those who identify themselves as being homosexual; but not in the context of interacting with other homosexuals, are more likely to have guilt feelings than those who identify themselves as being homosexual in the context of interacting with other homosexuals. Interaction with other homosexuals facilitates the learning of a vocabulary that will not simply explain but will also justify the homosexual behavior.

Identifying oneself as homosexual is almost uniformly accompanied by the development of certain techniques of neutralization (Sykes and Matza).[9] In this self-identification, it would be incorrect to state that the homosexual accepts himself as being deviant, in the evaluative sense of the term. The subject may know he is deviant from the societal standpoint but often does not accept this as part of his self-definition. Lemert (1951) has defined secondary deviation as the situation in which ". . . a person begins to employ his deviant behavior or a role based upon it as a means of defense, attack or adjustment to the overt and covert problems created by the consequent societal reaction to him." Once the subject identifies himself as being homosexual, he does develop means, often in the process of the change in self-definition, of adjusting to the societal reaction to the behavior. The means employed usually involve the denial, to himself and to others, that he is really deviant. Becker explained the situation when he stated:

> But the person thus labeled an outsider may have a different view of the matter. He may not accept the rule by which he is being judged and may not regard those who judge him as either competent or legitimately entitled to do so. [pp. 1-2]

The societal reaction to homosexuality appears to be expressed more in a mental health rhetoric (Bieber; Hadden; Ovesey; Socarides; Szasz), than in a rhetoric of sin and evil or crime and criminal behavior. In order to determine how the subjects adjusted to this societal reaction to homosexuality, they were asked to react to the idea that homosexuals are sick or mentally ill. With very few exceptions, this notion was rejected.

> SUBJECT 1: I believe this idea to be very much true, if added that you are talking from society's standpoint and society has to ask itself why are these people sick or mentally ill. . . . In other words, you can't make flat statements that homosexuals are sick or mentally ill. I do not consider myself to be sick or mentally imbalanced.
> SUBJECT 2: That's a result of ignorance; people say that quickly, pass quick judgments. They are not knowledgeable, fully knowledgeable about the situation.
> SUBJECT 3: I don't feel they are. I feel it's normal. What's normal for one person is not always normal for another. I don't think it's a mental illness or mental disturbance.
> SUBJECT 4: Being a homosexual does not label a person as sick or mentally ill. In every other capacity I am as normal or more normal than straight people. Just because I happen to like strawberry ice cream and they like vanilla, doesn't make them right or me right.

It is the learning of various ideas from other homosexuals that allows the subject to in effect say, "I am homosexual, but not deviant," or, "I am homosexual, but not mentally ill." The cognitive category of *homosexual* now becomes socially acceptable, and the subject can place himself in that category and yet preserve a sense of his self-esteem or self-worth.

It should be emphasized that coming out often involves an entire transformation in the meaning of the concept of homosexual for the subject. In these cases the subject had been entirely unaware of the existence of gay bars or an organized gay society, of economically successful homosexuals, of homosexually "married" homosexuals, and so on. In the words of one subject:

> I had always thought of them as dirty old men that preyed on 10-, 11-, 12-year-old kids, and I found out that they weren't all that way; there are some that are, but they are a minority. It was a relief for me 'cause I found out that I wasn't so different from many other people. I had considered consulting professional help prior to that 'cause at the time I thought I was mentally ill. Now I accept it as a way of life, and I don't consider it a mental illness. It's an unfortunate situation. . . . I consider myself an outcast from general society, but not mentally ill.

Public Labeling

It should be made clear that the self-identification as a homosexual does not generally take place in the context of a negative public labeling, as some labeling theorists imply that it does (Garfinkel; Lemert, 1951; Scheff). No cases were found in the interview sample in which the subject had come out in the context of being arrested on a charge involving homosexuality or being fired from a job because of homosexual behavior. In the questionnaire sample, 4 percent (7) had just been arrested and 1 percent (2) had just been fired from a job. A total of 8 respondents or 4.5 percent of the sample came out in the context of public exposure.

It can be hypothesized that the public labeling of an actor who has not yet identified himself as being homosexual will reinforce in his mind the idea that he is not homosexual. This is hypothesized because it is to be expected that at the time of the public labeling the actor will be presented with information that will present homosexuals and homosexuality in a highly negative manner. For example, the following subject was arrested for homosexual activities at the age of 11. Both before and after the arrest he did not consider himself to be a homosexual. His reaction to the arrest was:

> SUBJECT: The officer talked to me and told me I should see a psychiatrist. It kind of confused me. I really didn't understand any of it.
> INTERVIEWER: And were you thinking of yourself at that time as a homosexual?
> SUBJECT: I probably would have said I wasn't. 'Cause of the way the officer who interrogated me acted. It was something you never admit to. He acted as if I were the scum of the earth. He was very rude and impolite.

If the actor has not yet identified himself as being homosexual, it can probably be assumed that to a significant degree he already accepts the negative societal stereotype; the new information accompanying the public labeling will conform to the societal stereotype, and the actor consequently will not modify his decision not to place himself in the homosexual category. This is not to say that public labeling by significant others and/or official agents of social control does not play a significant role in the life of the homosexual; all that is hypothesized is that public labeling does not facilitate and may in fact function to inhibit the decision to label oneself as being homosexual.

The Closet Queen

There are some persons who may continue to have homosexual desires and may possibly engage in homosexual relations for many years, but yet do not have a homosexual identity. Self-admitted homosexuals refer to such persons as "closet queens."[10] Such persons may go for many years without any contact with or knowledge of self-admitted homosexuals. The subject previously cited who came out in prison was a closet queen for 20 years.

An interval of 10 or more years between first awareness of sexual attraction toward males and the decision that one is a homosexual, would probably classify one as having been a closet queen. As Table 2 shows, the questionnaire sample included 35 respondents (20 percent of the samples) who at one time were closet queens.

It is the closet queen who has most internalized the negative societal stereotype of the homosexual. It is to be expected that such persons would suffer from a feeling of psychological tension, for they are in a state of cognitive dissonance (Festinger)—that is, feelings and sometimes behavior are not consistent with self-definition.

The following subject was a closet queen for over 50 years. He had his first homosexual experience at the age of 12, has had homosexual desires since that time, and has been exclusively homosexual for 53 years. At the time the subject was interviewed, he expressed amazement that he had just come out during the last few months. Over the years, his involvement with the gay subculture was peripheral; at the age of 29 for about one year he had some involvement with overt homosexuals, but otherwise he had had only slight contact with them until recently. During that earlier involvement:

> I was not comfortable with them. I was repressed and timid and they thought I was being high hat, so I was rejected. It never worked out; I was never taken in. I felt uncomfortable in their presence and I made them feel uncomfortable. I couldn't fit in there, I never wanted to, never sought to; I was scared of them. I was scared of the brazen bitches who would put me down.

During the years as a closet queen he was plagued with feelings of guilt; for varying periods of time he was a patient in over twenty mental hospitals. His social life was essentially nil; he had neither gay friends nor straight friends. His various stays in mental hospitals relieved continuing feelings of loneliness. At the age of 65 he attended a church whose congregation was primarily homosexual. It was in the context of interacting with the gay persons who were associated with this church that after 53 years this subject came out.

SUBJECT: I had never seen so many queens in one place; I was scared somebody would put me down, somebody would misunderstand why I was there. I had this vague, indescribable fear. But all this was washed away when I saw all were there for the one purpose of fellowship and community in the true sense of the term. . . . I kept going and then I got to be comfortable in the coffee hour. . . . Then out in the lobby a young fellow opened his heart to me, telling me all his troubles and so forth, and I listened patiently, and I thought I made a couple of comforting remarks. Then I went out to the car, and when I got in the car I put my hand out to shake hands and he kissed my hand. . . . it's hard for you to understand the emotional impact of something like this—that I belong, they love me, I love them.

Until the last few weeks, in all my life I had never been in a gay bar for more than a few minutes. I was actually uncomfortable. But now I can actually go into it; this is the most utterly ludicrous transformation in the last few weeks. . . . there's no logic whatsoever. I'm alive at 65.

It's a tremendous emotional breakthrough. I feel comfortable and relieved of tensions and self-consciousness. My effectiveness in other fields has been enhanced 100 percent. I have thrown off so many of the prejudices and revulsions that were below the surface. . . . I'm out of the closet. In every way, they know, where I work, in this uptight place where I work; I've told them where I live; I've written back east. What more can I do?

INTERVIEWER: Do you think you are now more self-accepting of yourself?

SUBJECT: Brother! I hope you're not kidding. That's the whole bit. How ironical it would come at 65. The only thing that I wouldn't do now is to go to the baths. I told the kids the other day; it's the only breakthrough I cannot bring myself to.

One can only speculate why after all these years this subject came out. The reason may have been that he had had a very religious upbringing and could not conceive of homosexuals in a religiously acceptable manner. The church he attended for the first time at age 65 presented homosexuals as being religiously acceptable, and presented to the subject highly religious homosexuals.[11] Contact with this church may have helped change the meaning of the category homosexual so that he could now include himself.[12]

In a sense the closet queen represents society's ideal homosexual, for the closet queen accepts the societal stereotype of the homosexual and feels guilt because he does the same sort of things that homosexuals do, yet believes he is really different from homosexuals in some significant way. This inability of the closet queen to see himself in other homosexuals prevents him from placing himself in the cognitive category of *homosexual,* and he will not come out until some new information is given to him about homosexuals which permits him to say, "There are homosexuals like myself," or "I am very much like them."

There may be significant differences between ex–closet queens and those closet queens who never come out. Of course, I had contact only with ex–closet queens, and they uniformly reported that their own psychological adjustment has been much better since coming out. Their only regret was that they had not come out sooner. Possibly the closet queen who remains a closet queen reaches some sort of psychological adjustment that ex–closet queens were unable to reach.

The Role of Knowledge

The change of self-identity to *homosexual* is intimately related to the access of knowledge and information concerning homosexuals and homosexuality. Hoffman has observed:

> Society deals with homosexuality as if it did not exist. Although the situation is changing, this subject was not even discussed and was not even the object of scientific investigation until a few decades ago. We just didn't speak about these things; they were literally unspeakable and so loathsome that nothing could be said in polite society about them. . . . [p. 195]

The traditional silence on this topic has most probably prevented many persons with homosexual feelings from identifying themselves as being homosexual. Lofland has noted that the role of knowledge in creating a deviant identity is an important one. If significant others or the actor himself does not know of the deviant category, his experience cannot be interpreted in terms of that category; or if his experience appears to be completely alien from that category he will not interpret his experience in terms of that category. If the societal stereotype of homosexuals is one of dirty old men, perverts, Communists, and so on, it should not be surprising that the young person with homosexual feelings would have difficulty in interpreting his experience in terms of the homosexual category.

The greater tolerance of society for the freer circulation of information concerning homosexuality and homosexuals has definite implications in reference to coming out. The fact that there is greater overt circulation of homophile magazines and homophile newspapers, that there are advertisements for gay movies in newspapers, and that there are books, articles, and movies about gay life, permits the cognitive category of homosexuals to be known to a larger proportion of the population and, most importantly, permits more information to be circulated that challenges the negative societal stereotype of the homosexual.

Since there has been a freerer circulation of information on homosexuality during the past few years, it can be hypothesized that the development of a homosexual identity is now occurring at an increasingly earlier age. Indeed, older gay informants have stated that the younger homosexuals are coming out at a much earlier age. In order to test this hypothesis, the sample was dichotomized into a 30-and-above age group and a below-30 age group. It can be seen in Table 4 that the below-30 mean age for developing a homo-

Table 4 RELATIONSHIP OF RESPONDENT AGE TO AGE AT HOMOSEXUAL SELF-IDENTIFICATION

Age at homosexual self-identi- fication	Age of respondents			
	30 and above		Below 30	
	N	(%)	N	(%)
5-9	0	(0)	1	(1)
10-14	8	(9)	19	(22)
15-19	35	(38)	44	(50)
20-24	29	(32)	23	(21)
25-29	10	(11)	1	(1)
30-39	7	(8)	0	(0)
40-49	1	(1)	0	(0)
50-59	0	(0)	0	(0)
60-69	1	(1)	0	(0)
Total	91	(100)	88	(100)
Mean	21.4*		17.2*	
Standard Deviation	7.7		3.8	

Coming Out in the Gay World

* Means significantly different at .01 level

sexual identity was significantly lower (at the .01 level) than the above-30 mean age; the drop in mean age was from approximately 21 to 17.[13]

Indications are that the present trend toward greater circulation of information that is not highly negative about homosexuals and homosexuali will continue. The fact that a mass circulation magazine such as *Time* gave its front cover to an article entitled "The Homosexual in America" (Oct. 31, 1969) and that this article was not highly negative represents a significant breakthrough. The cognitive category of homosexual is now being presented in a not unfavorable manner to hundreds of thousands of people who previously could not have been exposed to such information through conventional channels. This is not to say that more information about homosexuals and homosexuality will lead to a significantly greater prevalence of persons engaging in homosexuality. What is being asserted is that a higher proportion of those with homosexual desires and behavior will develop a homosexual identity, and that the development of that identity will continue to occur at an increasingly younger age.

Conclusion

This study has suggested that the development of a homosexual identity is dependent on the meanings that the actor attaches to the concepts of homo-sexual and homosexuality, and that these meanings are directly related to the meanings that are available in his immediate environment; and the meanings that are available in his immediate environment are related to the meanings that are allowed to circulate in the wider society. The commitment to a homosexual identity cannot occur in an environment where the cognitiv category of homosexual does not exist. Hoffman in essence came to the same conclusion when he hypothesized that the failure to develop a homo-sexual identity is due to a combination of two factors:

> ... the failure of society to make people aware of homosexuality as an existent way of life (and of the existence of the gay world), and the strong repressive forces that prevent people from knowing what their real sexual feelings are. One might consider this a psychological conspiracy of silence, which society insists upon because of its belief that it thereby safeguards existent sexual norms. [p. 138]

Homo-sexuality

In an environment where the cognitive category of homosexual does not exist or is presented in a highly negative manner, a person who is sexually

244

attracted to persons of the same sex will probably be viewed and will probably view himself as sick, mentally ill, or queer.

It can be asserted that one of the main functions of the viewpoint that homosexuality is mental illness is to inhibit the development of a homosexual identity. The *homosexuality-as-mental illness* viewpoint is now in increasing competition with the *homosexuality-as-way-of-life* viewpoint. If the homosexuality-as-way-of-life viewpoint is increasingly disseminated, one would anticipate that the problems associated with accepting a homosexual identity will significantly decrease, there will be a higher proportion of homosexually oriented people with a homosexual identity, and this identity will develop at an earlier age.[14]

If the homosexuality-as-way-of-life philosophy does become increasingly accepted, the nature of the homosexual community itself may undergo a radical transformation. To have a community one must have members who will acknowledge to themselves and to others that they are members of that community. The increasing circulation of the homosexuality-as-way-of-life viewpoint may in fact be a self-fulfilling prophecy. It may lead to, and possibly is leading to, the creation of a gay community in which one's sex life is becoming increasingly less fragmented from the rest of one's social life.

References

ACHILLES, NANCY. "The Development of the Homosexual Bar as an Institution," in John H. Gagnon and William Simon (Eds.), *Sexual Deviance*; Harper & Row, 1967.

BECKER, HOWARD S. "Becoming a Marihuana User." *Amer. J. Sociology* (1953) 59:235-242.

BECKER, HOWARD S. *Outsiders: Studies in the Sociology of Deviance*; Free Press, 1963.

BERGLER, E. *Neurotic Counterfeit-Sex*; Grune & Stratton, 1951.

BIEBER, IRVING, et al. *Homosexuality. A Psychoanalytic Study of Male Homosexuals*; Vintage Books, 1965.

BRYAN, J. H. "Apprenticeships in Prostitution," *Social Problems* (1965) 12:287-297.

CAMERON, MARY O. *The Booster and the Snitch: Department Store Shoplifting*; Free Press, 1964.

CHAMBLISS, WILLIAM J. "Two Gangs: a Study of Societal Response to Deviance and Deviant Careers," unpublished manuscript, 1967.

CORY, DONALD W. *The Homosexual in America*; New York, Greenberg, 1951.

DANK, BARRY M. "Why Homosexuals Marry Women," in *Medical Aspects of Human Sexuality,* in press.

ERICKSON, KAI T. "Notes on the Sociology of Deviance," *Social Problems* (1962) 9:307-314.

FELDMAN, H. W. "Ideological Supports to Becoming and Remaining a Heroin Addict," *J. Health and Social Behavior* (1968) 9:131-139.

FESTINGER, LEON, *Theory of Cognitive Dissonance;* Harper & Row, 1957.

FREUD, SIGMUND. *Three Contributions to the Theory of Sex;* Dutton, 1962.

GAGNON, JOHN H., and SIMON, WILLIAM. "Homosexuality: The Formulation of a Sociological Perspective," in Mark Lefton et al. (Eds.) *Approaches to Deviance,* Appleton-Century-Crofts, 1968.

GARFINKEL, HAROLD. "Conditions of Successful Degradation Ceremonies," *Amer. J. Sociology* (1956) 61:420-424.

GEBHARD, PAUL, et al. *Sex Offenders, An Analysis of Types;* Hoeber-Harper, 1965.

GIALLOMBARDO, ROSE. *Society of Women: A Study of a Women's Prison;* Wiley, 1966.

GOFFMAN, ERVING. *Asylums;* Doubleday Anchor, 1961.

GOFFMAN, ERVING. *Stigma;* Prentice-Hall, 1963.

HADDEN, SAMUEL B. "A Way Out for Homosexuals," *Harper's Magazine,* March, 1967, pp. 107-120.

HOFFMAN, MARTIN. *The Gay World, Male Homosexuality and the Social Creation of Evil;* Basic Books, 1968.

HOOKER, EVELYN. "Male Homosexuals and Their 'Worlds'," in Judd Marmor (Ed.), *Sexual Inversion: The Multiple Roots of Homosexuality;* Basic Books, 1965.

HOOKER, EVELYN. "Parental Relations and Male Homosexuality in Patient and Non-Patient Samples," *J. Consulting and Clin. Psychology* (1960) 33:140-142.

HUMPHREYS, LAUD. *Tearoom Trade;* Aldine, 1970.

KRICH, A. M. (Ed.). *The Homosexuals;* Citadel Press, 1954.

LEMERT, EDWIN M. *Social Pathology;* McGraw-Hill, 1951.

LEMERT, EDWIN M. "Paranoia and the Dynamics of Exclusion," *Sociometry* (1962) 25:2-20.

LEMERT, EDWIN M. *Human Deviance, Social Problems and Social Control;* Prentice-Hall, 1967.

LOFLAND, JOHN. *Deviance and Identity;* Prentice-Hall, 1969.

MATZA, DAVID. *Becoming Deviant;* Prentice-Hall, 1969.

MCCALL, C. J., and SIMMONS, J. L. *Identities and Interactions;* Free Press, 1966.

MERTON, ROBERT, *Social Theory and Social Structure* (rev. ed.); Free Press, 1957.

)VESEY, LIONEL. *Homosexuality and Pseudo-homosexuality;* Science House, 1969.

²OLSKY, NED. *Hustlers, Beats and Others;* Aldine, 1967.

RUITENBEEK, HENDRIK (Ed.). *The Problem of Homosexuality in Modern Society;* Dutton, 1963.

³CHEFF, THOMAS. *Being Mentally Ill.;* Aldine, 1966.

³CHOFIELD, MICHAEL. *Sociological Aspects of Homosexuality;* Little, Brown, 1965.

³IMMONS, J. L. "Public Stereotypes of Deviants," *Social Problems* (1965) 13:223-232.

³OCARIDES, CHARLES W. "Homosexuality and Medicine," *J. Amer. Med. Assn.* (1970) 212:1199-1202.

³TOLLER, ROBERT. *Sex and Gender;* Science House, 1968.

³YKES, GRESHAM M. *Society of Captives;* Princeton Univ. Press, 1958.

³YKES, GRESHAM M., and MATZA, DAVID. "Techniques of Neutralization: A Theory of Delinquency," *Amer. Sociol. Review* (1957) 22:664-670.

SZASZ, THOMAS. *The Manufacture of Madness;* Harper & Row, 1970.

Time. "The Homosexual in America," Oct. 31, 1969, pp. 56, 61-62, 64-67.

TITTLE, CHARLES R. "Inmate Organization: Sex Differentiation and the Influence of Criminal Subcultures," *Amer. Sociol. Review* (1969) 35:492-505.

WARD, DAVID A., and KASSEBAUM, GENE G. *Women's Prison: Sex and Social Structure;* Aldine, 1965.

WEINBERG, MARTIN S. "The Male Homosexual: Age-Related Variations in Social and Psychological Characteristics," *Social Problems* (1970) 17:527-537.

WERTHMAN, C., and PILIAVIN, I. "Gang Members and the Police," in David Bordua (Ed.), *The Police: Sex Sociological Essays;* Wiley, 1967.

WEST, DONALD J. "Parental Figures in the Genesis of Male Homosexuality," *Internat. J. Social Psychiatry* (1959) 5:85-97.

WESTWOOD, GORDON. *A Minority: A Report on the Life of the Male Homosexual in Great Britain;* London, Longmans Green, 1960.

1. In homosexual argot, "gay" means homosexual and "straight" means heterosexual. These terms are acceptable to homosexuals whether used by gay or straight persons.
2. Sometimes homosexuals use the expression "to bring out" or "bringing out." The meaning attached to these expressions varies: they are sometimes used interchange-ably with "coming out." However, as used by my informants, they usually refer to the first complete homosexual act which the subject found enjoyable. The statement, "He brought me out," usually means, "He taught me to enjoy real homosexual acts."
3. Some homosexuals are parents. In the homosexual social networks that I am involved in, there are many persons who once played the role of husband and father —generally before they decided they were homosexual. In addition, there are homo-

sexual couples who are raising children they adopted or children from a former heterosexual marriage; however, such couples tend to be lesbian. In some cases one parent has decided that he or she is homosexual, but both parents have remained together as husband and wife. "Front" marriages also occur, in which a male homosexual marries a female homosexual and they adopt children or have children of their own; such marriages are generally for purposes of social convenience. What the effects are, if any, of being raised by at least one homosexual parent have not been determined. In this sample, there were no cases in which a subject had a homosexual mother or father.

4. First sexual desire toward persons of the same sex was chosen instead of first sexual contact with persons of the same sex since it is quite possible for one to have homosexual desires, fight against those desires, and have no homosexual contacts of any type for an extensive period of time. The mean age of first homosexual contact of any type was 13, which was not significantly different at the .01 level from age of first homosexual desire. In reference to which came first, homosexual act or homosexual desire, 31% (56) had desire before the act; 49% (87) had act before desire; 20% (36) had first homosexual desire and first homosexual act at approximately the same time.

5. In gay argot, the meaning of the term "queen" is variable. Depending on the context, it can mean any homosexual or a homosexual on the feminine side.

6. YMCAs have not been studied in their relation to homosexual society. It appears that YMCAs function as meeting places for homosexuals and for those desiring homosexual relations but defining themselves as straight. This is not a regional phenomenon but is, according to my informants, true for almost all YMCAs in large metropolitan areas. YMCAs are often listed in gay tourist guides.

7. This subject later admitted that he had previously been attracted to other males.

8. In gay argot, "nellie" means feminine or feminine-appearing. The word is not usually used in a complimentary manner.

9. Particularly, denial that there is a victim and denial of injury.

10. In gay argot, the meaning of the term "closet queen" varies, but usually it is applied to one who does not admit to being homosexual. However, the term is sometimes used to refer to a self-admitted homosexual who does not like to associate with other homosexuals, or who may be trying to pass as straight most of the 24 hours of the day.

11. It may be that among closet queens, or those who have been closet queens for many years, one would find a disproportionately high number of very religious persons; the traditional negative religious reaction would probably prevent highly religious persons from easily placing themselves in the homosexual category. It would therefore be expected that clergymen who have homosexual feelings would tend to be closet queens for many years. Not only do clergymen have a more difficult time in resolving problems of guilt, but also interaction with other homosexuals could lead to their losing their jobs. In this sample, there were 10 respondents who were ministers or who were studying for the ministry at the time they came out. Their mean age for coming out was 22, and the mean time interval between first homosexual desire and the homosexual self-identification was 10.4 years. I hope to publish a report in the near future on the social life of homosexual ministers.

12. There have been some recent actions that challenge the traditional religious reaction against homosexuality and homosexuals. Particularly, see: John Dart, "Church for Homosexuals," *Los Angeles Times,* Dec. 8, 1969, Part 2, pp. 1–3; Edward B. Fiske, "Homosexuals in Los Angeles . . . Establish Their Own Church," *New York Times,* Feb. 15, 1970, Sec. 1, p. 58; "The Homosexual Church," *Newsweek,* Oct. 12, 1970, p. 107. Some churches have openly accepted homosexuals; I am currently preparing an article on such a church.

13. It can be argued that this was not a meaningful test because of sample bias, since the sample could not include subjects of the younger generation who had still not come out. However, the age of 30 was chosen as the dividing point because only 9 respondents (5%) had come out after the age of 30. Any remaining bias in the sample from this source should presumably be insignificant.
14. Weinberg has recently reported that younger homosexuals have on the whole a worse psychological adjustment than older homosexuals. As the age for the development of a homosexual identity drops, the psychological adjustment of younger homosexuals may significantly improve.

Part 5
SOME
PUBLIC ISSUES

ABORTION IN AMERICA

Vera Borosage

The abortion issue has aroused considerable public concern in the last decade. Although some observers believe the problem is on the road to solution because seventeen states have liberalized their rigid antiabortion laws to permit aborting a fetus, in most cases under certain specified conditions, no new states have been added to the roster since 1971, and many embattled state legislatures still resist putting the question to popular vote.

The central issue is the moral view of abortion as murder. When is the fetus a human being with a soul—at conception, at "quickening," or at birth, when it can function independently? While this emotionally-laden, controversial question persists, statistics reveal that an estimated million illegal abortions are performed every year. The illegal abortion industry can no longer be swept under the carpet.

How can society resolve this question with justice for all concerned? Professor Borosage lists some of the variables that have led to the impasse: (1) the ambivalent attitudes toward growing sexual permissiveness in this country; (2) the shifting alliances of physicians, lawyers, feminists, and theologians on both sides of the issue; (3) the inferred threat to the male ethic extant in law and medicine; and (4) the powerful antiabortion stance of the Catholic church hierarchy.

Before the 1960s, abortion—both the word and the practice— lay deeply enshrouded in a conspiracy of silence.[1] Although most states had laws permitting "legal" abortion in a hospital, such abortions were performed only to "save the life" of the mother. Occasionally medical men would expand this narrow legal interpretation to include the mother's mental health if it was believed that the unwanted pregnancy might cause her to commit suicide. But the ten-year-old victim of incest, the young rape victim, the grandmother in her menopause, the indigent woman with more children than financial

---

Written expressly for this volume.

means to care for them—none of these was able to obtain a legal abortion.

Statistically, such cases made up only a tiny percentage of the estimated total number of abortions performed in any given year. Only a few accurate statistics on the incidence of abortion are based on empirical evidence; the rest are based on educated guesses, but the figures range from a half-million to 1.2 million largely illegal abortions performed annually in the U.S. Only about 8,000 "therapeutic" abortions were performed under hospital auspices each year.

Then, in 1962, the Sherri Finkbine case exploded in newspapers across the land. Mrs. Finkbine, a young, pregnant mother of four, was horrified to learn that she had inadvertently taken the drug thalidomide in the early months of her pregnancy. Reports of tragic cases of deformed children born in Germany and England with "flippers" instead of arms and legs had been traced to the use of this tranquilizing drug by pregnant women. Distraught over the prospect of producing a deformed child, Mrs. Finkbine obtained approval for an abortion from a hospital board in Phoenix, Arizona. But when the case was reported in the press, a furor of opposition rained down upon the principals involved. Yielding to the religious and political pressures brought about by the national publicity, the medical board rescinded its approval.

After several desperate attempts to secure an abortion in the U.S. failed, the Finkbines finally obtained approval from a hospital in Sweden, where Mrs. Finkbine was aborted of a deformed fetus. Echoes of this case still persist in the current national controversy over the drive to liberalize, or to repeal, the antiquated antiabortion laws still extant in most states. According to Lawrence Lader: "The most disturbing outcome of the case was that religious and political passions became inextricably entwined with the practice of medicine. The case took place in an election year. . . ."[2]

The "Problem" of Abortion

The practice of inducing abortion has existed since antiquity and has not always aroused such passion. The ancient Greek and Roman civilizations practiced both infanticide and abortion as a means of doing away with unwanted progeny, with the responsibility of decision making resting on the family rather than on the state.[3] Christianity would, of course, oppose both practices. Although infanticide was never countenanced in America, abortion has been less clearly defined and is now enmeshed in a tangled web of legal and theological circumscriptions.

Like most issues compounded by moral and value perplexities, abortion becomes a "problem" when diametrically opposing views are held by groups large and powerful enough to determine parameters for its acceptance. Abortion intersects with medicine, law, morality, religion, and the question of the individual's rights as against the rights of society. Alice Rossi calls it "a major unsolved problem in the United States," largely because our culture, which has so many "unresolved attitudes toward sex," endorses punitive attitudes when sex is employed for playful rather than for pro-creative purposes.[4]

Lucille Newman, writing from the anthropological point of view, claims that American society tends to tolerate a gap between "ideals unlikely of realization, and to legislate laws unlikely of enforcement."[5] Thus, very few abortionists are brought to trial although more than a million women annually risk their lives and health at the hands of illegal abortionists, rarely knowing whether they are licensed and capable physicians performing abortions as a "sideline" or unscrupulous, minimally-trained butchers. This is, indeed, a very basic aspect of the abortion "problem." Edwin Schur calls it a "crime without a victim" wherein "an attempt is made to proscribe through criminal law the willing and private exchange between adults of socially disapproved but widely demanded goods or services."[6]

Widespread unavailability of legal abortion becomes a problem when unwanted children are allowed to be born. The literature in the behavioral sciences offers abundant evidence of the tragic consequences of being unwanted. Such persons become "battered" children; they fill the welfare rolls; they become inadequate parents themselves, thus perpetuating a vicious circle from generation to generation.

Medically, abortion is a relatively simple procedure. For years the most popular method was the "D and C" (dilation and currettage). This method, usually performed under general anesthesia, consists of dilatihg the opening of the uterus (cervix), then scraping the lining of the uterus with a spoon-like instrument called a curette until all fetal matter has been removed. Done by a physician, it can take less than fifteen minutes; women can return to their homes or jobs within a day.

A new method increasingly in use, if abortion is performed before the twelfth week of pregnancy, is vacuum aspiration. This procedure can be performed on an outpatient basis and completed within five minutes or less. The cervix is dilated, a metal tube attached to a small vacuum pump is inserted, and the suction draws the fetal material into a bottle.

A third method, which can be used between the sixteenth and twenty-fourth week of pregnancy, is a more drastic procedure. The doctor inserts a needle through the patient's abdomen into the uterus, draws off most of the amniotic fluid in which the fetus floats, and replaces it with a salt solution. The saline solution kills the fetus and induces labor for twenty-four to seventy-two hours until the fetus is expelled.

The mortality rate in *legal* abortions is known to be lower than the general maternal mortality rate in the U.S. (which is 27.4 per 100,000 births). It is the *illegal* abortion, with its greater risks of perforation of the uterus, hemorrhage, and infection, that is a medical problem. The horrors reported by doctors trying to save the lives of desperate women who have attempted self-abortion through drugs, by inserting knitting needles and other blunt instruments into the uterus, only add fuel to the impetus for abortion law reform.

Present Status of Abortion Laws

Concerned about stringent abortion laws leading to inhumanity in practice and criminal charges if disregarded, in 1962, after a ten-year study, the American Law Institute approved a Model Penal Code in which it was proposed that a licensed physician may terminate a pregnancy within the first sixteen weeks, providing that two physicians certify its necessity for one of the following reasons: (1) the risk of endangering the mother's physical or mental health; (2) the possibility of mental or physical deformity in the child; (3) pregnancy as a result of "rape, incest, or other felonious intercourse" (including illicit intercourse with a girl under sixteen years of age).[7]

To date (July 1972), led by Colorado in 1967, seventeen states have liberalized their abortion laws based on variations of this ALI code; theoretically, safe, legal abortions are obtainable in these states. Most states, however, have established restrictions of legal residence and approval by a board of doctors for each abortion to be performed. California, for example, in a last-minute concession to the Catholic church, added a further restriction by striking out the ALI provision of fetal deformity as a legal reason for abortion. The effect of these restrictions has been to hobble the practice of abortion in these states while only minimally changing the actual number of legal abortions performed. New York State alone has no residency requirement, which is reflected in the great increase in legal abortions being performed there.

Although the ALI version is now being endorsed as the result of intense campaigns in other states, it is also being increasingly attacked for failing to cover any substantial number of abortion cases. Most women do not want abortions because of their health or because of rape, incest, or fetal deformity. Statistical evidence obtained in the 1950s indicated that most women seeking abortion were married women who did not want a third, fourth, or fifth child.[8] More recent statistics indicate that an increasing number of abortees are single white women between the ages of twenty and thirty. In New York, where there are no restrictions, the incidence of abortion among the unmarried is now over 50 percent, although this figure may reflect the large number of out-of-state residents who come to New York for abortions —120,000 in New York City alone.[9]

For many of these women, pregnancy is the result of the increasing sexual freedom of women. Young unmarried women are living openly with men; career plans are still top priority, and, to their way of thinking, an accidental pregnancy should not be allowed to disrupt these plans. On this basis Alice Rossi claims that the ALI reforms miss the point. They may alleviate misery and unhappiness in unusual cases, but they show "very little recognition of the major reason so many American women seek illegal abortions."[10] Many critics regard the ALI proposal as merely a "paper reform" designed to legitimize a practice already current in hospitals under the rubric of "therapeutic abortion."

New York's liberal "abortion on demand" law has been in operation since 1 July 1970. Reports of its first year reveal that 57 percent of the abortions were performed on women with a first pregnancy and 26 percent on women already having one or two children. It was therefore concluded that abortion is being used "to prevent unwanted first pregnancies—which would accord with legitimacy data—or to limit family size, in line with a national trend toward smaller families."[11] At present, however, only New York, Hawaii, Alaska, and the state of Washington have "abortion on demand."[12]

Abortion and the Law

Antiabortion laws are being nationally challenged on several counts, most of which impinge upon other current "hot" issues. Cases are pending in New York, California, Texas, and elsewhere that challenge the very constitutionality of abortion laws. Appeals will undoubtedly go to the U.S. Supreme Court for final resolution, and at that time the Court may well render the whole issue "academic" by striking out all abortion laws across the nation.

Four points compose the major issues in the continuing controversy: legal vagueness, marital privacy, "women's lib," and the "murder-of-the-fetus" argument.[13]

Legal vagueness. Under due process, every citizen is entitled to know the precise regulations to which he is subject under any law. Most states permit abortion to "save the life" of the mother, but what exactly does this mean, asks Roy Lucas, representing the Association for the Study of Abortion. "Does it mean that without an abortion a woman has to die immediately, or that she will have her life span shortened by two days?"[14] What about her physician, who is liable to criminal prosecution if he decides wrong? The law is too ambiguous and too susceptible to personal interpretation that may be contrary to opinions held by the courts.

Marital privacy. In a landmark decision in 1965, the U.S. Supreme Court declared all birth control laws unconstitutional on the grounds that they infringed upon the right to marital privacy. The decision that no state could deny its constituents the use of contraceptives struck down the law against their sale in Connecticut, which had initiated the court appeal. Lucas argues that the right of marital privacy should logically be extended to include the right to abortion if contraceptives fail. It has also been argued that restrictive state abortion laws violate a patient's right to privacy in the doctor-patient relationship without infringement from the state.[15]

The "equality of the sexes" issue. Laws that restrict and control sexual behavior and its results have heretofore been made by men; but the Women's Liberation movement has made the repeal of all abortion laws its *cause celebre,* and its writings on the issue reflect both the changing attitudes of women and increased militancy for women's rights. One can only speculate whether abortion would be regarded as simply another, private health problem if it were not inextricably involved in a sexual context. As it is, however, the undercurrent of power struggle between the sexes is nowhere more evident than at state hearings in consideration of new abortion legislation. Natalie Shainess eloquently describes the setting.

> In most of the discussions on abortion, there is so little consideration of the woman. It is as if a complex, learned debate goes on while the woman, hanging in air and regarded as nothing more than an encapsulating amniotic sac, is threatened with falling or splitting, but the learned gentlemen seem not to notice and find no cause for hurry.[16]

Sexual freedom and equality are now being debated at all levels of American society, from the corporation boardroom to the marriage bed. Dr. Wardell B.

Pomeroy, the noted marriage counselor, asserts that it is a "moral" issue "whether half of the human race is going to continue telling the other half what it may and may not do."[17]

The American ambivalence toward sexuality is clearly illustrated in the attitudes toward abortion of many doctors (mostly male) and nurses (mostly female). Even in New York, as Patricia Fishbein of the New York City Health Services Administration reports:

> It is appalling, but true, that even some professionals who participate in abortions disapprove of the procedure and reveal their attitudes to their patients by unsympathetic or downright cruel and abusive behavior. . . . Women who are criticized, and made to feel guilty by their own doctor or nurse are, unfortunately, not a thing of the past.[18]

Some women disapprove of abortion and consider it morally wrong even though they make use of the practice. They hesitate to approve abortion as a means of solving the problem of a contraception failure, although religious orientation may not be of crucial importance in their thinking.

A recent Louis Harris poll in which three thousand women were questioned indicated little difference between Catholic and Protestant women regarding approval of abortion as a solution to an unwanted pregnancy. The poll reports that 44 percent of the Protestant and 43 percent of the Catholic women favored legalizing abortion, while 41 percent of the Protestant and 43 percent of the Catholic women "disagreed," which suggests that the traditional attitudes regarding sex and the sanctity of motherhood that girls internalize early in our society are not easily disregarded. Interestingly, 63 percent of the women in the same poll believed that single women "are entitled to the same sexual freedom as men." Since many current studies reveal that widely used, effective contraceptives, such as "the pill," are influential in changing sexual standards toward greater permissiveness, it seems reasonable to assume that abortion will eventually be accepted as a basic individual right for women.[19]

Militant women libbers are campaigning for free abortions, a goal unlikely to be soon realized. There is no doubt, however, that glaring socioeconomic differentials at present block access to abortion for the poor of all colors and nationalities. Studies clearly indicate that high socioeconomic status largely determines whether a woman will get a legal "therapeutic" abortion in a private hospital. Even in the public hospitals, far fewer abortions are performed on the indigent ward patients, the ratio being generally about four private patients to one ward case. The affluent can also, in many instances, pay handsomely for a well-trained doctor to perform a clandestine abortion.

Abortion is expensive, and poor women who live in states with restrictive abortion laws are not able to travel to New York or Hawaii. Even if travel were possible, they would not be able to afford the professional fees, of which $500 to $1,000 are not unusual. In some areas, hospital and medical insurance plans like Blue Cross and Blue Shield will pay the hospital and surgical expenses of abortion; in other areas, a confusing array of restrictions persist.

To ease the financial burden, outpatient clinics are currently being established in increasing numbers. New York City has a nonprofit Women's Services as well as the profit-making Parkmed service, the latter charging about $150. In Washington, D. C., abortion clinics are legal, and costs are held to a minimum. A totally nonprofit clinic called Preterm, opened in early 1971, charges $150 for those who can afford it and less or nothing for those who cannot. These early successful efforts are examples of what honesty, humanity, and equity can mean when the practice of abortion is within the law.

The opposition. Opposition to abortion law reform is extensive and organized on many fronts. It is still largely carried on by the Roman Catholic church hierarchy (as distinct from the Catholic laity), some fundamentalist Protestants, and Orthodox Jews. Organized citizens' groups are also gaining momentum; these include the Right to Life committees (nationwide), Voice for the Unborn (Washington State), Citizens Concerned for Life (Minnesota), and many others who are dedicated to forestalling and defeating any legislation aimed at liberalizing the abortion laws extant in the majority of states. Campaigns mounted by these groups in New York State and well-supported by the Catholic power structure came within a hairbreadth of rescinding New York's liberal abortion law. Only a veto by Governor Nelson Rockefeller saved it: "I can see no justification," he said, "for condemning hundreds of thousands of women to the dark ages once again." [20]

The crucial argument centers upon two questions: (1) when does human life begin? and (2) is abortion murder? The confusion about the nature of the fetus and its rights under law is far from being resolved. Medical, legal, and religious experts have so far failed to produce a definitive answer. For some, human life begins at the moment of conception; for others, the live cells of a fetus are a "potential rather than an actual human being." In civil law, "only the 'quick' fetus of five or six months is regarded as a viable or potential human being" with legal rights. [21]

The murder argument, with its moralistic overtones, has assumed excessive proportions as organized opposition to reform has pressured legislators to come to grips with the issue, often at the cost of political office. Dr. Robert Hall, a leader in New York's abortion movement, regards the murder argument as tangential: "The question is whether women have a fundamental right to bear or not to bear children, and incidentally, whether a church should be free to impose its beliefs on the state."[22] To many citizens, however, the separation of church and state is not an incidental issue. Many liberal Catholics feel that "it would be difficult to justify the imposition of the monolithic moral stance of official Catholicism . . . by legal means on society at large."[23]

Major opposition is fueled by the Catholic church hierarchy, whose traditional position has been that to abort a fetus, even from the moment of conception, is to take a human life endowed with a soul and deserving of respect and reverence. Interestingly, the question of when a soul enters the embryo was not always clearly resolved by the church. It was not until 1869 that the Catholic church established by fiat the tenet that "animation," or the soul, is established at the moment of conception and that abortion is therefore murder.

This view is by no means held by all Catholics, however. Studies have shown repeatedly that Catholic women avail themselves of abortion (both in the U.S. and in largely Catholic Latin countries) and generally favor removing the question of abortion from the context of criminal law, leaving the decision to the conscience of the woman involved. Other Catholics believe that the physical, mental, and spiritual wellbeing of the mother and her family should take priority over the rights of the fetus, certainly in the months before "quickening." This view is held by Daniel Callahan, former executive editor of *Commonweal*, who, following a detailed study published in his book *Abortion: Law, Choice and Morality*, has advocated abortion reform.

> This is the way I argue against my conservative Roman Catholic brethren. I say precisely that there is far more to the question of abortion than the question of fetal life. There is the problem of the battered child. Let's get this into the equation. There is the probability of the terribly depressed woman. There is the problem of her wishes.[24]

Prospects for the Future

New statistics beginning to appear as a result of the 1970 abortion reform law in New York show that although the number of abortions has "skyrocketed" to approximately 200,000 a year, the maternal mortality rate has gone down by 50 percent, the death of infants at childbirth has decreased by 20 percent, and the number of illegitimate births has dropped as well. There is growing evidence that women do not suffer trauma as a result of abortion, when it is done legally in hospitallike conditions and especially where there are supportive counseling services.

Support to separate the practice of abortion from criminal law and to relinquish it to the medical profession is widespread and cuts across lines of sex, age, and religion. The impetus in the last decade for social change in civil rights, students' rights, and women's rights may well result in women being accorded the right to control the fruits of their sexuality and to choose maternity or abortion without having to justify their decision to a hospital board composed largely of male doctors.

The church opposition, though well-organized and well-financed, has the right to oppose abortion for its own faithful; but to impose its views upon everyone in a pluralistic society such as ours is not only unrealistic but in violation of the separation of church and state.

No woman can be forced to have an abortion if she does not wish it; conversely, therefore, no woman should be forced to bear a child against her wishes. No child should be born unwanted to endure the subsequent problems in the parent-child relationship. Perhaps with the U.S. Supreme Court currently adjudicating the constitutionality of all abortion laws, more rational and equitable policies regarding the practice of abortion can be expected in the near future.

POSTSCRIPT

After two years of deliberation, the United States Supreme Court, in a seven to two decision in February of 1973, struck down the abortion laws of Texas and Georgia, both hedged with restrictions limiting the practice of abortion. These restrictions had formed the substance of the appeal before the Court.

The ruling barred the states from interfering between a woman and her physician if they decided that a pregnancy should be terminated within the first three months. The Court's decision was based predominantly on the constitutional "right of privacy," a concept which evolves from the Fourteenth Amendment's guarantee of due process of law. The Court also recognized medical data which indicate that abortion in the first trimester of pregnancy is a relatively safe procedure. In effect, the seven justices in favor of the ruling rejected the "right to life" theory that the fetus is a person with legal rights.

According to the Supreme Court decision, a state may, if it chooses, regulate abortion procedures to protect maternal health. During the last trimester, the state may regulate and apply increasing restrictions as the period of pregnancy lengthens, even to the point of prohibiting abortion in the last three months.

The practical effect of this ruling is a repeal of the anti-abortion laws in the forty-six out of the fifty states where they now exist. Only time will determine what the full impact of this ruling will have on family life, the role of women in society, the extent of population growth, and other health and welfare trends.

1. Lawrence Lader, *Abortion* (Indianapolis, Ind.: Bobbs-Merrill, 1966), p. 1.
2. *Ibid.*, p. 16.
3. Alan Guttmacher, "Abortion—Yesterday, Today and Tomorrow," in *The Case for Legalized Abortion Now*, ed. Alan Guttmacher (Berkeley, Calif., Diablo Press, 1967), p. 2.
4. Alice Rossi, "Public Views on Abortion," in Guttmacher, *Legalized Abortion*, p. 26 and p. 34.
5. Lucille Newman, "Between the Ideal and Reality: Values in American Society," in Guttmacher, *Legalized Abortion*, p. 62.
6. Edwin M. Schur, "Abortion," *The Annals* of the American Academy of Political and Social Science, Vol. 376, March 1968, p. 140.
7. Based on the Model Penal Code of the American Law Institute, copyright 1962.
8. Mary S. Calderone, ed., *Abortion in the United States* (New York: Harper & Row, 1958), p. 60.
9. Portia Worden, "Current Opinions on Abortion," *PTA Magazine*, May 1972, p. 13.
10. Rossi, "Public Views on Abortion," p. 29.
11. Patricia Fishbein, "Abortion on Demand," *Sexual Behavior*, June 1972, p. 37.
12. The writer can attest to this fact for New York. In the year 1971–72, four women students from Michigan confided that they had used a commercial referral service and flown to Niagara Falls, New York, for abortions. "Package deals" covered all costs: air flight round trip, a professional fee for medical services, and incidental fees for other ancillary services provided.
13. Paul Blanshard and Ed Doerr, "Is Abortion Murder?," *The Humanist* 32, No. 3 (May/June, 1972): 8.
14. Linda J. Greenhouse, "Constitutional Question: Is There a Right to Abortion," *New York Times Magazine*, 25 January 1970, p. 30.
15. *Ibid,* p. 31.
16. Natalie Shainess, Panel Discussion in *Abortion in a Changing World*, vol. 2, ed. Robert Hall (New York: Columbia University Press, 1970), p. 210.
17. Wardell Pomeroy, *Abortion in a Changing World*, p. 97.
18. Fishbein, "Abortion on Demand," p. 41.
19. Martin Cohen, "You've Come a Long Way Baby . . . or Have You?," *Sexual Behavior*, June 1972, p. 51.
20. New York: Backlash on Abortion," *Newsweek*, 22 May 1970, p. 32.
21. Blanshard and Doerr, "Is Abortion Murder?," p. 9.
22. Robert Hall, "The Abortion Revolution," *Playboy*, September 1970, p. 112.
23. Testimony of Dr. Mary Daly before Social Welfare Committee of the Massachusetts Legislature, 23 March 1971, report in NARAL (National Association for Repeal of Abortion Laws), New York, N. Y., 1971.
24. Daniel Callahan, *Abortion in a Changing World*, p. 114.

THE EXPERIENCE OF ABORTION

Rosalie Taylor

A British marriage counselor describes her experiences in advising both married and unmarried women about abortion. Suggesting the numerous reasons that women have for seeking abortion and the variety of feelings that accompany it, Dr. Taylor comments that changes in the abortion la in England have brought about changes in public attitude toward abortion. On this basis, she speculates about future attitudes.

Since the change in the Abortion Law, doctors, like myself working with young people in the field of family planning and sex counselling have found ourselves in a particularly vulnerable and exposed position.

In the past, despite the apparently obvious immediate expediency of the abortion, I had basically felt very uncertain about the abortion, fearing particularly its negative long-term effects on the woman's full potential for successful and happy personality development. I would always try very hard to dissuade her from having an abortion, and since I could shelter behind the law, I could always invoke it to justify my refusal.

Now that I can no longer escape from the full confrontation of the distres —demand on one hand and my own uncertainty of judgment and conscience on the other—I have had to rethink my attitudes.

I am, of course, writing here particularly of the young unmarried women who form the large proportion of those I see asking for an abortion. I do not think that experience of abortion for the older married woman with children and within the ambience of a stable family relationship is likely to prove so serious or so traumatic in its effects.

It is claimed that it is every woman's right to decide whether she has the baby or not, but this decision cannot be objectively arrived at, at the momer

Reprinted from *Marriage Guidance*, published by the National Marriage Guidance Council, Little Church Street, Rugby, England, November 1971, Volume 13, Number 6, pp. 748–753. Reprinted by permission of publisher.

when she first presents herself, in a state of panic and only wanting to have the clock put back and just to wipe out the terrifying threat.

I have come to realise that at such a moment for me to try and dissuade her or offer her alternative solutions simply puts me in the enemy camp. She is likely to see me as inimical and indifferent to her needs and with the face of the moralist, ranged with society against her, and my potential to give her effectual help is greatly reduced.

It is important, therefore at the outset of the interview to establish that if abortion is the only acceptable solution for her, it will not be refused. It is also important that she should be able to feel that we are seeing her as a decent human being in distress whom we are trying to help and not as a degraded creature who now has to submit herself to a humiliating and rightfully punishing experience.

Once it has been established that her request for abortion will not be refused she is likely to lose some of her panic, relax, and it may become possible to talk together about her situation in a more objective way and discuss some of her conflict of feelings. Then she may even be able to look at her other feelings—feelings, perhaps of *wanting* the baby very much, and her distress at having to give up the idea of having it because of external circumstances. She may be able to talk about her feelings, about her parents and especially about her relationship with the boyfriend. She would certainly be more likely to agree to come again before the abortion, perhaps, and after it.

It is particularly valuable if she is able to come to a better understanding of how she came to find herself in this predicament, and if she can come to understand some of the underlying motives, hopes and blind compulsions which had propelled her into it. An unplanned pregnancy is by no means always the result of ignorance or lack of sexual education—in point of fact it happens quite often amongst girls who are well informed and have adequate contraception available. It seems that people are not always motivated by rational considerations; it is the irrational, unacknowledged motives that can be the more powerful ones in creating these unhappy situations.

If she can be helped to an understanding of her underlying anxieties and attitudes, she may be in less danger of repeating the same mistakes blindly.

For instance, it is surprising how often a girl may have quite a deep conviction that she is infertile and may be compulsively putting it to the test.

On the other hand, under a complacent exterior, she may be carrying around a basic feeling of expectation of exploitation by men. Somewhere perhaps there is already an incipient bitterness, an inherited chip on the shoulder: the logic of her childhood experiences of an unhappy mother, a "selfish" father, leads her compulsively to repeat the pattern of woman exploited and betrayed by man. Such girls are potential victims. They particularly need to re-examine and reappraise their relationship with the boyfriend If he does not want the baby, this is felt by them to be an absolute uncompromising refusal and rejection and immediately reinforces the feeling that "men will always let you down." At the same time the anger with the boyfriend's refusal to sponsor the baby allows her to escape from facing her own negative feelings and any responsibility for her own "not wanting" is never faced but is all blamed onto him, and she can cling to the picture of women essentially being victimized by men.

Sometimes she may be feeling trapped by the pregnancy into a relationship for which she does not really feel ready and feels very guilty about wanting to escape both from motherhood, which she does not yet want, and from an involvement of a permanent kind when she was only using the man as a playfellow. It is not always the man who doesn't want the baby. Sometimes he tenderly and deeply longs for it and it is the girl who turns it down.

On a simpler, immediate level the girl is also having to contend with the actual fear of the operation and the dread of permanent damage to her body and her future fertility.

This aspect of the problem was vividly brought home to me some years ago (before the change in the Law). A young woman, unmarried and pregnant came to ask me to arrange for an abortion. Despite my efforts to dissuade her, she went elsewhere and then came back to tell me it was all arranged, she was determined to go through with it, but could I give her a tranquilizer to relieve her terror.

At this point I accepted the situation as inevitable and instead of trying again to dissuade her, asked her if she would like me to explain to her exactly how the abortion would be carried out and in as simple and reassuring a way as I could, I described the details of the operation, drawing diagrams for her and particularly stressing the smallness of the foetus, the ease of its evacuation from the womb and the extremely small risk of damage to her body and her future fertility. She went away much calmed. Shortly after the abortion she came back to see me, mainly, she said, to thank me because not only had I taken her fears away but I had also helped three other girls who had shared her nursing home room with her, and who were initially as afraid as she had been, but she had repeated my explanations to them and redrawn my diagrams and they too were assured and comforted.

In any case we have to accept that whether we like it or not, abortions are here and here to stay. It is necessary, therefore, that we should now concern ourselves with finding ways and means of making the experience minimally traumatic for each individual woman. Let us remember that legalizing of abortion was largely brought about in order to minimize the risks of physical damage to which women are exposed by the illegal abortion. It is now, therefore, imperative that we minimize the equally important risks of damage to the emotional constitution of the woman, damage to which she is still as largely exposed in the present legalized situation as before.

It is strange to consider that in the present day permissive society, it is no longer sinful to have extra-marital sexual intercourse, but it is a sin to become pregnant as a result!

To offer abortions, however skilfully performed, is surely not enough and if we are offering them, surely we must be prepared to see our patients through and to offer them support and understanding and opportunity to understand what has been happening to them and to come to terms with it. Also they should be enabled by our support to make a real choice, to examine alternative solutions and not feel that they have been forced into this way out, because they are frightened, lost and lonely and there is no alternative for them.

Ideally, a girl's best friend is her mother, and such a mother can say— "I will stand by you whether you decide to keep the baby or to have an abortion. In either decision I will be behind you and give you every help."

But so often this is not what happens. It is the mother who cannot tolerate or accept the situation of the illegitimate pregnancy. It is such a mother who may be supportive and loving only in so far as she will help to provide the money for an abortion without even considering any possible alternative. Then the girl accepts her help and decides for the abortion but this will not have been a free choice, but only acceptance that she is not allowed an alternative.

I would like to illustrate this situation.

A young woman of twenty became my patient at an FPA clinic. She was then at the beginning of her second year as a student at University and had just married a fellow student, following a termination of pregnancy shortly before (his baby). At our first interview she told me how good her mother had been in immediately arranging for her to have an abortion privately by a gynaecologist and paying all the expenses. Recently this girl came to see me and told me that she and her husband were off to Africa for a year to look around and travel. I said, "What about your studies?" She said they were young, had plenty of time and might probably come back to do the third year later. When I asked her if her mother had not been upset by thi decision to interrupt their education, she admitted that her mother was rather upset. I said, "Perhaps you are wanting to let your mother see how little you think of the importance of the studies, for the sake of which you were not allowed to have your baby." She agreed it might be so, and then with tears in her eyes told me that her cousin had recently had an illegitimat baby, was managing very well and added that she knew that she, too, could have coped, and managed to care for the baby she was not allowed to have. She had never been given a real choice and now a year later her bitterness was breaking through, and she was making nonsense of the reasons for which she had been forced to sacrifice her potential motherhood.

Generally speaking, the experience of the abortion is an experience of confusion, great emotional disturbance, dramatic build-up with a sudden ending, with a sense of flatness and emptiness and sometimes an absence o feeling. It is a sort of "open-shut" experience, and there is bewilderment and a lack of opportunity to come to any emotional terms with it.

I think that this may be why the first abortion is so often followed by a second pregnancy and a second request for abortion, and this, despite well-meaning proffered advice on contraception and often the admonishing finger of the gynaecologist: "Do not let me see you here again!"

Just as a child will sometimes repetitively play out in a game some inciden or situation he has experienced and not been able to understand fully— gradually through the play digesting and integrating the experience; so per haps the repeated pregnancy and abortion may be a blind effort to fix and take in the experience that they have not been able to experience fully and digest.

Sometimes the repetition is in order to play it differently the next time. I have been struck by the fact that it often happens that a girl who has had an illegitimate pregnancy, seen it through and had the baby adopted will turn up again pregnant but this time she will utterly refuse to see the pregnancy through and demands an abortion. It is as if she is asserting that she'd made the wrong decision the first time and this time she will play it a better way.

Or, the opposite situation—having had an abortion the first time, she will decide to see the pregnancy through this time. What is manifest is that either solution has been unsatisfactory and traumatic. Had the girl had hel to integrate the experience and been supported through the painfulness of her emotions, she might have come to accept the experience and come to terms with it, put it behind her and got on with her life and its next natural step.

There are many, however, who appear to experience only a great sense of relief from the abortion. The abortion is not, as with some others, followed by a depression or any obvious ill effects—and it does not seem to interfere with a successful continuation of their lives. Yet in the course of my practice I do from time to time come across a particular type of patient complaining of obscure gynaecological symptoms which seem irrelevant to her seemingly good health, and which do not yield to reassurance but tend to have an insistent repetitive anxiety quality about them. It is in this group that one often discovers that there has been an abortion in the past, apparently successfully weathered at the time. Once she has been able to tell me that she has had an abortion the real nature of the anxiety reveals itself. It is always a dread that her fertility has been impaired.

It is not enough to open Pregnancy Advisory Centres where girls can be helped to make arrangements for safe abortions with reputable doctors and clinics; it is just as important to make available for them Abortion Advisory Centres where they can be put in touch with informed professional people who will help to protect them from the emotional traumas to which they will be so largely exposed in their experience: this service should be available as part of the regular Abortion package deal.

It would seem that increased permissiveness in society appears to be one jump ahead of the natural emotional evolution of full acceptance of the new permissiveness.

So people are now bringing the same moral opprobrium to the new easing of the Abortion restrictions as they brought to the Family Planning Association in its early days which is now so universally accepted.

However, I am aware how much in myself the change in the law has been bringing about a change of my attitudes to abortion, and I think, in the same way it is also bringing about a gradual change with lessening of guilt and sense of its awfulness to many of the women who undergo abortion.

It is interesting to speculate on the future of abortion with the further development of the use of prostaglandins. All the strain of physical intervention is likely then to be taken out of abortion; it might mean just a vaginal pessary inserted at the expected time of menstruation or an injection when it is delayed, and then perhaps abortion will lose all its emotional significance and importance.

ABORTING A FETUS:
THE LEGAL RIGHT,
THE PERSONAL CHOICE

Suzannah Lessard

Exaggerated and simplistic dogmatisms from both the feminist and the Right to Life movements have obscured the necessary distinctions between the legal and the personal issues involved in abortion. The question of the value of the life of the fetus is a matter of faith, a realm in which argument and counterargument are of little avail. Where issues of faith are concerned, it is essential that personal choice be a free one; it is also essential that careful and reflective thought be given to avoiding a utilitarian attitude toward human life.

Although written before the Supreme Court decision legitimizing abortion in this country, this article's major concerns are as relevant as they were before the legal issue was settled by the court. The closing sentence of the article is an interesting presage of judicial action.

Arguing that abortion as a *legal option* must be available to women, Lessard emphasizes the extreme importance of serious and responsible *personal decision-making* (with the help of counseling, if necessary) to clarify such matters as: the motivations for unwanted pregnancy, ambivalences about violation of one's maternity, conflicts about one's sexuality, the woman's self-picture and her readiness to assume responsibility for herself, and other personal ambivalences.

According to Lessard, eliminating the social duplicity and personal isolation related at present to most unwanted pregnancies are difficult but achievable goals.

The belief that abortion must be legally available to those who want it comes to many of us first as a gut certainty, not that the procedure itself is morally acceptable, but that to deny women the option is intolerable and

Reprinted from *The Washington Monthly*, August 1972. Reprinted by permission of publisher.

nsane. That intuitive recognition is most likely to spring either from experience, or having been close to people who have been through it—from one way or another having gotten into the shoes of an individual faced with the dilemma of an unwanted pregnancy. The intimate appreciation of what's involved is why so many women, sometimes to the jeopardy of the cause, take the issue so personally. A friend of mine, who has had an abortion and who considers the moral implications insoluble, described coming out of a museum into a demonstration against legal abortion. "There they all were with little children, chanting these slogans, and I just sat down and cried. I thought they were trying to stamp on me, that if they had their way I wouldn't have any choice." In print this attitude looks childishly selfish and petulant, but it is a primal and very honestly expressed feeling. While it won't get one very far in the attempt to build a philosophical edifice justifying abortion, understanding the strength of that feeling is the key to understanding why so many women appear irrationally certain about a question which is patently conflict-ridden and inescapably charged with ambiguities. The feeling doesn't say "I have a right to an abortion"; it says "you have no right to decide for me one way or the other and your presumption to do so is violently offensive."

Twilight Zone

Moving backward from this gut certainty, one blunders into a wilderness of intellectual constructs built in the attempt to either condemn or justify abortion in a rational, consistent manner. Many of them are cockeyed; some, on both sides, are orderly and impressive, but none of them contain the matter satisfactorily because the basic question—what is the value of the life of a fetus—is unanswerable and therefore a matter of faith. The second thing one notices about both sides is that besides being ferociously dogmatic and blind to each other's points, the emotional pitch of the battle is deafeningly high. That, no doubt, is because if it's difficult to discourse with someone you consider a murderer, it's equally, if not more difficult, to be open-minded toward a person who is calling you one.

Looking at the inadequacy of the constructs on either side, there seems little point in trying to erect a more perfect one, since at bottom it is a matter of faith and people who hold the opposite faith are not likely to be persuaded otherwise. At best one can hope that the Right to Lifers will acknowledge that the question is ultimately imponderable, and that those who press the case for abortion have as much right to their belief as their opponents. At most, the fetus exists in a twilight zone of humanity. Despite their repeated use of the word murder, even the most virulent of the abortion opponents aren't arguing that abortionists and consenting mothers be given prison terms remotely like those given murderers. A miscarried fetus is not mourned the way even a one-day-old child would be. So to the rhetorical question put by the Right to Lifers—does the human creature suddenly undergo some absolute transformation in the short passage from the womb to the outside world—the answer is yes, at least people have always behaved as though that is what they believe. According to Kinsey, one out of four American women has privately wrestled with that question in a very immediate sense and has decided to have an abortion. The law which forced them to take the often high physical risk of going to illegal practitioners was passed in the 19th century, not for the protection of the fetus, but, ironically, for the woman's protection, because it was at that time a far more dangerous operation than normal childbirth. The transformation of the legal issue into a debate over the right to life of the fetus as opposed to the safety of the procedure for the woman has occurred not through legal process but in the minds of the latter-day opponents of abortion. Now that abortion is eight times safer than childbirth, the only question that remains is whether a woman has a right to decide on her own what course to take in this intensely personal matter of such far-reaching consequence to herself. The right to privacy is the basis of the case pending before the Supreme Court, and so it should be.

"A Mass of Protoplasm"

The failure of both sides to distinguish between the legal and the personal aspects of the issue has been one of the reasons, I think, for the bad blood and seemingly hopeless division on fundamental principles between the two groups. I don't understand the strident ferocity of the Right to Lifers, so I can only say that their absolute refusal to even acknowledge that there might be a matter of separation between state and private life indicates that they have confounded the two perspectives. I do understand the stridency of the feminist position. Their doctrinaire intensity is due in part to the fact that the way the still-fragile crusade ends will vitally, drastically, affect the lives of millions of women, and in part to the rage which an intrusion of the state into this area inspires. But I don't think I'm alone in being acutely uncomfortable with many of the arguments and descriptions of the issue as they have evolved on the pro-abortion side, or in feeling that many of the positions taken serve only to tie the knot more tightly in the minds of opponents and waverers. I can best describe the source of that discomfort as the failure of the "movement," not unlike the opposition, to distinguish between abortion as a legal option and abortion as a personal decision.

For instance, the tenet that the state has no more right to interfere in an abortion than it does in a tonsillectomy (or any other form of minor surgery) is often transformed into a description of abortion as the equivalent of a tonsillectomy. At least for an awful lot of women, their belief that the state should keep out notwithstanding the psychological, emotional, and just plain personal elements involved in deciding to have an abortion make such an equation outlandish. Another point of wild confusion between personal questions and political questions has involved the description of the fetus. A fetus, even at two months, is a good deal more than a "mass of dependent protoplasm," as Gloria Steinem recently wrote in *Newsweek*. It has a very well-defined human shape—head, back, legs, arms, sometimes hands and feet. It's growing, and it is highly likely to become a separate human being if left alone, a fact which certainly can't be said of just any blob of protoplasm, and which any intelligible description of the fetus would have to be based on. To describe it that way is either extraordinarily ignorant, as an absurd reduction of all protoplasmic—i.e. "living"—forms which renders any distinctions between them impossible, or a blatantly false description of reality in order to make it conform to ideological lines.

Reaction formation along ideological lines has cropped up in several areas of the new feminist movement. In the early stages of most revolts, the self-overhaul into a catechism of "correct" responses is prevalent, and often for good reasons. I think a lot of women need to go fanatically ideological for a while because they can't in any other way overthrow the insidious sense of themselves as inferior, nor otherwise live with the rage that comes to the surface when they realize how they have been psychically mauled. But I don't think that state of mind—hopefully temporary—is the strength of the movement. It has very little to do with working out a new, undamaging way of living as women. Specifically with regard to abortion, just because it's an essential goal in building a new world for women to convince the state that it has no right to see abortion any differently than a tonsillectomy, it does not mean that whatever feelings a woman having an abortion might experience over and above what she experiences when undergoing a tonsillectomy are counterrevolutionary.

Brainwashed Plumbing

A critically important part of the movement has been the de-mystification of a woman's sexual and reproductive life and the substitution of scientific education where fear, uncertainty, guilt and ambivalence, existed before. It's been a great help to learn to look at our bodies as plumbing rather than as mysterious, at once glorified and faintly disgusting things, as it's a great help to any human being undergoing a physical-medical operation to overcome fear by thinking of what is going on in those terms. Knowing what's happening scientifically helps put you on top of it. But to carry this revelation to the point where you insist that it's nothing but plumbing, that bearing a child or aborting a fetus are different only in a neutral sense, to me turns what should be a liberation into a denial of the real self as violent and as destructive as the old mystique in its heyday. There is little question that many of our reactions, particularly those relating to sex and reproduction, have been formed by social pressures under which we grew up, and there's little question that many of them are unhealthy and imprisoning. Nevertheless, I am not only affronted when, for example, it's suggested to me that all my feelings about abortion, since they don't conform to ideology, are the result of brainwashing, but I think it's an absurd accusation, which, taken to its logical limits, reduces the human being to a blank.

To dictate how women "should" feel about abortion—to say they "shouldn't" feel it's as inconsequential to their inner life as having a tooth pulled—would be to fall into the same fallacy as the positions under criticism. I will admit, however, that I suspect any grown woman who claims that deciding to have an abortion was a totally neutral act of either being afraid of the truth, of having artificially overhauled her emotions to conform with ideology, or, as Simone de Beauvoir suspected 20 years ago when she wrote *The Second Sex,* of being protected from her true feelings by her political environment. I'm not implying that the experience must be a great agonizing tragedy, just that more is involved than the removal of a blob of protoplasm and that most women know that and react accordingly.

"Nobody on the Table with You"

Since legal abortion is relatively new, the only sources of collected informa tion on how women react to the experience are limited to a few formal studies and the cumulative wisdom of counselors. (Many clinics maintain a large staff of counselors to deal with physical fears and psychological conlicts.) Since counselors are immersed daily in the actuality of going through with an abortion, they tend to be less interested in doctrine and focus instead on trying to understand all the dimensions of an experience which is only beginning to be systematically explored. Conflict, psychological and moral, is what much of their work is about. From their descriptions of what concerns their patients, two categories of conflict emerge. First were conflicts clearly related to the shame attached to illicit sex—in other words, the violation of social mores—in terms of which getting pregnant and having an abortion are more punishment than anything else. The second category concerns the abortion itself, quite separate from guilt about the act which resulted in the predicament. As described by counselors, those battles seem much more prone to line up within the patient herself, rather than as an attempt to come to terms with a gap between private practice and public standards of behavior. This makes good sense, since awareness of abortion has been pushed so far back in the public consciousness that moral repulsion from it isn't likely to have been ingrained very deeply in the average American. The rusty coat hanger and the physical fears it conjures up, not the red letter A, is likely to be the strongest socially-ingrained association. (Catholics are an exception, though there, too, the concern is separate since the relevant teaching relates to abortion itself, not illicit sex, which will be listed under a different heading on Judgment Day.)

The two levels of conflict are often mixed up, as one quickly learns sitting in on a counseling session. Very often, for instance, a young woman has gotten pregnant because she was so ambivalent about her violation of sexual mores that she didn't face up to what she was doing and its possible consequences, and therefore didn't use contraception. For the same reason, she doesn't want to face the fact that she is having an abortion or any other evidence of sex and her sexual nature. The most well-defined object of this kind of counseling is to get patients to confront this lapse and to take responsibility for their actions by using adequate contraception in the future. Sometimes the blocks are formidable, condensing into: "I don't need it. I got caught. I'm taking my punishment, and I'm never going to have sex again." A good counselor works hard on such patients as experience indicates their attitude makes them highly prone to getting into the predicament a second time.

Though frequently entangled with the outside influences of sexual mores, making the decision to have an abortion tends to precipitate a woman into an unusually unencumbered confrontation within herself, because being pregnant isolates a person, particularly if she's single and doesn't want to

Aborting a
Fetus: the
Legal Right,
the Personal
Choice

275

have a child. If you live in a society where bearing an illegitimate child is something to be ashamed of, and where, on the other hand, abortion is illegal, you are suddenly cut off from all the support, advice, information, and facilities which have diluted the immediacy of previous crises in your lif This compounds the isolation which accompanies pregnancy under any circumstances. Whatever you decide to do, you are ultimately alone. As one young patient put it. "Nobody is going to get on that operating table with you." You have to decide for yourself. This is true of any medical procedure one has to go through, but most of them don't present such a serious and complex choice.

No Hold on Her Life

The discomfort with having violated social mores, and a person's consequent ambivalence about her sexual nature in general, if very strong, will probably preclude getting in touch with real self—completely. But insofar as patients do wrestle with questions about abortion itself, their concerns are often cast precisely in this kind of internal frame of reference and therefore can be especially "pure" or "unsocialized." From descriptions, the iss in such cases takes shape not so much in terms of "murder" (though fetal size and characteristics are points of great interest) but of violating one's maternity (in a very broad sense). Insistence that "I really love children," or "I definitely want to have children," for instance, is a common patient protestation. In other words, the question is often more one of "what am I doing to myself" than consideration of the fetus as an independent entity: the perspective is one from which the fetus is more the fruition of a part of the woman's nature which she values highly and doesn't want to grow calluses over, than it is a creature to be considered separately from herself. Along these lines, it's common for an abortion patient to be in one way deeply pleased at being pregnant, even though the whole business has been a nightmare, even though she definitely doesn't want to bear a child at this point, and fervently wishes the pregnancy had never happened. That contradictory pleasure—surely independent of social mores, independent even of a disastrous, personal predicament—and the fear of frustrating the nature which generates it, is the most explicit expression of irreducible conflict in making the decision to have an abortion which I have come across.

Patients, most of them very young and new to this whole side of themselves, are also not likely to identify their feelings, much less the distinctions I am making here, very clearly. Counselors, however, who usually suffer very little from concern with social mores or aversion to sex, have often thought a lot on this level. "There's a conflict, no question about it, you can't think it away. The best you can do is to face it," said Vicki Simons, head counselor in one of New York's largest clinics.

> Many of the counselors had to deal with their feelings about their own abortions all over again when they first started work here. . . . They might not admit it, but I think many have deep feelings of ambivalence about abortion. . . . We've had some counselors who have had to have abortions while working here and it was a crisis in their lives. At a workshop for abortion counselors, many of them said they would not have abortions now, and a majority said that it would be a very very difficult decision for them . . . because they wanted to have children even though it wouldn't fit very well into their lives right then.

I'm not setting up this particular attitude as a norm beyond which lies only abnormality. Some women are genuinely uninterested in bearing children and others may want children but simply have no problem at all with abortion. My point is that many women, who could not possibly be called reactionary, see the personal decision in very serious terms, and that it's significant that among them are people who have been heavily exposed to the experience and have had occasion to think about it especially hard. Secondly, this attitude doesn't weaken the feminist case. Awareness of an irreducible conflict and personal resistance to having an abortion in no way dilutes these peoples' conviction that abortion must be legal and unconditionally accessible. Following them through a day's work lets you know why.

The frame of mind which considers abortion a morally acceptable option yet would lean heavily towards carrying an unexpected pregnancy to term despite grave difficulties depends on a very important factor—a sense of being fundamentally in command of personal destiny so that making way for an unexpected child, however disruptive, is still possible without throwing the mother's life beyond her control. Women in their mid-twenties and older often have developed that stability and, according to observations, they are the ones who are most likely to come to a decision to have an abortion with sorrow and difficulty. The average patient who comes through a clinic is not in this category, however. She is under 20, definitely not in command of her life, and the consequence of bearing a child clearly may mean that she will never gain command.

After getting to know, however slightly, a number of teen-age patients, the insanity of compelling them to give birth crashes through whatever vestiges of doubt one might have harbored. For most of them "getting pregnant"

Aborting a
Fetus: the
Legal Right,
the Personal
Choice

277

really is an event that somehow happened to them. Not having been brought up to look directly at their own sexuality, they seem to have fallen into it sideways, having looked even less directly at its possible consequences. Abortion counselors talk about how having an abortion can be a positive experience, which sounds a little strange at first, but what they mean is that the experience can be more than an ordeal or even the solution to a particular predicament. It can mean facing a crisis, sorting it out, through the question that sorting leads one to ask, taking control of one's own life. It can change a person from being menaced and therefore evasive of this whole side of their nature into someone who willingly takes responsibility for what previously was shadowed with threat.

In a lecture at Berkeley, Garrett Hardin, a professor of biology, said.

> Critics of abortion generally see it as an exclusively negative thing, a means of nonfulfillment only. What they fail to realize is that abortion, like other means of birth control, can lead to fulfillment in the life of a woman. A woman who aborts this year because she is in poor health, neurotic, economically harassed, unmarried, on the verge of divorce, or immature may well decide to have some other child five years from now—a wanted child. If her need for abortion is frustrated, she may never know the joy of a wanted child.

It Happened to Them

In *It Happens to Us,* a documentary film by Amalie Rothschild on people who have had abortions (legal and illegal), one interview brings this home especially vividly. A young, unmarried couple talk about what they've been through in these terms. The man tells how sex had always been presented to him as something that was going to get him in trouble—before he went on his first date at fourteen, his parents had warned him, "Now don't get her pregnant." The nightmare having finally come true, confronted, and worked out with an abortion, "my attitude towards marriage, having children, and sex have benefited." These things have become matters of choice, he said, not forces of circumstance. Needless to say, it would be preferable to work these problems out beforehand, thereby greatly reducing the chances that an abortion will be needed. But given the predicament, the sanity of solving it with an abortion cannot be denied. As they themselves said, Betsy and her boyfriend have a much better chance of being good parents some day: not people who feel they have been forced into something, and basically blame a child for it, but people who have freely chosen the responsibilities of parenthood. The forces of desperation which involuntary parenthood can create are starkly documented in that victim who inhabits all levels of the social structure in horrifyingly high numbers, the physically battered child.

The Betsys come to the clinics in hordes, hopefully leaving behind the combination of ignorance and evasion which got them into the predicament. Another kind of patient comes less often but with alarming frequency none-theless. She's younger and would be even more vulnerable to permanent psychic damage if she bore a child. Unlike the 19- or 20-year-old who gen-erally just wants to stop being pregnant as fast as she can, causing the least possible disruption in her life (the straightforward personal crisis attitude seems to come with maturity), the younger teenager often wants desperately to have the baby. Somebody else has pressed her into the abortion. A theory about this phenomenon, advanced in several studies, is that the subcon-scious reason she got pregnant was that she felt rejected, and sees in the future baby a substitute for herself on which she will lavish the love she her-self needs badly. None of this has the remotest connection with what taking care of a child actually entails, and it's through pushing her to face the gulf between her fantasy and what motherhood would really be like for her that she can be led to understand her motivations, As a young girl said in *It Happens to Us:* "Now I know that I don't want a baby until I'm taking care of myself, until I'm fully responsible for myself," an insight many older women have failed to perceive.

Ulterior motivation behind unwanted pregnancies is not limited to teen-agers. The complex forces which motivate a woman who does not have room in her life for a child to become lax about contraception, or fail to use it at all when it is available, are only just beginning to be explored. But even the rudimentary knowledge which has been gained reinforces, as in the case of the rejected teenager, the gut sense that prohibiting abortion does violence to sanity, and, on the other hand, that there's a lot more than plumbing involved. A study was made by Lawrence Downs and David Clayson of abortion patients at New York Hospital after the psychiatric department was called in to help a medical staff beset by this new kind of patient who "presented with tremendous emotionality that ran the gamut from extreme sadness, fear, and guilt through various psychotic and border-line' conditions to those patients who demonstrated a bizarre euphoria, making a social event of their hospitalization" [Not, in other words, your average tonsillectomy patients]. Several characteristics distinguished the test group from the population at large. Sixty-six per cent of them recently had suffered either some kind of traumatic separation, such as termination of

Aborting a
Fetus: the
Legal Right,
the Personal
Choice

279

a marriage, or a death, recent or anticipated, in the immediate family. Fifty-one per cent had either felt disturbed enough to seek psychiatric help around the period when they conceived, or habitually used hard drugs or tranquilizers. Eighty-five per cent suffered from at least one of these situations. Other patterns emerged, such as a high incidence of women coping with unstable love relationships in which they were extremely dependent. Thirty-seven per cent had been recently troubled by a gynecological abnormality, and more than half of these thought they might be infertile. Seven per cent of the patients were teenagers whose mothers had recently had hysterectomies. The study opens only the tiniest chink towards truly understanding what might be going on in our heads when we ill-advisedly get ourselves pregnant. The glimmer that comes through, however, not only suggests that the points in our life when we make that mistake are likely to be the points when we are least able to cope with a child, but that the pregnancy is likely to be tied up with deep feelings about life, death, and generativity which would have to be dealt with in any healthy decision to end or go ahead with it.

An Aborted Calvinist

Of all the counterarguments made by Right to Lifers, one reaches me with force. You cannot, they say, use social utility as the ultimate criterion in matters which involve life and death and essential liberties. There is one point on which abortion proponents switch from focusing entirely on the mother, take the fetus as a separate entity, and talk about its right not to be subjected to the misery which it is likely to suffer if born unwanted, and here, I think, they get into very deep water. While a huge proportion of the unhappy lives, and a whole network of social ills can most likely be traced to a common condition, the unwanted child, when you start arguing that the person a fetus is going to become should not exist because he or she will be unhappy and/or will be a trouble to society— because they will be damaged goods—I bale out. Most of us would rather be alive than not, even if being alive also means being deformed, battered, half-crazy, or poor.

In *Abortion Rap* by Florence Kennedy and Dianne Schulder, Rabbi David Feldman's testimony in a federal suit challenging the constitutionality of New York's pre-1970 abortion laws is quoted. He makes the distinction between the two ways of thinking very clear:

... if the woman were to say that she had taken thalidomide during pregnancy (and the chances of a risk of deformity are very great) and she wanted an abortion, because a deformed life is not very good, the

Rabbi would dismiss such talk of the future on grounds of "Well, you don't know what's going to be, whether the child is going to be deformed and whether being deformed is worse or better than not being born."

But if the same woman were to phrase the question differently and say that "the possibility of deformity is driving me to anguish or distraction" then the Rabbi would say: "Well, now, you're talking about someone who is here and alive and real and all of Jewish tradition says . . . if a woman asks for compassion in that respect, then she is entitled to it."

The distinction may seem like a philosophical nicety, but to me if the answer to the two ways of asking the question were "Have an abortion," the difference between those two ostensibly identical answers is a matter of opening the door to a utilitarianism in which the human life is reduced to the value of a machine—how well does it work.

I'm not suggesting that abortion should be accessible to women on a basis of how they answer questions. But these considerations are crucial as we build a case for, and tradition around, abortion, because how we think about its function and the function of other medical advances which introduce previously unimagined subtleties about the borderlines of life, is going to determine in the end how we think about all life.

Rabbi Feldman also said, "One thing emerges from the writings of all rabbis . . . that the welfare of the woman is primary, and that welfare, of course, is not limited to saving of life, but even to saving of mental health and to saving of welfare. It might even be extended to saving her the anguish of shame or embarrassment." Later he quotes a 19th century Hungarian rabbi: "No woman is required to build the world by destroying herself." An understanding of pregnancy, wanted and unwanted, and what it means for a woman to decide whether to go through with it or not, is the proper ground on which to base a case for abortion—not the social value of unwanted children, over-population, or any other overview which is based on conjecture of whether or not the growth of the fetus into a human being ought to be canceled. Aside from opening the door to an abhorrent utilitarianism, such arguments lead as surely as the Right to Lifer position into an intolerable intrusion into the privacy of woman's choice in matters of maternity.

The hypocrisy this civilization has managed to maintain in its attitude towards unwanted pregnancies is unmatched. From the homes for unwed mothers where the inmates have pressed upon them first of all the importance of secrecy—the child will be whisked away at birth and lucky-lucky you will be able to resume life as though nothing had happened—to the gynecologists who refuse to help a woman who comes to them to get an abortion yet tells her to come back when it's all over for a checkup, the social duplicity about this age-old, widespread, and drastic predicament is astounding. No less mystifying has been the silence of women; the fact that no bond grew between the millions who journeyed either into those treacherous regions of undefined conscience, illegality, and physical risk, or through the traumatic experience of bearing a child and giving it up. Now that it's all out in the open at last, we are faced with building new attitudes and principles which integrate this experience honestly into the social picture almost from scratch.

The centuries of acquiescence by women to the old attitudes, demonstrate that we can dupe ourselves into believing almost anything: it would be sad indeed if in the process of rejecting the notion that abortion is something to be guilty about we substituted the equally unstraightforward mindset that it is something that shouldn't entail any feelings at all. Should I have a daughter, I want a world for her in which abortion is as available to her as a tonsillectomy. But I don't want her to grow up in an atmosphere which propels her into aborting an unwanted pregnancy without considering it a matter for deep and careful thought. To make that reflection truly free of social pressure, I also want the option of having the child, and the help and care she would need, openly presented to her and considered a respected and a viable alternative in the society she lives in. I hope she will reflect, not because I'm a Calvinist and want her to suffer where, if left alone, she would feel perfectly unconcerned about an abortion, but because I think she would otherwise be closing off to a part of herself if she didn't. Women have been closed off to themselves for too long.

THE LAW AND SEXUAL RELATIONSHIPS

Robert Veit Sherwin

That the law is often inappropriate and inconsistent is nowhere more apparent than in the area of laws pertaining to sexual relationships. Usually based upon long-existing attitudes and customs, the law, in times of changing norms and revolutions of thought and practice, often finds itself obliged to defend tenets long discarded or otherwise ignored by the public—an example being the law condemning fellatio, cunnilingus, and mutual masturbation, even though these are performed by married couples in the privacy of their bedrooms. In most states, many sexual acts that induce orgasm are crimes, and any professional counselor advising couples to adopt these practices would be commiting a felony. For obvious reasons, these laws are rarely, if ever, enforced.

Mr. Sherwin, an attorney, gives an account of the subtle male values that permeate the laws in its discrimination against women in cases of divorce, abortion, prostitution, and so on, although—in cases of homosexuality, for example—men may fare no better. He suggests some causes and remedies and calls to attention the fact that only the state of Illinois has to date enacted a criminal code pertaining to sexual practices between consenting adults. The reader will find substantial information in this selection and may be stimulated to seek reform in the legal administration of human sexual behavior.

Introduction

It is most embarrassing to any lawyer, who is proud of being a member of the legal profession, to write an analysis of the law as it pertains to sex, especially when this analysis must be part of a group of articles written by

Reprinted from *The Journal of Social Issues*, a publication of the Society for the Psychological Study of Social Issues, Volume XXII, Number 2, April 1966. Reprinted by permission of the publisher.

representatives of other disciplines, such as psychiatry and sociology. The greater availability and the greater depth of professionalism in research materials in the fields of psychology, psychiatry, and sociology make most evident the lack of comparable data concerning law and sex.

There are many reasons for this. In the first place, the laws concerning sex are much like public highways that surround large cities. By the time a much needed public highway gets built, it is often already outmoded on the very day that it is opened. In the same way, the laws concerning sex, which are actually codifications of attitudes and customs already long in existence, may very quickly be inappropriate very shortly after the enactment of said laws.

Secondly, unlike outmoded highways, sex laws can be ignored as if they did not exist, which can and does aggravate the situation instead of improving it. It must be remembered that the problem of sex administration straddles two houses, the courthouse and the church, and each tends to blame the other for the violation of sexual mores.

Thirdly, there are certain elements present in the legal administration of sexual mores that are absent in other phases of the law which cause many of the difficulties to be outlined in this article. For one thing, lawyers depend upon the decisions written by the judges concerning the judicial interpretation of the law. Very few cases involving the violation of sex laws get beyond the Police Court or the Magistrate's Court level, and are thus not recorded in official books available to the legal profession. It is only when the occasional case is appealed to an Appellate Court that a record is made of that case for purposes of study and analysis. Because of the embarrassment to the accused's family, lack of funds, etc., appeals are seldom taken by convicted defendants.

Even when cases are appealed, in many instances, the case will be reported as follows: "No opinion—conviction affirmed." In still other cases, the court's opinion will be recorded in the following manner: "The facts of this case are so reprehensible and disgusting that the court sees fit not to record same—25 years imprisonment." Thus, the criteria of how and why the degree of punishment was selected, the question of what elements were present in order to comply with the statutory requirements for a conviction are all missing, and are unavailable to anyone who wishes to appraise the science of legal administration.

A further difficulty arises from the fact that many district attorneys, aware of the inappropriateness and severity of the available statutes applicable to the facts of the alleged crime, are often willing to "make deals" with the accused's attorney, not in the dishonest sense but in the humane sense. The effect of which is to distort any accurate measurement of the degree of success in the field of law enforcement. For the same reason, the accused is often acquitted by a judge because he is unable to apply a law which he feels is unnecessarily harsh and inappropriate.

There are two major effects resulting from what has just been described. Many persons, whose minor infraction of a law indicates a serious need for medical and psychiatric treatment, are acquitted for the reasons stated above, and, therefore, released upon society only to be apprehended at a later date for perhaps a major infraction of the criminal law this time involving first degree rape or murder. And, conversely, many who should only receive therapy as a result of their minor infraction are treated as felons and are sent to prisons, which tends to aggravate whatever maladjustments have caused them to violate the laws of society.

The second major effect concerns the public's attitude towards law enforcement in general. When everyone knows that nobody gets arrested these days except very occasionally, there is engendered a general disrespect for the law as such. This diminishes, in the classic sense, the whole preventive purpose of the Criminal Code.

One further point must be made in order to make clear much of the material to be presented. Two major arguments are raised by those in the field who feel that the laws concerning sex, as they presently exist, are outmoded and ineffective. The first point concerns sex laws that attempt to control behavior that should be controlled by the church, the school, or the home. In this category would be many forms of sexual expression to be discussed, which Justice Learned Hand deemed to be "questions of taste" rather than an act to be punished by law. Various forms of sexual expression when performed by consenting adults in the privacy of the home would be in this category. The second point raised is that there are certain acts, although criminal in a minor sense, are impossible to enforce with any degree of effectiveness and, therefore, should be deleted from the Criminal Code to improve the effectiveness of the Criminal Code in the preventive sense. An illustration of this point would be the act of adultery. In New York State alone, there have been something less than five convictions of the act of adultery in 66 years, despite the fact that thousands of divorces are granted by the New York Courts every year on the grounds that an adulterous act has been committed.

It is, therefore, the purpose of this article to dissect the law in action, as it is applied to sexual behavior under the current pressures that affect the sexual mores of the community at large.

Legal Approach to the Sexual Problems of the Female

The emphasis, for better or worse, during the last fifty years concerning the sexual emancipation of the female has been to change the position of the female from that of a mere receptacle for the male penis, in return for her support and maintenance, to that of an equal sex partner fully entitled to all the various forms of sexual satisfaction, in accordance with her own needs. In view of the complexity of female anatomy and, more specifically, in view of the emergence of the clitoris as one of the more important means of achievement of sexual satisfaction for the female, serious results have been created when the attempt is made to apply a law which is appropriate only if one pretends that there is no such thing as a clitoris.[1] Since the function of sexual administration was originally in the hands of the church, sexual intercourse (in the penis-vagina sense of the word) was considered strictly as a means of propagation; questions of pleasure and emotional fulfillment were uncontemplated. The omission of pleasure was reenforced so as to avoid sexual satisfaction at the expense of failure to propagate. Hence a typical statute reads:

> Every person who shall carnally know, or shall have sexual intercourse in any manner with any animal or bird, or shall carnally know any male or female by the anus (rectum) or with the mouth or tongue; or shall attempt intercourse with a dead body is guilty of Sodomy.[2]

This type of statute, with many variations in as many jurisdictions, represents a typical example of a law which is usually entitled "Crime Against Nature," "Lewd and Lascivious Behavior," or "Sodomy." Some jurisdictions even include the specific act of mutual masturbation in the category of crimes against nature. The fact that all such statutes do not differentiate between people who are married to one another and those who are not (such as is done in adultery statutes) results in categorizing as a crime any of the various forms of sexual expression generally recommended to aid and induce the female orgasm even though the man and woman are married to each other. As if the above were not patently disturbing enough, such illegal acts in most jurisdictions are classed as felonies and bring, in many instances, imprisonment of sixty years to life and, in one jurisdiction, a minimum sentence of life at hard labor. It is interesting to note in passing, that in this same jurisdiction the penalty for having intercourse with a cow brings only five years of imprisonment. (Sherwin, I, 1951)

As an illustration, the following case within the author's own experience should be noted. In a Midwestern town, a young couple, the groom being twenty-two years and his bride nineteen, were experiencing sexual difficulties: premature ejaculation and difficulties in the wife's achieving an orgasm. Through their own experimentation they finally solved the problem by means of sexual intercourse plus the use of cunnilinctus to help her achieve her orgasm. Some months thereafter, the husband brought home the news to his young wife that the act of cunnilinctus was a crime in their state, punishable by sixty years in prison or more. They actually arrived at a point of hysteria, which caused them to have themselves arrested by the police authorities. Family contacts averted any court decision on the case.

Comment should also be made about the legal dilemma faced by the psychiatrist (or psychologist, marriage counsellor, etc.). Assuming that a wife is seeking to become a more satisfactory sexual partner both for the sake of her husband and herself, she may well seek professional help. Under the law of most jurisdictions, to advise the commission of a criminal act is, in and of itself, a criminal act. Thus when a psychiatrist advises precoital techniques[3] to a patient, he is committing a crime by so advising. Because of the period of hostile patient attitudes toward the psychiatrist which often happens in the natural progress of therapy, many psychiatrists, psychologists, and marriage counsellors hesitate to prescribe forms of sexual expression that violate the state law. This may be due to the psychiatrist's own concern for the jeopardy in which he would be placed if a patient publicly accused him of advocating the commission of criminal acts. In other cases, the psychiatrist may feel that to advocate behavior which the patient knows is listed as a crime might help the patient sexually, but that such behavior might do harm to the patient, therapeutically speaking, if the patient were to accept it as being illegal.

One need only mention in passing the effect of these laws on the planning of any high school or college course in domestic sciences, such as family relations. Any detailed discourse on sexual relationships would necessarily jeopardize the instructor for the same reasons which affect the psychologist and psychiatrist.[4]

An equally important legal area which aggravates the problems of the female is the area of divorce negotiations. In those marriage relationships in which the wife has a far greater sexual drive and need than the husband, the husband's chronic failure to satisfy his wife may lead him to justify his own position, describing himself as being normal and his wife as being a nyphomaniac. This can lead to a frightening situation, in which the husband lawyer will threaten to "expose the wife's infamous and degenerate needs via certain deviate and criminal sexual acts." Accompanied with these threat the husband's lawyer may further suggest the removal of the children from the wife's custody, implying that she is unfit to care properly for the childre The fraudulence of the husband's attorney's claim is usually graphically illustrated when the entire claim is speedily dropped the moment the wife agrees to accept support terms from the husband that are far below that which the Court would have granted to her if the accusations had not justifiably frightened her out of her wits. The fact that the said "degenerate acts" are condoned and prescribed in most sex hygiene texts does not comfo her, nor, as a matter of fact, would this entirely comfort her attorney. Any experienced attorney knows that all the usual methods of predicting a Court ruling do not apply when the question before the Court concerns the subject of sex.

Similarly in the two-headed problem (paternity suits and abortion) of the unwed mother, almost insurmountable problems face the social worker, the physician, and the attorney in trying to arrive at a logical and appropriate solution that is in keeping with the latest knowledge of the various scientific disciplines involved. Paternity suits, popularly considered a hopeless trap for the innocent male, are in the author's opinion devastatingly rigged, again the female. The requirements in most jurisdictions are barbaric in terms of consideration for human dignity. For example, in a paternity trial, the femal must describe, in open Court in very explicit terms how, when, and where the male defendant's penis entered her vagina and the Court record must show that she used those terms. The entire procedure implicitly indicates that the Court regards her as a whore, and that the only reason the Court listens to her at all is for the sake of the taxpayer, in that support for the child (not for her) should be obtained from the father rather than from welfare. The ultimate is reached in at least one state, where, if the girl wishe to give up her baby for adoption, she must somehow persuade the alleged father to sign permission for the adoption, or must publicly state on the record in Court that she has no idea who the father is or what his name may be, thus publicly confessing that she is promiscuous. This situation is especially unfair since it is generally conceded that the lady of commercial virtue avoids pregnancy with a high degree of efficiency, as does the girl who is habitually active sexually. More often than not, however, the unwed mother cannot be classed as promiscuous. (Rosen, Vincent)

As to the problem of abortion, the law is fraught with lack of appropriateness and what most would agree is out-and-out cruelty. In jurisdictions where the law permits a therapeutic abortion when the life of the mother is in danger either for physical or for psychiatric reasons, physicians and psychiatrists, as well as various "abortion boards" of hospitals, are fearful enough that permission is granted to only a very small percentage of those cases which fit into the narrow definitions described by law. Very little success has thus far been achieved in changing the law to more liberal proportions; the reasons for this will be discussed in more detail. Suffice it to say at the moment that the fear of opening the door to multitudes of pregnancies among the unwed and the immoral seems to force the retention of the punitive and irrational aspect of the abortion laws. There are many cases on record where permission to abort had actually been granted by a hospital board because of serious danger to the life of the mother, only to be withdrawn when the members of the board discovered that the mother in question was unmarried. (Rosen) By some odd method of reasoning, the members of each of these boards felt that it was within their province to sentence the mother to possible death because of her lack of marital status.

In the area of homosexuality, even though most statutes are sufficiently general in terms to include both men and women, there have been few, if any, recorded convictions of females for such activity. As a matter of curious fact, in a recent article in a publication (entitled *The Ladder*—1965) published by The Daughters of Bilitis, a group consisting of lesbians and those interested in lesbian problems, the author actually complained about this. Even in matters of crime, the author felt, the woman is listed as second rate in our society, in that she is not considered important enough to be prosecuted for engaging in homosexual acts. A very well-known, now deceased, gynecologist of the author's acquaintance quite seriously advocated a homosexual experience for women prior to marriage, on the theory that no one can teach a woman about her sexual sensitivities better than another woman. It may well be that the good doctor was simply finding another way to cry out against the ignorance concerning sex and the lack of education and preparation for mature sexual activities in our society. Many among the doctor's female patients wrote him letters of gratitude, stating how much the homosexual experience had helped in developing and promoting a better heterosexual relationship with their husbands. Regardless of the actual value of such advice, it is mentioned in passing as an indication of incredible lack of education and understanding in what should be an objective approach to the administration of sex.

Yet another form of discrimination against the female is in the preponderance of laws concerning prostitution. Minutely detailed statutes are devoted to punishing cab drivers who direct a passenger to a prostitute, to depriving employment agencies of their licenses if they send an employee to clean a house or home used as the scene of prostitution, and to the punishing of a person who lives off the proceeds of a prostitute or who merely consorts or is seen in public with a known prostitute. All these and more make more blatant the fact that what allows the crime of prostitution to survive as one of our leading industries (in terms of blackmail, bribery of public officials, and tax deductible expense accounts of big business) is the absence of the one law that is most appropriate—namely, the law that punishes the customer who uses the prostitute. In all but a very few jurisdictions, the use of a prostitute is not a felony or a misdemeanor.[5] This simple fact encourages the prostitute to assume the calculated risk to earn large sums of money, and to use occasional periods of imprisonment for purposes of a well needed rest. If the customer were in similar jeopardy of imprisonment, the payment of large sums of money to the prostitute would be discouraged for the customer would then stand to lose with little or no chance to gain. Because of the structure of sex administration in the area of prostitution, the real problems involved in the relevant fields of psychiatry, sexology, and sociology affecting both the customer and the prostitute are almost completely ignored, and the world of prostitutes remains deeply buried in the atmosphere of judicial impotency.[6]

Legal Approach to the Sexual Problems of the Male

There are, of course, legal problems involved in the male's sexual expression similar to those described above concerning females. Except for the State of Illinois, whose new code of laws will be described later, all states hold that almost any form of sexual expression not involving the connection of the male penis with the female vagina is illegal; this is either so stated specifically, or is implied by virtue of the vagueness of the statutes. The male problem of premature ejaculation is professionally dealt with, in part, by advising the man to cause the female orgasm prior to the connection of the penis within the vagina; here again the problem of being advised to commit crimes arises. Also, there are other problems concerning the male which would necessitate that professional advice be given to the female concerning precoital techniques she might perform for her husband, thus again violating the criminal code. But there are several further problems created that are uniquely problems of the male. The first of these, though perhaps not directly concerned with sexual desire, fulfillment, and satisfaction, nevertheless is of sufficient import and is similarly affected by the emotional pressures of public opinion so as to cause danger in its practice: the process known as artificial insemination.

Whereas the problems arising from artificial insemination do pertain in part to the female, it is the behavior of the male that can cause problems of a destructive nature that should be handled by legal administration. This is perhaps due to the fact that artificial insemination obviously would be used only because of the husband's lack of capacity to make his wife pregnant. By definition, it is a male who is the donor of the semen to artificially inseminate a woman other than his wife. There have already been cases in both England and the United States that have granted a husband a divorce from his wife on the grounds of adultery, based on the fact that she had been artificially inseminated. (Pilpel, Williams) Space does not allow for a full discussion of the problems involved, but it is sufficient to mention in passing that statutes are urgently needed to protect the physician, the donor, the wife, the husband, and the resulting child. It is sufficient to note that no jurisdiction seems to have made even a beginning in the creation of proper legislation that would appropriately protect all those involved. The problem is mentioned here because it would seem that the same pressures, which thwart proper revision of the law in the area of sexual behavior, exist to retard progress in this important field.

Another topic too vast for more than passing mention is the problem of pornography and the law. Although the placing of this problem in this section is not meant to indicate that the female has no use for, and is not aroused by pornography, the chief purchaser and user of pornography appears to be the male. Confusion caused by the collision between the concepts of freedom of the press, censorship, license, and the right of the state to police in the name of law and order is just as great today as it was fifty years ago. The problem of defining terms such as "literary art," "obscenity," and "hardcore pornography" practically ensure an incredibly large traffic in so-called illegal pornography for many years to come. Despite the fact that progress (to be described below) has been made in certain other areas of sex administration, very little progress, if any at all, can be demonstrated in the area of pornography.

Although the original concept of statutory rape may have been more than justified (protection of the female in spite of herself), the method of carrying out this concept has proved a dismal failure and one most harmful to the legal safety of the male.

In the first place, in the light of today's knowledge of the discrepancy between the actual emotional maturity of a person and that person's chronological age, the oversimplified device of specifying the exact age of consent of the female entirely defeats the well-intentioned purpose of the statute. It has resulted, for instance, in the conviction of a boy fifteen years of age for having sexual intercourse with a girl seventeen and one-half years of age for the sole and insufficient reason that the girl was under eighteen.[7] In some states even though the statute's wording was changed to avoid the situation just described, the original concept behind the statute was recommended without a single protest. To illustrate, New York State amended the statutory rape law by stating that no male under twenty-one years of age could be indicted or convicted for statutory rape. Nevertheless, to single out one particular case, five boys were indicted and convicted as youthful offenders, even though the girl in question was a known prostitute, was older than all of the boys involved, and but three weeks short of her eighteenth birthday at the time of the crime. One might add in passing that in spite of the admission on the part of the girl that she had received monies from all five boys, no legal action of any kind was taken against her. No one would suggest that the young female be left unprotected, but the time is long overdue for a reappraisal of this particular statute (which is of comparatively recent origin, compared to other biblically oriented sex statutes) by rewriting the statutory rape law, incorporating psychiatric, psychological, and social materials at our disposal.

Just as the cruelty of the law towards females is most intense in its treatment of unwed mothers, the equivalent of such inquisition is present in the legal treatment of the male homosexual. The entrapment of homosexuals by police officers in plain-clothes has been too often described for repetition here. Suffice it to say that the masochistic aspect of the desire of the homosexual to subconsciously trap himself, and thus alleviate his guilt through the punitive atmosphere of the average criminal court is evidence of the complete ineptness of the present laws concerning the homosexual. One could say that the law must have been designed to specifically aggravate the condition of homosexuality, rather than to protect society and the individual homosexual, as all criminal codes are supposed to do.[8] So great is the hostility of society-at-large that as of this writing, the Section that would have made homosexual acts between consenting adults in private legal has been eliminated from the Proposed Revised Criminal Code of the State of New York by an overwhelming vote. As a further example, although the entrapment of a person by law enforcement officers is unconstitutional both in the Federal Constitution and in most State Constitutions, no lawyer, to the author's knowledge, would dare use entrapment as a defense for his client when the charge concerns homosexuality, because even the most blatant set of facts indicating obvious entrapment would be categorically denied by most Courts as constituting entrapment.

The subjects of transvestism and transexualism in re the legal treatment available indicate to a greater degree the discrepancy between psychiatry and law. No specific statutes exist, as yet, that actually deal with the two subjects mentioned. When necessary, completely inappropriate statutes[9] are used regardless of the results obtained. Statutes such as disturbing the peace, disorderly conduct, and mayhem have all been used even though the deeper aspects concerning the individual and society are completely ignored and, if anything, both the individual and society are left in far greater danger[10] than if nothing had been done at all.

Causes and Remedies

It would be fair to say that to be alive is to have a sexual problem. This statement is not meant to be facetious, but rather it indicates the magnitude of the task of making society come face to face with deep-seated feelings of conflict concerning sex. The expressions "Let George do it," and "There ought to be a law" are in this instance synonymous; the reason for the perpetuation of laws concerning sex for interminable periods of time lies in the individual's "Let George do it" feeling that all you have to do to solve such "evil," "dirty," and "ungodly" problems is to make a law which prohibits them. The individual's false security is further enhanced by the law's provision for severe penalties for violations. The impossibility of enforcement of such laws, and their devastating results, are seldom, if ever, understood by the community. The need to create appropriate laws is constantly branded with the desire to create lawlessness. Many commissions have been formed to study and recommended revisions and, except in one State, all such recommendations have been "swept under the rug."

Only in the State of Illinois was a revised code actually passed, becoming effective January 1, 1962. (Sowle) This code reflects great credit on those who wrote the code, and on the Illinois Legislature. The code can be briefly summarized as follows: All laws prohibiting sexual acts between consenting adults in privacy were eliminated from the criminal code. Those laws which remain concern themselves with sexual crimes performed (a) in public, (b) against children, and (c) with force. It is interesting to note that even though a crime of adultery remains in the Illinois Code as a misdemeanor, it must be proven that the behavior of the offenders was "open and notorious. . . ."[11] It should also be noted that no change was made concerning the crime of abortion and "lawful abortion," such abortion being lawful only if performed by a licensed physician, in a licensed hospital or other licensed facilities, and necessary for the preservation of the woman's life.

The habit of ignoring problems rather than making a law appropriate is so ingrained that it would seem, at the moment, that there is little hope for widespread changes in the various State Codes in the United States. It is too early to properly evaluate the success or failure of the Illinois Code. The method of change was a quiet one, so that a general "hue and cry" may yet be forthcoming in Illinois, depending on the skill of the law enforcement agencies, the type of cases which may arise and be reported in the daily papers, and the resulting public demand for "backward" revision of the criminal statutes.

In general, permitting of archaic laws—archaic since they no longer serve their purpose because of changes in public mores, and increased knowledge in the social sciences—to remain as part of the criminal code means they will remain unenforced for the most part, despite the fact that they are violated openly every hour of the day. To fail to enforce any law is to automatically affect the enforceability of all law.

The Illinois Code, therefore, has caused a long step to be taken toward improving the efficiency of law enforcement, by restricting those acts of a sexual nature to be called a crime to those which do not depend on the invasion of personal privacy for their discovery and allow for the most part freedom of will between consenting adults. It is already difficult to maintain a large enough police force to enforce the law in public places, to protect the individual from violence, and the child from harm without the additional thousands that would be needed to police the internal areas of one's home. As the late Justice Learned Hand consistently maintained years ago, all sex practices (except those involving force, public view, or the participation of children) are matters of taste, and should not be administered or regulated within the provisions of the law, but rather through the school, the church, and the home. The Illinois Code is designed around this concept.

Conclusion

Reference should be made to a distinction existing in the legal administration of sex between unenforce*able* and unenfor*ced* laws. A clear recognition and understanding of this distinction would be a very real step forward in achieving fairness and efficiency in the structure of laws concerning sex. In the category of unenforceable laws, one finds statutes which are concerned with prohibiting various forms of sexual expression between consenting adults (such as oral-genital contacts, etc.). By eliminating (as the Illinois Code does) those statutes which are obviously unenforceable, the problem of dealing with the remainder becomes clarified and, therefore, much simpler.

As to the category of the unenforced statute, the causes of such unenforcement are largely twofold. First, there are those cases in which the prescribed penalties for the crime committed are so outlandishly inappropriate that a judge simply refuses to inflict cruelty on a sick defendant and indulges in the fiction that the facts of the case really indicate some lesser crime (such as the crime of rape being reduced to the crime of simple assault), and thus imposes a lesser punishment. Second, in many cases the facts really do not fit into any of the statutes presently "on the books," so that the judge is forced to select some statute at random, whether it is appropriate or not, so as to satisfy public opinion in the community over which he presides.

As to the immediate future, there is no question that there is evidence of a sexual renaissance, but such evidence would seem to be least observable in the area of legal administration of sexual expression. There are glimmers of important changes in the near future. The normal forty to sixty year lag which has always existed between the creation of mores and codification of such mores into statute seems about up, so that one has hope that the dawn of appropriate legal administration of human sexual behavior is closer at hand than would appear on the surface.

References

Cases and Readings on Law and Society. St. Paul: West Publishing Co., 1948-1949.
CHESSER, EUSTACE. *Sexual Behavior, Normal and Abnormal.* New York: Roy Pub., 1949.
DONNELLY, RICHARD C., GOLDSTEIN, JOSEPH, AND SCHWARTZ, RICHARD D. *Criminal Law.* New York: The Free Press of Glencoe, 1962.

DRZAGA, JOHN. *Sex Crimes.* Springfield, Illinois: Charles C. Thomas, 1960.
ERNST, MORRIS, AND LINDEY, ALEXANDER. *The Censor Marches On.* New York: Doubleday, Doran, 1940.
GUTTMACHER, M. S., AND WEIHOFEN, H. *Psychiatry and the Law.* New York: W. W. Norton, 1952.
HALL, GLADYS M. *Prostitution in the Modern World.* New York: Emerson Books, 1936.
KARPMAN, BENJAMIN. *The Sexual Offender and His Offenses.* New York: Julian Press, 1954.
PILPEL, HARRIET F. AND SAVIN, THEODORA. *Your Marriage & The Law.* New York: Rinehart, 1952.
REINHARDT, JAMES MELVIN. *Sex Perversions and Sex Crimes.* Springfield, Illinois: Charles C. Thomas, 1957.
ROSEN, HAROLD. *Therapeutic Abortion.* New York: Julian Press, 1954.
SHERWIN, ROBERT V. *Sex and the Statutory Law.* New York: Oceana Pub., 1949.
SHERWIN, ROBERT V. "Some Legal Aspects of Homosexuality." *Internat. J. Sexology,* 1950, 4; 22-26.
SHERWIN, ROBERT V. "Sex Expression and the Law. The Law of Rape." *Internat. J. Sexology,* 1951, 4; 206-210.
SHERWIN, ROBERT V. "Sex Expression and the Law. II. Sodomy: A Medico-Legal Enigma." *Internat. J. Sexology,* 1951, 5; 3-13.
SHERWIN, ROBERT V. "Prostitution: A Study of Law and Disorder." *Internat. J. Sexology,* 1952, 5; 201-205.
SHERWIN, ROBERT V. "Laws on Sex Crimes." *The Encyclopedia of Sexual Behavior, Vol. II,* pages 622-630; New York: Hawthorn Books, 1961.
SHERWIN, ROBERT V. "The Legal Problems in Transvestism." *American Journal of Psychotherapy,* 1954, 8, 243-244.
SOWLE, CLAUDE R. *A Concise Explanation of the Illinois Criminal Code of 1961,* Chicago, Illinois: Burdette Smith, 1961.
VINCENT, CLARK. *Unmarried Mothers.* New York: The Free Press of Glencoe, 1961.
VOLLMER, AUGUST. *The Police and Modern Society.* Stanford, California: Bureau of Public Administration, University of California, 1936.
WILDERBLOOD, PETER. *Against the Law.* New York: Julian Messner, 1959.
WILLIAMS, GLANVILLE. *The Sanctity of Life and the Criminal Law.* New York: Alfred A. Knopf, 1957.

Some Public
Issues

296

1. Illustrations are numerous; one need only contemplate the effect on a woman patient with a conservative background, religious training, etc., when she is told that she has committed a felony while making love to her husband by permitting term "Sodomy," or the titles "Crime Against Nature" and "Lewd-Lascivious

Behavior" contain acts within them that include, either by specific mention or vague reference, the acts of fellatio, cunnilinctus and mutual masturbation.

2. This example is a composite statute based on the average "Crime Against Nature" type of statute that appears in most states. It is important to note that all states have some form of this statute, with the exception of Illinois. In some states such as New York, the statute has been expanded to include first degree, second degree, and third degree gradations of crime. Note too that no distinction is made as to whether or not the participants are married or single.

3. If a psychiatrist advises a female patient that certain precoital acts described in Footnote (1) would aid her in her physical fulfillment and in her marriage, he is advising her to commit the crimes of Sodomy, etc. If the act is a felony in the state in which the psychiatrist practices, his act of so advising becomes a felony.

4. It is important to note here that most states have what is called in the vernacular a "catchall" statute, which is so vague that it jeopardizes almost anyone who is engaged in any kind of behavior from advising to functioning in the field of sex. For example a statute from the New York Criminal Code reads: "a person who willfully and wrongfully commits any act . . . which openly outrages public decency, for which no other punishment is specifically prescribed, . . . is guilty of a misdemeanor." Some of the cases caught up in these catchall statutes border on the absurd, and would be deemed so even by the most conservative observer.

5. In some states, notably New York state, the actual act of prostituting herself (as compared with the acts of soliciting, pandering, etc.) is not defined as a misdemeanor or a felony, but comes under the vagrancy statute and is regarded as an "offense" an oral-genital contact to help her achieve orgasm. It is important to note that the which is considered less than a misdemeanor. Certain rules and regulations concerning repeated convictions, parole, etc. are not applied to an "offense" in the same way that they are to a misdemeanor or a felony. (See Sherwin, 1949 and 1952.)

6. The permitted existence of known houses of prostitution and the more modern "call-girl" version of the prostitution industry by law enforcement officers, and the wide-spread system of "payoffs," would seem to give ample evidence of the absence of enforcement of the multiple laws concerning prostitution.

7. Statutory rape is usually defined as having sexual intercourse with a female under the age of consent. Even though she may have acquiesced to and actually solicited the physical relations engaged in, if she be under the age of consent as prescribed by the law of the particular state in which the act occurs, the male can be convicted of rape. Some states have more detailed statutory rape laws in that they specify several ages of the female such as 13, 15, and 18, and increase the penalty as the age decreases. Thus, the least penalty is where intercourse is with an 18 year old and the most severe when the female is 13 or under. Only a handful of states takes into account the age of the male. Also, see Sherwin, 1949.

8. It would seem to the author that the incarceration of the homosexual, without any specific treatment being available, reenforces his homosexuality. Both the assaults made upon him in person, and the so-called "special treatment" the homosexual may receive from the guards and the inmates if he acquiesces to their seductive approaches, all serve to reenforce his homosexual desires. In addition, blackmail derived from the entire entrapment situation (in some instances the homosexual pays the police officer in his neighborhood weekly to be allowed his freedom to "cruise") allows the homosexual to become an even greater problem to both himself and the public at large.

9. Very little is known as yet regarding the nature and problems of the transvestite and the transexualist. Despite this, arrests have been made under vagrancy statutes, disorderly conduct statutes, and statutes concerning the act of masquerading on a

public street with the intent to conceal one's identity or for other purposes of fraud. Convictions have been obtained in spite of the fact that the statutes mentioned were clearly not appropriate to the act and basic proofs of intent to commit a fraud were absent. See Sherwin, 1954.

10. It goes without saying that the basic purpose of the law and its enforcement is for the protection of society, and the protection of the individual against himself. So long as inappropriate laws are all that exist, individuals who may well be potentially harmful both to society and to themselves will remain at large or temporarily incarcerated; either of which defeats the purpose of law and order. To arrest a person for the wrong reason may secure him his freedom when he should be apprehended. The same applies to a person who is released for the wrong reason because of the inappropriateness of the statute under which he was arrested and convicted.

11. *Illinois Crime Code:* Sec. 11-7.

FACTS VERSUS FEARS: WHY SHOULD WE WORRY ABOUT PORNOGRAPHY?

W. Cody Wilson

The U.S. Commission on Obscenity and Pornography was created by Congress in 1968. Its main task was to gather facts—information, not rhetoric—on the "determinants and effects" of pornography on the public. Prior to 1968, reports of the public's experiences with pornography were mostly based on speculation, on personal experiences, or hearsay of personal experiences—hence, the reason for the commission.

In 1970 the commission reported that explicit sexual materials have been available to, and used by, people for many years with no apparent harmful effects either to themselves or as agents of delinquency to others. It was also discovered that sex offenders generally had had "significantly less experience with explicit sexual materials in adolescence" than the normal control subjects.

This finding, and others like it, was so contrary to the expected linking of pornography with the increasing incidence of crime in this country that political leaders denounced the commission, including President Nixon who called it "morally bankrupt".

According to Dr. Wilson, the real issue is that a sizable minority of the public finds the commission's facts irrelevant and claim that the government should control pornography and uphold the moral standards and values important to this society. Putting this kind of power into the political structure is to invite catastrophe, and this is why Dr. Wilson says we should worry about pornography.

> The publication and distribution of salacious materials is a peculiarly vicious evil; the destruction of moral character caused by it among young people cannot be overestimated. The circulation of periodicals containing such materials plays an important part in the development of crime among youth of our country.[1]

Reprinted from *The Annals of the American Academy of Political and Social Science*, September, 1971, Volume 397. Reprinted by permission of publisher.

If a case is to be made against 'pornography' in 1970, it will have to
be made on grounds other than demonstrated effects of a damaging
personal or social nature. Empirical research designed to clarify the
question has found no reliable evidence to date that exposure to explic
sexual materials plays a significant role in the causation of delinquent
or criminal sexual behavior among youth or adults.[2]

Thus is the issue drawn: popular rhetoric versus the findings of empirical
science—fears versus facts. This issue is, of course, much larger by far than
the issue of pornography. But the issue of pornography may serve as a case
study which illuminates the larger issue—and, indeed, pornography is an
issue of considerable interest in itself.

This paper will review the "facts" about pornography as they are revealed
by empirical research in the social, behavioral, and medical sciences, and
then explore some of the implications of these "facts" for our society.

Many of the data that exist at the present regarding pornography are eith
the direct or indirect products of the needs and interests of the U.S. Commission on Obscenity and Pornography which began its work in 1968 and
made its report in 1970.[3] The Commission, created by Congress, was
assigned four specific tasks: (1) to analyze existing laws, (2) to ascertain
the volume of traffic and patterns of distribution for obscene and pornographic materials, (3) to study the effects of these materials on the public,
and (4) to recommend policy. A review of the existing empirical literature
in 1968 concluded that

> we still have precious little information from studies of humans on the
> questions of primary import to the law. . . . the data 'stop short at the
> critical point'. Definitive answers on the determinants and effects of
> pornography are not yet available.[4]

The Commission spent two years and nearly one million dollars in research
on these tasks. The result was not a "definitive answer"—but there are, now,
a few facts with which to think about the issues.

PATTERNS OF EXPERIENCE WITH
EXPLICIT SEXUAL MATERIAL

Some Public
Issues

Extent of Exposure

In retrospect it may seem incredible that in 1968 there were no "facts" abou
people's experience with erotic materials. Alfred C. Kinsey and his associate

had collected information on this topic, but it had never been adequately analyzed and reported. Any estimate was necessarily a projection of one's own personal experience or one's own private fears and fantasies. Each individual was a repository of information about such experiences, but this experience had never been collated to provide a description of the typical experience in our society.

In 1969 several investigators began to ask selected individuals about their experiences with pornography or explicit sexual materials.

Approximately 20,000 readers of *Psychology Today* responded to the question, "Have you voluntarily obtained or seen erotic or pornographic books, movies, etc?" In this sample (obviously not representative of the general population since 77 percent were less than 35 years old and 89 percent had some college experience), 92 percent of the males and 72 percent of the females said, "Yes." [5]

The same question was asked of 450 members of professional and community service groups in metropolitan Detroit, and 80 percent indicated that they had voluntarily obtained erotic materials. [6]

A questionnaire submitted to several hundred predominantly middle-class men and women members of social, professional, service, and church groups in Denver revealed that 83 percent had seen at some time in their lives depictions of people engaged in a sex act. [7]

Intensive clinical interviews regarding experience with a variety of sexual materials were conducted with predominantly lower middle-class, black and white, normal males in the age range 20-40 in Los Angeles. Over 90 percent of the group reported that they had seen photographs of fully nude females, and 86 percent of the whites and 76 percent of the blacks reported having been exposed to photographic depictions of sexual intercourse. [8]

These several studies of selected samples are quite consistent in their results and suggest that experience with explicit sexual materials sometimes called pornography is rather widespread in our society.

This hypothesis was tested by conducting face-to-face interviews with approximately 2,500 adults selected in such a way that their responses could be generalized to the total adult population of the United States. This survey asked questions about seeing pictorial depictions and reading verbal depictions of the following five types: emphasizing the sex organs of a man or woman; mouth-sex organ contact between a man and woman; a man and woman having sexual intercourse; sexual activities between people of the same sex; and sex activities which included whips, belts, or spankings. Eighty-four percent of the men and 69 percent of the women in this representative national sample reported having been exposed to at least one of these kinds of depictions.[9]

Experience in the United States is very similar to that in Denmark. In a survey of a representative sample of 398 men and women in Copenhagen, 87 percent of men and 73 percent of women reported that they had "consumed" at least one "pornographic" book, and similar percentages had "consumed" at least one "pornographic" magazine.[10]

Correlates of Exposure

Experience with explicit sexual materials varies according to the characteristics of both the material and the person.

People are more likely to have experience with depictions of sexual activity which conform to our society's general cultural norms than with portrayals of sexual activity which deviate from these norms.[11] The rank ordering of depictions in terms of their likelihood of being seen in our society is: full nudity, heterosexual intercourse, oral sex, homosexual activity, and sadomasochistic activity. Portrayals of combinations of sex and violence are relatively rare in the experience of normal adults in our society.

People with different characteristics have differential experience with explicit sexual material. It was reported above that men are more likely to have had experience with sexual materials than are women. Younger adults are more likely to have been exposed to erotic materials than are older adults; and the more education one has, the more likely one is to have been exposed to such materials. These two relations hold for both men and women. For men, but not for women, those who live in large metropolitan areas are more likely than those who do not to have had experience with explicit sexual materials. People who read general books, magazines, and newspapers more and who see general movies more, also see more erotic stimuli. People who are socially and politically active are exposed to more erotic material. Both these latter two findings hold for both men and women. People who attend religious services more often are somewhat less likely to be exposed to erotica.[12]

These differences in experience with sexual materials may be summarized by the following profiles. Persons who have had greater amounts of experience with erotic materials tend to be younger, better educated, better read, urban males who are more socially and politically active, but less involved in religious affairs. Those who have had less experience with erotic materials tend to be older, less educated and less well read females who live in smaller communities and are more isolated socially, less politically active, but more active in religious affairs.

Similar profiles have been reported for Sweden.[13]

Although some experience with explicit sexual materials is almost universal among males in our society, only about one-fifth to one-quarter of the population have somewhat regular experience as adults with materials as explicit as heterosexual intercourse.[14]

Age of First Experience

The representative sample of American adults was also asked to try to recall the age at which they had first been exposed to explicit sexual materials. Roughly three-quarters of the males reported having been exposed before age 21, one-half before age 18, and one-third before age 15; females report being exposed to these materials about two years later than do males. These figures may report later exposure than actually occurred, however, because it may be difficult for older people to make differentiations of a few years when recalling teenage experience. For example, although 19 percent of all male adults report first exposure at 12 years of age or younger, 34 percent of men age 21-29 report first exposure at age 12 or younger. This difference in reporting may reflect errors in recall among older respondents, or it may reflect actual changes in experience in more recent decades.[15]

The clinical interviews with normal subjects in Los Angeles confirm these findings that adult males report considerable experience with explicit sexual materials in adolescence. Three-quarters of the subjects reported having seen photos of heterosexual intercourse in adolescence, and two-thirds reported having seen photos of mouth-genital activity in adolescence.[16]

Three studies of college students indicate a greater degree of exposure to explicit sexual materials during adolescence than do retrospective reports of older adults. Again, it is not clear whether this reflects more precise recall or a change in cultural experience over time.

A report of a survey of a national random sample of college students conducted in 1967 concluded that over 90 percent of college students have exposure to explicit sexual materials before reaching college.[17]

Another study found that over two-thirds of students in five different universities in New York, Providence, and Boston reported first exposure to "pornography" in any form by age 13.[18]

The third study found that 49 percent of male students in 8 colleges in Westchester County, New York, report having been exposed to "pornography" before age 13, and 50 percent of the females report having been exposed before age 15.[19]

Three sets of investigators have inquired into the experience of adolescents with explicit sexual materials using selected convenient samples.

One researcher submitted a questionnaire to more than 300 eleventh and twelfth grade students in a public school in a working-class suburb of Chicago. The respondents were nearly all white and Christian, with slightly more than half belonging to the Roman Catholic Church. Eighty-one percent of the boys and 43 percent of the girls reported having seen photographs of nude males and females engaging in sexual behavior, and 95 percent of the boys and 72 percent of the girls reported having been exposed to printed material describing sexual intercourse.[20]

A study of 473 working-class, white, predominantly Roman Catholic adolescents aged 13 to 18 obtained similar results. Seventy-seven percent of the boys and 35 percent of the girls (the girls in this study were on the average a couple of years younger than the boys) had seen pictures of sexual intercourse, and 79 percent of the boys and 78 percent of the girls had been exposed to books describing sexual activities in slang terms.[21]

The third investigator studied inmates of a youth reformatory in a Northeastern city; the subjects were males ages 17 to 20 and predominantly from minority ethnic groups (67 percent black and 21 percent Puerto Rican). Eighty-four percent had seen pictures of heterosexual intercourse. [22]

The national survey described earlier also included a sample of more than 750 adolescents age 15 to 20 who were living at home. This group, while more representative than the other groups of adolescents reported on above, is not representative of all adolescents in the United States this age, because it leaves out those who were not living at home, such as those who were away at school or in the armed services. Ninety-one percent of the males and 88 percent of the females reported having been exposed to depictions of sex at least as explicit as nudity with genitals exposed and emphasized.[23]

These various studies are quite consistent among themselves in finding that there is considerable exposure to explicit sexual materials on the part of minors. One may rather conservatively estimate from all these figures that 85 percent of boys and 70 percent of girls have seen visual depictions or read textual descriptions of heterosexual intercourse by the time they finish high school, or reach the age of 18. Substantial proportions of adolescents have had more than an isolated experience or two, although the rates of exposure do not indicate an obsession with erotic materials. A great deal of exposure to explicit sexual materials occurs in the pre-adolescent and early adolescent years. More than half the boys would appear to have some exposure to depictions of sexual intercourse by age 15. Exposure on the part of girls lags behind that of boys by a year or two. Exposure to depictions of nudity with genitals occurs earlier and more often. Exposure to oral-genital and homosexual materials occurs later and less frequently. Experience with depictions of sadomasochistic material is much rarer, although it does occur.[24]

Source of Exposure

The most common source of exposure to sexual materials is a friend; and this exposure appears to be a part of the "normal" social activity centered around home and school.[25] Young people rarely purchase explicit sexual materials; most of their exposure occurs in a social situation where materials are freely passed around among friends.

Few adults report that they buy erotic materials, also. In the national survey only 5 percent of the men report having bought the pictorial depiction they most recently had seen, and 26 percent of men report having bought the most recent textual depiction that they read; most report having obtained these from someone else (it was shown or given to them by a friend) at no cost.[26] The study of social, professional, service and church groups in Denver found that only 26 percent of those who had seen depictions of sex acts with full exposure of sex organs had also bought these materials at some time. The principal source was a friend or acquaintance.[27]

Patrons of "Adult" Bookstores

Although a small proportion of people buy sexual materials, nevertheless, customers of "adult" bookstores and movie theaters probably constitute a sizable absolute number of people. Several studies have attempted to document the characteristics of these people.[28]

In these studies nearly 14,000 "customers" were observed in 12 different cities. The profile that emerges from all these observations is: middle-aged, middle-class, married, white, male, dressed in business suit or neat casual attire, shopping alone. More intensive studies using questionnaires and interviews with smaller groups confirm the characterizations of patrons derived from external observation.[29]

People in pornography shops in Denmark were found to be very similar in characteristics to customers of adult book stores in the United States.[30]

EFFECTS OF EXPLICIT SEXUAL MATERIALS

In 1968, the state of our factual knowledge about the consequences of exposure to explicit sexual materials was quite circumscribed; the existing empirical knowledge generally was limited to sexual arousal responses. Briefly, pictures and words depicting various aspects of human sexuality produce sexual arousal in a considerable proportion of the adult population; the amount of arousal is a joint function of the characteristics of the stimulus, the characteristics of the viewer, and the context in which the viewing occurs. There was no empirical information concerning the duration of the arousal or how this stimulation might affect overt behavior, attitudes governing behavior, or such things as mental health.[31]

Opinions

Lack of empirical information often encourages people to speculate and project their own fears to fill the void. The Commission on Obscenity and Pornography reviewed the popular literature concerning pornography and collected a variety of presumed consequences of exposure to explicit sexual materials such as: sexually aggressive acts of a criminal nature, unlawful sexual practices, sexually perverse behavior, adultery, deadly serious pursuit of sexual satisfaction, obsession with sex, moral breakdown, homicide, suicide, delinquency, indecent personal habits, unhealthy thoughts, ennui, information, attitudes, draining off of illegitimate sexual desires, release of strong sexual urges without harming others, pleasure, and assistance in consummation of legitimate sexual responsibilities.[32]

Many of these presumed consequences of exposure to explicit sexual materials receive rather widespread acceptance among the public. The earlier cited survey of a representative sample of American adults asked for "opinions about the effects of looking at or reading sexual materials." The most widely held opinion about effects, subscribed to by two-thirds of the adults in the United States, is one supported by empirical research, namely, that these materials excite people sexually. Three-fifths of those asked feel that these materials provide information about sex. Approximately half the sample are of the opinion that sexual materials provide entertainment, lead to rape, lead to a breakdown in morals, and improve sex relations of some married couples.[33] The same 50 percent do not necessarily subscribe to all these opinions!

The opinions that sexual materials excite people, provide information about sex, provide entertainment, and improve sex relations of some married couples seem to be grounded in experience; that is, people who hold opinions that these are consequences of exposure to such materials tend to report that the materials have had this effect on them or on someone they know personally, and they also report more experience with such materials in the past two years. On the other hand, the opinions that sexual materials lead to rape, or to a breakdown in morals, seem to be based more on hearsay, since the people who hold these opinions tend to report that these effects have not occurred to them nor to anyone they know personally, and also report less experience with such materials.[34]

Empirical Studies of Adult Sex Criminals

Although there has been for some time a considerable amount of concern about possible harmful and anti-social consequences of exposure to explicit sexual materials, almost no controlled empirical studies had been carried out until relatively recently.

In 1964, one study reported no significant differences between matched groups of delinquent and nondelinquent youth in the number of "sensational" books they had read.[35] In 1965, a book from the Kinsey Institute reported no significant differences in exposure to sexual materials among white male sex offenders, males who were not sex offenders, and volunteer non-offender males from the general population.[36]

More recent research provides elaboration on these findings.

Long intensive clinical interviews regarding sexual history were conducted with sex offenders in a California state hospital for the criminally insane and with a group from the general population which was similar in age, ethnic group membership, and socio-economic status. Particular attention was paid to experience with explicit sexual materials during adolescence and pre-adolescence, with the aim of checking out the idea that early exposure to sexual materials produces sexual deviance and sexual criminals. The investigators did find a correlation between exposure to sexual materials in adolescence and pre-adolescence and the committing of sexual offenses—but it was in a direction opposite to that embodied in our cultural myths. Sex offenders (rapists and pedophiles) had had significantly *less* experience with explicit sexual materials in adolescence and pre-adolescence than had the normal control subjects from the general population![37]

Similar results were obtained independently by investigators in other geographical regions using other research methods: one group compared offenders and non-offenders in the prison system of Wisconsin using a brief face-to-face interview;[38] a second study compared sex offenders with non-offenders, college students, and business men's service club members in Texas;[39] a third compared probationed sex offenders in Pennsylvania with a national sample of men of similar age and socio-economic status using survey interviews.[40] All these studies indicate that sex offenders have somewhat later and relatively less experience with explicit sexual materials than do people who have not committed sex offenses.

The California study also included groups of homosexuals, trans-sexuals, and customers of adult bookstores and movie theaters. These groups also reported less experience with explicit sexual materials in adolescence and pre-adolescence than did the control subjects.[41]

These several investigators also inquired about more recent experience, as adults, with sexual materials. In general, the results indicate that the recent experience of sex offenders and other population subgroups with depictions of sex is very similar. When differences are observed they are usually in the direction of the sex offender having less experience.

Sex Crime Statistics

Additional data regarding the relationship between explicit sex materials and sex crimes come from a "natural field experiment" that occurred in Denmark as a result of recent changes in the law. The Danish Parliament voted to remove erotic literature from its obscenity statute in June, 1967, and then two years later, in 1969, repealed the statute entirely. It is now legal in Denmark to disseminate sexually explicit materials to persons sixteen years of age or older. An analysis of sex crimes reported to the police in Copenhagen over a 12-year period, 1958 to 1969, was undertaken at the request of the U.S. Commission on Obscenity and Pornography. This time period included nine years prior to the change in the law, two years subsequent to the first change, and one year subsequent to the second change. The statistics indicate that the number of sex crimes decreased by 40 percent in the two years following the first liberalization of the availability of pornography as compared with the relatively stable average of the previous nine years; the number of sex crimes reported to the police decreased 30 percent further in the year in which the second liberalization of the pornography law occurred.[42]

This decrease in reported sex crimes did not include obscenity offenses, and cannot be attributed to changes in police procedures in recording nor to changes in legal definitions of crimes. Indeed, each separate type of sex crime (rape, intercourse on threat of violence, sexual interference with adult women, sexual interference with minor girls, coitus with minors, exhibitionism, peeping, verbal indecency, and homosexual offenses) decreased by more than 30 percent over the interval from 1958 to 1969.

A Danish criminologist conducted a survey of a random sample of Copenhagen residents in order to try to explain the dynamics of this change in the number of reported sex crimes.[43] Some, but not all, of the change *may* be attributable to changes in public attitudes about sex crimes and the willingness to report such events to the police. However, there does seem to be a real decrease in the number of occurrences of certain of the acts, such as peeping and sexual interference with minor females.

At the very least, the data from Denmark contradict the widely held assumption that explicit sexual materials *cause* sex crimes.

Juvenile Crime

Reliable information regarding the relationship between exposure to explicit sexual materials and crime on the part of non-adults is more difficult to find. A review of available social indicator statistics provides some indirect evidence on this topic. Although the availability of sexual materials increased severalfold over the period 1960-1969 in the United States, the number of juvenile arrests for sex crimes decreased.[44] This study also reports that the rate of increase of illegitimate births among adolescent females aged 15 to 19 years was considerably less, over the period 1960-1965, than the rate for unmarried women aged 19 to 44 years.

Another group attempted to study the relationship between experience with explicit sexual materials and various types of delinquency among the juveniles seen by the juvenile court of a large Eastern city. The research was stymied, however, when an examination of approximately 800 records, selected at random from the files for one recent year, revealed no information from police, psychiatric, or social work records regarding sexual material.[45]

A third study collected data on the experience of 476 incarcerated delinquent juvenile males with explicit sexual materials.[46] Although this study did not collect similar data on nondelinquents for comparison, the data on the delinquents are comparable to data collected by other investigators of nondelinquents.[47] The amount of exposure to sexual materials on the part of the delinquents is generally not distinguishable from that of nondelinquents.

Other Antisocial Consequences

Two other "antisocial orientations" have been studied in terms of their relationship to exposure to explicit sexual material: "bad moral character" and "calloused sexual attitudes toward women."

Psychologists found a moderate correlation between exposure to explicit sexual materials and "bad moral character," but pointed out that the raw correlation tells nothing about the direction of causation. After a further complicated causal analysis they concluded that bad moral character "causes" exposure to explicit sexual materials—not that exposure to sexual materials leads to development of bad moral character![48]

An experimental investigation tested the hypothesis that "calloused" sexual attitudes in males would increase after exposure to explicit sexual stimuli. Results showed that exposure to two erotic films did not increase already established frequencies of exploitive sexual behavior; and "calloused" sexual attitudes toward women *decreased* immediately after viewing the erotic films, and continued to decrease slightly 24 hours and two weeks later![49]

Other Consequences

A number of experimental studies have been conducted recently to investigate the effects of exposure to explicit sexual materials.[50]

As a group these studies indicate: (1) exposure to explicit sexual stimuli produces sexual arousal in most people; (2) there is no general increase in sexual behavior following exposure to sexual stimuli; (3) there is no change in the type of sexual behavior one engages in as a result of exposure to sexual materials; (4) there is no change in attitudes regarding what is acceptable sexual behavior; (5) there is a marked increase in the likelihood of individuals talking about sex in the 24-hour period following exposure to explicit sexual materials—many subjects, especially married people, rate this a highly desirable consequence, since it often results in a breakdown of communication barriers that have retarded the solving of marital conflicts; and (6) attempts to censor by cutting out more explicit depictions tend to increase the arousal value of sex-related materials.

Finally, a representative sample of American adults reports that, on the basis of their own knowledge regarding the consequences of exposure to explicit sexual materials, these consequences tend to be positive or harmless rather than harmful. For example, approximately 40 percent report that such materials have provided information about sex to themselves or someone they know personally; roughly 35 percent report on the basis of their own knowledge that these materials excite people sexually, and a similar number say they provide entertainment; and approximately 25 percent report that these materials improve the sex relations of some married couples, and a similar number report that exposure to sex materials produces boredom with such materials. On the other hand, few people report first-hand knowledge of harmful consequences such as breakdown of morals, rape, or driving people sex crazy.[51]

Conclusions

The facts that have been summarized here would appear to be sufficient to begin to reassure and calm most reasonable and rational people regarding the threat and danger of pornography. Mr. Hoover's fears may now be replaced by empirical facts. Indeed, the majority of the members of the Commission on Obscenity and Pornography concluded that explicit sexual materials could not be considered to play a significant role in the causation of delinquent or criminal behavior among youth or adults. Rather, they concluded that much of the "problem" regarding materials which depict explicit sexual activity stems from the inability or reluctance of people in our society to be open and direct in dealing with sexual matters.[52]

The response of the Commission on Obscenity and Pornography was in many respects a conservative one. In the past half decade, five other nations have had official commissions study and make recommendations in this area: Denmark, Sweden, West Germany, Great Britain, and Israel. Each of these commissions had many fewer empirical facts to guide their considerations than did the United States Commission. Yet each of these commissions arrived at essentially similar conclusions and recommendations: there is no evidence that explicit sexual materials are harmful, and legal restrictions which inhibit freedom of the press and of speech should be repealed.[53]

THE IRRELEVANCE OF FACTS

Why, then, should we worry about pornography?

We should worry about pornography because there is a segment of our society for whom facts are not relevant and who cling, for some reason or other, to fears.

Facts and Attitudes toward Restriction

The national survey that has been cited previously asked a series of question about attitudes toward the control of availability of explicit sexual materials.[54] The authors report that there is a "hard-core" minority of adults in our society, amounting to roughly one-third of the adult population, which is opposed to the existence of explicit sexual materials—even if these materials are shown to have no harmful effects and the availability is limite to being looked at or read by adults in their own homes!

Political Response to the Commission's Facts

The above group is, perhaps, the constituency to which the President and the U.S. Senate were addressing themselves in October 1970 in response to the *Report* of the Commission on Obscenity and Pornography, which contained a more detailed presentation of facts similar to those briefly reviewe in this paper and a set of recommendations consistent with these facts.

Mr. Nixon called the Commission "morally bankrupt" and promised to ignore its findings and recommendations.[55] The Senate passed by a vote of 60 to 5 "a resolution declaring that the Senate rejects the findings and recommendations of the Commission on Obscenity and Pornography."[56]

Three of the eighteen members of the Commission also felt that empiric facts are irrelevant to the discussion, and issued vigorous dissents to the majority report with its emphasis on facts.

> The fundamental "finding" on which the entire report is based is: that "empirical research" has come up with "no reliable evidence to indicate that exposure to explicit sexual materials plays a significant role in the causation of delinquent or criminal behavior among youth or adults. . . . [but] The basic question is whether and to what extent society may establish and maintain certain moral standards. If it is conceded that society has a legitimate concern in maintaining moral standards, it follows logically that government has a legitimate intere in at least attempting to protect such standards against any source which threatens them.[57]
>
> For those who believe in God, in His absolute supremacy as the Creator and Lawgiver of life, in the dignity and destiny which He has conferred upon the human person, in the moral code that governs sexual activity—for those who believe in these "things," no argument against pornography should be necessary.[58]

Characteristics of Those for Whom Facts May Be Irrelevant

Three empirical studies provide some data on the characteristics of the constituency for whom facts appear to be irrelevant.

In the U.S. national adult population, people who are more restrictive in their orientation to explicit sexual materials are significantly more likely to be: older, less educated, female, frequent churchgoers, and conservative (in their own opinion) on other issues. They are less supportive of free expression in terms of the First Amendment: for example, they are more likely to reject the idea that newspapers have the right to print articles which criticize the police, or that people should be allowed to make speeches against God, or that people should be allowed to publish books which attack our system of government. They also tend to perceive widespread support within the public for their own position; that is, the majority think that other people in the community want either about the same amount or more restriction on sexual materials than they themselves do.[59]

Sociologists have studied intensively two ad hoc anti-pornography organizations, one in the Midwest and the other in the Southwest. The characteristics of the participants and the dynamics of the operation of these two organizations were very similar. In comparison with individuals who opposed these organizations' activities, the members were: more likely to be raised in rural communities, older, more active religiously, family oriented, politically conservative, traditional, and restrictive in their sexual attitudes. They were also more likely to score higher on scales of authoritarianism and dogmatism, and to be intolerant of individuals whose political views differed from their own. They tended to feel that there was widespread community support for their position, and to dismiss people who did not agree with them as not representative of the real community.[60]

A national survey of prosecuting attorneys indicates that these law enforcement officials are quite divided in their opinions regarding the helpfulness of citizen action groups to law enforcement in the area of obscenity and pornography, with roughly half feeling that such groups are not helpful. The key to this opinion seems to be the representativeness of the group in terms of the total community. The more representative the group is of the total community the more likely it is to be judged helpful. Unfortunately, the prosecuting attorneys do not report such groups as being very representative of their communities.[61]

In the analysis of the two ad hoc anti-pornography organizations, the authors interpret the actions of these groups and the motives of their members as an attempt to reinforce and reinstate value systems and behavioral norms which are perceived to be in danger of eroding away. Because a number of people will no longer conform to the norms, an attempt is made to arouse the community to a reaffirmation of its values and impose these on the straying ones. Thus, pornography becomes a lightning rod which attracts a variety of not very well defined status anxieties, and its control provides the hope of a simple and sovereign solution to a variety of social ills. The authors draw a number of parallels between the anti-smut movement and the Prohibition movement of the early part of this century.[6]

Conclusion

In the appeals of the politicians and the characteristics of that "hard-core" constituency for whom facts are not relevant, one may perceive the ingredients of a moral crusade. Moral crusades and political repression often go hand-in-hand.

And that is the reason why we, perhaps, should worry about pornography

1. J. Edgar Hoover, Statement, in Interim Report of the Committee on the Judiciary, *Obscene and pornographic literature and juvenile delinquency.* 84th Congress, 2nd Session. June 28, 1956.
2. O. N. Larsen, G. W. Jones, J. T. Klapper, M. A. Lipton, and M. E. Wolfgang, "The impact of erotica: report of the effects panel," in Commission on Obscenity and Pornography, *The Report of the Commission* (Washington, D.C.: U.S. Government Printing Office, 1970).
3. *Ibid.*
4. R. B. Cairns, "Psychological assumptions in sex censorship: an evaluative preview of recent (1961–68) research," in Commission on Obscenity and Pornography, *Technical Reports,* vol. 1 (Washington, D.C.: U.S. Government Printing Office, 1971)
5. R.Athanasiou, P. Shaver, and C. Tavis, "Sex," *Psychology Today,* July, 1970, pp. 39–52.
6. D. Wallace and G. Wehmer, "Contemporary standards of visual erotica," in *Technical Reports,* vol. 6.
7. M. E. Massey, "A market analysis of sex-oriented materials in Denver, Colorado, August, 1969—a pilot study," in *Technical Reports,* vol. 7.
8. M. J. Goldstein and H. Kant, "Exposure to pornography and sexual behavior in deviant and normal groups," in *Technical Reports,* vol. 4.
9. H. Abelson, R. Cohen, E. Heaton, and C. Slider, "Public attitudes toward and experience with erotic materials," in *Technical Reports,* vol. 3.
10. B. Kutschinsky, "Pornography in Denmark: Studies on producers, sellers, and users," in *Technical Reports,* vol. 7.
11. Abelson et al., op. cit.; Goldstein and Kant, op. cit.; Massey, op. cit.
12. Abelson et al., op. cit.; Wallace and Wehmer, op. cit.
13. H. L. Zetterberg, "The consumers of pornography where it is easily available; the Swedish experience," in *Technical Reports,* vol. 7.

14. Abelson et al., op. cit.; Goldstein and Kant, op. cit.
15. Abelson et al., op. cit.
16. Goldstein and Kant, op. cit.
17. A. Berger, J. Gagnon, and W. Simon, "Pornography: high school and college years," *Technical Reports*, vol. 4.
18. D. M. White, "College students' experience with erotica," in *Technical Reports*, vol. 1.
19. W. J. Roach and L. Kreisberg, "Westchester college students' views on pornography," in *Technical Reports*, vol. 1.
20. J. Elias, "Exposure to erotic materials in adolescence," in *Technical Reports*, vol. 4.
21. A. Berger, J. Gagnon, and W. Simon, "Urban working-class adolescents and sexually explicit media," in *Technical Reports*, vol. 4.
22. M. Propper, "Exposure to sexually oriented materials among young male prison offenders," in *Technical Reports*, vol. 4.
23. Abelson et al., op. cit.
24. Abelson et al., ibid.
25. Abelson et al., ibid.; Berger et al., op. cit.; Elias, op. cit.; Popper, op. cit.
26. Abelson et al., ibid.
27. Massey, op. cit.
28. M. M. Finkelstein, "Traffic in sex oriented materials: adult bookstores in Boston, Massachusetts," in *Technical Reports*, vol. 7; Massey, op. cit.; H. Nawy, "The San Francisco erotic marketplace," in *Technical Reports*, vol. 7; C. Winick, "Some observations of patrons of adult theaters and bookstores," in *Technical Reports*, vol. 7.
29. Massey, op. cit.; Nawy, op. cit.; Winick, op. cit.
30. Kutschinsky, op. cit.
31. Cairns, op. cit.; R. B. Cairns, J. C. N. Paul, and J. Wishner, "Sex censorship: the assumptions of anti-obscenity laws and the empirical evidence." *Minnesota Law Review*, vol. 46 (1962), pp. 1009–1041.
32. W. T. Johnson, L. R. Kupperstein, W. C. Wilson, O. N. Larsen, G. W. Jones, J. T. Klapper, M. A. Lipton, M. E. Wolfgang, and W. B. Lockhart, "The impact of erotica; report of the effects panel," op. cit., p. 144.
33. Abelson et al., op. cit.
34. Abelson et al., ibid.
35. D. K. Berninghausen and R. W. Faunce, "An exploratory study of juvenile delinquency and the reading of sensational books." *Journal of Experimental Education*, vol. 33 (1964), pp. 161–168.
36. P. H. Gebhard, J. H. Gagnon, W. B. Pomeroy, and C. V. Christenson, *Sex Offenders: An Analysis of Types* (New York: Harper & Row, 1965).
37. Goldstein and Kant, op. cit.
38. R. F. Cook and R. H. Fosen, "Pornography and the sex offender; patterns of exposure and immediate arousal effects of pornographic stimuli," in *Technical Reports*, vol. 4.
39. C. F. Walker, "Erotic stimuli and the aggressive sexual offender," in *Technical Reports*, vol. 4.
40. W. T. Johnson, L. Kupperstein, and J. Peters, "Sex offenders' experience with erotica," in *Technical Reports*, vol. 4.
41. Goldstein and Kant, op. cit.
42. R. Ben-Veniste, "Pornography and sex crime—the Danish experience," in *Technical Reports*, vol. 6.
43. B. Kutschinsky, "Sex Crimes and pornography in Copenhagen: a survey of attitudes," in *Technical Reports*, vol. 3.
44. L. Kupperstein and W. C. Wilson, "Erotica and anti-social behavior; an analysis of selected social indicator statistics," in *Technical Reports*, vol. 5.

45. T. P. Thornberry and R. A. Silverman, "The relationship between exposure to pornography and juvenile delinquency as indicated by juvenile court records," in *Technical Reports*, vol. 5.
46. Propper, op. cit.
47. Abelson et al., op. cit.; Berger et al., op. cit.; Elias, op. cit.; Goldstein and Kant, op. cit.
48. K. E. Davis and G. N. Braucht, "Exposure to pornography, character, and sexual deviance: a retrospective survey," in *Technical Reports*, vol. 4.
49. D. L. Mosher, "Sex callousness toward women," in *Technical Reports*, vol. 6.
50. D. M. Amoroso, M. Brown, M. Preusse, E. E. Ware, and D. W. Pilkey, "An investigation of behavioral, psychological, and physiological reactions to pornographi stimuli," in *Technical Reports*, vol. 6; D. Byrne and J. Lamberth, "The effect of erotic stimuli on sex arousal, evaluative responses, and subsequent behavior," in *Technical Reports*, vol. 6; Cook and Fosen, op. cit.; K. E. Davis and G. N. Braucht, "Reactions to viewing films of erotically realistic heterosexual behavior," in *Technical Reports*, vol. 6; J. L. Howard, C. B. Reifler, and M. B. Liptzin, "Effects of exposure to pornography," in *Technical Reports*, vol. 6; B. Kutschinsky, "The effect of pornography—an experiment in perception, attitudes, and behavior," in *Technica Reports*, vol. 6; J. Mann, J. Sidman, and S. Starr, "Effects of erotic films on sexual behaviors of married couples," in *Technical Report*, vol. 6; D. L. Mosher, "Psychological reactions to pornographic films," in *Technical Reports*, vol. 6; V. Sigusch, G. Schmidt, R. Reinfeld, and I. Sutor, "Psychosexual stimulation: sex differences," *The Journal of Sex Research*, vol. 6 (1970), pp. 10–24. P. H. Tannenbaum, "Emotional arousal as a mediator of communication effects, in *Technical Reports*, vol. 6.
51. Abelson et al., op. cit.
52. The Commission on Obscenity and Pornography, op. cit.
53. T. D. Gill, M. A. Hill, B. Scott, W. B. Lockhart, P. Bender, J. M. Friedman and W. C. Wilson, "Legal considerations relating to erotica: report of the legal panel," in *The Report of the Commission*, op. cit.
54. Abelson et al., op. cit.
55. *The Washington Post*, October 26, 1970.
56. *The Congressional Record*, October 13, 1970, pp. 17903–17922.
57. M. A. Hill and W. C. Link, Separate statement, in *The Report of the Commission*, p. 385.
58. C. H. Keating, Jr., Separate statement, in *The Report of the Commission*, p. 515.
59. Abelson et al., op. cit.
60. L. A. Zurcher and R. G. Cushing, "Some individual characteristics of participants in *ad hoc* anti-pornography organizations," in *Technical Reports*, vol. 8; L. A. Zurcher and R. G. Kirkpatrick, "Collective dynamics of *ad hoc* anti-pornography organizations," in *Technical Reports*, vol. 8.
61. W. C. Wilson, B. Horowitz, and J. Friedman, "The gravity of the pornography situation and the problems of control," in *Technical Reports*, vol. 3.
62. L. A. Zurcher and R. G. Kirkpatrick, op. cit.

PORNOGRAPHY, OBSCENITY, AND THE CASE FOR CENSORSHIP

Irving Kristol

Mr. Kristol argues cogently and potently on behalf of censorship. It is not eroticism that offends him but the tendency of commercial pornography to dehumanize people by representing them as obscene animals. Sexual privacy, he says, "is indigenous to the human race," and to violate it is both obscene and reductive of humanness. Many people contend that pornographic overkill ultimately induces boredom and that the mature person can take it or leave it. Not so, says Kristol, pornography strikes at the very heart of civilization as we know it. It is power politics, and its intent is to subvert our institutions.

Whether the reader agrees or not, Kristol presents a forceful argument for censorship based on a concern for a quality of life which the laws of a democracy should defend and enhance. He supports the feminists' view that pornography is usually exploitative of women and also supports the recommendation of the U.S. Commission on Obscenity and Pornography that young people should be protected by law against pornography. The question then becomes whether we should have a "little censorship" law. How much, exactly, is a "little" censorship?

Being frustrated is disagreeable, but the real disasters in life begin when you get what you want. For almost a century now, a great many intelligent, well-meaning and articulate people—of a kind generally called liberal or intellectual, or both—have argued eloquently against any kind of censorship of art and/or entertainment. And within the past ten years, the courts and the legislatures of most Western nations have found these arguments persuasive—so persuasive that hardly a man is now alive who clearly remembers what the answers to these arguments were. Today, in the United States and other democracies, censorship has to all intents and purposes ceased to exist.

From *On the Democratic Idea in America*, by Irving Kristol, © 1972 by Irving Kristol (Harper & Row). Reprinted by permission.

Is there a sense of triumphant exhilaration in the land? Hardly. There is, on the contrary, a rapidly growing unease and disquiet. Somehow, things have not worked out as they were supposed to, and many notable civil libertarians have gone on record as saying this was not what they meant at all. They wanted a world in which *Desire Under the Elms* could be produced, or *Ulysses* published, without interference by philistine busybodies holding public office. They have got that, of course; but they have also got a world in which homosexual rape takes place on the stage, in which the public flocks during lunch hours to witness varieties of professional fornication, in which Times Square has become little more than a hideous market for the sale and distribution of printed filth that panders to all known (and some fanciful) sexual perversions.

But disagreeable as this may be, does it really matter? Might not our unease and disquiet be merely a cultural hangover—a "hangup," as they say? What reason is there to think that anyone was ever corrupted by a book?

This last question, oddly enough, is asked by the very same people who seem convinced that advertisements in magazines or displays of violence on television do indeed have the power to corrupt. It is also asked, incredibly enough and in all sincerity, by people—e.g., university professors and school-teachers—whose very lives provide all the answers one could want. After all, if you believe that no one was ever corrupted by a book, you have also to believe that no one was ever improved by a book (or a play or a movie). You have to believe, in other words, that all art is morally trivial and that, consequently, all education is morally irrelevant. No one, not even a university professor, really believes that.

To be sure, it is extremely difficult, as social scientists tell us, to trace the effects of any single book (or play or movie) on an individual reader or any class of readers. But we all know, and social scientists know it too, that the ways in which we use our minds and imaginations do shape our characters and help define us as persons. That those who certainly know this are nevertheless moved to deny it merely indicates how a dogmatic resistance to the idea of censorship can—like most dogmatism—result in a mindless insistence on the absurd.

I have used these harsh terms—"dogmatism" and "mindless"—advisedly. I might also have added "hypocritical." For the plain fact is that none of us is a complete civil libertarian. We all believe that there is some point at which the public authorities ought to step in to limit the "self expression" of an individual or a group, even where this might be seriously intended as a form of artistic expression, and even where the artistic transaction is between consenting adults. A playwright or theatrical director might, in this crazy world of ours, find someone willing to commit suicide on the stage, as called for by the script. We would not allow that—any more than we would permit scenes of real physical torture on the stage, even if the victim were a willing masochist. And I know of no one, no matter how free in spirit, who argues that we ought to permit gladiatorial contests in Yankee Stadium, similar to those once performed in the Colosseum at Rome—even if only consenting adults were involved.

The basic point that emerges is one that Prof. Walter Berns has powerfully argued: no society can be utterly indifferent to the ways its citizens publicly entertain themselves.[1] Bearbaiting and cockfighting are prohibited only in part out of compassion for the suffering animals; the main reason they were abolished was because it was felt that they debased and brutalized the citizenry who flocked to witness such spectacles. And the question we face with regard to pornography and obscenity is whether, now that they have such strong legal protection from the Supreme Court, they can or will brutalize and debase our citizenry. We are, after all, not dealing with one passing incident—one book, or one play, or one movie. We are dealing with a general tendency that is suffusing our entire culture.

I say pornography *and* obscenity because, though they have different dictionary definitions and are frequently distinguishable as artistic genres, they are nevertheless in the end identical in effect. Pornography is not objectionable simply because it arouses sexual desire or lust or prurience in the mind of the reader or spectator; this is a silly Victorian notion. A great many nonpornographic works—including some parts of the Bible—excite sexual desire very successfully. What is distinctive about pornography is that, in the words of D. H. Lawrence, it attempts "to do dirt on [sex] . . . [It is an] insult to a vital human relationship."

In other words, pornography differs from erotic art in that its whole purpose is to treat human beings obscenely, to deprive human beings of their specifically human dimension. That is what obscenity is all about. It is light years removed from any kind of carefree sensuality—there is no continuum between Fielding's *Tom Jones* and the Marquis de Sade's *Justine*. These works have quite opposite intentions. To quote Susan Sontag: "What pornographic literature does is precisely to drive a wedge between one's existence as a full human being and one's existence as a sexual being— while in ordinary life a healthy person is one who prevents such a gap from opening up." This definition occurs in an essay defending pornography—

Miss Sontag is a candid as well as gifted critic—so the definition, which I accept, is neither tendentious nor censorious.

Along these same lines, one can point out—as C. S. Lewis pointed out some years back—that it is no accident that in the history of all literatures obscene words, the so-called "four-letter words," have always been the vocabulary of farce or vituperation. The reason is clear; they reduce men and women to some of their mere bodily functions—they reduce man to his animal component, and such a reduction is an essential purpose of farce or vituperation.

Similarly, Lewis also suggested that it is not an accident that we have no offhand, colloquial, neutral terms—not in any Western European language at any rate—for our most private parts. The words we do use are either (a) nursery terms, (b) archaisms, (c) scientific terms, or (d) a term from the gutter (i.e., a demeaning term). Here I think the genius of language is telling us something important about man. It is telling us that man is an animal with a difference: he has a unique sense of privacy, and a unique capacity for shame when this privacy is violated. Our "private parts" are indeed private, and not merely because convention prescribes it. This particular convention is indigenous to the human race. In practically all primitive tribes, men and women cover their private parts; and in practically all primitive tribes, men and women do not copulate in public.

It may well be that Western society, in the latter half of the twentieth century, is experiencing a drastic change in sexual mores and sexual relationships. We have had many such "sexual revolutions" in the past—the bourgeois family and bourgeois ideas of sexual propriety were themselves established in the course of a revolution against eighteenth-century "licentiousness" —and we shall doubtless have others in the future. It is, however, highly improbable (to put it mildly) that what we are witnessing is the Final Revolution which will make sexual relations utterly unproblematic, permit us to dispense with any kind of ordered relationships between the sexes, and allow us freely to redefine the human condition. And so long as humanity has not reached that utopia, obscenity will remain a problem.

II

One of the reasons it will remain a problem is that obscenity is not merely about sex, any more than science fiction is about science. Science fiction, as every student of the genre knows, is a peculiar vision of power: what it is really about is politics. And obscenity is a peculiar vision of humanity: what it is really about is ethics and metaphysics.

Imagine a man—a well-known man, much in the public eye—in a hospital ward, dying an agonizing death. He is not in control of his bodily functions, so that his bladder and his bowels empty themselves of their own accord. His consciousness is overwhelmed and extinguished by pain, so that he cannot communicate with us, nor we with him. Now, it would be, technically, the easiest thing in the world to put a television camera in his hospital room and let the whole world witness this spectacle. We don't do it—at least we don't do it as yet—because we regard this as an *obscene* invasion of privacy. And what would make the spectacle obscene is that we would be witnessing the extinguishing of humanity in a human animal.

Incidentally, in the past our humanitarian crusaders against capital punishment understood this point very well. The abolitionist literatures goes into great physical detail about what happens to a man when he is hanged or electrocuted or gassed. And their argument was—and is—that what happens is shockingly obscene, and that no civilized society should be responsible for perpetrating such obscenities, particularly since in the nature of the case there must be spectators to ascertain that this horror was indeed perpetrated in fulfillment of the law.

Sex—like death—is an activity that is both animal and human. There are human sentiments and human ideals involved in this animal activity. But when sex is public, the viewer does not see—cannot see—the sentiments and the ideals. He can only see the animal coupling. And that is why, when men and women make love, as we say, they prefer to be alone—because it is only when you are alone that you can make love, as distinct from merely copulating in an animal and casual way. And that, too, is why those who are voyeurs, if they are not irredeemably sick, also feel ashamed at what they are witnessing. When sex is a public spectacle, a human relationship has been debased into a mere animal connection.

It is also worth noting that this making of sex into an obscenity is not a mutual and equal transaction but rather an act of exploitation by one of the partners—the male partner. I do not wish to get into the complicated question as to what, if any, are the essential differences—as distinct from conventional and cultural differences—between male and female. I do not claim to know the answer to that. But I do know—and I take it as a sign that has meaning—that pornography is, and always has been, a man's work; that women rarely write pornography; and that women tend to be indifferent consumers of pornography.[2] My own guess, by way of explanation, is that a woman's sexual experience is ordinarily more suffused with human emotion than is man's, that men are more easily satisfied with autoerotic activities, and that men can therefore more easily take a more "technocratic" view of sex and its pleasures. Perhaps this is not correct. But whatever the explanation, there can be no question that pornography is a form of "sexism," as the women's liberation movement calls it, and that the instinct of women's liberation has been unerring in perceiving that when pornography is perpetrated against them, as part of a conspiracy to deprive them of their full humanity.

But even if all this is granted, it might be said—and doubtless will be said —that I really ought not to be unduly concerned. Free competition in the cultural marketplace—it is argued by people who have never otherwise had a kind word to say for laissez-faire—will automatically dispose of the problem. The present fad for pornography and obscenity, it will be asserted, is just that, a fad. It will spend itself in the course of time; people will get bored with it, will be able to take it or leave it alone in a casual way, in a "mature way," and, in sum, I am being unnecessarily distressed about the whole business. *The New York Times*, in an editorial, concludes hopefully in this vein.

> In the end . . . the insensate pursuit of the urge to shock, carried from one excess to a more abysmal one, is bound to achieve its own antidote in total boredom. When there is no lower depth to descend to, ennui will erase the problem.

I would like to be able to go along with this line of reasoning, but I cannot. I think it is false, and for two reasons, the first psychological, the second political.

The basic psychological fact about pornography and obscenity is that it appeals to and provokes a kind of sexual regression. The sexual pleasure one gets from pornography and obscenity is autoerotic and infantile; put bluntly, it is a masturbatory exercise of the imagination, when it is not masturbation pure and simple. Now, people who masturbate do not get bored with masturbation, just as sadists don't get bored with sadism, and voyeurs don't get bored with voyeurism.

In other words, infantile sexuality is not only a permanent temptation for the adolescent or even the adult—it can quite easily become a permanent, self-reinforcing neurosis. It is because of an awareness of this possibility of regression toward the infantile condition, a regression which is always open to us, that all the codes of sexual conduct ever devised by the human race take such a dim view of autoerotic activities and try to discourage autoerotic fantasies. Masturbation is indeed a perfectly natural autoerotic activity, as

o many sexologists blandly assure us today. And it is precisely because it is
o perfectly natural that it can be so dangerous to the mature or maturing
person, if it is not controlled or sublimated in some way. That is the true
meaning of Portnoy's complaint. Portnoy, you will recall, grows up to be a
man who is incapable of having an adult sexual relationship with a woman;
his sexuality remains fixed in an infantile mode, the prisoner of his autoerotic fantasies. Inevitably, Portnoy comes to think, in a perfectly *infantile*
way, that it was all his mother's fault.

It is true that, in our time, some quite brilliant minds have come to the
conclusion that a reversion to infantile sexuality is the ultimate mission and
secret destiny of the human race. I am thinking in particular of Norman
O. Brown, for whose writings I have the deepest respect. One of the
reasons I respect them so deeply is that Mr. Brown is a serious thinker who
is unafraid to face up to the radical consequences of his radical theories.
Thus, Mr. Brown knows and says that for his kind of salvation to be achieved,
humanity must annul the civilization it has created—not merely the civilization we have today, but all civilization—so as to be able to make the long
descent backward into animal innocence.

And that is the point. What is at stake is civilization and humanity, nothing
less. The idea that "everything is permitted," as Nietzsche put it, rests on the
premise of nihilism and has nihilistic implications. I will not pretend that the
case against nihilism and for civilization is an easy one to make. We are here
confronting the most fundamental of philosophical questions, on the deepest
levels. In short, the matter of pornography and obscenity is not a trivial one,
and only superficial minds can take a bland and untroubled view of it.

In this connection, I must also point out those who are primarily against
censorship on liberal grounds tell us not to take pornography or obscenity
seriously, while those who are for pornography and obscenity on radical
grounds take it very seriously indeed. I believe the radicals—writers like
Susan Sontag, Herbert Marcuse, Norman O. Brown, and even Jerry Rubin—
are right, and the liberals are wrong. I also believe that those young radicals
at Berkeley, some seven years ago, who provoked a major confrontation
over the public use of obscene words, showed a brilliant political instinct.
And once Mark Rudd could publicly ascribe to the president of Columbia a
notoriously obscene relationship to his mother, without provoking any kind
of reaction, the S.D.S. had already won the day. The occupation of Columbia's buildings merely ratified their victory. Men who show themselves unwilling to defend civilization against nihilism are not going to be either
resolute or effective in defending the university against anything.

*Pornography,
Obscenity,
and the Case
for Censor-
ship*

323

III

I am already touching upon a political aspect of pornography when I suggest that it is inherently and purposefully subversive of civilization and its institutions. But there is another and more specifically political aspect, which has to do with the relationship of pornography and/or obscenity to democracy, and especially to the quality of public life on which democratic government ultimately rests.

Though the phrase "the quality of life" trips easily from so many lips these days, it tends to be one of those clichés with many trivial meanings an no large, serious one. Sometimes it merely refers to such externals as the enjoyment of cleaner air, cleaner water, cleaner streets. At other times it refers to the merely private enjoyment of music, painting, or literature. Rarely does it have anything to do with the way the citizen in a democracy views himself—his obligations, his intentions, his ultimate self-definition.

Instead, what I would call the "managerial" conception of democracy is th predominant opinion among political scientists sociologists, and economists, and has, through the untiring efforts of these scholars, become the conventional journalistic opinion as well. The root idea behind this "managerial" conception is that democracy is a "political system" (as they say) which car be adequately defined in terms of—can be fully reduced to—its mechanical arrangements. Democracy is then seen as a set of rules and procedures, and *nothing but* a set of rules and procedures, whereby majority rule and minority rights are reconciled into a state of equilibrium. If everyone follows these rules and procedures, then a democracy is in working order. I think this is a fair description of the democratic idea that currently prevails in academia. One can also fairly say that it is now the liberal idea of democracy par excellence.

I cannot help but feel that there is something ridiculous about being this kind of a democrat, and I must further confess to having a sneaking sympathy for those of our young radicals who also find it ridiculous. The absurdity is the absurdity of idolatry—of taking the symbolic for the real, the means for the end. The purpose of democracy cannot possibly be the endless functioning of its own political machinery. The purpose of any political regime is to achieve some version of the good life and the good society. It is not at all difficult to imagine a perfectly functioning democracy which answers all questions except one—namely, why should anyone of intelligenc and spirit care a fig for it?

There is, however, an older idea of democracy—one which was fairly common until about the beginning of this century—for which the conception of the quality of public life is absolutely crucial. This idea starts from the proposition that democracy is a form of self-government, and that if you want it to be a meritorious polity, you have to care about what kind of people govern it. Indeed, it puts the matter more strongly and declares that if you want self-government, you are only entitled to it if that "self" is worthy of governing. There is no inherent right to self-government if it means that such government is vicious, mean, squalid, and debased. Only a dogmatist and a fanatic, an idolater of democratic machinery, could approve of self-government under such conditions.

And because the desirability of self-government depends on the character of the people who govern, the older idea of democracy was very solicitous of the condition of this character. It was solicitous of the individual self, and felt an obligation to educate it into what used to be called "republican virtue." And it was solicitous of that collective self which we call public opinion and which, in a democracy, governs us collectively. Perhaps in some respects it was nervously oversolicitous—that would not be surprising. But the main thing is that it cared, cared not merely about the machinery of democracy but about the quality of life that this machinery might generate.

And because it cared, this older idea of democracy had no problem in principle with pornography and/or obscenity. It censored them—and it did so with a perfect clarity of mind and a perfectly clear conscience. It was not about to permit people capriciously to corrupt themselves. Or, to put it more precisely: in this version of democracy, the people took some care not to let themselves be governed by the more infantile and irrational parts of themselves.

I have, it may be noticed, uttered that dreadful word "censorship." And I am not about to back away from it. If you think pornography and/or obscenity is a serious problem, you have to be for censorship. I'll go even further and say that if you want to prevent pornography and/or obscenity from becoming a problem, you have to be for censorship. And lest there be any misunderstanding as to what I am saying, I'll put it as bluntly as possible: if you care for the quality of life in our American democracy, then you have to be for censorship.

IV

But can a liberal be for censorship? Unless one assumes that being a liberal *must* mean being indifferent to the quality of American life, then the answer has to be: yes, a liberal can be for censorship—but he ought to favor a liberal form of censorship.

Is that a contradiction in terms? I don't think so. We nave no problem in contrasting *repressive* laws governing alcohol and drugs and tobacco with laws *regulating* (i.e., discouraging the sale of) alcohol and drugs and tobacco. Laws encouraging temperance are not the same thing as laws that have as their goal prohibition or abolition. We have not made the smoking of cigarettes a criminal offense. We have, however, and with good liberal conscience, prohibited cigarette advertising on television, and may yet, again with good liberal conscience, prohibit it in newspapers and magazines. The idea of restricting individual freedom, in a liberal way, is not at all unfamiliar to us.

I therefore see no reason why we should not be able to distinguish repressive censorship from liberal censorship of the written and spoken word. In Britain, until a few years ago, you could perform almost any play you wished, but certain plays, judged to be obscene, had to be performed in private theatrical clubs which were deemed to have a "serious" interest in theater. In the United States, all of us who grew up using public libraries are familiar with the circumstances under which certain books could be circulated only to adults, while still other books had to be read in the library reading room, under the librarian's skeptical eye. In both cases, a small minority that was willing to make a serious effort to see an obscene play or read an obscene book could do so. But the impact of obscenity was circumscribed and the quality of public life was only marginally affected.[3]

I am not saying it is easy in practice to sustain a distinction between liberal and repressive censorship, especially in the public realm of a democracy, where popular opinion is so vulnerable to demagoguery. Moreover, an acceptable system of liberal censorship is likely to be exceedingly difficult to devise in the United States today, because our educated classes, upon whose judgment a liberal censorship must rest, are so convinced that there is no such thing as a problem of obscenity, or even that there is no such thing as obscenity at all. But, to counterbalance this, there is the further, fortunate truth that the tolerable margin for error is quite large, and single mistakes or single injustices are not all that important.

This possibility of error, of course, occasions much distress among artists and academics. It is a fact, one that cannot and should not be denied, that any system of censorship is bound, upon occasion, to treat unjustly a particular work of art—to find pornography where there is only gentle eroticism, to find obscenity where none really exists, or to find both where its existence ought to be tolerated because it serves a larger moral purpose. Though most works of art are not obscene, and though most obscenity has nothing to do with art, there are some few works of art that are, at least in part, pornographic and/or obscene. There are also some few works of art that are in the special category of the comic-ironic "bawdy" (Boccaccio, Rabelais). It is such works of art that are likely to suffer at the hands of the censor. That is the price one has to be prepared to pay for censorship—even liberal censorship.

But just how high is this price? If you believe, as so many artists seem to believe today, that art is the only sacrosanct activity in our profane and vulgar world—that any man who designates himself an artist thereby acquires a sacred office—then obviously censorship is an intolerable form of sacrilege. But for those of us who do not subscribe to this religion of art, the costs of censorship do not seem so high at all.

If you look at the history of American or English literature, there is precious little damage you can point to as a consequence of the censorship that prevailed throughout most of that history. Very few works of literature —of real literary merit, I mean—ever were suppressed; and those that were, were not suppressed for long. Nor have I noticed, now that censorship of the written word has to all intents and purposes ceased in this country, that hitherto suppressed or repressed master pieces are flooding the market. Yes, we can now read *Fanny Hill* and the Marquis de Sade. Or, to be more exact, we can now openly purchase them, since many people were able to read them even though they were publicly banned, which is as it should be under a liberal censorship. So how much have literature and the arts gained from the fact that we can all now buy them over the counter, that, indeed, we are all now encouraged to buy them over the counter? They have not gained much that I can see.

And one might also ask a question that is almost never raised: how much has literature lost from the fact that everything is now permitted? It has lost quite a bit, I should say. In a free market, Gresham's Law can work for books or theater as efficiently as it does for coinage—driving out the good, establishing the debased. The cultural market in the United States today is being pre-empted by dirty books, dirty movies, dirty theater. A pornographic novel has a far better chance of being published today than a non-pornographic one, and quite a few pretty good novels are not being published at all simply because they are not pornographic, and are therefore less likely to sell. Our cultural condition has not improved as a result of the new freedom. American cultural life wasn't much to brag about twenty years ago; today one feels ashamed for it.

Just one last point which I dare not leave untouched. If we start censoring pornography or obscenity, shall we not inevitably end up censoring political opinion? A lot of people seem to think this would be the case—which only shows the power of doctrinaire thinking over reality. We had censorship of pornography and obscenity for 150 years, until almost yesterday, and I am not aware that freedom of opinion in this country was in any way diminished as a consequence of this fact. Fortunately for those of us who are liberal, freedom is not indivisible. If it were, the case for liberalism would be indistinguishable from the case for anarchy; and they are two very different things.

But I must repeat and emphasize: what kind of laws we pass governing pornography and obscenity, what kind of censorship—or, since we are still a federal nation, what kinds of censorship—we institute in our various local ties may indeed be difficult matters to cope with; nevertheless the real issue is one of principle. I myself subscribe to a liberal view of the enforcement problem: I think that pornography should be illegal *and* available to anyone who wants it so badly as to make a pretty strenuous effort to get it. We have lived with under-the-counter pornography for centuries now, in a fairly comfortable way. But the issue of principle, of whether it should be over or under the counter, has to be settled before we can reflect on the advantages and disadvantages of alternative modes of censorship. I think the settlement we are living under now, in which obscenity and democracy are regarded as equals, is wrong; I believe it is inherently unstable; I think it will, in the long run, be incompatible with any authentic concern for the quality of life in our democracy.

1. This is as good a place as any to express my profound indebtedness to Walter Bern's superb essay, "Pornography vs. Democracy," in the winter, 1971 issue of *The Public Interest.*
2. There are, of course, a few exceptions—but of a kind that prove the rule. *L'Histoire d'O* for instance, written by a woman, is unquestionably the most *melancholy* work of pornography ever written. And its theme is precisely the dehumanization accomplished by obscenity.
3. It is fairly predictable that some one is going to object that this point of view is "elitist"—that, under a system of liberal censorship, the rich will have privileged access to pornography and obscenity. Yes, of course they will—just as, at present, the rich have privileged access to heroin if they want it. But one would have to be an egalitarian maniac to object to this state of affairs on the grounds of equality.

Part 6

SOME PERVASIVE SEXUAL MISCONCEPTIONS

MYTHS AND FALLACIES

James L. McCary

n spite of wide dissemination of the results of significant research about human sexuality in the past few years, many misconceptions, myths, and fallacies persist. Notions having absolutely no basis in fact are tenaciously affirmed and passed along to friends and offspring, and these are by no means limited to the ignorant or uneducated. Professional people, university professors, and university students harbor ideas which blight and distort their understanding of sexuality, sexual functioning, and their own sex lives. Some of the most widely circulated and persistent misconceptions are examined here. For the student who wishes to pursue this topic further, James McCary has complied an entire book on sexual misinformation (*Sexual Myths and Fallacies*. New York: Van Nostrand Reinhold Co., 1971).

When any facet of the human condition becomes as shrouded in misinformation and downright superstition as human sexuality has, it is almost inevitable that a welter of myths and fallacies should mushroom. And the tragedy is that misinformation not only becomes perpetuated by the distortions of truth communicated laterally by the peer group to its members, but also by those legitimately in a position to educate. Scientists have made notable advances in sex research, yet the educators—parents, teachers, clergymen—because of their own equivocal sex education, or their fear of freedom of expression on what they consider the hypersensitive subject of sex, ignore modern scientific contributions toward greater understanding in this vital area. Just as contradictory maternal attitudes toward sex are transmitted through successive generations of daughters, so sexual illogicality and bigotry become the bequest of one generation to the next.

Beliefs for which there is no conceivable foundation in truth are by no means limited to the uneducated and the unsophisticated. Highly educated professional people, as has been said, can harbor a rather harrowing collec-

From *Human Sexuality* by James Leslie McCary. Copyright © 1967 by James Leslie McCary. Reprinted by permission of Van Nostrand Reinhold Company.

tion of sexual misconceptions that, if not corrected, will almost certainly be handed down as indisputable truth to those whom they influence and instruct. This book has emphasized the vital importance of possessing accurate sex information, and the dispensing of that knowledge in an honest, direct manner to those under one's charge. This same approach can be used successfully when one encounters anyone caught up in some of the mythology obscuring the realities of sex. Some of the most common of these myths will now be discussed.

1. That each individual is allotted just so many sexual experiences, and that when they are used up, sexual activity is finished for that person.

This notion has troubled mankind for centuries, yet it is totally false. In fact, the degree of sexual activity that humans are capable of maintaining throughout the years seems to be correlated in quite an opposite manner: the earlier men or women mature physically, the longer their sexual reproductive ability continues; and the more sexually active a person is and the earlier the age at which he begins that activity, the longer it continues into old age. These observations do not mean necessarily that if a person starts his sex life early he will be guaranteed a longer and consistently vigorous sex life; it means that ordinarily the person with a stronger sex drive than average will commence sexual activity earlier in life and continue it longer.

A similar fallacious assumption is that men have only a certain amount of semen or a certain number of sperm cells in their bodies, and that once the supply has been discharged, no further reservoirs remain and no further manufacture is possible. Certainly this argument has been used—often with detrimental results—by adults in an attempt to discourage boys from masturbating. Most boys have heard that each ejaculation takes from his body some fantastic amount of protein, blood, strength, and the like, most of which, they are warned, will be difficult to replace—if replacement is possible at all. Experts in hormonal functioning have shown that the chemical constituents of semen are constantly being replenished by a normal intake of food, and that the production of sperm is also a continuing process. Ejaculated sperm are, therefore, easily and quickly replaced in the healthy body, much in the same way that saliva is constantly replenished.

It is a physical near-impossibility for a person to experience orgasm or ejaculation too often. When one has functioned to his or her physiological limit, the sexual act becomes repelling; and for the man, it becomes impossible to perform. After a normal rest or recovery period, however, both the desire and ability to engage in sexual activity return to normal.

2. That an unborn child can be "marked."

Because of the close connection between fetus and mother, it is understandable why many people assume that such experiences as sudden shocks or fright to the mother would cause her baby to be born with some physical or emotional "mark," most commonly a birthmark. There is no direct connection between the nervous systems or between the blood systems of mother and fetus, and the idea of prenatally "marking" the child in the manners mentioned is, therefore, completely false.

Most often when a child is born with an unusual birthmark—for example, a skin discoloration in the general shape of a bird—the parents' faulty memory processes will cause them to "remember" an incident while the mother was pregnant wherein she was attacked or in some way frightened by something of that shape.

Misinformed scientists have also been party to perpetuating the "marking" myth. For example, in 1836, eight physicians signed a report, which appeared in an American medical journal, that a man had a face like a snake and could coil and uncoil his arm in a snakelike fashion because a rattlesnake had frightened his mother during her sixth month of pregnancy.

It is true, of course, that the mother supplies nourishment for the fetus; her diet and chemical intake can have a direct effect on certain physiological reactions of the child, both before and after birth. For example, if the mother grossly overeats certain foods, it is sometimes possible to cause an allergic condition in the child that continues after birth. Also, it is well known that the physical condition of infants whose mothers smoked tobacco during their pregnancies will be affected by the smoking. However, these reactions are not the same as those ordinarily considered when one discusses "marking" a baby; the latter theory is a physiological and psychological impossibility, so far as scientific investigation has been able to determine.

3. That sexual intercourse should be avoided during pregnancy.

Considerable investigation has been made into the pregnant woman's physiologic and psychologic patterns of response to sexual stimulation. In general, there is little change from the nonpregnant state in sexual interest or capacity for satisfying coition during the first three months (first trimester) of pregnancy; and during the second trimester, there is usually an increase in erotic feelings, even beyond those of the nonpregnant state. During the third trimester, most women show a loss in sexual interest. There is no evidence to indicate that the pregnant woman with no unusual complications should not regularly engage in sexual intercourse or automanipulative activity to orgasm until late in the third trimester. Quite naturally, sensible precautions should be taken against excessive pressure on the abdomen, deep penile penetration, and infection.

It is now well known that there are rather strong contractions of the uterus during a woman's orgasmic response that are not unlike those experienced during labor. Couples should be warned, therefore, that the uterine contractions of orgasm may cause labor contractions to begin if the woman is within three weeks of term.

On the whole, sexual intercourse during pregnancy is valuable for both the wife and husband. The nature of a man's sex drive, and the psychological stresses he experiences during the pregnancy and immediate postpartum period cause him to be more likely to seek out extramarital sexual activity in the last six weeks of his wife's pregnancy and the first six weeks after delivery than at any other time. Continuing sexual activity as long as possible during pregnancy is, therefore, quite likely a hedge against future marital discord and unhappiness if the husband would otherwise feel driven during these weeks to seek sexual release elsewhere.

Sexual intercourse may continue up to the time of labor if three conditions are met: (1) if there is no pain during the act, (2) if the fetal membrane is intact, and (3) if there is no spotting or bleeding. It now appears that unless these adverse conditions exist, coital abstinence during pregnancy and after delivery (that is, after the time postpartum vaginal bleeding has stopped and any vaginal incisions have healed) is not called for. To the contrary, sexual intercourse during this period probably should be encouraged, if the woman is psychologically disposed toward it. However, whether or not sexual intercourse should take place during the third trimester and the early postpartum period is an *individual* matter that should be decided by the woman and her physician, without the latter's arbitrarily following a set of rules that are not equally applicable to all women. If for some reason coitus is contraindicated, most couples would benefit from an understanding of the value of automanipulation and of mutual sexual stimulation to relieve both the husband's and the wife's sexual tensions during this time.

4. That oral-genital sex between a man and woman indicates homosexual tendencies.

Homosexuality involves sexual contact between members of the same sex. The choice of a partner of the same rather than of the opposite sex is the determinant in homosexuality, *not* the technique used in sexual activity. Some of the most genuinely masculine of men and feminine of women often enjoy oral-genital contact. But unless that type of outlet is preferred with a member of the same sex, it is no more an indication of homosexual tendencies than if sexual intercourse were the technique of choice.

Probably this idea is an outgrowth of the fact that homosexuals often employ oral-genital techniques in their sex-play activities. It does not follow, however, that the same technique cannot be employed by heterosexual partners with pleasure and without the implication of the slightest trace of homosexuality.

5. That repeated sexual experiences with one man will leave a mark on a child later fathered by another man.

The influence of a "previous sire" on a later conception is a theory known as *telegony*. Despite its rather widespread acceptance among breeders of animals, and regardless of the writings of such scientists as the great Charles Darwin, there is no scientific basis for the theory, whether one is discussing humans or animals. Inadequate knowledge of the laws of heredity and unscientific methods of observation and control in animal breeding have led some people to the conclusion that, on the human level, the offspring of a second husband might be affected by the fact that the wife was impregnated by her first husband or simply had sexual intercourse with him. There are cases wherein a woman, who had previously borne children of a Negro man and then had later married a white man, subsequently bore children with "Negro traits." However, these latter children were either fathered by a man with "Negro traits," or the woman had some Negro blood in her own heritage. It is a genetic impossibility that there could be a causal relationship between her previous Negro husband and the fact that children born after her marriage to a white man have Negroid features.

A common occurrence that appears to give credence to the telegony theory concerns female dogs. Bitches remain in heat for several days, during which time they may mate with several males. Since female dogs have the maddening capacity for escaping the watchful eye of their owners and mating with almost any male that happens along, it is quite possible to find a litter of puppies of which none resembles the intended sire. There is in this instance no "carry-over" from the bitch's previous matings; it is simply that the puppies of the same litter have been sired by different dogs.

6. That heart patients need not worry that sexual activity will be detrimental to their health, as long as they remain physically inactive and quiet during coitus.

Heart patients who do not understand the marked changes that inevitably occur in heart rate and blood pressure during human sexual response may be endangering their lives or health by sexual arousal. During sexual excitement and fulfillment, the heart rate may increase from 70 beats per minute to 150 or more, and blood pressure may rapidly increase from 120 to 250 or more. Both husband and wife should understand that even if the heart patient plays a passive and physically inactive role during the sexual act, the heart beat and blood pressure will unquestionably rise to very high peaks as a result of the sexual response alone.

This is not to say that considerable benefit cannot accrue from sensible sexual behavior. What the heart patient *is* warned against is prolonged coition, fatiguing sexual positions, and extended sex play. Control of these factors can allow him the fulfillment and release of coitus with no undue threat to his health. Death can be (and has been) caused by violent coronary reaction to sexual acts, and the increase in blood pressure may lead to rupture of blood vessels, especially in older persons. Such severe reactions, however, are rare, and the admonition to observe total (or near total) sexual abstinence is not applicable to most patients suffering from heart disease; the advice, rather, is directed to those with serious coronary involvement.

It is quite possible for heart patients under proper circumstances to lead an active sex life; but in this as in other medical questions, a physician should be consulted and his prescriptions (and proscriptions) followed carefully. In addition to controlling physical factors of sex play and coition, one should be reminded that control of anxiety from any source is of utmost importance in the management of cardiac conditions. Tensions can frequently be alleviated by the patient's discussing whatever is disturbing him with his wife (or wife with husband, as the case may be) and with the physician; in severe or persistent cases of tension, a psychotherapist should probably be consulted.

7. That the virginity of the woman is an important factor in the success of a marriage.

Most of the scientifically sound investigations into the effect of a woman's premarital sexual experiences on marital adjustment show that there is only a slight correlation between happiness in marriage and premarital experience. However small the correlation, the indications are nevertheless slightly in favor of premarital chastity.

The importance to either men or women of their prospective marriage partner's chastity at the time of marriage is apparently diminishing gradully. Studies were made at the University of Wisconsin in 1939 and 1956 to determine the components that students considered important in a happy marriage. In the intervening years between the two surveys, chastity dropped in importance from tenth to fourteenth place. Kinsey's studies indicate that over 40% of men wanted to marry virgins, while only 23% of women expected their prospective husbands to be without coital experience.

As indicated earlier, even though mothers who had premarital sexual intercourse admit they are not sorry for their actions and would do the same thing again, they do not want their daughters to experience sexual intercourse before marriage. Mothers are more rigid in their attitude toward premarital coitus than their daughters are. When both groups were asked "How important do you think it is that a girl be a virgin when she marries?" 88% of the mothers replied "very important," and 12% said "somewhat important"; none indicated that it was "not important." The percentage of the daughters replying in the same three categories was, respectively, 54%, 33%, and 13%.

During the early part of marriage, those women who have had premarital coitus seem to enjoy sexual intercourse more than those who have not, but the differences eventually diminish as the marriages grow older. Because sexual compatibility in marriage is dependent upon compatibility at the many levels of a couple's day-by-day living together, having premarital sexual intercourse, however satisfactory, will not assure them of a happy sex life after marriage. This truth stands in opposition to the arguments many young men present to sexually reluctant girl friends, and to their threadbare cliche that "only a foolish person would purchase shoes without trying them on."

In summary, whether or not a woman has premarital coitus is not nearly so important to marital adjustment as are other factors, such as adequate sex education, emotional stability, dependability, and economic security.

3. That there is a difference between vaginal and clitoral orgasms.

Since the time of Sigmund Freud (and perhaps before), there has been considerable controversy over the difference between vaginal and clitoral orgasm—that is, orgasm produced by penile penetration of the vagina, as opposed to orgasm produced by some form of manipulation of the clitoris. Indeed, in the early days of the controversy it was considered—especially by the psychoanalysts—that only mature women had vaginal orgasms, while clitoral orgasms were sure signs of narcissism and sexual inadequacy. Freud taught that a girl can achieve orgasm by clitoral stimulation, but that as she matures into a "real" woman, she will transfer her sexual response from the clitoris to the vagina.

For years, physiologists have recognized that the vaginal walls contain few erogenous nerve endings and that it is *only* stimulation (direct or indirect) of the clitoris that produces orgasmic responses in women. It has taken, however, the recent Masters and Johnson research to convince many medical men and scientists that "from an anatomic point of view, there is absolutely no difference in the response of the pelvic viscera to effective sexual stimulation, regardless of whether stimulation occurs as a result of clitoral area manipulation, natural or artificial coiton, or, for that matter, from breast stimulation alone."

Many women have been concerned over their sexual adequacy because they are unable to achieve orgasm through coition. The research findings of Masters and Johnson should once and for all dispel the myth that women have two kinds of orgasms—one clitoral and the other vaginal. From a purely physiological viewpoint, direct clitoral stimulation usually produces a somewhat stronger orgasmic response than does the indirect stimulation of the clitoris in vaginal penetration; but many women find the latter more satisfying because of various psychological factors. Apparently these women feel that orgasm by vaginal penetration places them in a more traditional female role, and allows more "togetherness" with their husbands during the sex act, producing more satisfaction. Other women receive more gratification from clitoral stimulation alone; in fact, many women are unable to achieve an orgasm in any manner other than direct stimulation of the clitoral area.

9. That menopause or hysterectomy terminates a woman's sex life.

Kinsey and other researchers have shown that a woman's sexual desire ordinarily continues undiminished until she is sixty years of age or older. This is long after menopausal changes in hormonal functioning have occurred, and clearly indicates that ordinarily no physical reasons exist for a woman's sex life to end because of menopause or hysterectomy.

It is understandable that in the relatively unenlightened medical world of the 1800s, physicians would reason that since the ovaries dwindle in their production of female sex hormones at and after the climacteric, women's sex drive would accordingly decrease. It is now known that women's sex drive often does not diminish even when the ovaries are surgically removed. Hormones are only one of many factors affecting the capacity for sexual response; more crucial factors are the woman's emotional stability and attitude toward sex.

Total hysterectomy is the removal of the uterus; panhysterectomy is removal of uterus, Fallopian tubes, and ovaries. In the first instance, there would not even be the reason of hormonal imbalance to account for loss of sex drive; if the woman's surgeon carefully explains the effects of the operation, neither should she have any diminution of sex drive because of psychological factors. If any change does occur, in fact, it might be in the direction of increased drive, since fear of pregnancy is now removed. If ovaries and tubes are also removed, some hormonal changes will occur, although medication can make up any deficiencies.

Considering all the factors, a woman can expect to maintain her sex drive at approximately the same level between the ages of about thirty to sixty years, despite menopause or hysterectomy.

10. That Negroes have greater sex drive than whites, and that the penis of the Negro male is larger than that of the white male.

There is no scientific evidence to support the contention that one race is more sexually active than another. The basis for the prevalent notion that Negroes are more sexually immoderate than whites to a great extent lies in certain conclusions of research groups. Their findings reveal a greater amount of sexual activity among poorly educated Americans of low socio-economic status than among those who are more fortunate. Since a greater number of Negro citizens—sadly, a majority—fall into the first group than whites do, many people erroneously conclude that racial rather than environmental or class factors account for the differences in sexual activity. The recent Duke University investigation into sexual behavior during the human aging process demonstrated that Negro subjects between the ages of sixty and ninety-three were more active sexually than were whites, but the researchers also pointed out that the Negro subjects were of the lower classes.

We have also been taught—mistakenly—that people from culturally and economically deprived strata are more primitive and aggressive (and thus, presumably, more sexually potent) than are people from higher strata. This prejudicial belief exaggerates in many people's minds the sexual powers of the Negro.

Many people have the notion that the Negro's penis is larger than the white man's, and that the larger the penis, the greater the man's sexual powers. Many studies have proven that the size of the penis has absolutely nothing to do with the sexual ability of a man, except, of course, in those cases where hormonal deficiency has stunted both penile growth and sexual drive. It is believed by some that because body configurations of Negro and white males are somewhat different, the flaccid penis of the Negro is accordingly somewhat larger than that of the white man. However, even if this were true, there appears to be little or no relationship between the largeness or smallness of the penis when it is flaccid and when it is erect. This misconception has helped in the evolution of a related fallacy, which is discussed next.

11. That a large penis is important to a woman's sexual gratification, and that the man with a large penis is more sexually potent than the man with a small penis.
. . . The size of the penis has practically no relationship to a man's ability to satisfy a woman sexually. The only exceptions would be these: the instances in which there is the psychological influence of a woman's *thinking* penile size makes a difference, or when sexual pleasure is diminished because the penis is too large and causes the woman pain; or when the penis is so pathologically small that peneration and pelvic contact cannot be maintained.

The vaginal walls themselves have few nerve endings. But it is true that in penetration, the penis that is larger in circumference will be more likely to make contact with the labia minora and vestibular tissue, pulling them in and out during coital movements. This contact causes a tugging of the clitoris which stimulates it and produces erotic pleasure. A very long penis may also put pressure on the cervix, producing pain and detracting from some women's excitement. Yet other women will report that such pressure gives added pleasure, apparently because of psychological reasons, or because the pressure pushes the uterus in such a way that the erogenous nerve endings of the inner abdominal wall are stimulated. With the exceptions stated, however, the size of the penis is not related to the sexual gratification experienced by a woman.

To recapitulate what has been said earlier, there is little correlation between body and penile size—far less correlation, in fact, than there is between the dimensions of other organs and body size. Penile size is dictated by heredity, and in no way affects, either adversely or favorably, sexual potency. The mystique surrounding the large penis no doubt has its beginnings in the prepuberal boy's awe at the postpuberal boy's larger penis —an awe augmented, quite likely, by the braggadocio of adolescent youths in their accounts (usually fantasied) of herculean sexual achievements. The

ounger boys thereby come to associate larger genitals with extraordinary
exual ability, and the attitude is carried into adulthood.

2. That today's young adults are "going wild" sexually.
   Since the beginning of recorded history, older generations have been in
a state of shock and horror at the immorality and other unacceptable
behavior of younger generations. It is not surprising, then, that newspaper
and magazine articles, organized groups, and individuals are crying out
that the nation is on the brink of ruin because of the sexual misconduct of
its young people. There are, to be sure, those incidents that incite public outrage and that are offered as evidence of general moral degeneration among
the young. But there have always been such occurrences, and there are no
more now—if as many—than in the past. . . . The evidence is overwhelming
that the young people of today are as well-adjusted mentally, as mature in
their responsibilities, and as decent a group of citizens as America has
ever known.
   Sociological and psychological investigations indicate that very few
changes are occurring in the sexual mores of boys and girls of today,
although, as one expects of members of any new generation, they are working out new standards of thinking, believing, and behaving. Americans are
not having sexual relations at an earlier age than before, promiscuity is not
rampant among college students (only about 20% of college girls, for
instance, are not virgins), and there has been no great leap forward in
sexual permissiveness since about 1920. There is, on the other hand,
considerable evidence that today's young people—especially the college
populations—are behaving responsibly. Indeed, they demonstrate moral
strength in their concern for the welfare and rights of others.
   There will always be rebellious youth whose behavior will outrage certain
segments of the citizenry, and such outrage has a tendency to radiate to
include all youth. But every new generation has contained a core of
rebellion, and the only surprise is that today there are not more rebellious
acts—certainly there are no more than in past generations. As a matter
of fact, group rebellion has often forced some of our most needed social
reforms, although when such insurgence begins, it is interpreted by many
simply as further evidence of the failure of adults to maintain proper
control of their charges.

Myths and
Fallacies

**13. That frigid women, promiscuous women, and prostitutes are not so
likely to conceive as women whose sexual activity is more normal.**

Since frigidity in women is practically always based on psychological factors, and since conception has nothing whatever to do with whether or not a woman enjoys sexual activity, it is obvious that there is no foundation to the first part of this myth. If in an attempt to prevent conception a woman holds herself back from orgasm, or remains passive and indifferent during coition, she is running the risk of pregnancy. Neither orgasm nor active participation in coition is in the slightest degree necessary to conception.

If promiscuous women and prostitutes do not appear to become pregnant as readily as the average woman does, it is because they take better precautions against the possibility. Sometimes promiscuous women begin their coital activity at a very early age, even before they produce mature ova. They are not, of course, able to conceive at that time of their lives, which perhaps leads to the false notion that a woman's "sexual excess" will cause her to be sterile. (Men *do* lower their ability to impregnate by frequent ejaculations because their sperm count is thereby reduced. The average man requires about thirty to forty hours to regain his normal sperm count after ejaculation.)

Prostitutes who allow themselves to become pregnant are putting themselves out of business; one would quite naturally expect them to take extra precautions against such an eventuality, which they probably do. Furthermore, some prostitutes are sterile because of present or past venereal infection. But frequent sexual intercourse of itself will not lessen the likelihood of these women becoming pregnant, nor strengthen the possibility of their becoming sterile.

14. That it is dangerous to have sexual intercourse during menstruation.

This erroneous idea, along with other myths about menstruation, has been with mankind for centuries. As early as 60 A.D., the Roman historian Pliny declared that the mere presence of a menstruating woman will cause "new wine to become sour, seeds to become sterile, fruit to fall from trees, and garden plants to become parched." Furthermore, according to Pliny, menstrual fluid can blunt the edge of steel, kill a swarm of bees, instantly rust iron and brass (causing an offensive odor); and if, by chance, dogs were to taste the menstrual flow, they would become mad, and their bite venomous and incurable. Small wonder, then, that couples shy away from sexual intercourse during menses. The taboo against "wasting sperm" by having intercourse during the "safe period" of menstruation undoubtedly has added to the cluster of misinformation surrounding coition during this time.

Menstrual blood is perfectly harmless in content to both man and woman; the source of the flow is uterine rather than vaginal, and no tissue damage occurs from penile penetration; and a woman's sex drive ordinarily does not diminish during the menstrual period: these facts point up the irrationality of any arguments against coition during menses, if the couple desire it at that time.

A related myth concerning menstruation is that women should not bathe during the time of flow. It is true that sharp changes in temperature during bathing may temporarily stop the bleeding, but a woman should take precautions against any abrupt temperature changes. Otherwise, there is no reason why bathing, as well as other normal everyday activity, should not be carried on.

15. That humans can get "hung up" (i.e., experience penis captivus) during sexual intercourse.

This is another faulty notion that results from man's observing the behavior of animals and attributing the same possibility to himself. Dogs do get "hung up" because of the peculiar anatomical structure of the male dog's sexual organs. There is a bone in the animal's penis (os penis) that enables him to penetrate the bitch's vagina before full erection. With ensuing tumescence, the head of the penis fills the vaginal barrel and at the same time the walls of the bitch's vagina swell, all of which serves to "trap" the penis and prevent its withdrawal before ejaculation.

Most people have heard stories of couples who became locked together while copulating, the services of a physician being required before the penis could be released. The story is characteristically told as the truth and as having happened to a friend (or to a friend of a friend), although no one has ever witnessed the phenemenon or experienced it. It is, of course, theoretically possible for a woman to experience sudden strong muscle spasms of the vagina (vaginismus) during sexual intercourse, and the vagina may momentarily tighten around her partner's penis. But even in these circumstances, the pain or fear the man would experience would cause loss of erection, permitting easy withdrawal of the penis. There are no scientifically verified cases of penis captivus among humans in modern medical literature.

16. That nature compensates for the number of males killed during time of war.

For his own stability, man depends upon the laws of nature to keep his life in balance. Particularly after the shattering experiences of recent wars, he finds some comfort in the notion that nature compensates for the combatants killed during hostilities by increasing, in some mystical way, the ratio of male to female births. Indeed, at first sight, it seems that just such a miracle occurred after World War I and II when there was, in fact, an increase in male births. Scientists, however, have fairly sound explanations for this phenomenon.

It is an established fact that many more males than females are conceived, whatever the reason may be. From this point on, the female survival ratio is higher than that of the male: the conception ratio is about 160 males to 100 females, the zygote implantation ratio is about 120 males to 100 females, and the birth ratio is 105 males to 100 females. The noted biologist and anthropologist, Ashley Montagu, offers this explanation for what happens in wartime. People marry, he points out, at a younger age; the younger mothers, being strong and healthy, give fertilized ova a greater chance for survival and implantation, and hence tend to give birth to a higher percentage of males than older mothers do. Furthermore, since these young mothers are separated from their husbands, the enforced spacing between births is longer than usual, leaving the wives in a stronger physical condition to carry the next child to term, and thereby increasing the likelihood of a male birth. Following Montagu's reasoning, what actually happens is that more male zygotes are implanted in the uterus and fewer male embryos die, producing a greater male to female ratio of births.

17. That circumcision makes it difficult for a man to control ejaculation.

Until the recent Masters and Johnson research, this fallacy was frequently accepted as a biologic fact. The assumption had been that the glans of the circumcised penis is more sensitive to the frictions of masturbation or coitus; the circumcised man cannot, therefore, delay ejaculation as long as the man whose foreskin is still intact. Neurological and clinical testing of tactile discrimination has failed, however, to reveal any differences in the sensitivity of a circumcised and an uncircumcised penis. In most instances of the latter, the foreskin retracts from over the glans during a state of penile erection, especially during coition, permitting the same exposure of the glans that the circumcised glans receives during the sex act. But even in those cases where the prepuce does not fully retract, the response to stimulation of the uncircumcised penis is the same as that of the circumcised penis.

18. That urination by the woman after coitus, or having sexual intercourse while standing, will prevent pregnancy.

Since the bladder does not empty through the vagina, urine cannot possibly wash out sperm deposited in the vaginal canal during sexual intercourse. There is some remote possibility that the position assumed for urination, if the woman voids immediately after coitus, might aid in preventing the sperm from entering the uterus. But the act of urination itself will not prevent impregnation.

Sexual intercourse, whether experienced in a lying, standing, sitting, or some more unusual position, can produce a pregnancy. Sperm are deposited at or near the cervix upon ejaculation and almost immediately afterwards they begin to move toward and into the uterus. The standing position is not likely to cause the sperm to spill out of the vagina before they can enter the uterus and make their way towards the ovum, if one is present in the uterine tubes.

19. That humans and infrahuman animals can crossbreed.

Not only is it impossible for humans to crossbreed with infrahuman animals, but interbreeding among the various genera of lower animals is equally impossible, although members of different species of the same genus may produce crossbred offspring. For example, a man and an ape cannot interbreed, nor can an ape and a tiger; but two members of different species in the cat family, for example, may crossbreed.

Undoubtedly, our knowledge of the wondrous creatures of Greek and Roman mythology—the centaurs, sphinxes, mermaids, and satyrs—has given status through the years to the myth that humans and lower animals can interbreed.

20. That simultaneous climaxes are necessary if conception is to take place.

The best proof of the erroneousness of this belief is that a woman can be made pregnant through artificial insemination, at which time no orgasm—alone or simultaneous—occurs. The presence or absence of orgasmic response on the part of the woman has nothing to do with whether or not she becomes pregnant. If she produces a mature healthy egg that is penetrated by a normal sperm, conception has taken place.

There are many other myths and fallacies revolving around human sexuality. There now follows a list of several more of them, and in each instance, the statements are false as set out. . . .

Myths and Fallacies

1. That an intact hymen is proof of virginity, and the absence of a hymen proves nonvirginity . . .
2. That masturbation is dangerous, and causes pimples or acne . . .
3. That men and women lose their sex drive after the age of fifty . . .
4. That alcohol is a sexual stimulant . . .
5. That sterilization diminishes the sex drive . . .
6. That castration completely destroys the sex drive . . .
7. That removal of a man's prostate gland will keep him from attaining and maintaining an erection, from having children, and from enjoying sex . . .
8. That it is the woman who determines the sex of the child . . .
9. That there is an absolute "safe" period for sexual intercourse insofar as conception is concerned . . .

FALSE ASSUMPTION 3:
THAT LOVE IS NECESSARY FOR
A SATISFACTORY MARRIAGE

William J. Lederer and Don D. Jackson

Lederer and Jackson attack a cherished American notion—that romantic love is necessary for a viable marriage. While their interpretation of the meaning of love is very specialized, it deserves careful attention, for the mystique of romantic love is seldom challenged, especially by the young. While generally disagreeing with both the basic assumptions and definitions offered here, students nevertheless find that this selection cannot be easily dismissed.

Even though people are reluctant to admit it, most husbands and wives are disappointed in their marriages. There is overwhelming evidence to confirm this.

At least one person out of every three who gets married will be divorced within about ten years. Many of these will indulge in legal polygamy—that is, they will marry and divorce several times. All told, the divorce rate in the United States is 41 per cent.

Marriage is so turbulent an institution that articles on how to patch up disintegrating marriages can be found in almost every issue of our family magazines and daily newspapers, with titles such as "How to Keep Your Husband Happy," "How to Make Your Wife Feel Loved." Surveys show that this sort of article frequently attracts more readers than anything else in the publication. It appears because of public demand, a demand which must originate from millions of unhappy, confused, and dissatisfied couples. Evidently the dreamed-of marriage often does not materialize. There are unexpected shortcomings, bickerings, misunderstandings. Most spouses to varying degrees are frustrated, confused, belligerent, and disappointed.

Almost every expression of our culture, including advertisements, has something to say about how to improve female-male relationships. Motion pictures, plays, television, radio, feature the friction between wife and husband more than any other subject.

The offices of marriage counselors, psychologists, and psychiatrists are crowded with clients who are concerned over problems which mainly involve marriage, and who pay from twenty-five dollars to fifty dollars an hour for assistance. But these troubled people usually cannot identify their problems; even worse, they usually do not sincerely seek solutions. What each one wants is confirmation that he is correct and good, and that his spouse is the one at fault!

One reason for this marital disenchantment is the prevalence of the mistaken belief that "love" is necessary for a satisfying and workable marriage. Usually when the word "love" is used, reference is actually being made to romance—that hypnotic, ecstatic condition enjoyed during courtship. Romance and love are different. Romance is based usually on minimum knowledge of the other person (restricted frequently to the fact that being around him is a wonderful, beatific, stimulating experience). Romance is built on a foundation of quicksilver nonlogic. It consists of attributing to the other person—blindly, hopefully, but without much basis in fact—the qualities one *wishes* him to have, though they may not even be desirable, in actuality. Most people who select mates on the basis of imputed qualities later find themselves disappointed, if the qualities are not present in fact, or discover that they are unable to tolerate the implication of the longed-for qualities in actual life. For example, the man who is attracted by his fiancée's cuteness and sexiness may spend tormented hours after they are married worrying about the effect of these very characteristics on other men. It is a dream relationship, an unrealistic relationship with a dream person imagined in terms of one's own needs.

Romance is essentially selfish, though it is expressed in terms of glittering sentiment and generous promises, which usually cannot be fulfilled. ("I'll be the happiest man in the world for the rest of my life." "I'll make you the best wife any man ever had.")

Romance—*which most spouses mistake for love*—is not necessary for a good marriage. The sparkle some couples manage to preserve in a satisfying marriage—based on genuine pleasure in one another's company, affection and sexual attraction for the spouse as he really is—can be called love.

If romance is different than love, then what *is* love? We do best to return to the definition of Harry Stack Sullivan: "When the satisfaction or the security of another person becomes as significant to one as is one's own satisfaction or security, then the state of love exists." In this sense, love consists of a devotion and respect for the spouse that is equal to one's own self-love.

We have already shown that people usually marry on a wave of romance having nothing to do with love. When the average American (not long from the altar) lives with the spouse in the intimacy of morning bad breath from too much smoking, of annoying habits previously not known, when he is hampered by the limitations of a small income (compared with the lavishness of the honeymoon), or encounters the unexpected irritability of premenstrual tension or of business frustration and fatigue, a change in attitude begins to occur. The previously romantic person begins to have doubts about the wonderful attributes with which his spouse has been so blindly credited.

These doubts are particularly disturbing at the start. Not very long ago, after all, the spouse believed that "love" (romance) was heavenly, all-consuming, immutable, and that beautiful relationships and behavior were *voluntary* and *spontaneous*. Now, if doubts and criticism are permitted to intrude upon this perfect dream, the foundations begin to shake in a giddy manner. To the husband or wife the doubts seem to be evidence that one of them is inadequate or not to be trusted. The doubts imply that the relationship is suffering from an unsuspected malignancy.

To live with another person in a state of love (as defined by Sullivan) is a different experience from whirling around in a tornado of romance. A loving union is perhaps best seen in elderly couples who have been married for a long time. Their children have grown, the pressure of business has been relieved, and the specter of death is not far away. By now, they have achieved a set of realistic values. These elderly spouses respect each other's idiosyncracies. They need and treasure companionship. Differences between them have been either accepted or worked out; they are no longer destructive elements. In such instances each has as much interest in the well-being and security of the other as he has in himself. Here is true symbiosis: a union where each admittedly feeds off the other. Those who give together really live together!

But it is possible to have a productive and workable marriage without love (although love is desirable) as well as without romance. One can have a functioning marriage which includes doubts and criticisms of the spouse and occasional inclinations toward divorce. The husband or wife may even think about how much fun it might be to flirt with an attractive neighbor. Such thoughts can occur without being disastrous to the marriage. *In many workable marriages both spouses get a good deal of mileage out of fantasy.*

False Assumption 3: That Love Is Necessary for a Satisfactory Marriage

349

How, then, can we describe this functional union which can bring reasonable satisfaction and well-being to both partners? It has four major elements: tolerance, respect, honesty, and the desire to stay together for mutual advantage. One can prefer the spouse's company to all others', and even be lonely in his absence, without experiencing either the wild passion inherent in romance, or the totally unselfish, unswerving devotion that is basic in true love.

In a workable marriage both parties may be better off together than they would have been on their own. They may not be ecstatically happy because of their union, and they may not be "in love," but they are not lonely and they have areas of shared contentment. They feel reasonably satisfied with their levels of personal and interpersonal functioning. They can count their blessings and, like a sage, philosophically realize that nothing is perfect.

We must return once again to the meaning of the word "love," for no other word in English carries more misleading connotations. The following is an actual example of how distorted the thinking of an individual may become when he believes he is in love.

A young woman and her fiancé visiting a marriage counselor had completed an interpersonal test which told much about their behavior and how they viewed each other. The counselor, after studying the data, asked why the woman wished to marry this man, who was an admitted alcoholic. She said she had sought the counselor's help because she did have some doubts. Her previous husband, from whom she had recently been divorced, was weak and passive. Now she was looking for a man strong enough to take care of her.

The marriage counselor explained that he could not understand why she has picked an alcoholic—obviously a weak man who could not possibly look after her. She would have to look after *him*.

Her fiancé sat passively by and did not enter the conversation.

The counselor asked again, "Why do you want to marry this man who appears to be just the opposite of the spouse you say you need?"

The young woman shrugged her shoulders, smiled happily, and said, with dogmatic conviction, "Because I love him."

Her fiancé smiled and nodded in support of her unsupportable statement.

It is obvious that this woman did not know what she meant by "I love him." She did not even know how she felt about him. Because of her complex neurotic needs she had a desire for this man—and it could probably be shown that this was a unilateral and totally selfish desire. Her choice of someone to "love" had nothing to do with her prospects for having a workable or satisfying marriage. The word "love" was a cover-up for an emotional mix-up which she did not understand.

Often "I love you" is an unconscious excuse for some form of emotional destructiveness. Sometimes it is a camouflage for a status struggle, which may continue even after a couple has separated. A spouse who has been deserted (especially for another) may covertly or unconsciously wish to be identified and applauded as the good and loyal partner. The jilted spouse assumes a saintly, pious behavior—especially in public—and makes certain everyone knows he still "loves" the other and will lovingly and patiently wait forever until the other comes to his senses. This can be accomplished with operatic flamboyance while the individual simultaneously has a well-hidden affair with someone else's husband or wife; and the apparent inconsistency later can be rationalized away: "After John's [or Mary's] departure there was such a hole in my life I *had* to do something to stay on an even keel. If I had had a breakdown it would have hurt the children. But my behavior didn't alter the fact that I loved him."

This type of "love" is especially likely to manifest itself when one spouse believes he received ill-treatment from the other for some years prior to the final desertion. The "injured" spouse (for so he regards himself no matter what he did to hurt and destroy the other) will loudly maintain with grief: "But I still love him." It takes little clinical experience or psychological brilliance to recognize that usually this person really is exhibiting hurt pride and rage at being the one who was left, rather than the one who did the leaving.

"Love" may also be used as an excuse for domination and control. The expression "I love you" has such an immutable place in our traditions that it can serve as an excuse for anything, even for selfishness and evil. Who can protest against something done "because I love you," especially if the assertion is made with histrionic skill and in a tone of sincerity? The victim—the one on the receiving end—may intuitively realize that he is being misused. Yet he often finds it impossible to remonstrate.

Sullivan's definition of love is important. It describes not a unilateral process, but a two-way street, a bilateral process in which two individuals function in relation to each other as equals. Their shared behavior interlocks to form a compages[1] that represent *mutual* respect and devotion. One spouse alone cannot achieve this relationship. Both must participate to the same degree. The necessity for both spouses to "give" equally is one of the reasons that a marriage built upon mutual love is so rare.

People naturally wish to have a happy marriage to a loving spouse. But such a union is hard to come by without knowledge of the anatomy of marriage, plus much patience, work—and luck. Many people fail to face the fact that if their parents' marriage was unhappy or their childhood was neurotic, they do not possess the prerequisite experience for choosing the correct mate. Where have they observed a good model for marriage? How can they possibly know what a loving marriage is like—and what elements must be *put into* it?

Most Americans enter marriage expecting to have love without having asked themselves the question, Am I lovable? Following close behind is another question: If I am not lovable, is it not likely that I have married an unloving person?

There is another misuse of the word "love." Some people believe that they can love generously even if doing so requires behaving like a martyr. They believe their rewards will come not on earth but in heaven, or at least in some mystical, unusual way. Therefore they seem able to love unilaterally and want nothing for themselves. They suffer happily and enjoy making sacrifices while pouring their love out on another. The more undeserving the other is, the more of this love there is to be poured.

This situation is deceptive. Martyrdom is actually one of the most blatant types of self-centeredness. No one can be more difficult to deal with than the one-way benevolent person who frantically, zealously, and flamboyantly tries to help someone else, and apparently seeks nothing for himself.

Nathan Epstein, William Westley, Murray Bowen, John Workentin, Don Jackson, and others who have conducted research on couples who are content with their marriages and have reared apparently healthy, successful children, agree that *companionability* and *respect* are the key words in the lexicon these couples use to describe their marriages. A husband interviewed in one study stated: "In love? Well, I guess so—haven't really thought about it. I suppose I would, though, if Martha and I were having troubles. The Chinese have a saying, 'One hand washes the other.' That sort of describes us, but I don't know if that's what you mean by love."

The happy, workable, productive marriage does not require love as defined [here], or even the practice of the Golden Rule. To maintain continuously a union based on love is not feasible for most people. Nor is it possible to live in a permanent state of romance. Normal people should not be frustrated or disappointed if they are not in a *constant* state of love. If they experience the joy of love (or imagine they do) for ten per cent of the time they are mar-

ied, attempt to treat each other with as much courtesy as they do distinguished strangers, and attempt to make the marriage a workable affair—one
where there are some practical advantages and satisfactions for each—the
chances are that the marriage will endure longer and with more strength
than the so-called love matches.

1. "A whole formed by the compaction or juncture of parts, a framework or system of
conjoined parts, a complex structure."—*O.E.D.*

False As-
sumption 3:
That Love Is
Necessary
for a
Satisfactory
Marriage

THE ALLEGORY OF THE BLACK EUNUCHS

Eldridge Cleaver

Many middle-class white people regard Black people with sexual envy and fear, and it hardly needs to be said that racial stereotyping persists in this country. The Black is seen as sexually spontaneous, free and virile and at the same time as sexually sinister, animallike, evil, and threatening to sexual "values". This ambivalent attitude of fear and envy predates slavery by some centuries and continues into the present, spawning some very destructive and punitive practices along the way.

Some responsible scholars of race relations feel that sex is, in fact, the root cause of racism. Certainly there is much in our past and present to substantiate this thesis; in his documentary *The Algiers Motel Incident*, John Hersey exposes a contemporary example of the intertwining of sex and racism. And a close look at history reveals many illustrations of the link: the use of castration as a punishment for some male slaves (unheard of in any other slave culture); the lynching of Black men for alleged sexual overtures to white women; the double standard that allowed white men to have illicit relations with Black women without ever permitting the reverse; the antimiscegenation laws that denied the Black woman the dignity of legal marriage when involved in a white-Black liaison.

According to Calvin Hernton, author of *Sex and Racism in America*, both Blacks and whites have ignored the sexual component of race relations to their mutual detriment. But as everything in this country is increasingly sexualized, the relationship between the races cannot escape.

In this brief allegory, Eldridge Cleaver explores some of the myths about Black-white relations and takes an overt look at Black and white sexual issues. McCary discussed the myth of the Black male's endowment with an extralarge penis that makes him sexually more competent than

Some Pervasive Sexual Misconceptions

From *Soul on Ice* by Eldridge Cleaver; excerpt from the chapter, "The Allegory of the Black Eunuchs." Used with permission of McGraw-Hill Book Company.

white men. Cleaver constructs an allegory upon this notion, telling how it came to be and what its results are for Black and white alike.

The war going on between the black man and the white man is not the only war. Life is full of little wars and you fight them all at the same time. You have to have a grand strategy designed to cope with all hostilities, you have to have a style, and if there is someone making war on you and you don't know it, well, you are in big trouble, you're lost from the go. . . . There is a war going on between the black man and the black woman, which makes her the silent ally, indirectly but effectively, of the white man. The black woman is an unconsenting ally and she may not even realize it—but the white man sure does. That's why, all down through history, he has propped her up economically above you and me, to strengthen her hand against us. But the white man is a fool because he is also fighting a war against the white woman. And it doesn't end there: white men have a war going on against each other.

The myth of the strong black woman is the other side of the coin of the myth of the beautiful dumb blonde. The white man turned the white woman into a weak-minded, weak-bodied, delicate freak, a sex pot, and placed her on a pedestal; he turned the black woman into a strong self-reliant Amazon and deposited her in his kitchen—that's the secret of Aunt Jemima's bandana. The white man turned himself into the Omnipotent Administrator and established himself in the Front Office. And he turned the black man into the Supermasculine Menial and kicked him out into the fields. The white man wants to be the *brain* and he wants us to be the muscle, the *body*. All this is tied up together in a crazy way which was never too clear to me. At one time it seems absolutely clear and at other times I don't believe in it. It reminds me of two sets of handcuffs that have all four of us tied up together, holding all black and white flesh in a certain mold. This is why, when you get down to the root of it, the white man doesn't want the black man, the black woman, or the white woman to have a higher education. Their enlightenment would pose a threat to his omnipotence.

Haven't you ever wondered why the white man genuinely applauds a black man who achieves excellence with his body in the field of sports, while he hates to see a black man achieve excellence with his brain? The mechanics of the myth demand that the Brain and the Body, like east and west, must never meet—especially in competition on the same level. When it comes to the mechanics of the myth, the Brain and the Body are mutually exclusive.

There can be no true competition between superiors and inferiors. This is why it has been so hard historically for Negroes to break the color bar in sport after sport. Once the color bar falls, the magic evaporates, and when the black man starts to excel in a particular sport the question starts floating around: "Is boxing dying?" "Is baseball through?" "What happened to football?" "What is basketball coming to?" In fact, the new symbol of white supremacy is golf, because there the Brain dominates the Body. But just as soon as the Body starts ripping off a few trophies, they will be asking the question, "What happened to golf?"

All this became clear when Joe Louis cleaned out Max Schmeling in their second fight. Schmeling stood for the very thing the white man nursed and worshiped in his own heart. But the whites applauded Joe for crushing Schmeling. Why? Because Joe's victory over Schmeling symbolized the triumph of capitalistic democracy over nazism? No! There may have been a little of that to it, but on a deeper level they applauded Joe for the same reason they despised Ingemar Johansson, while rewarding him handsomely, for knocking out Floyd Patterson. Joe's victory over Schmeling confirmed, while Floyd's defeat contradicted, the white man's image of the black man as the Supermasculine Menial, the personification of mindless brute force, the perfect slave. And Sonny Liston, the mindless Body, is preferred over loud-mouthed Cassius Clay, because, after all, it takes at least a birdbrain to run a loud mouth, and the white man despises even that much brain in a black man. And when Clay, the loud-mouthed clown, abdicates his image as the Body and becomes Muhammad Ali, the Brain, whitey can't hold his mud! The white man loves the Supermasculine Menial—John Henry, the steel-driving man, all Body, driven to his knees by the Machine, which is the phallus symbol of the Brain and the ultimate ideal of the Omnipotent Administrator. To the white man's way of thinking, this was a perfect system of social imagery. But like all perfect systems, it had a great big flaw right in the middle of it.

The Omnipotent Administrator conceded to the Supermasculine Menial all of the attributes of masculinity associated with the Body: strength, brute power, muscle, even the beauty of the brute body. Except one. There was this single attribute of masculinity which he was unwilling to relinquish, even though this particular attribute is the essence and seat of masculinity: sex. The penis. The black man's penis was the monkey wrench in the white man's perfect machine. The penis, virility, is of the Body. It is not of the Brain: the Brain is neuter, *HOMO, MACHINE.* But in the deal which the white man forced upon the black man, the black man was given the Body as his domain while the white man preempted the Brain for himself. By and by, the Omnipotent Administrator discovered that in the fury of his scheming he had blundered and clipped himself of his penis (notice the puny image the white man has of his own penis. He calls it a "prick," a "peter," a "pecker"). So he reneged on the bargain. He called the Supermasculine Menial back and said: "Look, Boy, we have a final little adjustment to make. I'm still going to be the Brain and you're still the Body. But from now on, you do all the flexing but I'll do all the fucking. The Brain must control the Body. To prove my omnipotence I must cuckold you and fetter your bull balls. I will fetter the range of your rod and limit its reach. My prick will excel your rod. I have made a calculation. I will have sexual freedom. But I will bind your rod with my omnipotent will, and place a limitation on its aspiration which you will violate on pain of death. . . . I will have access to the white woman and I will have access to the black woman. The black woman will have access to you—but she will also have access to me. I forbid you access to the white woman. The white woman will have access to me, the Omnipotent Administrator, but I deny her access to you, you, the Supermasculine Menial. By subjecting your manhood to the control of my will, I shall control you. The stem of the Body, the penis, must submit to the will of the Brain."

It was the perfect solution, only it didn't work. It only drove the truth underground. You can't really dissociate the penis from the Body! Not even the Brain, the Omnipotent Administrator, can do that! *But you can seize the Body in a rage, in violent and hateful frustration at this one great flaw in a perfect plan, this monkey wrench in a perfect machine, string the Body from the nearest tree and pluck its strange fruit, its big Nigger dick, pickle it in a bottle and take it home to the beautiful dumb blonde and rejoice in the lie that not the Body but the Brain is the man.*

THE MYTH OF THE IMPOTENT BLACK MALE

Robert Staples

Both in social science literature and in society, one of the most prevalent notions about the Black family is that it is "matriarchal"—headed and dominated by women. The Moynihan Report (*The Negro Family: The Case for National Action*, 1965) supported and perpetuated this stereotype; but what Moynihan and many other researchers overlook is that more than two-thirds of the Black families in this country are two-parent families. Why, then, the focus on, and tendency to generalize from, a minority of families?

Staples, who calls the idea of female dominance a "cruel hoax," examines some of the roots of this persistent stereotype, especially with regard to its implications for the Black male. Insofar as the pattern of female strength is characteristic of any family, is this an inherent attribute, or is it a survival-oriented adaptation to the realities of Black life in a white-dominated culture? Does a focus on the historical antecedents of present Black and white family and sexual patterns facilitate understanding, or does it only exacerbate the misunderstanding and stereotypic thinking?

In white America there is a cultural belief that the black community is dominated by its female members, its men having been emasculated by the historical vicissitudes of slavery and contemporary economic forces. This cultural belief contains a duality of meaning: that black men have been deprived of their masculinity and that black women participated in the demasculinization process. Black female dominance is a cultural illusion that disguises the triple oppression of black women in this society. They are discriminated against on the basis of their sex role affiliation, their race and their location in the working class.

Some Pervasive Sexual Misconceptions

Reprinted from *The Black Scholar* 2, no. 10 (June 1971):2–9. P.O. Box 908, Sausalito, California 94965. $10 (ten issues); $8 for students. Reprinted by permission of publisher.

The assumption that black men have been socially castrated has yet to be challenged. Before examining the fallacies of black male castration, it is important to understand the function of these cultural images of black men and women for maintaining the level of black deprivation and white privilege. Most of these theories of black life come from the field of social science, a discipline ostensibly dedicated to the pursuit of truth. It would be more realistic to view social-science research as a form of ideology, a propaganda apparatus which serves to justify racist institutions and practices.

Stereotypes of the black male as psychologically impotent and castrated have been perpetuated not only by social scientists but through the mass media and accepted by both blacks and whites alike. This assault on black masculinity is made *precisely because black males are men,* not because they are impotent, and that is an important distinction to make. As one sociologist candidly admits, "Negro men have been more feared, sexually and occupationally, than Negro women." She further admits that the Negro man had to be destroyed as a man to "protect" the white world. It should be added that the attempt to destroy him failed but the myth of his demasculinization lingers on.

From a historical perspective, the black male's role has changed as he has traversed from the African continent to the shores of North America. This span of time has introduced the forces of slavery, racism and wage exploitation in the determination of his masculine expressions.

In Africa, he resided in a male-dominated society. Taken forcibly from his African roots, the black man experienced radical changes in his status. In the beginning of the period of slavery, black men greatly outnumbered black women. It was not until 1840 that there was an equal sex ratio among blacks. As a result of this low sex ratio, there were numerous cases of sex relations between black slaves and indentured white women, until interracial marriages were prohibited. Previously, black men were encouraged to marry white women in order to augment the human capital of the slave-owning class.

After black women were brought over to the New World they served as breeders of children, who were treated as property, and as the gratifiers of the carnal desires of white plantation owners. More importantly, the woman became the central figure in black family life. The black man's only crucial function within the family was that of siring the children. At most he was his wife's assistant, her companion and her sex partner. He was often thought of as her possession, as was the cabin in which they lived. It was common for a mother and her children to be considered family without reference to the father.

Under slavery the role of father was, in essence, institutionally obliterate Not only was the slave father deprived of his sociological and economic functions in the family but the very etiquette of plantation life eliminated even the honorific attributes of fatherhood from the black male, who was addressed as boy—until, when the vigorous years of his prime were past, he was permitted to assume the title of uncle. If he lived with a woman, "married," he was known as her husband (e.g., Sally's John), again denying him a position as head of the household.

There are those who say that slavery prevented black men from coming to emotional maturity, that they were childlike, docile creatures who were viewed not as objects of fear or hatred but as a source of amusement. In conflict with this view is B. A. Botkin's observation in *Lay My Burden Dow* that:

> In spite of all attempts to crush it, the slave had a will of his own, which was actively, as well as passively, opposed to the master's. . . . The slave expressed his hatred of enslavement and his contempt for hi enslaver in less subtle and more open ways, such as taking what belonged to him, escaping or assisting others to escape, secretly learni* or teaching others to read and write, secret meetings, suicide, infanti-cide, homicide, and the like.

In addition to this covert resistance the so-called "docile" slave put togeth a number of elaborate conspiracies and insurrections. According to Herbert Aptheker, over 250 slave revolts were planned. After slavery, however, the black male continued to encounter assaults on his manhood. The historical literature, for instance, suggests that Jim Crow was directed more at the black male than the black female. Black women, in a very limited way, were allowed more freedom, suffered less discrimination, and were provided mo* opportunities than black men.

The structural barriers to black manhood were great. In a capitalistic society, being able to provide basic life satisfactions is inextricably interwove with manhood. It is the opportunity to provide for his family, both individuall and collectively, which has been denied the black man. After emancipation, the economic role of the black woman was strengthened as blacks left the rural areas and migrated to the cities, where it was difficult for black men to obtain employment. Although they had previously held jobs as skilled crafts men, carpenters, etc., they were forced out of these occupations by a coalition of white workers and capitalists.

Through this systematic denial of an opportunity to work for black men, white America thrust the black woman into the role of family provider. This pattern of female-headed families was reinforced by the marginal economic position of the black male. Economically destitute black families may be forced into a welfare system where it makes "sense" in terms of daily security for black men to leave their families. An example is this black woman who refused to permit her husband back into the family after he got a job. She said:

> Not me! With him away I've got security. I know when my welfare check is coming and I know I can take him to court if he doesn't pay me child support. But as soon as he comes back in, then I don't know if he's going to keep his job; or if he's going to start acting up and staying out drinking and spending his pay away from home. This way I might be poor, but at least I know how much I got.

White society has placed the black man in a tenuous position where manhood has been difficult to achieve. Black men have been lynched and brutalized in their attempts to retain their manhood. For them it is not so much a matter of acquiring manhood as a struggle to feel it their own.

After placing these obstacles to manhood in the black man's way, white America then has its ideological bearers, the social scientists, falsely indict him for his lack of manhood. There are various sociological and psychological studies which purport to show how black males are demasculinized, in fact may be latent homosexuals. The reason they cite is that black males reared in female-centered households are more likely to acquire feminine characteristics because there is no consistent adult male model or image to shape their personalities.

Much of this supposition of the effeminate character of black men is based on their scores on the Minnesota Multiphasic Inventory Test (MMPI), a psychological instrument that asks the subject the applicability to himself of over five hundred simple statements. Black males score higher than white males on a measure of femininity; the researchers cite the fact that black men more often agreed with such "feminine" choices as "I would like to be a singer" and "I think I feel more intensely than most people do."

The only thing this demonstrates is that white standards cannot always be used to evaluate black behavior. Singers such as James Brown and others represent successful role models in the black community. Black male youth aspire to be singers because this appears to be an observable means for obtaining success in this country—not because they are more feminine than white males.

One can easily challenge the theory that black males cannot learn the masculine role in father-absent homes. Black people are aware—if whites are not—that in few female-headed households in the black community are adult males totally absent. A man of some kind is usually around. He may be a boyfriend, an uncle, or just the neighborhood bookie. Even if these men do not assume a central family role, the black child may use them as source material for the identification of masculine behavior.

Furthermore, men are not the only ones who teach boys about masculinity. Sex roles can also be learned by internalizing the culturally determined expectations of these roles. Consequently, a black mother can spell out the role requirements for her fatherless sons. He will be shown the way men cross their legs, how they carry their books, the way they walk, etc. Through the culture's highly developed system of rewards for typical male behavior and punishment for signs of femininity, the black male child learns to identify with the culturally defined, stereotyped role of male.

The myth of the black matriarchy is accompanied by the falsehood that the model black father has abdicated his paternal responsibilities. That this is untrue is confirmed in a study by Schulz which found that most black men assume a very responsible quasi-father role vis-à-vis their women and their children. Black men, however, have to spend a large part of their lives bargaining for a familial relationship, the major impediment being a limited income that cannot equal the combined resources of their present job plus their woman's welfare check.

Black women are charged with complicity with white men to subordinate the black male to his lowly position. Contrary to this assumption, one finds that when the Afro-American male was subjected to such abject oppression, the black woman was left without protection and was used—and is still being used—as a scapegoat for all the oppression that white racism has perpetrated on black men. The system found it functional to exploit them and did so without the consent, tacit or otherwise, of black women. Moreover, while black men may be subjected to all sorts of dehumanizing practices, they still have someone who is below them—black women.

Nevertheless, black women have had a variety of responses to the plight of black men. Some black women accepted the prevailing image of manhood and womanhood that depicted black men as shiftless and lazy if they did not secure employment and support their families as they ought to. Other black women have ambivalent feelings about black men and remember painful experiences with them. They believe that black men do not appreciate the role of black women in the survival of the race. Some even internalize white society's low regard for black men but are bothered by their appraisals.

These attitudes on the part of black women are understandable. There are many black male-female conflicts which are a result of the psychological problems generated by their oppressed condition. Under a system of domestic colonialism, the oppressed people turn their frustrations toward each other rather than their oppressor. Being constantly confronted with problems of survival, blacks become more psychologically abusive toward their spouses than perhaps they would under other circumstances.

On the other hand, some black women are very supportive of their men. As Hare notes, the black woman realizes that she must encourage the black man and lay as much groundwork for black liberalization as he will let her. She realizes that it is necessary to be patient with black men whenever they engage in symbolic assertions of manliness. Her role is to assist strongly but not dominate. Black women, however, may not realize the contradiction between their desire for a comfortable standard of living and wanting the black man to exercise his masculinity. The expression of black masculinity can frequently be met with the harshest punishment white society can muster. Physical punishment and economic deprivation are frequently the white responses to expressions of black manliness.

Whatever the role of the black woman, she realizes that the mythical castrated black male can rarely be dominated. In the dating situation, he has the upper hand because of the shortage of black men in the society. The henpecked black husband is usually a mythical figure. The fact that black wives carry a slightly larger share of the housework than white wives—while not a particularly desirable situation—effectively dispels any notion of the black husband in the role of a servant.

It was mentioned earlier that the attempt to emasculate the black male was motivated by the fear of his sexual power. One needs a deep understanding of the importance of sex in the United States in order to see the interrelationship of sex and racism in American society. In a society where white sexuality has been repressed, the imagined sexual power of the black male poses a serious threat. As Fanon comments, the white man fears that the black man will "introduce his daughter into a sexual universe for which the father does not have the key, the weapons, or the attributes."

What can we say about the sexual abilities of white men and black men? First, it must be acknowledged that sexual attitudes and behavior are culturally determined—not inherent traits of a particular group. But sex relations have a different nature and meaning to black people. Their sexual expression derives from the emphasis in the black culture on feeling, of releasing the

natural functions of the body without artificiality or mechanical movements.
In a concrete sense, this means that black men do not moderate their
enthusiasm for sex relations as white men do. They do not have a history of
suppressing the sexual expression of the majority of their women while
singling out a segment of the female population for premarital and extramarital adventures. This lack of a double standard has also unleashed the
sexual expression of black women.

The difference between black men and white men in sexual responses may
be explained by realizing that for white men sex has to be fitted into time
not devoted to building the technological society, whereas for black men it is
a natural function, a way of life.

It is this trait of the black male that white society would prefer to label
sexual immorality. The historical evidence reveals, however, that the white
man's moral code has seldom been consistent with his actual behavior. The
real issue here is one of power. In a society where women are regarded as a
kind of sexual property, the white male tries to insure that he will not have
to compete with black men on an equal basis for any woman. Not only may
the white male experience guilt over his possession of black womanhood
but he fears that as the black man attains a bedroom equality he will gain a
political and economic equality as well.

Sexual fears, however, do not totally explain the attempted castration of
black men. White society realizes quite well that it is the men of an oppressed
group that form the vanguard, the bulwark, of any liberation struggle. By
perpetrating the myth of the impotent black male on the consciousness of
black and white people, they are engaging in wishful thinking. It is patently
clear that men such as Nat Turner, Denmark Vesey, Frederick Douglass and
Malcolm X were not impotent eunuchs. The task of black liberation has been
carried out by black men from time immemorial. While black women have
been magnificently supportive, it is black men who have joined the battle.

White Americans will continue to perpetuate the myth of the impotent
black male as long as it serves their purpose. Meanwhile, the task of black
liberation is at hand. It will continue to be in the hands of black men. While
racists fantasize about the impotency of the black man, his childlike status,
the liberation struggle will proceed, with one uncompromising goal: total
freedom for all black people, men and women alike.

THE MYTH OF INNATE
FEMININE GOODNESS

Myron Brenton

One of our enduring myths, accepted and perpetuated by men and women alike, has its source in differentiated child-rearing practices based on the assumption that little girls are "good" while "boys will be boys." In subtle ways, this misconception of the fullness and complexity of the female personality has hobbled women in their social interaction with men, especially in political and other competitive settings, and has fostered an unfair image of the male as well. Culturally, the myth of "pure white womanhood" has been at the root of many racial sexual proscriptions. Reinhold Neibuhr's warning that "the chief engine of injustice in this world is the self-deception of the righteous" should help women see the trap inherent in the myth of innate feminine goodness.

The feeling that it's unmanly to work for peace is part of the idealization of women. From it stems the myth that women are inherently good and men inherently destructive. It's a mischievous notion, which has served highly destructive ends, for not only does it freeze the male in the essentially negative role in human relationships, but it also tends to minimize his personal responsibility for his actions. When it becomes exclusively woman's function to socialize him—to make him fit to live in human society—doing so robs him somewhat of his own initiative. When the mother is the sole or even the principal agent in the task of civilizing the little boy, the adult male he finally turns into is not all that at ease with his civilized self. He in turn leaves civilizing to the mother of his children, and the cycle continues. Maybe that's one reason that the myth of innate feminine goodness has persisted throughout the centuries. It certainly is still very much alive today, kept steaming hot and ready to serve by such ardent partisans of womanhood

Reprinted by permission of Coward, McCann and Geohegan, Inc., from *The American Male* by Myron Brenton, pages 197–201. Copyright © 1966 by Myron Brenton.

as Ashley Montagu ("Woman is the creator and fosterer of life; man has been the mechanizer and destroyer of life. . . . Women love the human race; men are on the whole hostile to it") and novelist J. B. Priestley ("In a true matriarchy, love, personal relationships, homemaking, family-creating and taking root in a settled society are at the top of all lists of priorities . . . and all the things that men are always arguing about come a very bad second").

It cannot be denied that a woman's upbringing and her deep involvement in child care activities lead her to develop to a greater degree humanistic traits like sympathy, understanding, and patience and that the male's struggle in the competitive arena leads him to develop to a greater degree other traits, which give him the strongest supports in meeting the demands of his particular challenges. But that's not at all the same thing as saying that woman's genius lies on the side of the angels and man's on the side of death and destruction. The unintended—but unavoidable—result of such polarization is to keep men displaying their masculinity in negative ways and to place unfair requirements on the conduct of women simply because they *are* women.

The myth of feminine goodness has given rise to the saying that this is a man's world and that if women had a free hand, things would be a lot different—needless to say, a lot better. In this context, Mr. Priestley comes right out and unashamedly plumps for an honest-to-goodness matriarchy to replace the present pattern. Although no one can deny that men have steadfastly held the balance of power between the sexes and that women have been cast into the inferior role, it's by no means a clear-cut case of men and women having vastly different psyches. Women have been the socializers of men; but they have also wielded their own power, behind the scenes, covertly, and their power has in the main not been pitted against the men's supposed demonic drives. In point of fact, if the psyches of the two sexes were actually as starkly differentiated, as totally unalike, as the idealizers of womanhood make them out to be, then there couldn't possibly be a meeting of minds between men and women.

It's true that men have generally done the killing, at least on the basis of a mass war. That men are biologically much better equipped to fight than women is obvious; it may also be the case that men are on the whole more aggressive than women. But not to be dismissed is the fact that the restrictions placed on women have inhibited them from any direct outward displays of mass violence in the manner of men. Random examples of women warriors do exist, of course: there were female battalions in the Soviet Union during World War II, for instance, and in Cuba during the revolution, and here are reports of women fighting on the North Vietnamese side at present. Biology might have combined with cultural restraints to prevent the vast majority of females from waging active war. As a group, females may be less prone to violence than males, but this doesn't mean they aren't potentially violent. It doesn't mean they're morally superior. It doesn't mean nature has exclusively endowed them with humanitarian impulses.

Evidence that women aren't innately morally superior to men isn't so very difficult to find, after all, now that women as a group have so much more freedom to express the various aspects of their personalities than they did before and now that they are doing so in a time of social upheaval. Each year, at least in the United States, the alcoholism rate for women climbs. So does the rate of narcotics addiction. So does the suicide rate. So does the crime rate. In fact, F.B.I. *Crime Report* figures show that robberies executed by women have increased a whopping 60.3 percent in recent years. Aggravated assault with women as the aggressors has increased 10.1 percent. Thirty years ago only 9 percent of all the people arrested for murder were women. Today, according to a study recently completed by New Jersey's Fairleigh Dickinson University, 17 percent of all such arrests involve women. Here, for example, is the not so pretty picture of family murder in New York City in 1964:

Sixteen husbands were killed by their wives; twenty-seven wives were killed by their husbands.

Nine sons were killed by their mothers; five sons, by their fathers.

Twelve daughters were killed by their mothers; four, by their fathers.

Eighteen common-law husbands were killed by their common-law wives; twenty-nine common-law wives were killed by their common-law husbands.

Certainly anyone who has seen the twisted faces of some of the women who attend prizefights and wrestling matches, faces contorted with the lust for blood; anyone who has witnessed the hate-filled glitter in the eyes of women on both sides of the fence at a racial clash; anyone who has borne the brunt of corrupting bitterness that flows from some of the female activists in the camps of political extremism; and anyone who has observed the frenzy of women at a rummage sale—anyone who, for that matter, has read a history of the feminist movement—might have understandable doubts about the gentler sex necessarily being so gentle, the loving sex necessarily being so loving.

I am not suggesting that women are morally inferior to men, but that neither sex is inferior or superior to the other. It's only to be expected that the more women emerge from the cloistered walls of home to participate in the activities of the outside world, a highly competitive, contradictory world that both sexes have created, the more women will exhibit the traits now so commonly and exclusively attributed to men.

For that matter, even a surface display of idealism and humanitarianism is—at times—used to cover up less noble inclinations. Counselors in social agencies see many upper-middle-class women who appear to be concerned with humanity, with relationships, with cultural values. Money doesn't seem to be all important to them. In many instances, however, a closer look shows something quite different. According to psychiatric social worker Ruth Fizdale:

> She's gotten hold of a man who'll drive himself like mad to get money, and denigrates him for being too interested in money, and not interested in music, or the arts, or in spending time with the children. But at the same time she's subtly driving him—and doesn't know it.

Miss Fizdale explained that in many cases of this kind both the husband and the wife hold identical values. The difference is that the woman really doesn't like these materialistic values in herself and so gets someone else— her husband—to act them out for her. By disliking him, she can feel better about herself.

Myths die hard, and the ones that spring from the idealization of women still have plenty of bounce to them. That women would save the world if they would only go into the scientific arena or would grasp the reins of government is a well-meaning but unworkable idea. Men will always resist values labeled feminine, and so long as men resist, women will continue to be swept along by the social values that prevail.

Both men and women have an enormous range of possibilities within themselves for good and ill. If the aim is to eliminate war, abate crime, and foster a more humanitarian and corporative society, it cannot be accomplished on the basis of sex-differentiated roles or attitudes. Responsibility for such a choice is individual, not sexual. Humanistic values have no sex. The idealization of women notwithstanding, they're simply human.

Part 7

THE QUESTION
OF RELATIONSHIP

WHAT IS OUR PROBLEM?

Rollo May

Bombarded as we are today with sex merchandising in advertisements and TV commercials, how-to-do-it books, what-you-want-to-know books, and the forthright man-as-machine school of fiction, we arrive at last at satiation. The psyche can absorb no nore stimuli, and apathy or boredom takes over. Has this happened to sex in our society? Psychotherapist and author Rollo May thinks it has, and at the expense of man's sense of his own humanity.

Unlike the "old" Puritans, among whom sexual expression was covert and inhibited, our "new" Puritans are driven by a fear of not feeling or performing *enough.* How paradoxical, observes May, that in this age of sexual amorality, man has simply exchanged one yoke for another and has thus still denied his human need of passion with love.

Women complain that they are treated as sexual objects, but can men be any happier regarded as machines of sexual performance? If we genuinely value freedom of choice in lifestyles, can we allow the "new" Puritans to decry those who do not fit the hedonistic stereotype glorified in today's' popular literature? What do we most value, *Eros* or *agape*? May suggests that modern man must come to terms with both the "destructive and uniting possibilities" of sex and love.

Our problem today is set by several strange and interesting dilemmas in which we find ourselves with respect to sex in our society. When psychoanalysis began in Victorian times half a century ago, repression of sexual impulses, feelings, interests, and drives was the accepted situation. It was not nice to feel sexual, one would not talk about sex in polite company and an aura of sanctifying repulsiveness surrounded the whole topic, so that males and females dealt with each other as though neither possessed sex organs. Freud was right in his clinical assessment of this repression of sex with its allied hysterical symptoms.

Reprinted from *Review of Existential Psychology and Psychiatry,* Volume III (July 7, 1963), with the permission of the author.

Then in the 1920s it became widely believed in liberal circles that the opposite to repression—namely, sex education, freedom of talking, feeling, and expression—would have healthy effects, and was obviously the only stand for the enlightened person. An amazingly radical change occurred in four decades: our society shifted from acting as though sex did not exist to placing the most emphasis on sex of any society, according to Max Lerner, since the Roman. Far from not talking about sex, we might seem, if a visitor from Mars came to Times Square, to have no other topic. It remin me of the lady from Boston who, on visiting her elderly friends in Chicago, said, "Back East we place much emphasis on breeding." The ladies from Chicago answered, "We like it too, but we also have other interests."

Partly as a result of this radical change, many of us therapists rarely get i our consulting offices any more patients who exhibit repression of sex in the pre–World War I sense. In fact we find just the opposite: a great deal of talk about sex, a great deal of sexual activity, practically no one complainin of any cultural prohibitions over his going to bed as often or with as many partners as he wishes. But our patients do complain of lack of feeling and passion; so much sex and so little meaning or even fun in it. Whereas the Victorian person didn't want anyone to know that he or she had sexual feelings, now we are ashamed if we do not. Patients may have problems of impotence or frigidity, but they struggle desperately not to let anyone know they don't feel sexually. The Victorian nice man or woman was guilty if he or she did perform sexually; now we are guilty if we don't.

Our first dilemma is, therefore, that enlightenment has not at all solved the sexual problems in our culture. Some problems are eased: sexual knowl-edge is available in any bookstore, contraception is available outside Boston external social anxiety is lessened. But *internalized anxiety and guilt have increased*, and in some ways these are more morbid, harder to handle, and impose a heavier burden than external anxiety and guilt.

A second dilemma is that the new emphasis on technique in sex and lov making backfires. It often seems to me that there is an inverse relationship between the number of how-to-do-it books perused by a person or rolling of the presses in a country, and the amount of sexual passion or even pleasure experienced. Nothing is wrong certainly with technique as such, in playing golf or acting or making love. But the emphasis beyond a certain point on technique in sex makes for a mechanistic attitude toward love-making, and goes along with alienation, feelings of loneliness, and depersonalization.

The third dilemma is that our highly vaunted sexual freedom is, in my judgment, simply a new form of Puritanism. I define Puritanism as a state alienation from the body, separation of emotion from reason, and use of the body as a machine. This was moralistic Puritanism in Victorian times; industrialism expressed these characteristics of Puritanism in economic guise. Our modern sexual attitudes have a new content, namely, full sexual expression, but in the same old Puritan form—alienation from the body and feeling, and exploitation of the body as though it were a machine. In our new Puritanism bad health is equated with sin. Sin used to be "to give in to one's sexual desires"; now it is "not to have full sexual expression." It is immoral not to express your libido. A woman used to be guilty if she went to bed with a man; now she feels vaguely guilty if after two or three dates she still refrains from going to bed; and the partner, who is always completely enlightened (or at least plays the role) refuses to allay her guilt by getting overtly angry at her sin of "morbid repression," refusing to "give." And this, of course, makes her "no" all the more guilt-producing for her.

This all means, of course, that people must learn to perform sexually, but have to make sure they can do so without getting involved, without letting themselves go in passion or unseemly commitment, which latter may be interpreted as exerting an unhealthy demand on the partner. *The Victorian person sought to have love without falling into sex; the modern person seeks to have sex without falling into love.*

Some time ago I amused myself by drawing an impressionistic picture of the attitude of the contemporary enlightened person toward sex and love. I would like to share with you this picture of what I call the new intellectual:

> The new intellectual is not castrated by society, but like Origen, is self-castrated. Sex and the body are for him not something to be and live out, but tools to be cultivated like a T.V. announcer's voice. And like all genuine Puritans (very passionate underneath) the new intellectual does it by devoting himself passionately to the moral principle of dispersing all passion, loving everybody until love has no power left to scare anyone. He is deathly afraid of his passions unless they are kept under leash, and the theory of total expression is precisely his leash. His dogma of liberty is his repression; and his principle of full libidinal health, full sexual satisfaction, are his Puritanism and amount to the same thing as his New England forefathers' denial of sex. The first Puritans repressed sex and were passionate; our new man represses passion and is sexual. Both have the purpose of holding back the body, both are ways of trying to make nature a slave. The modern man's rigid principle of full freedom is not freedom at all but a new straitjacket as compulsive as the old. He does all this because he is afraid of his body and his compassionate roots in nature, afraid of the soil and

his procreative power. He is our latter day Baconian deviated to gaining power *over* nature, gaining knowledge in order to get more power And you gain power over sexuality (like working the slave until all zes for revolt is squeezed out of him) precisely by the role of full expression. Sex becomes our tool like the caveman's wheel, crowbar, or adz. Sex, the new machine, *Machina Ultima*.

Fortunately I do not have to solve all these dilemmas. I only want to point out that the existential approach is very much concerned with sex and love. There are several reasons for this concern. The first is that existentialism has always stood strongly against the dehumanizing trends in our society—indeed, the contemporary form of existentialism may be said to have been born in the revolt against dehumanization in our Western society, and the movement takes its decisive form therefrom. It stands against depersonalizing tendencies in all forms, making man into a machine in industrialism or making him into a technical tool in sex.

Second, the existential approach sees the body as an inseparable aspect of being-in-the-world. Thus the body is not a machine but a relatedness, a communion, a participation with and in nature and other persons. The body is one expression of being.

Third, the existential approach places a new emphasis upon passion and feeling. Not passion in the sense of being compulsively driven by sex or eroticism but passion as commitment and involvement of one's total (I speak *qualitatively, not quantitatively* here) centered self.

Fourthly, this approach brings a new dimension of depth and dynamism to the understanding of sex and love. We have tended particularly in America to over-simplify sex and love; one way of our doing this has been to let our too-easy view of *agape* cover up and rationalize the demonic aspects of *eros*. Like most of us, I find my own "definitions" of love written some years ago too superficial, and not giving enough recognition to the powerful non-rational forces of sex and love—powerful both with destructive and uniting possibilities. Freud certainly helped us greatly in appreciating the varied and almost omnipresent channels by which powerful erotic drives express themselves. But I think Freudianism was bound to oversimplify sex and love because it had no norm of I-Thou relationship, or norm of *agape* which is not sublimation of *eros* but a transcendence of it. We need a new appreciation of the demonic aspects of sex and love, particularly of *eros*. The tragic emphasis present in existentialism also makes a contribution at this point: tragic as meaning not only the negative possibilities but the positive, creative, ennobling possibilities of sex and love as well.

TANDY: A LITERARY IMAGE OF LOVE

Truman A. Morrison

Illustrating with a story by Sherwood Anderson, Truman Morrison takes the position than man-woman love relationships require that both individuals be strong, positive, and courageous. Many people disagree with this notion, however, believing that it is sexual *in*equality that precipitates a viable interaction and that the strong-weak, dominant-subordinate, leader-follower inequality is precisely what makes man-woman relationships enjoyable and preserves the "valid" distinctions between masculine and feminine. Morrison gives the *personal* priority over the *sexual,* indicating that one must first be a strong, authentic person and only second a member of a particular sex.

Until she was seven years old she lived in an old unpainted house on an unused road that led off Trunion Pike. Her father gave her but little attention and her mother was dead. The father spent his time talking and thinking of religion. He proclaimed himself an agnostic and was so absorbed in destroying the ideas of God that had crept into the minds of his neighbors that he never saw God manifesting himself in the little child that, half forgotten, lived here and there on the bounty of her dead mother's relatives.

A stranger came to Winesburg and saw in the child what the father did not see. He was a tall, red-haired young man who was almost always drunk. Sometimes he sat in a chair before the New Willard House with Tom Hard, the father. As Tom talked, declaring there could be no God, the stranger smiled and winked at the bystanders. He and Tom became friends and were much together.

The stranger was the son of a rich merchant of Cleveland and had come to Winesburg on a mission. He wanted to cure himself of the habit of drink, and thought that by escaping from his city associates and living in a rural community he would have a better chance in the struggle with the appetite that was destroying him.

Written expressly for this volume.

His sojourn in Winesburg was not a success. The dullness of the passing hours led to his drinking harder than ever. But he did succeed in doing something. He gave a name rich with meaning to Tom Hard's daughter.

One evening when he was recovering from a long debauch the stranger came reeling along the main street of the town. Tom Hard was sitting in a chair before the New Willard House with his daughter then a child of five, on his knees. Beside him on the board sidewalk sat young George Willard. The stranger dropped into a chair beside them. His body shook and when he tried to talk his voice trembled.

It was late evening and darkness lay over the town and over the railroad that ran along the foot of a little incline before the hotel. Somewhere in the distance, off to the West, there was a prolonged blast from the whistle of a passenger engine. A dog that had been sleeping in the roadway arose and barked.

The stranger began to babble and made a prophecy concerning the child that lay in the arms of the agnostic. "I came here to quit drinking," he said, and tears began to run down his cheeks. He did not look at Tom Hard, but leaned forward and stared into the darkness as though seeing a vision. "I ran away to the country to be cured, but I am not cured. There is a reason."

He turned to look at the child who sat up very straight on her father's knee and who returned the look. The stranger touched Tom Hard on the arm. "Drink is not the only thing to which I am addicted," he said. "There is something else. I am a lover and have not found my thing to love. That is a big point if you know enough to realize what mean. It makes my destruction inevitable, you see. There are few who understand that."

The stranger became silent and seemed overcome with sadness, but another blast from the whistle of the passenger engine aroused him. "I have not lost faith. I proclaim that. I have only been brought to the place where I know my faith will not be realized," he declared hoarsely.

He looked hard at the child and began to address her, and to pay no more attention to the father. "There is a woman coming," he said, and his voice was now sharp and earnest, "I have missed her, you see. She did not come in my time. You may be the woman. It would be like fate to let me stand in her presence once, on such an evening as this, when I have destroyed myself with drink and she is as yet only a child."

The shoulders of the stranger shook violently, and when he tried to roll a cigarette the paper fell from his trembling fingers. He grew angry and scolded. "They think it's easy to be a woman, to be loved, but I know better," he declared. Again he turned to the child. "I understand," he cried. "Perhaps of all men I alone understand."

His glance again wandered away to the darkened street. "I know about her, although she has never crossed my path," he said softly. "I know about the struggles and her defeats. It is because of her defeats that she is to me the lovely one. Out of her defeats has been born a new quality in woman. I have a name for it. I call it 'Tandy'. I made up the name when I was a true dreamer and before my body became vile. It is the quality of being strong to be loved. It is something men need from women and that they do not receive."

The stranger arose and stood before Tom Hard. His body rocked back and forth and he seemed about to fall, but instead he dropped to his knees on the sidewalk and raised the hands of the little girl to his drunken lips. He kissed them ecstatically. "Be Tandy, little one," he pleaded. "Dare to be strong and courageous. That is the road. Venture anything. Be brave enough to dare to be loved. Be something more than man or woman. Be Tandy!" The stranger arose and staggered off down the street. A day or two later he got aboard a train and returned to his home in Cleveland.

On the summer evening, after the talk before the hotel, Tom Hard took the girl child to the house of a relative where she had been invited to spend the night. As he went along in the darkness under the trees, he forgot the babbling voice of the stranger and his mind returned to the making of arguments by which he might destroy men's faith in God. He spoke his daughter's name and she began to weep. "I don't want to be called that," she declared. "I want to be called 'Tandy' —Tandy Hard!"

The child wept so bitterly that Tom Hard was touched and tried to console her. He stopped beneath a tree and, taking her into his arms, began to console her. "Be good now," he said sharply; but she would not be quieted. With childish abandon she gave herself over to grief, her voice breaking the evening stillness. "I want to be Tandy! I want to be Tandy! I want to be Tandy Hard," she cried, shaking her head and sobbing as though her young strength were not enough to bear the vision the words of the drunkard had brought to her.*

This story by the great American writer Sherwood Anderson has always seemed to me a striking depiction of some of the deeper meanings of love and interpersonal relations. The stranger in the story speaks of a quality in women which he calls "Tandy"—the quality of "being strong to be

*From *Winesburg, Ohio* by Sherwood Anderson. Copyright © 1919 by B. W. Heubsch, Inc., renewed 1947 by Eleanor Copenhaver Anderson. Reprinted by permission of The Viking Press, Inc.

Tandy: A Literary Image of Love

loved' —and says that a man needs and desires this quality in the woman he would love. This is *not,* however, what many women (or men) would expect a man to say. For it is often assumed—and with much to substantiate it—that a man desires a woman who is pliant, indulgent, submissive, and dependent. One of our contemporary psychologists, by no means a Freudian, has observed that in erotic love relationships, today's average man takes the chorus girl for his "erotic ideal." He does so because her impersonality cannot burden him with responsibility. He can "have" her in much the way that he can possess other things involving no question of long-term commitments. As with a piece of property, the decision of having or disposing of her is felt to be basically *his* decision.

Perhaps this makes us think of the Geritol television commercial in which a man says of his wife, who has retained her health and beauty, "I think I'll keep her!" The tone and sentiment are about the same as if he had been speaking of his Karman Ghia or Irish Setter! That such an advertisement is used to sell Geritol to women is revealing. It seems to suggest that a great many women want to be "taken" but do not want to be "taken seriously", for what they truly are—unique and singular beings. As the psychologist I was quoting expresses it:

> She wants to be taken as a member of a sex, and therefore she puts her appearance, with all its un-specific character, in the forefront. She wants to be impersonal and to represent whatever type happens to be the fashion. She will attempt to imitate that popular type, and in doing so, she must necessarily be un-faithful to her Self. She is not concerned to assert the personality which is unique and incomparable in all human beings. She does not give herself. For the man who chooses her does not want *her;* he is, in reality, choosing only her type. Submissive to the man's desires, she gives him what he wants to "have". Instead of seeking one another and so finding each other's selves, they have settled for a fiction![1]

The fiction is that real love (and what we need and want at the deepest levels of our personality) has anything to do with the "relationship of having." To "have" a man or woman implies that what you "have," you can swap; what you possess, you can change or exchange. In the mutual giving and receiving of two people in love, however, the personality of each comes into its own. "The love impulse breaks through to that layer of being in which every individual no longer represents a 'type,' but himself (or herself) alone, not comparable, not replaceable, and possessing all the dignity of one's uniqueness.[2] The individual's quintessence is comprehended

ot just bodily and temperamental peculiarities of the sort that can be
ound in other persons.

Fictions about love and about the relationships between men and women
bound in our culture. Think of the image of women that one finds in
any of the women's magazines. Undoubtedly some changes are taking
lace in this regard as a result of the liberation movements of our time.
ut the traditional cultural concept of the woman as essentially secondary
nd subservient to the man is deeply embedded in our folkways, practices,
ttitudes, and values. The same kind of fiction is peddled in *Playboy*, which
urveys a shallow ethic of personal freedom and fulfillment. Some would
rite off the magazine as appealing mainly to men in a certain age range,
ut there is every reason to believe that the *Playboy* view of sexuality is
idely prevalent. This is serious because it perpetuates a concept of human
timacy and a view of men and women that is as depersonalizing as anything
roduced by the Victorians or the Puritans.

To *Playboy*, there is no necessary or proper connection between sex and
ve—i.e., sexual relationships may be pursued without concern for the
nterpersonal involvements, commitments, and obligations that such a
elationship would normally bring. Hugh Heffner, like the Victorians before
im, views sex as merely a function of the body that can be indulged (if one
ollows Heffner) or dispensed with (if one follows the ascetics) with no
mpact upon the real self. Heffner and those who think as he does fail to
ecognize the full psychological depth of the sexual relationship. As Richard
Iettlinger has commented:

> "By depicting sex as a simple, uncomplicated exercise in the enjoyment
> of the good life, *Playboy* misleads its readers into assuming that real
> women are as pliable, convenient and usable as 'the play-mate of the
> month'—quite ready to be folded up in three sections when the next
> attraction comes along. And the male reader is wrongly encouraged
> to assume that he can approach sex in this manner without danger
> to his own integrity and maturity."[3]

Certainly one of the things that people discover sooner or later—beyond
ll the relativities of moral codes—is that an act which makes another person
erely an instrument for the satisfaction of momentary desire not only
iolates the other's dignity but strikes against one's own dignity as well.
This is why Reinhold Niebuhr, among others who have specialized in the
ield of ethics, has said that the central problem of man's sexual life arises

from the fact that "sexual relationships are necessarily relationships *between persons* and that they also involve a degree of physical intimacy of the two parties, giving themselves to each other, which becomes intolerable if undertaken without mutual respect and ultimately without mutual fidelity." I think also in this regard of Erich Fromm's timeless definition in his *The Sane Society:* "Love is union with someone under the condition of retaining the separateness and integrity of one's own self."[5] Dr. Fromm has acknowledged his indebtedness to Martin Buber and to Buber's influential concept of "I and Thou"—i.e., there can be no real love between persons without the expression of "I-ness," the selfhood of each, or without respect for the "Thou-ness," the personhood and singularity of the other. If one is merely submissive to another, denying one's own uniqueness and worth, there can be no real communion, no creative interaction, no real love.

Two tendencies are operating here: one is our tendency to forfeit a sense of our own selfhood and singularity by subordinating our sense of ourselve to the function we perform. In that respect, we know ourselves essentially as a teacher, or lawyer, or businessman, as a wife, or mother, or social worker, and so forth. The other tendency is to escape the fatiguing burden of personal responsibility by responding to persons, individually or in groups, as essentially a "type". We are tempted to follow preconceived and overgeneralized patterns of thought and action. "In the whole mysterious gift of life," wrote William Shannon in the *New York Times* recently, "wha most astonishes and excites is diversity. No two human beings are the same . . . Overwhelmed by this profusion man's deepest intellectual drive is to understand, to classify, to find self-consistent structures. But this effort move strongly toward suppressing variety!"[6]—suppressing it for the sake of surmounting confusion and disorder and to establish control. We sometimes make it difficult for a person to change, because we continue to respond to him in stereotyped patterns of thought and action.

This takes us deeper into what the stranger in the Anderson story meant when he spoke of his need and desire for love and his recognition that genuine love presupposes a certain strength in both the loved and the lover. "Be Tandy!" he said. "Dare to be strong and courageous! That is the road. Venture anything. Be brave enough to dare to be loved!" Well, venture one must. For genuine love involves both courage and sensitivity, daring to care and to share, and extending one's self in this way, but sensitive at the same time to the dangers of enveloping the other, of denying or infringing upon his dignity as one asserts one's self.

If love is what we want, need, desire—and who would say differently—then we need strength and courage, sensitivity and honesty in the other person. As Rollo May has observed:

> "Our capacity to love depends upon our prior capacity to be persons in our own right. To love means essentially to give; and to give requires a maturity of self-feeling. One gives only if he has something to give, only if he has a basis of strength within himself from which to give. It is most unfortunate in our society that we have had to try to purify love from aggression and competitive triumph by identifying it with weakness. No wonder that tenderness—that yeast without which love is heavy and soggy as unrisen bread—has been generally scorned and often separated out of the love experience. What was forgotten is that tenderness goes along with strength: one can be gentle as he is strong; otherwise tenderness and gentleness are masquerades for clinging."[7]

When we associate love with strength this way, we think of other attributes of strength and human authenticity, such as freedom and self-awareness. Love which is coerced or propelled by dependency is not love. Love which is not freely given is not love.

Since love requires the ability to empathize with the other person, it presupposes a deep self-awareness in each party, a self that can enter into the life of another, feel his feelings, and think his thoughts. An infant or small child can care for his parents in his state of dependency, but real maturity and deep love must await the child's growth in self-awareness and his development of the kind of freedom that makes his love a personally chosen affirmation. The child's more spontaneous warmth and care can be seen in the way he treats his teddy bear or live pets; these do not force him beyond his present capacity to empathize with their needs.

We sense that "somethings is missing" if one cannot *do* something for the other, or give something, in an important relationship. Our giving and receiving are interdependent: if you cannot receive from the other, your giving will dominate him; if you cannot give, you will not be able to appropriate and make your own what you receive.

A new kind of human being may be emerging, and it would be like fate to allow us to stand in the presence of this new person in such times as these—when we are so close to massive destruction or to vast change for human good—when the new human being is present in only small numbers. But out of mankind's defeats and victories, a new quality in humankind is coming into being. It is the quality of "being strong to be loved"—self-affirmation and affirmation of the other in a new implicit covenant of human solidarity.

Dare to be strong and courageous—all of you. That is the road. Venture everything. Be brave enough to love and be loved. Be something more than man or woman, as we have conventionally thought of them. Be Tandy!

1. Viktor E. Frankl, *The Doctor and the Soul* (New York: Bantam Books, 1969), p. 116.
2. *Ibid.,* p. 109.
3. Richard F. Hettlinger, *Living With Sex: The Student's Dilemma* (New York: Seabury Press, 1966), p. 41.
4. Donald Parter Geddes, ed., *An Analysis of the Kinsey Reports* (New York: Mentor Books, 1954), p. 64.
5. Erich Fromm, *The Sane Society* (New York: Rinehart, 1955), p. 31.
6. William Shannon, *New York Times,* 25 September 1970.
7. Rollo May, *Man's Search for Himself* (New York: Norton, 1953), p. 245.

THE JUSTIFICATION OF SEX
WITHOUT LOVE

Albert Ellis

nsofar as sexual activity is the result of decision making rather than the result of blind drives, the question of values is important for the student of human sexuality. In this selection, Albert Ellis suggests that sex and love do not necessarily have to be linked, that sex without love is a viable option and ought to be both personally and socially acceptable. Speaking from his wide experience as a counselor and psychologist, his thesis is that sex *without* love is possible and quite satisfactory, though sex *with* love is probably "better".

A scientific colleague of mine, who holds a professorial post in the department of sociology and anthropology at one of our leading universities, recently asked me about my stand on the question of human beings having sex relations without love. Although I have taken something of a position on this issue in my book, *The American Sexual Tragedy*, I have never quite considered the problem in sufficient detail. So here goes.

In general, I feel that affectional, as against non-affectional, sex relations are *desirable* but not *necessary*. It is usually desirable that an association between coitus and affection exist—particularly in marriage, because it is often difficult for two individuals to keep finely tuned to each other over a period of years, and if there is not a good deal of love between them, one may tend to feel sexually imposed upon by the other.

The fact, however, that the co-existence of sex and love may be desirable does not, to my mind, make it necessary. My reasons for this view are several:

1. Many individuals—including, even, many married couples—*do* find great satisfaction in having sex relations without love. I do not consider it

Reprinted from Albert Ellis, *Sex Without Guilt*, Lyle Stuart, Inc. Used by permission of publisher.

fair to label these individuals as criminal just because they may be in the minority.

Moreover, even if they are in the minority (as may well *not* be the case) I am sure that they number literally millions of men and women. If so, they constitute a sizeable subgroup of humans whose rights to sex satisfaction should be fully acknowledged and protected.

2. Even if we consider the supposed majority of individuals who find greater satisfaction in sex-love than in sex-sans-love relations, it is doubtful if all or most of them do so for *all* their lives. During much of their existence, especially their younger years, these people tend to find sex-without-love quite satisfying, and even to prefer it to affectional sex.

When they become older, and their sex drives tend to wane, they may well emphasize coitus with rather than without affection. But why should we condemn them *while* they still prefer sex to sex-love affairs?

3. Many individuals, especially females in our culture, who say that they only enjoy sex when it is accompanied by affection are actually being unthinkingly conformist and unconsciously hypocritical. If they were able contemplate themselves objectively, and had the courage of their inner convictions, they would find sex without love eminently gratifying.

This is not to say that they would *only* enjoy non-affectional coitus, nor that they would always find it *more* satisfying than affectional sex. But, in the depths of their psyche and soma, they would deem sex without love pleasurable *too*.

And why should they not? And why should we, by our puritanical know-nothingness, force these individuals to drive a considerable portion of their sex feelings and potential satisfactions underground?

If, in other words, we view sexuo-amative relations as desirable rather than necessary, we sanction the innermost thoughts and drives of many of our fellowmen and fellowwomen to have sex *and* sex-love relations. If we take the opposing view, we hardly destroy these innermost thoughts and drives, but frequently tend to intensify them while denying them open and honest outlet. This, as Freud pointed out, is one of the main (though by no means the only) source of rampant neurosis.

4. I firmly believe that sex is a biological, as well as a social, drive, and that in its biological phases it is essentially non-affectional. If this is so, then we can expect that, however we try to civilize the sex drives—and civilize them to *some* degree we certainly must—there will always be an underlying tendency for them to escape from our society-inculcated shackle and to be still partly felt in the raw.

When so felt, when our biosocial sex urges lead us to desire and enjoy sex without (as well as with), love, I do not see why we should make their experiences feel needlessly guilty.

5. Many individuals—many millions in our society, I am afraid—have little or no capacity for affection or love. The majority of these individuals, perhaps, are emotionally disturbed, and should preferably be helped to increase their affectional propensities. But a large number are not particularly disturbed, and instead are neurologically or cerebrally deficient.

Mentally deficient persons, for example, as well as many dull normals who, together, include several million citizens of our nation) are notoriously shallow in their feelings, and probably intrinsically so. Since these kinds of individuals—like the neurotic and the organically deficient—are for the most part, in our day and age, *not* going to be properly treated and *not* going to overcome their deficiencies, and since most of them definitely *do* have sex desires, I again see no point in making them guilty when they have non-loving sex relations.

Surely these unfortunate individuals are sufficiently handicapped by their disturbances or impairments without our adding to their woes by anathematizing them when they manage to achieve some non-amative sexual release.

6. Under some circumstances—though these, I admit, may be rare—some people find more satisfaction in non-loving coitus even though, under other circumstances, these *same* people may find more satisfaction in sex-love affairs. Thus, the man who *normally* enjoys being with his girlfriend because he loves as well as is sexually attracted to her, may occasionally find immense satisfaction in being with another girl with whom he has distinctly non-loving relations.

Granting that this may be (or is it?) unusual, I do not see why it should be condemnable.

7. If many people get along excellently and most cooperatively with business partners, employees, professors, laboratory associates, acquaintances, and even spouses for whom they have little or no love or affection, but with whom they have certain specific things in common, I do not see why there cannot be individuals who get along excellently and most cooperatively with sex mates with whom they may have little else in common.

I personally can easily see the tragic plight of a man who spends much time with a girl with whom he has nothing in common but sex: since I believe that life is too short to be well consumed in relatively one-track or intellectually low-level pursuits. I would also think it rather unrewarding for a girl to spend much time with a male with whom she had mutually satisfying sex, friendship, and cultural interests but no love involvement. This is because I would like to see people, in their 70-odd years of life, have maximum rather than minimum satisfactions with individuals of the other sex with whom they spend considerable time.

I can easily see, however, even the most intelligent and highly cultured individuals spending a *little* time with members of the other sex with whom they have common sex and cultural but no real love interests. And I feel that, for the time expended in this manner, their lives may be immeasurably enriched.

Moreover, when I encounter friends or psychotherapy clients who become enamored and spend considerable time and effort thinking about and being with a member of the other sex with whom they are largely sexually obsessed, and for whom they have little or no love, I mainly view these sexual infatuations as one of the penalties of their being human. For humans are the kind of animals who are easily disposed to this type of behavior.

I believe that one of the distinct inconveniences or tragedies of human sexuality is that it endows us, and perhaps particularly the males among us, with a propensity to become exceptionally involved and infatuated with members of the other sex whom, had we no sex urges, we would hardly notice. That is too bad; and it might well be a better world if it were otherwise. But it is *not* otherwise, and I think it is silly and pernicious for us to condemn ourselves because we are the way that we are in this respect.

We had better *accept* our biosocial tendencies, or our fallible humanity— instead of constantly blaming ourselves and futilely trying to change certain of its relatively harmless, though still somewhat tragic, aspects.

For reasons such as these, I feel that although it is usually—if not always —*desirable* for human beings to have sex relations with those they love rather than with those they do not love, it is by no means *necessary* that they do so. When we teach that it *is* necessary, we only needlessly condemn millions of our citizens to self-blame and atonement.

The position which I take—that there are several good reasons why affectional, as against non-affectional, sex relations are desirable but not necessary—can be assailed on several counts. I shall now consider some of the objections to this position to see if they cannot be effectively answered.

It may be said that an individual who has non-loving instead of loving sex relations is not necessarily wicked but that he is self-defeating because, while going for immediate gratification, he will miss out on even greater enjoyments. But this would only be true if such an individual (whom we shall assume, for the sake of discussion, *would* get greater enjoyment from ffectional sex relations than from non-affectional ones) were *usually or always* having non-affectionate coitus. If he were *occasionally* or *sometimes* having love with sex, and the rest of the time having sex without love, he would be missing out on very little, if any, enjoyment.

Under these circumstances, in fact, he would normally get *more* pleasure from s*ometimes* having sex without love. For the fact remains, and must not be unrealistically ignored, that in our present-day society sex without love is *much more frequently* available than sex with love.

Consequently, to ignore non-affectional coitus when affectional coitus is not available would, from the standpoint of enlightened self-interest, be sheer folly. In relation both to immediate *and* greater enjoyment, the individual would thereby be losing out.

The claim can be made of course that if an individual sacrifices sex without love *now* he will experience more pleasure by having sex with love in the future. This is an interesting claim; but I find no empirical evidence to sustain it. In fact, on theoretical grounds it seems most unlikely that it will be sustained. It is akin to the claim that if an individual starves himself for several days in a row he will greatly enjoy eating a meal at the end of a week or a month. I am sure he will—provided that he is then not too sick or debilitated to enjoy anything! But, even assuming that such an individual derives enormous satisfaction from his one meal a week or a month, is his *total* satisfaction greater than it would have been had he enjoyed three good meals a day for that same period of time? I doubt it.

So with sex. Anyone who starves himself sexually for a long period of time—as virtually everyone who rigidly sticks to the sex with love doctrine must—will (perhaps) *ultimately* achieve greater satisfaction when he does find sex with love than he would have had, had he been sexually freer. But, even assuming that this is so, will his *total* satisfaction be greater?

It may be held that if both sex with and without love are permitted in any society, the non-affectional sex will drive out affectional sex, somewhat in accordance with Gresham's laws of currency. On the contrary, however, there is much reason to believe that just because an individual has sex relations, for quite a period, on a non-affectional basis, he will be more than eager to replace it, eventually, with sex with love.

From my clinical experience, I have often found that males who most want to settle down to having a single mistress or wife are those who have tried numerous lighter affairs and found them wanting. The view that sex without love eradicates the need for affectional sex relationships is somewhat akin to the ignorance is bliss theory. For it virtually says that if people never experienced sex with love they would never realize how good it was and therefore would never strive for it.

Or else the proponents of this theory seem to be saying that sex without love is so greatly satisfying, and sex with love so intrinsically difficult and disadvantageous to attain, that given the choice between the two, most peopl would pick the former. If this is so, then by all means let them pick the former: with which, in terms of their greater and total happiness, they would presumably be better off.

I doubt however, that this hypothesis *is* factually sustainable. From clinical experience, again, I can say that individuals who are capable of sex with love usually seek and find it; while those who remain non-affectional in their sex affairs generally are not particularly capable of sex with love and need psychotherapeutic help before they can become thus capable.

The
Question of
Relationship

NEW YARDSTICKS FOR OLD BEHAVIOR

Rustum and Della Roy

t takes time to build a relationship of depth and meaning, say the Roys, and he "right" sexual behavior is determined, or matched, by the length of the elationship—the longer and deeper the relationship, the freer and more omplete the sexual expression, with coitus being the ultimate surrender f self. To illustrate this thesis, the Roys develop an interesting graphic nalogy in the form of a cistern.

Another important component of the Roy's theory is that "in a developing elationship sexual expression should always lag behind the depth attained." n this way, a couple will become attuned to the many facets of personality efore the ultimate intimacy of coitus. Some students, both male and emale, feel impelled to "prove" themselves sexually on short acquaintance. or them, the "saturation relationship" described here may sound old-ashioned or unnecessarily demanding; for others, however, it may represent a desirable ideal.

We have said that sexuality is an important and integral part of human nature; that sexual expression and feeling are among the sublimest joys that man can know. It is believed by modern psychology—and expressed by the record of mankind's history—that for the body-spirit entity known as *man,* appropriate somatic expression of spiritual or psychic feelings is in general necessary. We affirm that deeply loving relationships between persons constitute the greatest good of human existence. If, then, men and women are to have loving relationships with each other, they must find the appropriate physical vehicles for expressing this love. Most importantly we have asserted that sexual expression can be part of the entire process of communication between two human beings. It behooves us now to attempt to speak

Reprinted from Rustum and Della Roy, *Honest Sex,* Kirkridge, Inc., 1966. Reprinted by permission of the publisher and the authors.

to the crucial question of the appropriateness of various types of sexual communication within a man-woman relationship.

First, we state the obvious when we say that it is the relationship that is primary, the independent variable; the sexual expression of it derives any meaning only insofar as it serves an existing relationship. In temporal terms this means that relationship—the concern of a man and a woman for each other—comes first, and its somatic expression *may* follow. In the case of two free agents, young people or otherwise, the time-lag between relationship-building and sexual expression is today all too short, but the sequence is crucial: sex comes after relationship. Sexual contact cannot generally be used to develop a relationship—it can enrich an existing one.

In order to develop our ideas regarding the appropriateness of various modes of sexual expression for various relationships, it is important to consider first of all the concept of a maximum or saturation level of physical sexual intimacy. This level includes the complete paraphernalia of sexual stimulation and expression, via all its stages to coitus in all its modes and variants, exercised with complete ease and freedom. Such sexual expression is obviously appropriate for the maximum or saturation level of relationship possible between a man and a woman, where two persons know and love each other with all the affection, friendship, Eros, and Venus available to human beings. Obviously it is within marriage that such relationships and concomitant sexual expressions are most often found. However, one should not fall into the trap of labeling such a relationship "marriage," since only a small percentage of marriages attain this level of relationship and not always do the same marriages find the fullest sexual expression. Moreover, it is also true that occasionally either the fullest sexual expression or the deepest relationships, or both together, can exist outside marriage.

We have indicated, therefore, the content of what we will call a saturation relationship and complete sexual expression. These two concepts are very important and should be thoroughly understood as they form a crucial part of the ethical argument. By defining a saturation relationship as that which each individual considers as the maximum he or she can attain at a particular time, or to put it another way, that which he or she would regard as necessary in order to enter into marriage, a personal factor is introduced. That is, a scale is constructed, which varies from person to person. The saturation relationship can be different, but each can with integrity spell out his or her dream or vision of such a saturation relationship.

We are continually told that if one makes such a statement, then every couple will interpret this to their own advantage—whatever that means.

Our answer is that every couple will doubtless interpret *any* statement to their advantage. However, in order to give some concrete expression to what one could see as the content of a saturation relationship for a typical American couple, below are listed some of the features which might well be present. All four love-strands of affection, friendship, Eros, and Venus should be present and well-developed. This can result from:

1. Knowledge of each other. To be thoroughly and completely known by another in both an I-it and I-Thou sense. This means that one has spent literally thousands of hours in the company of the other and knows the physical and spiritual roots as well as the trunk and leaves of the other personality.

2. Commitment to each other. It is necessary in a saturation relationship to have the kind of commitment which not only says that "I will die for you" but is willing to face squarely the question of living with and for the other: paying the bills, putting up with the mistakes, taking the rough with the smooth, "for better, for worse," etc.

3. Commitment to the same goals. Especially in our day of the new position of women, it is not enough to find only a deep face-to-face relation. There must also be in a saturation relationship a basic side-by-side relationship, where the chief commitments in life are shared.

4. The primary concern of each party for the good, the happiness and well-being of the other.

The basic sex ethic equation is: Wherever a saturation relationship exists, the maximum sexual expression is right and proper and even desirable. (However, since all things are possible but not all edify, other factors may also influence a particular course of action in a particular situation.) From this basic equation follow the rest of the considerations regarding appropriateness of various sexual expressions. Since maximum sexual intimacy is the proper expression of the saturation relationship, a corresponding decrease of the level of intimacy is appropriate for relationships which are not as deep, till we find that handshakes are the appropriate expression for acquaintanceship. One further factor must be introduced: We have indicated that in most cases it takes time in the order of several months to years to build a saturation relationship. Yet, it is possible to arrive at nearly a maximum sexual intimacy in a few evenings spent together. Hence a consideration which must enter in is the deliberate restraining of sexual expression below that which may be appropriate for a relationship for periods up to some months. Only after such lengths of time should the sexual expression gradually increase to the appropriate level.

There is a useful physical analogy by which one can elaborate on these ideas and thence deal with some real-life situations. Let us think of the depth of a relationship between a man and a woman being represented by the level of water in a cistern. The relationship grows and deepens and the level in the cistern rises as it is filled with hours spent together, with experiences shared, with common goals fought for or attained. The total height of the cistern (as distinct from the level of the water in it) represents the saturation relationship, or maximum involvement with each other, of which two particular persons are capable at a specific time. Not all cisterns involving even the same person are of the same height. Nor does the height of a cistern remain constant for a particular couple; usually it increases with age and maturity, but traumatic events and unfortunate circumstance can cause the total height of the cistern, representing the maximum relationship of which a couple is capable, actually to decrease.

Our first sketch (Fig. 1) illustrates, then, a typical relationship, showing it as the height of a column in a cistern the total height of which is determined by the individual and his circumstance. The increase or decrease of the depth of the relationship is then measured against a personalized standard

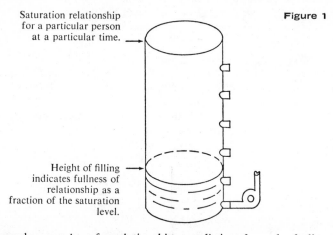

Saturation relationship for a particular person at a particular time.

Figure 1

Height of filling indicates fullness of relationship as a fraction of the saturation level.

Sexual *expression* of a relationship—as distinct from the feelings of Eros and Venus—is not essential to the existence of a relationship, although it can enrich it and strengthen it. Along one side of the cistern we show in Figure 1, a series of connections at different heights. We can now elaborate our analogy by using the idea of a circulating arm to represent sexual

xpression. The arm is permanently attached at the bottom of the cistern
nd comes equipped with its own motor—appropriately signifying both
1e ineradicable sexuality of man and the powerful force that is behind it.
n Figure 1 the arm goes nowhere, it is simply turned off at the valve—
epicting the condition that in many, many relationships all expressions of
exuality have been, and can be, eliminated. Figure 2 is concerned with
1e attachment of the arm of sexual expression. The other end of this arm
1ay be attached to the cistern at any one of the coupling points at different
eights. When a connection is completed and some sexuality expressed, it
auses an enriching circulation of the contents of the relationship in the
istern. Feelings are expressed, tension released, new reactions created, new
igor and beauty added when to the standing level of a relationship, we
dd and connect the invigorating arm of sexual expression.

In Figure 2, a full cistern is shown by analogy to a deep relationship such
s in good marriages with the hose attached at the topmost connection,
orresponding to completely free sexual expression. But there exist also a
arge number of connections all the way up the cistern, and they corre-

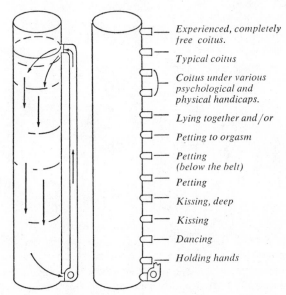

Experienced, completely
free coitus.

Typical coitus

Coitus under various
psychological and
physical handicaps.

Lying together and/or

Petting to orgasm

Petting
(below the belt)

Petting

Kissing, deep

Kissing

Dancing

Holding hands

Figure 2

spond, of course, to the different degrees of intensity of sexual expression, from holding hands through kissing and petting to intercourse. The labels are only illustrations of what one might consider as identifiable stages in this continuum. It is clear that the spacing of these connectors representing the stages depends on age, culture pattern, circumstance, and so on. In some communities, for instance, the gap between kissing and petting may be large, although petting and intercourse may be close to each other. In prewar middle-class America the biggest break came between petting to orgasm and intercourse, although the Kinsey study clearly showed that the former had already dropped much lower down our cistern wall in the postwar era.

The circulating arm of sexual expression can be attached at any level in the relationship cistern. Our basic equation or thesis is that *given sufficient time* the healthy and fulfilling relationships will have the arm attached at the level to which the cistern is filled. We repeat in this analogical format what we said earlier, when we say that because of the slow rate of filling of cisterns compared to the ease of attachment of arms, it is always wise to attach the hose first well below the height of the filling, and then to gradually move it up over a period of months—years. This is illustrated in Figure 3.

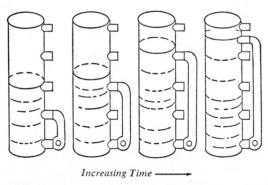

Increasing Time ⟶

Figure 3

Note here that not only is the point of attachment raised gradually over a period of months (up to a year or two) but that in this time and during this process the depth of the relationship itself may also be growing.

It is also quite possible in practice to have two other situations which are illustrated in Figure 4 for rather common cases. The first cistern corresponds to the situation of a good deep relationship between a man and a woman in which no sexual expression occurs. This is so common and in many circumstances so healthy that it may not at first appear to be of any consequence. However, it will transpire that in our day of the affluent society—affluent in opportunity, in time, in control over nature—this situation will pose the most subtle sex-ethic problem of them all. Such a situation between two persons both happily married for instance, has proved in the past to be both possible and creative. Between two unmarried persons in America today who are frequently together, this absence of any sexual expression is both tension-producing and possibly destructive. In the increasingly common situation of relationships developed at work, of a married pastor with a single parishioner, of a helpful married friend with needy single person, it is this imbalance between a deep relationship and no physical expression thereof which can create real problems. . . .

A   B

Figure 4

The last figure (4B) illustrates the common situation where the sexual expression arm has been connected at a level well above the height of filling. What happens? In our analogy the sexual expression then is expected to do more than it normally can, that is, it has to *pump* the liquid of relationship rather than just circulate it. Moreover, there can be many problems and disturbances connected with the "splash" as the forced expressions fall into a relationship not deep enough for it. The greater the disparity between height in the cistern and the sexual expression used, the less appropriate its use.

Let us summarize our basic sex-ethic equation. As relationships deepen, increasingly intimate sexual expressions become appropriate. At any given time, each individual recognizes for himself the maximum relationship of which he or she may be capable and regards as appropriate for *this* the expression of completely free intercourse. Right (or appropriate) sexual behavior, then, is that which matches the sexual expression (as a fraction completely free intercourse) to the depth of a relationship (as a fraction of that required, say, for marriage by that person at that time). A further crucially important part of this theory is the observation that sexual expression should always be brought rather slowly up to the appropriate level. In other words, in a developing relationship sexual expression should always lag behind the depth attained. Finally, these are necessary but not sufficient conditions for sexual expression. Whether or not *any* expressions should occur will need the consideration of many other factors also. . . .

There are two other related combinations of observation and intuition which have a profound bearing on sex ethics, and indeed on what one can reasonably expect to accomplish in altering society's sexual behavior pattern. They are concerned with the capacity of any particular human being to have deep relationships of friendship, Eros, and Venus, with others. The classical ethic was formulated as though every person had an equal capacity for love of any kind, including the outgoing, giving, active seeking of the other's good.

This is clearly a highly distorted view of reality. It may be put into the language of statistics by the diagram on the left in Figure 5, which simply expresses pictorially the unrealistic proposition that 100 percent of the people have the capacity to love just one person at a time and this capacity is equal for all. It would be wrong to pretend that social science has now, or could obtain easily, a more quantitative estimate of the distribution of this talent for loving among the entire population. However, it is certain that there are wide differences among human beings, in this capacity to love others. Furthermore, it is also very probable that if we were able by some study to measure this ability for each person, we would obtain a result expressed by our figure on the right. Similar distributions of values are characteristic of large numbers of other related measurements; for instance, of the height of males in the United States or of the intelligence of fourth-grade children.

We have drawn two curves to express the fact that while we do not know exactly where real Americans fit, we do know both that there is a spectrum of abilities to love and that this type of distribution is likely to be characteristic of this particular human capacity. Moreover, the curves drawn cannot be very far from the real situation and probably include the real situation

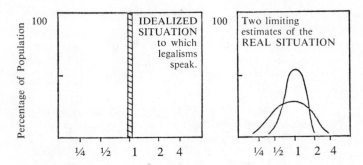

Capacity of loving (expressed as number of persons loved at one time)

Figure 5

Capacity for Loving Others. The "capacity" for loving is, of course a complex parameter which combines a function of intensity or depth, with another of extensiveness. The unit chosen for this parameter is the normative capacity implicit in contemporary ethical theory which is set equal to loving "one person." A symmetrical distribution is shown as the simplest assumption for such a crude model, for the two curves which attempt to present the outside limits of our estimates on what the real situation is today.

between them. If the narrower or sharper of the two curves corresponds more closely to reality, then it means that about 1 percent of the population can handle simultaneously twice as many relationships as the average or median person (who is assumed to be able to handle the equivalent of one). If the wider of the curves is more representative of reality, it indicates that 1 percent of the population can handle four or five times as many relationships as the average and perhaps 20 percent can handle two or more. It is our commonsense evaluation that these curves set the outside limits on the possibilities for the real situation.

But what does such a distribution have to do with sex ethics? A great deal. We have based our ethic on a proportionality between physical expression and depth of relationship. If these observations have any validity, it follows that it may be "unethical" to impose a uniform monogynous code on the whole population. If the median person, indeed, most of the persons who cannot even love one person adequately, nevertheless qualify on their own personalized scale for a full coital expression, then surely there are substantial numbers in our society for whom coitus with two or more persons would be legitimate. Detailed support for precisely this finding is contained in the study of Cuber and Harroff where it was found that a most remarkable percentage among "significant Americans" were able to be involved in meaningful, simultaneous dual relationships. Referring to the individuals who were involved with two persons of the opposite sex to such an extent that they approached marriage they write:

> ... these [persons] always seem to be extremely vital and energetic people—people who have the capacity and the desire to live unusually fully. They seem to want to live two lifetimes in one span. And it does seem as if a few of them are able to achieve such an ambition with more vigor than other people can muster for one mating.

SEMANTICS AND SEXUALITY

S. I. Hayakawa

The crucial role of communication in human sexuality is here explored by a renowned semanticist, who, in comparing and contrasting animal sex with human sexuality, takes some interesting and provocative value positions.

The reproductive system of many forms of life is extraordinarily wasteful, involving an infant mortality rate of just a shade under 100 per cent. The American brine shrimp, says Susan Michelmore, in a book called *Sexual Reproduction*, lay so many eggs that they form a thick encrustation around the edges of the salt ponds in which they live. She says, "The female cod may lay six million eggs in one breeding season, a salmon thirty million." I have been told, too, that certain species of oysters lay so many eggs that if by some miracle they were all to grow up to adult size the world would be knee deep in oysters.

There is an importtnt relationship between the wastefulness of the system of reproduction and the level of development of an animal. Leon Adams, in his book, *Striped Bass Fishing on the Pacific Coast*, says that "one female bass may have from 11,000 to more than 4,000,000 babies; that is by actual sample count of the eggs from her ovaries." When the eggs are released, the males release milt over them. Some eggs get fertilized; many do not. The fertilized eggs are preyed upon by many creatures of the sea. They are eaten as eggs, as larvae, as fry, as fingerlings. Every legally catchable striped bass —which by California law must be sixteen inches long and is therefore about five years old—is the sole survivor out of millions of his siblings.

Despite the enormous rate of reproduction among fish, their sexual life would appear, from the human point of view, to leave much to be desired. In the case of the trout, for example, the female selects a clear, gravelly, sheltered stream in which to lay her eggs. The gentleman trout then comes along and fertilizes them somewhat later—a most unsociable procedure.

Reprinted from *Etc.*, Volume 25, Number 2, by permission of the International Society for General Semantics.

A psychiatrist once told me that he had a patient who had heard about th trout's mating habits and sighed, "Ah, that's the way it should be!" Perhaps that's why he was a patient.

A much more advanced stage in sexual reproduction is represented by those creatures which give their offspring their start in life inside the body o the female, as is true of, for example, the viviparous perch of San Francisco Bay, birds and reptiles that lay hard-shelled eggs, and all mammals.

For fertilization to take place, certain interindividual processes must tak place: male and female must get each other's attention, stimulate each other, secure each other's cooperation or compliance, until the female finally assumes the appropriate position for receiving the sperm. This process of interindividual interaction, whether brief or protracted, and whether occurrin among fish, lobsters, reptiles, birds, elephants, or human beings, is known as courtship.

Perhaps I have said enough to indicate already that communication is a necessary part of sexual behavior of all but the most elementary forms of life

But human beings are the creatures who have specialized in communication as their specific means of survival. No other creature is able, as human beings are, to build languages involving vocabularies of hundreds of thousands of words if necessary in order to communicate the complexities of hi experiences. No other creature is able to send messages to his fellow creature at great distances—indeed, to all parts of the world. No other creature can encode his thoughts in permanent marks on paper in order to pass on messages from the dead to the living, from the living to those yet unborn. No other creature governs his life and social relations so completely by patterne networks of communication: religions, schools, governments, and laws. No other creature so freely utilizes the materials of his environment not only to increase his safety and comfort but also to send messages: by means of foo or flowers, by dress and personal adornment, by dance and ceremony, by architecture and music.

So if communication is necessary to the love life of the sparrow, the croco dile, or the Canadian elk, how much richer and more complex are the problems of communication in the love life of human beings! And general semantics, which is the study of communication and sign behavior and symbolic action in all their forms, must surely have something to contribute to the study of human sexuality.

There are many puzzles about human sexuality. I have already spoken of the wastefulness of the reproductive process in the lower forms of life. As one goes up the scale of biological complexity, the infant mortality rate goe teadily downward. In contrast to the millions that fish give birth to in order to ensure the continuance of their species, amphibians such as frogs reproduce in the thousands, reptiles in the hundreds, mammals and birds in the dozens.

The increasing complexity of organisms as they move up the evolutionary scale is accompanied by the increasing length of dependency of the young. The striped bass is on his own in the hostile waters of the San Joaquin river from the moment he is a fertilized egg. For him there is no period of maturation within a shelled egg, or inside the warmth of a maternal womb, before being thrown on his own resources.

But infants of higher forms of life are fed and nurtured in their nests in infancy. A puppy is well on his way to being a well-formed dog when he is born, but he is still suckled and cared for for many months after birth before he is on his own. During infancy, all mammals experience a period of dependency during which they undergo some kind of education from their elders.

The period of dependency has an enormously important function. The longer the period of infant dependency in any creature, the greater is his reliance in later life on information-gathering and processing as his survival mechanism and the less his reliance upon built-in reflexes, usually called instincts.

As we go up the scale of biological complexity, it is fascinating to observe to what degree this complexity is essentially a matter of the ability of an organism to take in and utilize for purposes of survival more and more information about the environment. The octopus and the oyster are both of the order Molluscs. They provide a fascinating contrast. Oysters, in the interests of survival, gave up locomotion; they attached themselves to rocks and covered themselves with hard shells, which, along with their fantastic birth rate, are their basic survival mechanisms. But oysters sacrificed a lot in order to achieve security. They have few adventures, and, as everyone realizes, if you stay in one place all your life, you don't get to know very much. That is the lesson of the oyster.

In contrast, the octopus remained without armor plating. With no shell to protect him, he had to keep moving. He went places and did things, developing techniques of rapid locomotion, concealment, and food entrapment in order to survive. The octopus, as the British biologist J. Z. Young has shown, is by far the smartest of the molluscs, being capable of learning and even of certain elementary kinds of problem-solving. In other words, mobility brings you in contact with many aspects of the environment and therefore inevitably develops intelligence.

Or take the matter of the warm-bloodedness of mammals. The cold-blooded animal is the prisoner of the temperature he happens to be in. In cold weather, he slows down to a complete halt—like the alligators that lie motionless at the bottom of the pool in the Sacramento zoo in January. The warm-blooded animals, including the birds, maintain their body heat regardless of outside temperature.

Able to stay cool in hot climates and to stay warm in cold climates, mammals have great mobility, and are able to live in and wander around in far more places than the reptiles.

Warm-bloodedness is inextricably connected with mobility, therefore expanded opportunities for information-gathering, and therefore intelligence. The anatomical and nervous structures necessary to take in and utilize a great abundance of information and the habits of sociability to ensure the sharing of that information—these are the dominant characteristics of the higher mammals.

These characteristics achieve their highest development in man, whom Weston La Barre calls *The Human Animal* in a book of that title and whom Desmond Morris in the title of a more recent book calls *The Naked Ape*. The sexuality of human beings is profoundly a part of, and an extension of, their mammalian and primate nature.

It is of enormous human consequence that our remote ancestors lived in trees. In the trees they were safe from prowling quadrupeds, such as tigers and jaguars. Anatomical adaptation made life in the trees possible: the grasping hands and feet to enable locomotion in the treetops; the ability to rotate the arms in their sockets; the eyes side by side at the front of the face and not at the sides of the head as in quadrupeds, so that there would be binocular vision essential to the accurate judging of distances when swinging from branch to branch.

Think for a moment about the hand. A horse cannot scratch its own back; monkeys and people can. With the hand at the end of a brachiating, jointed arm, monkeys and human beings grasp things, bring them close to inspect them with their binocular eyes, put things in their mouths to taste or bite. These are all primate ways of taking in detailed information about the world.

If you have a small baby who is always putting things in his mouth, don't slap him as stupid mothers do. The baby is merely being true to his basic nature. Simply don't leave things around that are unsafe—and make sure to

eave a number of things around that he may bite and taste and chew and spit
ut. It's all part of his education.

The big problem of tree-dwelling creatures is the danger of falling out. The
rasping hands and feet are, of course, insurance against this danger. But
heir babies too are in danger of falling out. Therefore the species of tree-
dwelling primates that survived developed out of necessity the principle of
aving one baby at a time and taking extremely good care of it—which is the
eason that ape and human mothers have one pair of teats high up on the
hest, rather than a long row of them along the whole under side, like sows.

Also, the baby of the tree-dwelling primate was born with an instinct,
which human babies are also born with, for grasping with its hands the fur
f its mother and sustaining its own weight. An extremely close interindi-
idual process develops between baby and mother. Babies hold their mothers
nd are held; they are cuddled and rocked and played with and carried from
lace to place. The mammalian process of suckling gives gratification to both
aby and mother, making them necessary to each other. Some larger quadru-
eds, for example the elephant, are like the higher primates in having one
aby at a time, and therefore developing an intense mother-child relationship.

The cherishing of each individual life is not simply a moral demand
eculiar to highly developed civilizations. It is a basic demand of uniparous
mammals, including elephants, who, as many readers will remember from
he accounts of the explorer Carl Akeley, attempt furiously to save each
ther's lives and mourn deeply the death of one of their group.

For the purposes of taking in information, human beings have great visual
cuity, excellent hearing, an extraordinarily delicate sense of touch (espe-
ially at the lips and tongue and fingertips), a nervous system that transmits
ata with great rapidity, but a very limited sense of smell—not one-tenth as
cute as that of the dog and even less acute than that of the elephant, who
olds up the wet tip of his proboscis and turns it from side to side like radar
o detect the faint odors from any direction.

Weston La Barre says that the sense of smell is subordinated in the tree-
dwelling primates because of the greater importance of vision to creatures
iving high above the ground. But he further suggests that the sense of smell
may well have been repressed. Baby primates clinging to their mothers would
eep her fur soiled. Nests would frequently be fouled. Perhaps the repression
f smell was necessary among higher primates so that they could endure
ach other at close quarters.

Whatever the evolutionary facts may be, Professor La Barre's suggestion
ertainly fits in with an observation we have all made at one time or another,

namely, that people usually prefer smelly company to no company at all—and as soon as they are absorbed in socializing they don't notice the smells any more. Any crowded dance hall or night club gives evidence of the ease with which human beings adjust to strong odors—to say nothing of the smell of New York City, even without a garbage men's strike.

But the most important fact about human beings is their nonseasonal sexuality. Almost all other creatures have a mating season, an estrous cycle—periods of being in heat interspersed with long periods of sexual quiescence or apathy. The female of many mammals is sexually receptive only during ovulation, which, as in the porcupine, according to Sally Carrighar in *Wild Heritage*, is only once a year.

Male sea lions attend their females during the mating season, but as soon as the mating is over, they take off, leaving the care of the young to the females. They go hunting, or go to the club to shoot pool, or whatever it is that menfolk do when they're by themselves, and the ladies don't see them again until next mating season.

But human beings are different. The adult male is capable of being sexually aroused with or without provocation at practically any time. Female receptivity is interrupted by childbirth, but not by pregnancy. Shortly after the pregnancy is over, the female is back in business again. Human beings are just about always interested in sex. "Never on Sunday" is not a biological rule—merely a professional one.

At first it seems quite illogical that human beings, with the great reproductive economy that enables them to continue the race and multiply while bearing only a few young, should be so permanently and obsessively interested in sex. The reason for this is that sexual activity in human beings, as Weston La Barre says, serves two purposes—not merely procreation, but recreation. With his nonseasonal sexual interest, the male does not leave the female to bring up the young by herself. Baby and mother are tied to each other by suckling and by the prolonged dependency of the human infant. The male is tied to the mother by sexual interest—and has to learn to get along with the children. The advantage to the species is that the young of an information-gathering class of life have much to learn from the father as well as the mother.

Thus the life-long patterns of human communication and interaction are learned in the family. Sons and daughters learn to relate to mothers and fathers and to each other. This basic training in communication will serve them all their lives. And Freudians are quite right in attributing many of the difficulties of adult life to unresolved problems of communication and inter-relationship left over from childhood experience.

Desmond Morris has an ingenious argument about the relation of man's sexuality to his way of life. "The naked ape," he writes, "is the sexiest primate alive." Because men were hunters, and because they had to cooperate in the hunt, and because sexual rivalries among weapon-using men would jeopardize cooperation, and because men had to take some share in the education of children, the pairing of one man with one woman made a lot of biological sense, says Morris. Such stable pairing would reduce jealousies among men, establish peace and cooperation in the group, and give the children the well-protected childhood necessary for them to develop their brain capacity.

"Given this situation as a starting point," Morris writes, "we can see how often things grew from it. The naked ape had to develop the capacity for falling in love, for becoming sexually imprinted on a single partner, for evolving a pair-bond."

What prepares the human being for the pair-bond is his own long childhood, involving deep attachment to his mother. As the child grows up he needs another relationship as stable and as strong.

Because in mature pairing a deep and lasting relationship is sought, human courtship is more protracted, more elaborate, than that of any other creature. There is a vast amount of small talk in courtship—the exchange of words not for the sake of transmitting information so much as for the sake of assessing the nature of the interpersonal relationship or evoking emotional states. If each hears in the voice of the other the affection and reassurance evocative of the sounds they heard as babies from their own parents, they feel more and more at ease with each other.

Courtship for human beings is an immense communicative process. Dancing together, picnicking, going to ball games or movies, talking and teasing and testing each other, the couple finds occasion after occasion for comparing each other's reactions to the world, adjusting to each other, trying to decide if there is enough depth to the relationship to make it a durable one.

All the senses are brought into play. Assessments of the partner's sincerity or insincerity, gentleness or callousness, thoughtfulness or selfishness are made by reading subverbal as well as verbal cues: the way your partner holds your hand, takes your arm, or returns your gaze. The long courtship is certainly an essential part of what Morris calls sexual imprinting. As the song-writers say, it is the touch of *your* hand, it is *your* smile, *your* hair, that mean so much to me—and not someone else's hand or smile or hair.

And when it comes to mating, this too, like courtship, is richer for human beings than for other animals. "In baboons," says Morris, "the time taken from mounting to ejaculation is no more than seven to eight seconds . . . the female does not appear to experience any kind of climax." For human beings, sex is infinitely sexier than for the baboon; "the hunting life that gave us naked skins and more sensitive hands has given us much greater scope for sexually stimulating body-to-body contacts. . . . Stroking, rubbing, pressing and caressing occur in abundance and far exceed anything found in other primate species. Also, specialized organs such as lips, ear-lobes, nipples, breasts and genitals are richly endowed with nerve-endings and have become highly sensitized to erotic tactile stimulation."

But just as important as the tactile signals are the visual signals—the responsive facial expression of the partner—and the auditory signals—the voice husky with sexual excitement.

Sexual union then is a profound person-to-person communication, the culmination of all the communications antecedent to it. The sexually attractive and the sexually sensitive areas of the body are largely in front. It is therefore by no means accidental that a vast majority of the human race unite sexually in face-to-face position. "The frontal approach means that the incoming sexual signals and rewards are kept tightly linked with the identity signals from the partner," writes Morris. "Face-to-face sex is 'personalized sex.' "

In other words we are so constructed as to derive additional sexual pleasure from knowing who we're sleeping with. The sexual act derives richness from all the prior imprintings of the valued partner. And sexual pleasure is cumulative, each imprinting reinforcing the effect of past imprintings.

Sexual anarchists and advocates of sexual freedom proclaim that the general attitudes and legislation in favor of durable monogamous relationships are merely cultural prejudices, and that monogamy is contrary to human nature. Although Morris uses the term "pair-bond" in place of "monogamy" and "imprinting" in place of "love," those who read his book will find new grounds for questioning the easy dogmatism of sexual freedom advocates about the nature of human nature.

For human beings sexual imprintings necessarily involve communicative imprintings. Reinforcing the sensual pair-bond for a couple who have lived together for many years are all the communications they have exchanged, the understandings they have established, the feelings they have shared. They have talked to each other about themselves, their friends, the adventures they ave had, their home, their financial problems, their children, their political decisions, and their philosophies.

For the talkative class of life, a pair-bond is never solely the result of conditioning to mutually pleasurable erotic sensations. In the human pair-bond the erotic is inextricably bound up with the semantic.

Nature has so distributed our nerve-endings and constructed our bodies and brains that the profoundest joy we can experience comes from an erotic-semantic attachment reinforced by repeated imprintings over a long period of time.

Like a work of art, a durable pair-bond is not instinctually given. It is an achievement, and like all other worth-while human achievements, it is the product of patience, thought, and self-discipline.

Good communication is therefore at the heart of good sexuality. How can it be nurtured?

Certainly training in communication and responsiveness begins in infancy. Babies need to be cuddled and held and patted and talked to—all through their babyhood. To deprive babies of this kind of stimulation is to leave them deprived of a necessary ingredient in their education. Even the understanding of language in later life may be impaired by lack of contact with the experiences language stands for. As Lawrence K. Frank has written: "Without tactile communication, interpersonal relations would be bare and largely meaningless, with a minimum of affective coloring of emotional provocation, since linguistic and much of kinetic communication are signs and symbols which become operative only by evoking some of the responses which were initially stimulated by the tactile stimuli for which these signs and symbols are surrogates."

Elementary lessons in interaction are begun from the first moment the mother tries to coax a smile from the baby and the baby learns to smile in response. A somewhat more advanced lesson is the game of pattycake (variants of which are found in all cultures) in which the mother elicits the baby's response and the baby, by responding, elicits the mother's response in a continuing interaction.

Certainly there is not space here to go into all the ingredients of child-rearing that bear upon the development of the child's communicative abilities, but one general rule can be stated: just as we learn to swim by swimming, so we learn to communicate by communicating. Children throughout their chldhood must have ample opportunity to interact with other children and adults of both sexes and, if possible, of many different ages. Our present culture segregates the old into retirement communities, the young married with their small children into tract homes, and the more prosperous middle-aged into fashionable suburbs. I think we are all deprived by this segregation—and small children most of all.

Television is a wonderful invention, bringing the whole amazing world into our living rooms. But valuable as television is, it must be used wisely. Too often, mothers use the television set as a pacifier, and millions of young children all over America are placed in front of television sets to be out of mother's way.

But the terrible thing about a television set is that you can have no interaction with it. No matter what the child says or does, the TV set continues to do what it was going to do anyway—so that the child gets no experience influencing behavior and being influenced in return.

Having a puppy is in this sense far more important to a child than having a television set, although of course there is no reason he should not have both. The great American tragedy is the family of parents and children sitting with their TV dinners in their laps, watching the program, *and not talking to one another!*

The child who watches TV for four hours daily between the ages of three and eighteen spends something like 22,000 hours in passive contemplation of the screen—hours stolen from the time needed to learn to relate to siblings, playmates, parents, grandparents, and neighbors. Is there any connection between this fact and the sudden appearance in the past few years of an enormous number of young people who don't know how to relate to anybody —and drop out?

The mother who thinks she is saving herself time and trouble by setting her child for hours and hours daily in front of the television set instead of telling him stories or reading him books is certainly deceiving herself. The time and trouble she saves now may be only a fraction of what she will lose in worries later on.

Fathers have their own way of evading their parental responsibilities— and one of them is to get terribly wrapped up in their business or career. They often justify their neglect by saying that it is not neglect at all—they are merely trying to provide for their children as well as possible. But children need emotional just as much as financial support; they need father's companionship even more than they need the private swimming pool paid for by father's absence.

And father, staying late at the office to plan a new strategy for the sale of automatic garage doors, doesn't know what he is missing: communication with his children, watching the growth of their bodies, the expansion of their minds, and the emergence of their unique and individual personalities.

I am afraid it must be clear from what I am saying that what makes for good adult sexuality is not essentially different from what makes for emotional stability and maturity. So let me expand on some aspects of the problem of maturity as they affect sexual relations.

One of the fascinating things that Dr. Eric Berne says in his famous book, *Games People Play*, is that we all have three ego states—states of mind—which he calls Parent, Adult, and Child. The Parent in you is protective, admonitory, often scolding or censorious, as your own parents were to you when you were a child. The Adult in you is busy taking in information about the environment and solving problems in the light of that information. The Child is playful, imaginative, mischievous, irresponsible, exasperating, and lovable. Dr. Berne's theory is most quickly illustrated by his own example. He bought an expensive car when his book became successful. He explained that his Child—that is, the Child in him—bought it; his Adult paid for it; his Parent tells him not to drive too fast.

Now, in any love relationship, all people have their emotional ups and downs. Couples who get along supremely well are those profoundly attuned to each other's moods. Most of the time the man and woman relate to each other as Adult, discussing realistically their finances, their children's education, their social obligations, or whatever.

Sometimes, however, the woman is ill or nervous or anxious or afraid and needs protection, in which case the man can be a Parent to her Child. She is "baby" who can depend on "Big Daddy" to protect her.

But sometimes it's the other way. The man has had reverses in business or career. He is anxious or discouraged. At this point, the woman is Parent, the wonderful, protective mother whose love protects and strengthens her little boy.

Sometimes, as they worry about their children—and especially about their children's friends—they talk as Parent to Parent; and the favorite remark of communication at this level is, "What *is* the younger generation coming to?"

Then when the man and woman make love, they may become teasing, giggly, playful, spontaneous, emotionally expressive—a Child-to-Child relationship.

A complete love relationship over a long period of time necessarily means, then, sensitivity to the moods of the other and the ability to respond to them. If the woman cannot be the big strong mother when her big strong husband is for the time being a frightened little boy, or if the man cannot be the protective father when his wife is a scared little girl, then there's something lacking in the relationship.

Even more seriously, if either one remains persistently the child when adult thinking and adult decisions are called for, there is something very much wrong in the relationship.

In courtship, one can easily be misled by a pleasant Child-to-Child relationship; the couple go to parties and dances and the girl can say, "But he's such *fun* to be with!" After marriage, however, it is sometimes discovered, too late, that the boy who was such fun to be with is incurably a boy, incapable of assuming adult responsibilities.

So to young people going steady but not yet married, perhaps it would be good advice to say, "It's nice that you have such good times together. But don't marry until you've faced some kind of big troublesome problem together—not interpersonal problems between you, but problems given by the world around you. If you can gain strength from each other by confronting this problem, if your respect for each other increases as you discover each other's emotional resources, maybe you *are* meant for each other."

Let me quote from a letter received by Mrs. Alice Kermeen, director of the San Francisco State College Faculty Program Series, from a lady in Oakland after a recent weekend seminar.

The lady is intellectually inclined. She goes to seminars and is excited by the ideas and wants to be friends on an intellectual basis with some of the fine lecturers she has heard. Invariably, she gets the door politely slammed in her face. The men seem terribly afraid of getting involved. "I am forced to the conclusion," she writes, "that if a man *doesn't* want 'to get involved,' then he sees no point in talking to a woman *at all*. A thinking woman is to most men some sort of contradiction in terms."

"I really don't think," the lady from Oakland continues, "that men decide deliberately to exclude women from intellectual discussions. It's more that it doesn't occur to them to include a woman among their circle of friends on the basis of the ideas she is able to contribute. Ideas are not what women are for."

At the end of her letter the lady adds, "My husband has just read this and he has a reply which may shed light on the male viewpoint. He said, 'You're too pretty to be friends with.'" (He's prejudiced.) I pursued this with, 'Why can't women be people to men?' His reply is that it is the male nature to be interested in the femaleness of the female rather than any other aspect of her. . . .

"Go fight *that!* I quit."

So my final question for discussion here is that raised by the lady from Oakland. Is it the male nature to be interested in the femaleness of the female to the exclusion of interest in her ideas?

I don't think so. We have in the United States long established the principle that women are as much entitled to a college education as men. But we don't in actual practice believe in the principle. On the whole, girls are not encouraged to pursue their intellectual interests—or even their interest in sports, mechanics, or anything else not specifically defined as a legitimate female interest by *Good Housekeeping Magazine*. If a young girl gets excited about mathematics or philosophy or sports car racing, her elders smile among themselves and say, "She'll soon get over all this nonsense when she has her own babies to take care of."

But today with child-spacing an almost universal practice and all sorts of electrical appliances in the home, babies and housework need not be full-time occupations, especially as the children grow to school age. Thousands of women take jobs today not because the family needs the extra money, but because they cannot endure the boredom of underemployed hands and minds.

Perhaps these working women in teaching, in office jobs, in industry, in public office, have part of the answer to the lady from Oakland. As men become more accustomed to dealing with women executives, women colleagues, women members of congress, women competitors in business, they will listen to them for their ideas as well as look over their charms.

If the highest levels of sexuality are achieved only through fullness of communication, it is clear that the more things a man and wife have to communicate about—not only children and food and neighbors, but also current events, the stock market, automobiles, politics, religion, philosophy, natural history, or science—the more enriched will be the relationship between them.

The real frustration of women, so well expressed by the lady from Oakland, is their exclusion from the mainstream. It is a frustration that women experience in common with Negroes. The solution to these frustrations lies partly in the re-education of menfolk on the one hand and white folk on the other to enable them to adjust gracefully to the inevitable changes that lie ahead. It also lies in the determination of courageous women and courageous Negroes to fight their way into the mainstream despite all attempts to keep them in their places.

References

ADAMS, LEON. *Striped Bass Fishing on the Pacific Coast.* Palo Alto: Pacific Books, 1958.

CARRIGHAR, SALLY. *Wild Heritage.* Boston: Houghton Mifflin, 1965.

FRANK, LAWRENCE K. "Tactile Communication." *ETC.,* XVI (1958), 31-79.

LA BARRE, WESTON. *The Human Animal.* Chicago: University of Chicago Press, 1954

MICHELMORE, SUSAN. *Sexual Reproduction.* New York: American Museum Science Books, 1964.

MORRIS, DESMOND. *The Naked Ape.* New York: McGraw-Hill, 1967.

YOUNG, J. Z. *Doubt and Certainty in Science.* New York: Oxford University Press, 1951.

AUTHENTIC SELFHOOD: BASIS FOR TOMORROW'S MORALITY

Lester A. Kirkendall and Peter B. Anderson

Kirkendall and Anderson take as their touchstone for valid sexual relationships the development of genuine interpersonal relationships between two
authentic selves. They examine some of the current and emerging trends in
sexuality and welcome them as fruitful harbingers rather than dire
forebodings of the future.

Students should critically examine this thesis alongside the writings
of Albert Ellis. Are personal relationships indispensible in satisfying and
enjoyable sexual interaction, or are they, as Ellis suggests, desirable but
unnecessary?

> *Prologue*
> *In my beginning is my end. In succession*
> *Houses rise and fall, crumble, are extended,*
> *Are removed, destroyed, restored, or in their place*
> *Is an open field, or a factory, or a bypass.*
> *Old stone to new building, old timber to new fire . . .*
> *. . . each venture*
> *Is a new beginning, a raid on the inarticulate*
> *With shabby equipment always deteriorating*
> *In the general mess of imprecision of feeling,*
> *Undisciplined squads of emotion . . .*
> *. . . In my end is my beginning.*
> *"East Coker"*
> T. S. ELIOT

In these poignant lines, Eliot reminds us that aspects of life are both
finished and never finished, always dying yet always being reborn, often with
great trauma. We are forever involved with endings and with beginnings,

Reprinted by permission from the November, 1970 issue of *Pastoral Psychology*
© Meredith Corporation, 1970.

and they are often one and the same. This seems to be our present condition as it relates to human sexuality.

In more measured academic voice, James Peterson also tells us this. He says,

> Life is a river in time, and while it flows around bends and becomes deeper and more calm in places, it carries with it both the force that comes from its past and debris it has accumulated with each mile traversed . . . some who, because of fear of change, rigidity of role playing, anxiety about health or love, long alienation from mate or children, are simply not able to move creatively into (middle age). They carry too heavily the weight of past defeats in their hearts. The price of venturing has been too poignant. They are crippled. Such individuals may never know the prime of life . . . they have indeed made of the best period of life a wasteland and they have laid it waste unnecessarily.[1]

We can live joyously only as we know and accept certain of our inevitable endings and at the same time others of our necessary beginnings. As we note the values we are leaving, we will peer toward those which, hopefully, are emerging. At the same time, perhaps we will recognize some of the "excessive psychological baggage" which needs to be shed.

I

We have come to the end of a time when morality will be accepted as an edict from a deity, a supernatural pronouncement which must be obeyed whether it appears appropriate or not. We are moving into a period (many people are already there) in which moral judgments are made in terms of emotional needs and rational processes, and in light of these, the effects that decisions will have on our lives. As an illustration, the Catholic Church is in turmoil over the bases for the acceptance of authority. It comes out most clearly in the birth control issue. Some of the priests, and even those above them in the hierarchy, are suggesting that such rules as the birth control ban cannot be imposed from above. A couple's decision, they say, is a "matter of conscience." This same debate is found in other religions. Note, too, the extent in religious writings and in discussions of the term "Christian humanism," as evidence of the direction in which we are moving.

In actuality, we have built behavior codes, not morality, based both upon the cultural conditions in which we live and upon certain principles which are basic and essential needs of human interaction. In a relatively slowly-hanging society these behavior codes served us well and they did put down eep roots. We have now institutionalized them; they seem right; they have ecome recognized as our morality. They are so dear to us that we cannot ear to see them go. But times do change, and when they do, we assume hat with shifts in behavior codes our morality is deteriorating, and the neanings of life we have prized are slipping away.

The mistake, however, is that we have failed to grasp in our now rapidly hanging world what morality actually is. Morality must reside in how we reat one another in our human relations—in our marriages, in our families, n our business, in our international affairs—and, of course, in sex as well. Ve will be talking about sex, since this is our assignment, but we must not orget that what is basic to sexual morality is also basic to the rest of human norality. Face-to-face, in small groups, in legislative bodies, and in inter- ational affairs, the principles of human morality are the same, and are rounded in our human interaction. Whatever changes may be made as a onsequence of science, of new insights into undiscovered developments of nteractions of daily living, the essential fact remains that morality has its ase in interpersonal relationships.

In human relations and human interactions there are always judgments nd decisions about what should and what should not be done; they can ever be escaped. These are very, very seldom merely simple conditions. Vhat seems to be a single straight-line principle turns out to be complicated y other important principles which are also highly important. It is rarely he case in human relationships that one and only one moral principle is nvolved. Unless one simply focuses on one or two elements of an act in a implistic way, many complexities must be taken into consideration. Knowledge of how to make these perplexing moral decisions wisely must utilize all of the insight we can derive about human nature and the needs f human beings

Our basis for judging what is moral and what is not is based upon the undamental nature of men and women and their needs. The purpose of norals is to enable us to survive and to survive joyously. Simply to live is not enough; we wish to enjoy our potentialities, to be pleased with our reativeness, to realize that which is in us. This is the foundation upon which ve rest authentic selfhood; this is the touchstone from which the knowledge f our various moral decisions will need to be reached.

This concept, of course, assumes that men and women are social beings nd that they respond meaningfully to social stimuli. We could get involved n extensive arguments here about the complex nature of man, but since time and space do not allow, we offer this brief illustration. Recently the head of an agency, which seeks out abandoned and institutionalized Korean children and brings them to the United States, emphasized that the greatest needs of these children are care, love, and attention. When they receive these, they are able to thrive and develop. Children everywhere have this same social need. They have their own egos to develop, their own strivings, yet they need the attention, love, and appreciation of others if they are to grow and attain maturity.

All human beings, regardless of age, need this social interaction. In small groups where people can touch, see, feel, and have physical contact with others, the evidence becomes clear enough that human beings prize and respond to these needs. It is when we get into conglomerate masses where we have no opportunity for closeness and intimacy that our troubles in human relationships begin.[2] All in all, man is essentially a social being who derives his deepest meaning from his success or failure in his interpersonal satisfactions.

Ashley Montagu, the renowned anthropologist, stresses this point very strongly. In his book, *Man Observed,* he has this to say:

> ... the whole course of human evolution has led to (the fact) that human beings shall relate to each other as a loving mother relates to her dependent child. Such relatedness has had the highest selective value for the human species in all societies and in all times, and if men fail to recognize this or once having learned this truth ever forge it they will from that moment on be in imminent danger of destroying themselves. . . . The evidence for this statement is now, I believe, bombproof and it is available to anyone who cares to take the trouble to verify it for himself.[3]

The foundations of moral judgments, we have begun to learn, cannot be divorced from our day-to-day human relations decision-making. The basis upon which satisfying decision-making about morals should be made comes when men and women work toward the well-being and welfare of others, and at the same time their own.

II

We are at the end of the time when sex might be considered only in terms of procreation. We are at the beginning of a time when the quality of sexual morality will be deeply and definitely changed by the increasing separation of sexual functioning from its procreative aspects. This is probably the mos profound of all the changes which face us in the sexual morality of the future. It sounds like a simple enough matter—through the use of sex relations a couple decides upon the number of children they want. And this is still an important point for married couples who are in the process of raising a family. This has long been the significant aspect of sex—its major purpose has been to provide children and to tie husband and wife together in this joint endeavor. The couple may enjoy sexual pleasure, they may delight in its sensual experience, but the procreative element is always there.

Mankind, of course, has always sought in one way or another to keep procreative experience within desired limits. This was a very uncertain venture until the last century. Medical knowledge then began to accumulate, and with it birth control became a genuine possibility. New technological devices have contributed to the diminishing fear of an unwanted pregnancy —one might well say there is hardly any fear on the part of those who are knowledgeable about the use of contraceptive devices.

In the past we have sought to keep young unmarried couples chaste by frightening them. One has only to talk to college level students to know that the fear is no longer there. As long as the contraceptive methods had a definite degree of inefficiency, as long as the dissemination of knowledge was curtailed by restrictive regulations, and public opinion stood against the spread of such knowledge, fright and repression followed. Even then, the restraint quite clearly didn't work for many, and survey after survey showed that the fear of pregnancy did not influence many to avoid intercourse, at least not for long.

As has been noted, this hope of repression has disappeared now for several reasons. First, there is much reliable information about contraceptives available to young persons who wish to have it. Secondly, better and better methods of contraception are being devised. It will soon be possible to make individuals infertile from the time of puberty, and to permit them to remain infertile for as long as they wish. In the future, instead of using condoms, diaphragms, or the pill to produce infertility, the individual will be made infertile to begin with, then undergoing medical processes in order to restore fertility.

And, with the diffused and cramped conditions of modern city life, why shouldn't a husband and wife remain infertile as long as desirable? Having six or seven children instead of one or two, does not have the same meaning today as it did fifty years ago. This change in the meaning and relationships of the family has been taking place for quite some time in the wake of social and cultural developments. In the past, children were economic assets.

Authentic Selfhood: Basis for Tomorrow's Morality

417

In the early years of our nation, when farm work had to be done by sheer physical hand power, children were essential to the well-being of the economic enterprise. The family was close-knit. Having been raised on a western Kansas wheat farm and being a child-laborer himself, the senior author of this article can well visualize what this meant. As a lad he often heard his father come in to announce the birth of a new baby boy in some family in the neighborhood. The wording was always the same—"Well, Jim (or some other male) has himself a new hired hand this morning."

Looking at the loosely-knit city family today, the contrast may be readily seen. The early country child was an economic asset, and an integral part of the common enterprise in which the family was involved. He didn't always like it (as the senior author didn't), but he was needed, and he took a certain pride in the obligations he had to meet. There were "generation gaps"—parents and children didn't always think alike, but the encompassing core of family responsibility, purpose, and community action involving everyone, did not leave the parent and child—and particularly the child—in the "alienated" situation which exists today. Lacking the essential developments which might bind family and community together, all we can now expect are disaffected youth and adults, who, themselves, ultimately marry and who, in having their own children, do not actually wish for them. It is circumstances like these that lead to the "battered child syndrome" talked about by psychologists. More than one young married couple puzzle over whether a child is a luxury they can afford under conditions they may face now and in the future.

Then there is another element of great importance—the vast overgrowth of population with which everyone is now familiar. While the United States is one of the least affected countries at this point, it is facing a situation in terms of population growth which is rapidly growing worse. The only countries with larger populations than the United States are China, India, and Russia. Our population is now increasing at the rate of three million annually. From April, 1953 to April, 1964, the growth of population was equal to the entire net growth of population from the time of the landing of the Pilgrims until the time of the Civil War, or from 1620 to 1860. And we are still growing. If our present population, which as 212 million, continues to grow at the same rate, the census will show 344 million in 2000, and 558 million in 2030.[4] This development will undoubtedly produce vast changes in sexual customs and patterns. In the first place, dealing with children in congested areas will create a tremendous problem. Where they will play, who will look after them, what will be their value to parents hen there is a relatively small and insignificant core to total family activity —these are major problems of the future. It is one thing to cope with a elpless, yet charming infant who draws from a parent what he has in the ay of nurturing care; it is quite another to cope with children and adolescents who have ideas about what they want to do, but no place in which o try them.

Sexual function will still be used to reproduce, but in what ways and to hat extent is problematic. Rosenfeld has said:

> The nature of human relationships (including the sexual) must be thoroughly reexamined—and, some think, reconstructed—if we are to manage sensibly the new controls that scientists will hand us as a result of their exploration of prenativity.[5]

The same ideas were expressed by Taylor,[6] in a book which would be of elp to readers trying to understand this problem.

II

In still another way, we are both at an end and at a beginning. We are t an end of an undeviating, monolithic judgment of the morality of sexual ehavior by acts, and we are moving into a pluralistic and diversified cceptance of patterns of sexual behavior. Jetse Sprey,[7] who wrote on this ecently, sees our sexual attitudes and morality as now coming to be set up round institutions which have different bases for being and existing within hemselves. Procreation and family life may be a part of it, but not the najor emphasis or purpose. One evidence is the number of childless couples nd the emphasis on smaller families. It has also been estimated that at least 50,000 children are born through the use of artificial insemination each ear. For many, their sexuality will be used in different directions and in vays other than in procreation.

Sex, as Dr. Sprey sees it, is becoming institutionalized autonomously "in its own right, rather than primarily within the institutional contexts of reproduction and child-rearing. . . . The accent (around which sex is focused) lies on its cultural dimension; the extent to which a given kind of social interaction is defined and legitimated as an end in itself." In other words, sex is coming to be something to be participated in because it is sex; not simply as an experience in procreation.

The writers of *The Future of the Family*,[8] speculating on the future of sexuality in family life, think there is not much doubt about it—sex life in the future will be better. "But it will be different because it will center less and less on the sex act as we have come to know it, what we call sexual intercourse. There will be a much broader range of sexuality in the family —and it will probably not be limited to the family or the home."

This divergency may be seen in many different ways. The writers have approached this by accepting the view that sex, in its most satisfying form, is a matter of interpersonal relationships. It is quite unsatisfactory to regard sex as a physical experience, or as an entity in itself. The most intimate and meaningful experience comes when it is as an integral part of a relationship in which people are trying to express care and love for one another. Sex is not simply an end, but is a part of a more encompassing relationship. The emphasis on sex would be subordinated by a greater concern for building trust, sincerity, integrity, and a capacity for communication between the partners. In one sense, sex may mean less, yet in another sense it comes to mean even more; more because it has been built into the whole relationship. When sexuality has something to contribute within itself it has to be associated integrally with other parts of the total relationship.

The senior author has worked too long in counseling to see how quickly sex as a wholly sensory relationship can become superficial and meaningless. No relationship, no marriage, can be held together by physical sexual experience alone. We would do well to have a semantic differential in which sex for physical pleasure alone is known as copulation, while the experience in which feeling and appreciation have been exchanged would be known as intercourse. Satisfying experiences in sexual intercourse are not achieved simply by wishing. They are attained by couples who, together, have given time to building them emotionally and physically. The senior author's studies,[9] show that such experiences came through the depth of emotional involvement, and the degree of affectional attachment. And they came not by chance, but through an understanding of how meaningful relationships are reached by communication, integrity, genuineness, and sincerity.

Although we are describing relationships of great significance to those involved in them, there are many male-female relationships of shorter duration and less significance, and their value also must be judged in terms of the relationship which exists. Sex plays a different part from time to time for people who are maintaining the same relationship, or moving from one relationship to another. In some instances, relationships may be minimized or absent. It may become casual experimental play, or an over riding concern in which the total major element is sexuality with no concern or protection, interest, or personality development of the other person. How are these to be evaluated?

There is at present an increasing emphasis on sex as an adult play experience. To many, sex as play will seem, without doubt, reprehensible, particularly outside of marriage. Yet the thought of sex as play has been discussed from time to time. For example, Nelson Foote, in writing on "Sex as Play," made some significant points on the topic. He especially noted that play was often regarded by many as irresponsible and self-centered. For many people, sex as play had no meaning beyond that of seeking individual satisfaction. He speculated on whether it was the puritan tendency either to frown upon play, or to regard sex as intrinsically sinful, or both, which in combination has caused the dislike which still confuses us. He points out that:

> . . . . play—any kind of play—generates its own morality and values. And the enforcement of the rules of play becomes the concern of every player, because without their observance, the play cannot continue; the spoilsport is sternly rejected.[10]

He also noted that a play relationship called for "the dynamics of obligation and commitment," for without these characteristics the play arrangements themselves would break down.

Yet here we are likely to find our gravest disappointment. We may eliminate the relationship-communicative function; yet we still expect to satisfy our sexual desires in full. It is easy to focus on physical, sensory pleasure alone but, again, and again, this as the only focus has failed to bring people enduring satisfaction.

Foote also makes the point that sex play and activity have a contribution to make as a development experience in the process of growing up. Dr. Harlow, of the University of Wisconsin, in his study of youthful rhesus monkeys, deprived them of various ordinary interpersonal relationships with their mates and later found them unable to copulate, or if they did, the females were inadequate and unsuccessful mothers. So at the subprimate level, as seen by Dr. Harlow, the meaning of sex as play seems to be a significant feature in development toward an adult level.

Still other aspects of pluralistic sexual behavior are being discussed increasingly. Some couples will continue to live within, and follow closely, the traditional arrangements. But beyond them there are increasing pluralistic developments within the society: couples living together without marriage for long or short periods of time; unmarried couples spending weekends or

Authentic
Selfhood:
Basis for
Tomorrow's
Morality

421

making trips together (as has been done in Europe for quite some time); communal living; couples having consecutive spouses; varying arrangements for children (as interracial adoption); childless couples; ceoducational college dormitory living, as well as evidences of increasing interests and activity in homosexual experiences and associations.

Pressures are building up, for example, in colleges and universities, for contraceptive devices to be made available to persons who want them and in an open and direct way. In some schools, this is already being done in either a subdued or subterranean fashion. The whole question of contraceptives for unmarried youth is an issue which we have so far been unwilling to face, but which inevitably must be confronted.

As explorations into the biological nature of man continue, still other problems will arise, which have significance for patterns of living and which will further challenge moral traditions. In a recent book, Lionel Tiger, an anthropologist at Rutgers University, explored male-male relations (in what he calls male-binding associations) in their political, work, family, and friendship associations. At one point he touched briefly upon the possibility of homoerotic relationships between males, saying:

> The effect of homoerotic relationships in work, political and other groups is of considerable interest in terms of the many questions I have raised in this book. From a strictly biological viewpoint, there is no good reason for forbidding or even discouraging homoerotic activities, though in terms of Euro-American family structure and sexual attitudes there may be sociological reasons. As I have tried to indicate, there are important inhibitions in much of Euro-American culture—if not elsewhere too—against expressing affection between men, and one result of this inhibition of tenderness and warmth is an insistence on corporate hardness and forcefulness which has contributed to a variety of 'tough-minded' military, economic, political, and police enterprises and engagements.[11]

Dr. Tiger's comments are interesting (though speculative) about what this inability of males to express affection and homoerotic feelings may do to other aspects of our culture. We should also note that his discussion is based on "strictly biological" reasons, though he does recognize the psychological or sociological reasons as significant. But if biological, and ultimately psychological and sociological factors also, make it clear that "no good reason for forbidding or even discouraging homoerotic activities" between males exists, again note the challenge to existing morals which would immediately arise.

Nor is Dr. Tiger the only one who is thinking in this direction. More
nd more one finds comments in which the writer suggests that an increase
n and openness toward homosexual arrangements, involving both the
nale-male and the female-female sexes, will become a part of this changing
exual orientation. Thus (in discussing how to cut down on population
ncrease) in *The Future of the Family*,[12] the writers comment, "Too, we
hall probably see a good deal more of homosexuality."[11] The same point
as made in the "Wall Street Journal," September 15, 1969. In a report
rom a Federal Government task force in October, 1969, it was suggested
nat legal penalties be reduced or eliminated for consenting adults perform-
ng homosexual acts in private. This is now the arrangement in England
nd in our own state of Illinois.

Actually, as a society alleviates these restrictions on the physical intimacy
f various acts, they would come to seen less and less as homosexual, and
nore and more clearly as expressions of care and closeness in everyday
ving. In our culture the restrictions have been more severe with male-male
nan female-female relations. But now there is an increasing acceptance of
nese male-male arrangements, even in our own society. Martin Hoffman[13]
oes an excellent job of helping people think through these hard-and-fast
arriers for men, and putting the patterns of male-male affection versus
aditional homosexuality in a clearer perspective. There is certainly a
rowing acceptance of touch and physical closeness in the expression of
fectional relationships in both male-male and female-female relationships.

/

e are at the end of assuming that sex is an uncontrollable urge, an impulse
hich can be only subdued, but never understood and directed. We are
ow recognizing it as one, but only one, of our impulses, and that how we
andle it is the result of our conditioning and learning. One of the reasons
r which control of sexuality has seemed so difficult is the manner in which
has been dealt with in our culture. People will still engage in sex, of
ourse, but it need not be the overpowering force we have thought it to be;
can be dealt with in the same way in which we deal with the rest of
ar rational and emotional needs.

Research has contributed to this more rational and balanced approach,
nd if space were available many details could be given. General illustrations
ust suffice. Remembering the horrifying and utterly untrue tales about the
maging effects of masturbation helps one to realize the changes which

*Authentic
Selfhood:
Basis for
Tomorrow's
Morality*

knowledge brings about. The damage to children who have experienced an unsolicited sexual approach is much more often the result of circumstances created by agitated, hysterical parents than by the experience itself. The consequences of a sexual experience, for example, nonmarital intercourse, are not universally guilt or distress, but will vary according to family background, cultural upbringing, and the degrees of emotional involvement of the persons involved.[14]

Counselors who work with people presenting problems of sexual maladjustment very often are of greater assistance when they help their counselees recognize that typically they are in trouble with their total life pattern, rather than with sex alone. Psychological and sociological disturbances upset people in several ways, of which the sexual may be only one, and often a very minor one. The major advantage enjoyed by authentic persons lies in the kinds of satisfaction they find in the other areas of their lives. The case files of individual counselors and the clinical psychology books make these relationships clear.

V

We are at the end of assuming that we can handle our sex problems by evasion, denial, and subterfuge. More and more clearly we can see that the lodestar of our striving, our moral efforts, must be in the direction of openness, honesty, and always concern with a genuine search for the truth. This is our essential compass point. The person who can handle his sexuality must have a sense of authentic selfhood, derived in part from his early life experiences, and also from his expressions of acceptance and appreciation for his total self as he grows. The person who has experienced this is one who has confidence in his ability, in the balance and direction of powers within himself, his appreciation and acceptance of others, his worth and value to society, his sense of dignity; this is the man or woman of authentic selfhood. In the future our efforts should not be devoted to denying all sexual expression, but in understanding how to make our lives more joyous, rich in relationships, and authentic, and in understanding how sex can contribute to these outcomes.

VI

We have arrived at a time when it seems better to stop talking about morality, particularly in the traditional judgmental, punitive, act-centered sense. Instead, we need to enlarge and deepen our discussion of how to elp individuals fulfill their human potentialities. How can they become ,yous, fulfilled human beings, respecting the rights of others and their own ghts as well? This is the problem the civilized world should now face.

The situation ethicists have made a strong, clear break with the rigid, egalistic approach to moral considerations. They wish to break away from iterpretations of customs and patterns of behavior which now no longer erve human beings. They are concerned with making the principle of ,ving care for others the basis for moral decisions. This concern is, of .ourse, certainly not new. Jesus himself protested the rigid, unyielding iterpretation of the meaning of the Sabbath, and many before and since .ave fought the same kind of legalism.

We find ourselves in much accord with this group, but we feel that ,orking with interpersonal relations, grounded as they are in the behavioral .ciences, makes it possible to explain more clearly how to develop responsible neaningful interpersonal relationships. This is the value framework the enior author used in his study, *Premarital Intercourse and Interpersonal Relationships*.[15] Our goal, through the understanding of behavioral inter-.eaction, should help us make decisions about the use of our sexuality, our ntellect, our physical strength, our speech, and any other such capacities ,r potentialities. The creation of meaningful interpersonal relationships is he criterion against which we need to check our decisions and our results.

The interpersonal relationship approach provides an element of specificity .nd clarity in behavioral relationships which is lacking in the "situation thics" discussions. Many persons who are in essential agreement with the .ituational ethicist seem to find themselves immobilized by the need to .nalyze each human relations situation from scratch. They are unsure in heir decision-making as to which factors need to be taken into account .nd which ones disregarded. They are not clear as to the meaning of .ommunication, motivation, or the need for candor. They do not understand he nature of love, or what it requires of them. So while they are tired of a .egalistic interpretation of regulations imposed by fiat, they are lost when t comes to knowing how to proceed within the area of broad and significant nterpersonal relationships.

Utilizing the qualities of an interpersonal relationship and understanding he processes involved in creating a good or bad relationship, there is no need for starting afresh with every situation. The relationship components .re present in the various situations, and with experience and developing nsight one can anticipate the impact they will have upon the relationship, .nd what outcomes are likely. Some guiding "generalizations" can be developed, not with absolute certainty, but with enough assurance to make genuine sense. One can never be fully sure of a generalization, but as an example, the chances are high enough that if one lies to a friend, if one seeks his own satisfaction at his friend's expense, if one thinks only of himself instead of the other, there will never be a relationship. Everyone knows this even if he has still to meet the person whom he would later like to call his friend.

This way of thinking is already familiar to anyone versed in the behavioral sciences. Students of human behavior who are concerned with understanding what people are like, how they have come to be what they are, and what they may become, are concerned with what goes on in all areas of life They are interested in the development of persons with whom we could all live securely and with satisfaction. The people these leaders envision are the kind needed in a humane, responsible, compassionate society. Some of the scholars who have been engaged in such studies have been mentioned in other articles, and at the expense of omitting some, we will mention several here. We have Erich Fromm talking about the productive man; Carl Rogers, the fully functioning person—the person open to all his experiences; Maslow, the self-actualizing person; Jourard, the authentic being who is able to disclose himself; Horney, the real self; Huxley, the fulfilled person; Glasser, the responsible person; Saul and Jahoda, the mature person; Szasz, the autonomous person. Mowrer is concerned with the person of integrity. Nelson Foote and Schultz discuss how persons may develop in their interpersonal relationships. Montagu emphasizes the importance of love and the role of the cooperative person in human relations. In the field of theology, Fletcher, Cox, and Robinson talk about the caring, loving person. The individuals they are hoping to see develop are people with whom one would like to associate, whom one would welcome as neighbors and as friends; they are the concerned, compassionate, responsible people.

This point of view is apparently what Girvetz had in mind when he wrote

> Whether it be "self-actualization," "positive freedom," "relief from tension and anxiety," "dynamism," "creative interchange," "human dignity," "total personality," or something else (all of them inadequately and almost caricaturishly denoted in a bare list like this and even by the naked labels themselves), the source of values appears to lie in an integrated experience where problems do not fester but are resolved . . . when a Karl Menninger, among others, demonstrates in detail the relation of mental health to the outgoing activities of what he does not hesitate to call "love." and the contrary pathological

tendencies involved in withdrawal and cruelty, it can be argued that experimental and verifiable knowledge about man and his relationships to others is helping in some cases to justify, and elsewhere even to establish, norms of conduct.[16]

As said before, if this view of man and his morals was to be accepted and implemented it would require pronounced changes in our ways of thinking. It would mark the end of traditional and conventional discussions about morals and morality. In the not-too-far-distant future, perhaps, discussions of morality in the traditional sense will seem as outdated as witchcraft and sorcery. Much more meaning can be derived and help given by discussing how we can move positively toward the realization of that which is best in our human potential. Our need is to talk about how individuals, families, schools, churches, and civic institutions can build autonomous, fully-functioning, loving persons; individuals with authentic selfhood, and depend upon this knowledge to take care of the moral issue.

1. Peterson, James A., *Married Love in the Middle Years.* New York: Association Press, 1968.
2. Hall, Edward T. *The Hidden Dimension.* New York: Doubleday, 1966.
3. Montagu, Ashley. *Man Observed.* New York: G. P. Putnam's Sons, 1968.
4. American Assembly. *The Population Dilemma.* Englewood Cliffs, New Jersey: Prentice-Hall, 1963. pp. 71–72.
5. Rosenfeld, Albert. *The Second Genesis: The Coming Control of Life.* Englewood Cliffs, New Jersey: Prentice-Hall, 1969. p. 162.
6. Taylor, G. Rattray. *The Biological Time Bomb.* World Book Company, 1969.
7. Sprey, Jetse. "On the Institutionalization of Sexuality." *Journal of Marriage and the Family,* 31:432–440, August 1969.
8. Farson, Richard D., *et al. The Future of the Family.* New York: Family Service Association of America, p. 61.
9. Kirkendall, Lester A. *Premarital Intercourse and Interpersonal Relationships.* New York: Julian Press, 1961.
10. Foote, Nelson. "Sex as Play." *Social Problems,* 1:159–163, April 1954.
11. Tiger, Lionel. *Men in Groups.* New York: Random House, 1969, p. 216.
12. *op cit.* p. 61.
13. Hoffman, Martin. *The Gay World.* New York: Basic Books, 1968.
14. Readers might like to reread *Sex Ways-in Fact and Faith,* the workbook put out by the North American Conference on Church and Family, 1961, to refresh their thinking on these points.
15. Kirkendall, Lester A. *op. cit.*
16. Girvetz, Harry, et al. *Science, Folklore and Philosophy.* New York: Harper and Row, 1966. p. 528–529.

Authentic Selfhood: Basis for Tomorrow's Morality

CONTRIBUTORS

VERA BOROSAGE is Professor of Family and Child Sciences at Michigan State University. She has written in the area of child development and family relationships.

MYRON BRENTON is the author of *The American Male* as well as numerous articles and books related to human sexuality, the most recent of which is *Sex Talk.*

ELDRIDGE CLEAVER is former Black Panther Minister of Information, revolutionary in exile, and author of numerous publications about Black experience in America.

JOHN F. CUBER is Professor of Sociology at Ohio State University and the author of numerous articles and books on marriage and related topics.

SIMONE de BEAUVOIR is a well known French novelist and existentialist philosopher whose latest book, *The Coming of Age,* deals with aging and sexuality.

ALBERT ELLIS is a practicing psychotherapist and author of numerous books on sexual matters.

JO FREEMAN is a well known feminist. She has written extensively on women and women's liberation in anthologies and professional and popular journals.

JOHN H. GAGNON is Professor of Sociology at The State University of New York at Stony Brook, New York, and the author of numerous articles and books dealing with human sexuality.

S. I. HAYAKAWA is President-Emeritus of San Francisco State College and a writer of note in the field of linguistics.

RICHARD HETTLINGER is Professor of Religion at Kenyon College and author of several works dealing with college students and their problems regarding personal decisions about sex.

MARTIN HOFFMAN is a psychiatrist and Professor at the University of California, Berkeley, and the author of several works dealing with sexual deviance.

DON D. JACKSON is the late psychiatrist and the author of several works on communication and marriage.

LESTER A. KIRKENDALL is Professor-Emeritus of Family Life at Oregon State University.

IRVING KRISTOL is Professor of Urban Values at New York University. He is a prolific author of books and articles dealing with social commentary.

WILLIAM J. LEDERER is an author, retired captain of the U.S. Navy and co-author of several books including *The Ugly American* and the *Mirages of Marriage* (with Don D. Jackson).

CAROL LE FEVRE, after some years as wife, mother, nursery school teacher and elementary teacher, returned to the University of Chicago for her doctorate and is currently Assistant Professor of Psychology at St Xavier College.

SUSANNAH LESSARD is an editor of *The Washington Monthly*, and a penetrating commentator on the American scene.

PHYLLIS LYON is co-founder of the oldest Lesbian organization in America, The Daughters of Bilitis. She has written articles about sexuality, and is co-author of a recent book, *Lesbian Women*.

DEL MARTIN, co-founder of The Daughters of Bilitis, co-authored with Phyllis Lyon the book, *Lesbian Women*. She has written numerous articles about Lesbianism and related concerns.

ROLLO MAY is a psychotherapist and Professor of Graduate Psychology at New York University, and the author of numerous articles and books about sex and the human dilemma, including *Love and Will*.

Contributors

JAMES L. Mc CARY is Professor of Psychology at the University of Houston and internationally known in the field of sex education. He is the author of several

430 books including the well known basic college textbook, *Human Sexuality*.

DESMOND MORRIS is a British zoo curator, painter, and author. *The Naked Ape* made a wide reputation for him, and his latest book is *Intimate Behavior.*

TRUMAN A. MORRISON is Visiting Professor in James Madison College, Michigan State University, and Minister of Edgewood United Church, East Lansing Michigan.

BARBARA RHODES is Associate Professor in International Education at California State University at Northridge.

DELLA ROY is Professor in Materials Science at Pennsylvania State University and co-author with Rustum Roy of numerous articles and books dealing with human sexuality.

RUSTUM ROY is Professor of Geochemistry at Pennsylvania State University and a writer about sexual topics from a humanistic and Christian viewpoint.

ROBERT V. SHERWIN is a practicing attorney in the city of New York, specializing in the law concerning family relations, sex administration, psychiatry and psychology. He is author of *Sex and the Statutory Law,* and a contributor to many publications relating to sex and the law.

WILLIAM SIMON is Director of Sociology and Anthropology Programs at the Institute of Juvenile Research of the State of Illinois Department of Mental Health. He has co-authored several articles and books on topics dealing with human sexuality with John H. Gagnon.

ROBERT STAPLES, prolific writer and student of Black family and sexual issues, is Associate Professor of Sociology at Howard University.

GLORIA STEINEM is a well known feminist, contributor to feminist literature, and currently editor and president of *Ms. Magazine.*

ROSALIE TAYLOR is a counselor with special emphasis on marriage and sexuality areas. She writes from experience with the British health system.

CODY WILSON was Executive Director and Director of Research for the Commission on Obscenity and Pornography.